SPORTSWOMEN
TOWARDS 2000

A CELEBRATION

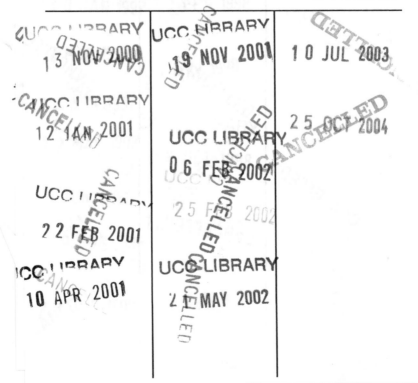

First published by Dr. Ken Dyer, University
of Adelaide, South Australia, 1989.

Printed in South Australia by:
   Hyde Park Press,
   4 Deacon Avenue, Richmond
   South Australia.

National Library of Australia
Cataloguing in publication data
ISBN 0 909120 93 5

Dyer, Ken (Kenneth Frank) 1939 —
   1. Sport, politics, sociology, law,
        medicine.
   2. Equal opportunity.

TABLE OF CONTENTS

The Contributors   vii
Tables   xi
Figures   xiii
Acknowledgements   xv

GENERAL INTRODUCTION

The background to the conference   1
    Wendy Ey

Where have we come from? Two views on the history of women's
    sport in Australia   2
    Ken Dyer

SECTION ONE — The Politics of Women's Sport

An introduction   17
    Ken Dyer

Women's sport: Sociology and politics   19
    Libby Darlison

Sport: A feminist perspective   21
    Lois Bryson

Strategies for change: Some thoughts from the Canadian experience   25
    Abby Hoffman

SECTION TWO — Women's Sport and the Law

An introduction   35
    Ken Dyer

The laws: Lead us or leave us alone   39
    Josephine Tiddy

Integrating sport: The Canadian experience   46
    Abby Hoffman

Sport and equality: Some issues, problems and possibilities in
    the interpretation of current legislation†   48
    Ken Dyer

SECTION THREE — Science, Medicine and Women in Sport

An introduction   63
    Ken Dyer

Eating for health and performance   64
    Angela Hehir

Medical problems of female athletes   69
    Peter Brukner

From science to performance: The use of sports science in
developing elite female athletes   72
    Julie Draper

    Appendix One: State of the art reviews completed and in
    preparation.

    Appendix Two: Some typical reference material on female
    track and field athletes as presented by the
    AIS SPORTSCAN service

Exercise and pregnancy   78
    Rosslyn Carbon

Striving for success: The role and significance of
personality development for the accomplishment of
high athletic achievement   81
    Ruth Fuchs

Predictions of records and elite performances   85
    Ken Dyer

SECTION FOUR — Recruitment and Participation of Female Athletes

An introduction   101
    Ken Dyer

Recruiting female athletes and keeping them   103
    Jackie Byrnes

Avoiding the 'drop out' syndrome   106
    Christina Lee and Neville Owen

Women's participation in exercise programs   110
    Tony Sedgwick

Talent development of elite sportswomen:
A retrospective picture of the process   113
    Sandy Gordon

Talent selection: The selection and development of gifted children
in the GDR   124
    Ruth Fuchs

SECTION FIVE — Training and Coaching for Women Athletes

An introduction   137
    Ken Dyer

Coaching women athletes   138
    John Daly

Women coaches and coaching women   141
    Shirley de la Hunty

Training for women   144
    Terry Dwyer

    Appendix: A one year training program for sprint women
    devised for Irena Szewinska

Women in sport: Some special considerations   153
    Richard Telford

The development of women's distance running: An Australian
   perspective   157
    Pat Clohessy

Some aspects of strength in women's field events   161
    Ruth Fuchs

SECTION SIX — Junior Sport

An introduction   167
    Ken Dyer

Back to basics: Getting off to a good start in athletics*   171
    Vern Gambetta

Turning on the turned off girl   175
    Henny Oldenhove

From research to practice in junior sport†   183
    Jeff Emmel

Children's sport: Where to now?   185
    Rosemary Crowley

The Commonwealth Sex Discrimination Act (1984) and children's
   sport: Policy implications †   188
    Henny Oldenhove

The role of sport in education and government in West Germany   192
    Ilse Bechtold

Young people and athletics in the GDR*   201
    Klaus Schonberger

    Appendix One: Children and long distance running: Policy
    Statement of the Australian Sports Medicine Federation,
    Children in Sport Committee*
        Dave Roberts, Allan Norton, Alex Sinclair and Peter Larkins

    Appendix Two: Children and Adolescents in Sport: Policy
    Statement of the Australian National Health and Medical
    Research Council*

SECTION SEVEN — Promoting Women's Sport

An introduction   219
    Ken Dyer

Women's sport: Treatment by the media   220
    Helen Menzies

The Women's Sport Promotion Unit   231
    Margaret Pewtress

    Appendix One: The recommendations from the Report to
    the Federal Government on Women in Sport 1985*

    Appendix Two: The Australian Sport Commission Policy on
    Women in Sport 1987*

Marketing and sponsorship of women's sport   246
    Julia Mourant

    Appendix: Women's sport and recreation in the media.

An Information Booklet prepared by the South Australian
Department of Recreation and Sport*

SECTION EIGHT — Success Stories

An introduction   259
  Ken Dyer

The joy of being a successful sportswoman   261
  Mary Peters

Women's distance running: Past, present and future
  — a participant's view   264
  Doris Heritage

Women, athletics and self-esteem: The athlete's view   273
  Gaylene Clews

Commitment   278
  Marjorie Jackson
  Irena Szewinska

Some questions and some answers   279
  Irena Szewinska, Ruth Fuchs and Mary Peters

REFERENCES   283

† Articles specially written for this volume
* Material previously published elsewhere

THE CONTRIBUTORS

Ilse Bechtold
> West Germany. Chairperson IAAF Women's Committee.

Doris Brown-Heritage
> Assistant Professor, School of Physical Education and Athletics,
> Seattle Pacific University, Oregon, USA.
> USA World Cross Country Champion 1967-71. World Masters Mile Record
> 1983.

Peter Brukner
> Medical Director, Olympic Park Sports Medicine Centre, Melbourne.
> Medical Officer to numerous local and national teams in a variety of sports.

Lois Bryson
> Associate Professor, School of Sociology, University of New South Wales.
> A widely published commentator on social issues in Australian society,
> including gender inequality in sport.

Jackie Byrnes
> State Coaching Director, New South Wales Athletic Association.
> World ranked 200m/400m runner 1967.

Rosslyn Carbon
> Inaugural CIBA-Geigy Fellow in Sports Medicine, Australian Institute of
> Sport, ACT.
> National Chairperson of Women in Sport Committee.

Gaylene Clews
> ACT Australian Cross Country Champion 1976/78.
> World Number One Sprint-Triathlete 1985.

Pat Clohessy
> Distance Coach, Australian Institute of Sport, ACT.
> Australian Athletic Union Coach of the Year 1982/83.
> Australian Athletic Union National Event Coach.

Rosemary Crowley
> Senator for South Australia. The first woman member of the ALP to be elected
> to the Commonwealth Parliament.
> Marathon Runner.

John Daly
> Principal Lecturer, Physical Education, South Australian College of Advanced
> Education.
> Australian track coach for 1976, 1980 and 1984 Olympic Games.
> Manager of Australian Track and Field Team for 1988 Olympic Games.

Libby Darlison
> Commissioner, Australian Sports Commission, ACT.
> Academic and Consultant.

Julie Draper

National Sports Research Co-ordinator, Australian Institute of Sport, ACT.

Terry Dwyer

Professor of Community Health, Director of Menzies Centre for Population Health Research. University of Tasmania.
Chairperson, Tasmanian Institute of Sport.
Chairperson, AAU Sports Science and Medicine Committee.

Ken Dyer

Senior Lecturer in Social Biology, Adelaide University.
Author of several books and many research papers on women, sport and physical education.

Jeff Emmel†

Senior Education Officer, Physical Education Branch, SA Education Department.
Previously Project Co-ordinator, Commonwealth Schools Commission Girls and Physical Activity Project.

Wendy Ey

Women's Adviser, South Australian Department of Recreation and Sport.
Silver Medallist, 1958 Commonwealth Games 4 x 100 m relay.
Manager, Australian Athletic Team 1984 Olympic Games.

Ruth Fuchs

East Germany.
Olympic Javelin Gold Medallist 1972 and 1976 Olympics.
Multiple Javelin world record holder.
Sports Scientist.
Member IAAF Women's Committee.

Vern Gambetta†

Editor of Track Technique.

Sandy Gordon

Lecturer, Department of Human Movement and Recreation Studies, University of Western Australia.

Angela Hehir

Project Officer, Nutrition Education, Health Development Foundation, South Australia.

Abigail Hoffman

Director General, Sport Canada.
Member of National Track and Field Team of Canada 1962-76.
Member of Executive Committee, Canadian Olympic Association.
Member IAAF Women's Committee.

Marjorie Jackson

Olympic Gold Medallist in 100 m and 200 m at 1952 Olympics.
Multiple World record holder.
Founded Peter Nelson Leukemia Research Fund for which she has raised more than one million dollars.

Christina Lee

Lecturer, Department of Psychology, University of Newcastle, NSW.

South Australian Schoolgirls Artistic Gymnastics 1972.
Captain/Coach SA Rhythmic Sportive Gymnastics 1977.

Helen Menzies
Community Education Officer, Office of the Commissioner for Equal Opportunity, South Australia.
Previously a sports journalist.

Julia Mourant
Publicity and Promotions Manager, Channel Nine Television Station, Adelaide.
Member Sponsorship Committee, Adelaide City Soccer Club.

Henny Oldenhove
Program Consultant, Women's Sport Promotion Unit, Australian Sports Commission.
Previously Project Officer, Girls and Physical Activity Project.
A Grade Women's Hockey player/coach.

Neville Owen
Senior Lecturer, Department of Community Medicine, Adelaide University.
Writer and researcher in the areas of health, behaviour modification and sport.

Mary Peters
Northern Ireland.
Gold Medallist Pentathlon, 1972 Olympic Games, Munich.
President, Northern Ireland Women's AAA.
Member of Sports Council GB.

Margaret Pewtress
Chairperson, Women's Sports Promotion Unit, Australian Sport Commission, ACT.

Klaus Schonberger†
Deputy Secretary General of the German Athletics Association, GDR.

Tony Sedgwick
Head, Institute for Fitness Research and Training, Adelaide, South Australia.

Shirley Strickland de la Hunty
Lecturer in Mathematics, Statistics and Computer Education, West Australian College of Advanced Education.
Gold Medallist at 1952 and 1956 Olympics.
Multiple World Record Holder.
Assistant Manager (Women) at 1968 and 1976 Olympics.
AAU National Event Coach.

Irena Szewinska
Poland.
Gold Medallist at the 1964, 1968 and 1976 Olympics.
The first woman to break 50 seconds in the 400 metres.

Richard Telford
Head, Department of Physiology and Applied Nutrition, Australian Institute of Sport, ACT.
Coach of international distance athletes.

Josephine Tiddy
 Commissioner for Equal Opportunity, South Australia.

† Authors of papers not presented at the Conference.

TABLES

1   Men's and women's world freestyle swimming records and the percentage difference between them in 1958 and 1988   52

2   Recommended dietary intake of iron for women, compared with available survey data of actual intake   66

3   Recommended dietary intake of calcium for women, compared with available survey data of actual intake   67

4   Numbers of men and women breaking world track records since the start of official record keeping   93

5   Numbers of men and women breaking world field event records since the start of official record keeping   94

6   Comparison of male versus female performance ratios for top 10 performers with world record performance ratios   94

7   Comparative improvement of world athletic records before and after the introduction of steroids   96

8   Female registrations in New South Wales Athletic Association   104

9   Sportswomen interviewed in the 'drop out project' listed by sport   115

10   The sample in the 'drop out project': personal details   115

11   Talent development of elite female sportswomen: summary of ingredients   123

12   Body fat for boys and girls of various ages   145

13   Strength measurements for boys and girls of various ages   145

14   The times recorded for a 50m run by boys and girls at various ages   146

15   The times recorded for a 1.6km run by boys and girls at various ages   146

16   A comparison of performance levels of men and women in track athletics as indicated by world records in 1958 and 1988   147

17   Two training regimes concerned with strength development   163

18   Strength training with advanced adolescent female athletes in the GDR   164

19   The treatment of women's sport in Australia by the capital city newspapers   222

20   Articles on women's sport carried in capital city morning papers, February 15-20, 1988   223

21   The number of women's sports given coverage by capital city morning papers, February 15-20, 1988   224

22   The response of capital city newspapers to a survey of women's sport coverage   225

23   The response of capital city radio stations to a survey of
     women's sport coverage   226

24   The response of capital city television channels to a
     survey of women's sport coverage   227

FIGURES

1   A front page headline story on mixed junior sport from
The Advertiser of Adelaide, September 1, 1988   37

2   A story on mixed junior sport from **The Sunday Mail**
of Adelaide, September 4, 1988   38

3   A story from **The Advertiser** of Adelaide, reporting an early
case on sex discrimination in sport in 1978   41

4   A story from **The Advertiser** of Adelaide, discussing the outcome
of the 1978 case of sex discrimination in sport   43

5   A story from **The News** of Adelaide, reporting the controversy
over mixed primary school sport in February, 1988   44

6   An article from **The News** of Adelaide, commenting on the
controversy over mixed primary school sport in February, 1988   45

7   The improvement in the average speed of the top 10 performers
in the women's 100 metres (1952-86)   88

8   The improvement in the average speed of the top 10 performers
in the women's 3000 metres (1972-86)   88

9   The improvement of performance in javelin throwing from
1960 to 1982 based on the average of the top 20 performers for
each year   89

10   The improvement of performance in the long jump from
1960 to 1982 based on the average of the top 20 performers for
each year   90

11   The change in the performance differential between the sexes
for three throwing events, two jumps and eight track
events between 1921 and 1984   91

12   The comparison of the change in sex differential in performance
in eight track events run by women since the 1920s
with those in events introduced more recently into
the women's program   92

13   The research structure: women's health and fitness program   112

14   The research project: 'Drop out phenomenon in organised sport'   114

15   Skinfold measurements in female Australian athletes   153

16   Ferritin and haemoglobin levels in netball players with and
without iron supplementation   155

17   A typical weekly training schedule for Australian swimmer
Janelle Elford   156

18   The development of power associated with javelin throwing   162

19   A structural model for the development of skills and
abilities in javelin throwing   163

ACKNOWLEDGEMENTS

I am grateful to the Adelaide **Advertiser**, the Adelaide **Sunday Mail**, and the Adelaide **News** for permission to reproduce a number of photographs and news headlines. I am grateful to the International Athletics Foundation, publishers of the journal *New Studies in Athletics* for permission to reproduce *Back to Basics: Getting Off to a Good Start in Athletics* by Vern Gambetta which appeared in Volume 1 (1986) and *Young People and Athletics in the GDR* by Klaus Schonberger which appeared in Volume 2 (1987). I am grateful to the Australian National Health and Medical Research Council for permission to reproduce their policy statement on Children and Adolescents in Sport. I am grateful to the South Australian Department of Recreation and Sport for permission to reproduce material from an Information Booklet on Women's Sport and Recreation in the Media. I am grateful to the Women's Sport Promotion Unit and the Australian Sport Commission for permission to reproduce material relating to the Unit and the Commission's Policy on Women in Sport (1987). The Australian Bicentennial Authority provided me with some photographic illustrations which first appeared in their publication *Sport 88*, and the Bicentennial Authority and the ACHPER Queensland Special Interest Group kindly made available the prize winning pictures from their 1988 National Photographic Competition. For that I thank them.

The Conference of which this book is a record was organised by Wendy Ey of the South Australian Department of Recreation and Sport. I, of course, thank her for her enormous hard work in organising that most successful conference, but I also thank her for her considerable help in many ways and her encouragement during the preparation of this book.

I thank all of the contributors to that Conference who agreed to allow their papers and talks to be reproduced in this volume. I thank in particular, Jeff Emmel and Henny Oldenhove who provided articles especially written for this volume describing their current endeavours. Jeff Emmel and Henny Oldenhove were also most helpful in assisting me to locate illustrations for this book.

The Conference itself was one of the activities of Women's Week in Adelaide in March, 1988. Another of the activities was the Women's 15K World Championship Road Race. Both events, and the visits to them of the overseas delegates, were supported financially by the International Amateur Athletic Federation, the Australian Athletic Union and the Rothmans Foundation. I thank Marlene Mathews, noted athlete and currently member of the IAAF Women's Committee and Athletics Co-ordinator on the Rothmans Foundation for help in various ways.

Finally, I thank Briony Barker and Margaret Hilliard who went far beyond the call of duty in their labours to typeset, design and undertake all the other chores associated with producing the book. Its final format is a tribute to their skills.

Ken Dyer
Adelaide, February, 1989

GENERAL INTRODUCTION

THE BACKGROUND TO THE CONFERENCE

Wendy Ey

The concept for the Conference which this book reports, was the brainchild of Ric Pannell, the General Manager of the Australian Athletic Union.

In Australia's Bicentennial year, the Australian Athletic Union sought to host a World Championship. They were successful in their bid for the Women's World 15km Road Running Championship, and to supplement the events the notion of 'Women's Week' was developed. The **Sportswomen Towards 2000** Conference was one of the major attractions of Women's Week.

In keeping with the tradition, the International Amateur Athletic Federation agreed to support the Conference as they have done for similar events in Europe and South America. The encouragement of the Chairperson of the IAAF Women's Committee, Ilse Bechthold and the Chairperson of the IAAF Foundation, Professor August Kirsch, is gratefully acknowledged.

A special sub-committee of the Organising Committee for the World Championship was established and comprised Wendy Ey (Chairperson), Henny Oldenhove, John Daly and Ken Dyer.

The planning was extensive and ambitious, and in consultation with Australian IAAF Women's Committee member, Marlene Mathews, negotiations were made to include the entire IAAF Women's Committee in the Conference. Although the entire Committee did not formally meet in Adelaide, several members were present. They were Ilse Bechthold, Irena Szewinska, Joshika Tanaka, Abigail Hoffman, Ruth Fuchs and Marlene Mathews. We are grateful for the contribution they made to the Conference. In particular we are grateful to Rothmans Foundation for sponsoring Ruth Fuchs from the German Democratic Republic.

The title and theme of the Conference were developed to focus on the future for women in sport, hence **Sportswomen Towards 2000** and **Increasing Participation**. One of the most significant barriers to increased participation by women in all aspects of sport is their relatively small numbers at present.

The speakers were selected to cover a wide range of areas: principally science, medicine, politics, law, coaching, training and media. Without any doubt they represented the very best in their field in Australia and never before has there been a conference where all of these experts have been present at the one time.

The Australian community appreciated the unique opportunity to meet some of the all-time greats of women's athletics, including two women who have the honour of having won the greatest number of Olympic medals in women's track and field history — Shirley Strickland de la Hunty and Irena Szewinska. Others included world record holders and Olympic Medallists Ruth Fuchs, Marlene Mathews, Mary Peters, Doris Heritage and Abigail Hoffman. They all contributed talks to the

1

Conference and/or took part in panel discussions. They are therefore all represented in this volume.

WHERE HAVE WE COME FROM? TWO VIEWS ON THE HISTORY OF WOMEN'S SPORT IN AUSTRALIA

Ken Dyer

There are several possible ways of writing the history of women's sport in Australia — setting out how we arrived at the situation typical of the late 1980s. I shall set out two contrasting accounts. The first will describe the setting up of the various women's sports associations, document the achievements of women in winning medals, and championships, setting records and improving their levels of participation. The problems which women have had to overcome in Australia as much as anywhere might be implied in all this but would not be emphasised. Indeed, the emphasis on success and achievement would suggest that although women may still have a lot to overcome, changes and improvement in areas such as discrimination and lack of opportunity will come gradually as participation and success also improve. In other words, change within sport is very much a function of sport itself.

The emphasis throughout such a description is on the progression of women's performances, opportunities and participation. It certainly mentions the deficiencies of the past both on and off the field, but suggests that with appropriate additions of money, science, goodwill and if necessary a little legal pressure, all will eventually be well. Sure, it will take longer than we would like; entrenched attitudes and economic difficulties are not that easily overcome. But eventually equality will be attained.

In the contrasting view, sport is seen as merely another manifestation of the social structure of society. The emphasis in this account is very much on those areas of sport in which women have hitherto not had equality of opportunity or achievement. The failure of women to progress as far in sport as their needs and potential demand and allow, are shown to be for the same reasons that their progress has been restricted in business, politics, medicine, the law, or indeed anywhere else that power and status are concentrated. Sport is seen not so much as a mirror of society or an area which follows social changes elsewhere, but as one which is absolutely central to society as a whole.

This sort of account asks **why** there has been so much emphasis on sex differences in performance and potential in sport. It asks why an activity, which in many aspects is so beneficial, has been denied to women in so many areas. And finally it asks what in particular was it that won various battles for women — allowed them into the Olympics, allowed them into golf clubs, gave them reasonable prize money at Wimbledon and so on — and what have been the consequences of these victories.

This approach also emphasises the need for legislation to deter the more overt forms of discrimination, the need for greater media attention to women's sport, the need for action in schools to provide girls with skill training and encouragement at an appreciably earlier age than is currently the case, if indeed such processes happen at all at present.

Echoes and implications of these differing views appear in the papers which follow in this volume. The papers on sports medicine, training, coaching and possible performance limits, all suggest that more effort from the women themselves, plus a little extra knowledge and maybe a little extra financial and media support, will enable women to finally show what they can do, destroy the myths of biological inferiority and reap all the rewards that sport brings. Other contributors to this book argue that success will by no means be so easily achieved. Indeed success may not be the right word at all if women merely succeed in entering a world which one writer has stated manifests *all the values of the capitalistic jungle . . . . virility, sexual athleticism, physical dominance, muscle worship, fascistic male chauvinism, racism, sexism, etc.*

There is room for, indeed a need for both approaches, provided it is recognised that neither tells the whole story, that neither has a monopoly of the truth. Sport itself is certainly not monolithic. The part that football or cricket, for example, play in our society is likely to be very different from that played by lawn bowls or or surfing. And social club cricket is likely to be very different from Sheffield Shield cricket or Test matches.

I propose to outline something of the history of athletics in Australia from both perspectives, since I have asserted that both are necessary. I will not restrict myself entirely to athletics, partly because athletics is but one aspect of sport and physical activity in general, and partly because the conference which was the starting point for this book was not itself restricted entirely to athletics.

Organised sport for women began in the late nineteenth century. I quote some paragraphs from Bushby and Jobling (1985) concerning the earliest days.

> *The first female tennis competition recorded was in 1884. Although first played in the spacious grounds of the wealthy, tennis soon became a very popular pastime among the middle class. It was considered suitable for women in their elaborate clothing because it was played in such a leisurely manner, and the activity was praised because it brought men and women together at play. It was reported in the Brisbane Courier that some ladies excelled at the game, however women were not included in the intercolonial competitions at that time. Lawson has noted that while there were some women's events in the Queensland titles from 1892, the newspapers reported the results only without any description or comment. Tennis might have been praised for assisting the 'social development of the sexes' but matches in which women participated were not considered newsworthy.*
>
> *Women were admitted as associate members of the Brisbane Golf Club in 1897 and, although denied access to the clubhouse, they were allowed to use the links on all week days except public holidays. As King has stated, golf and tennis were regarded as 'ladies sport since their graceful and charming movement complemented the overall cultural image of women', and their competitions were 'women's affairs' which posed no threat to male golfers and tennis players.*
>
> *Regular newspaper coverage was given to ladies' cycling clubs in the 1890s. Cycling complemented the growing social freedoms many women were seeking by giving them greater physical freedom. There were very few records of organised competition, however, and they seem to have been limited to the picnic type.*
>
> *Lawson has claimed that once games had been regularised, 'there was much less bombast and pugnaciousness in sport and women could participate without being considered unladylike'. Some of the activities they played included cricket, hockey, archery, skating and swimming, either in pools or in the sea where bathing boxes protected a lady's modesty.*

The first women's cricket match in Australia is reportedly a one innings match at Bendigo in 1874 and an international match was held in 1890 between Victoria and NSW in Sydney. By the 1890s it is reported that several strong sides were

3

established in Sydney and Melbourne. Not until 1923 was the Victorian Women's Cricket Association formed, however, and the New South Wales Women's Cricket Association followed in 1927. The Australian Women's Cricket Council was formed in 1931 with Victoria, Queensland and New South Wales as foundation members.

Some women's sports were performed in a less genteel and social atmosphere than is suggested in these sentences. The world's first cycle race for women was reportedly held in Ashfield NSW over a two mile course in 1888. By the 1890s two NSW women cyclists Barbara Whitcher (Newcastle) and Margaret McLachlan (Dulwich Hill) were barred from racing against male cyclists in their clubs after winning several events. And in 1899 a Mrs. McDonald set a record, cycling from from Sydney to Melbourne in 7 days 4 hours.

The Australian Women's Amateur Golf Championship played at Geelong Victoria in August 1894 preceded the Australian men's championship which was not held until November of that year. In bowls, however, although the first women's bowls match appears to have been played in 1881 at Stawell in Victoria and a women's bowls club was founded in 1898, national championships did not begin until 1919.

By the 1920s the women in Australia were active in a wide range of sports and had achieved some international successes. But not in athletics. The reasons for this delay relate to the fact that athletics for women was practised in few other countries, was not on the Olympic Program, and had little if any other international dimension until the 1920s.

However, as I relate in my book **Challenging the Men**, women's athletics began as an international sport in March 1921 when five nations competed at an international meeting in Monte Carlo. Later that year the Federation Sportive Feminine International (FSFI) was formed which proceeded to organise several Women's World Games (having been forbidden by the IOC to call them the Women's Olympic Games).

Continued pressure from the FSFI, and possibly a concern on the part of the IOC at the rapid rate of growth of the Women's World Games, resulted in track and field athletics being included on the program for the 1928 Olympic Games in Amsterdam. It was this decision which seems to have been the stimulus for the establishment of women's athletics in Australia.

The New South Wales Amateur Athletic Association became interested in the possibility of including women in the 1928 Australian Olympic Team and included three events for women in its 1926 State Championships — 75 yards, 100 yards and 4 x 110 yards relay. These championships were open to members of existing sports clubs formed by women's sports organisations, business houses, schools and to independent athletes. Edith Robinson from the Hordernian Club won both sprints in 1926 and also in 1927 and 1928 and as a result, duly became a member of the Australian Team for the 1928 Olympics. She was the only woman selected for the track team and competed in the 100m and 800m, although without winning a medal in either. At the 1932 and 1936 Olympic Games there was likewise only one woman competitor: A.E. Wearre, unplaced in the 100m in 1932 and D. Carter, also unplaced in the 1936 high jump.

The late 1920s and early 1930s were the formative years for athletics in most states. Three women's clubs affiliated with the NSW Amateur Athletic Association in 1928 and specifically women's associations were formed in Queensland and Victoria in 1929, South Australia in 1931, NSW in 1932, Western Australia in 1936 and Tasmania in 1937.

The straight forward facts and figures and the bald statistics of these early years can be found in **Women's Athletics in Australia. An official history of the Australian Women's Amateur Athletic Union.**

A better feel for some of the pioneering spirit of these early days and some of the difficulties which women had to face is given by a few paragraphs from John Daly's book **Ours Were the Hearts to Dare** which is a History of Women's Amateur Athletics in South Australia 1930-1980. He begins his story, in fact, a little before 1930.

On the first and second weekend in February 1928, the South Australian Amateur Athletic Association conducted its Tenth Annual Field and Track Games Championships at the Wayville Showgrounds. There were twenty-six events for men competitors each of whom represented one of five clubs — Adelaide Harriers, Plympton, South Australian Railways, University and the YMCA.

Included in the program for the second day of the championships was a race for women — the first State Championship for Ladies. The inclusion of this event was a token gesture acknowledging the fact that in the 1928 Olympic Games to be held in Amsterdam later that year women would be allowed to compete for the first time. The South Australian event was a 75 yard race and seven women competed, none of them representing a club but each ascribed a colour to identify them: Red - Gladys Batt; Blue - Maureen Carmody; Yellow - Florence Carr; Black - Norah Clutterham; Purple - Gerty Jennings; Brown - Dolly Swayne; White - Edna Thomson.

Dolly Swaine, who the press suggested appeared to get a good start won that race in 9.2 seconds and the event proved to be so popular that it was repeated in 1929 and 1930.

Gladys Batt was one of the few women in the state to train every day and her success was well-deserved. She was active in a wide range of sports —basketball (netball), tennis, swimming and roller-skating — but trained regularly at the Goodwood Oval with the professional men athletes under the guidance of coach, Wally Lapthorne. Such behaviour (training with men athletes) was considered risque at the time and the President of the Amateur Association, perhaps overly conscious of public opinion, was critical of men and women mixing at training.

Interest in men's amateur running diminished in the presence of an increasing number of picnic meetings arranged by lodges, trade unions and hotels both in the city and in the country. All offered substantial money prizes in preference to trophies and during the depression and unemployment days of the 'eighties big meets like those held at Glenelg, Norwood, Appila, Orroroo and Murray Bridge, enticed the aspiring and the talented.

This perhaps accounts for the existence and popularity of the Women's Professional Athletic League when women began running in the mid 'twenties. This Women's League had been formed in 1927 to match that of the men. Prior to the formation of this association women ran as amateurs at the various picnic meetings around the State but 'the pro's' included 'the odd race' for their ladies (sisters, daughters, girlfriends). These meetings were well-conducted, efficiently organised and extremely popular with the Adelaide public. A bookmaker, 'Dasher' Hewitt, whose sister Meg Hewitt ran in these early meetings, added excitement for both spectator and athlete by his presence.

The addition of women running at these sports added to their popularity for it was still considered 'scandalous' by some that women would compete publicly in shorts. On Good Friday and Christmas morning a crowd four or five deep lined the track to 'watch the girls'. It must have been an ordeal for some of the women. There were no changing facilities for women at the grounds (Jubilee, Norwood, Prospect, Glenelg, Alberton ovals) and they arrived already attired for running but modestly 'covered up by an overcoat'. Girls were warned to 'ignore the comments' from the spectators. Such advice came usually from Mrs. Muriel Wallace who was responsible for the formation of the Women's League, the only one in Australia at the time.

Muriel Wallace, was a skilful sportswoman interested in a wide variety of sports — hockey, netball, cricket and swimming. She competed in the 'Married Ladies' races in the mid 'twenties and later took an interest in young girls who showed talent when running in either schoolgirls or 'Single Ladies' races. In the absence of male coaches many of whom refused to coach girls, she looked after the youngsters who stayed on after their initial run.

Prior to the formation of the League in 1927 there were about twelve girls regularly competing in 'Ladies Races' which were confined to distances up to but not exceeding 100 yards. Seventy-five yards was described as the 'usual distance'. Races beyond that distance were considered 'too strenuous' and quite 'dangerous' for women. In 1931 a race over 220 yards was conducted in Sydney and much publicity was given to the 'distress and collapse' of the girl athletes.

Seven Adelaide girls contested the distance later that year at a Harriers meeting and all completed the race 'in fine style showing no signs of distress at the finish'. The race over 'a formidable distance' (for women) created much interest and controversy. The chairman of the Harriers stated that he was pleased with the 'success of the experiment' but would not advocate going 'beyond that distance'. The race, a handicap event, was won by Marjorie Turner who said afterwards that she 'did not find the distance too strenuous'. The State champion, Gladys Batt, also agreed that it was not too far to run but admitted that 'most of the girls were frightened and anxious at the start'. She confidently predicted that as the girls trained more and became accustomed to the distance it would become a regular event.

These attitudes strike one as curious and archaic in today's age of women's marathons and ultramarathons. Indeed Australia was somewhat behind the times, since even by the late 1920s and 1930s women were running 800m and 1000m races in various national and international events (see **Challenging the Men**: pp 120-128)

The first national championships for women were held in Melbourne in 1933. There were just 10 events in the program. These, with the winning times or distances were as follows: 100 yards, 11.3; 220 yards, 26.1; 880 yards walk, 4:00.3; 90 yards hurdles, 13.9; Shot, 30'4" = 9.25m; Discus, 91'8" = 27.94m; Javelin, 104'11" = 31.98m; High Jump, 4'11" = 1.49m; Long Jump, 16'5" = 5.00m; 4 x 110 yard relay, 50.1.

International competition for women was very restricted in these early years — and this was particularly so for Australia, subject so much in those days to 'the tyranny of distance'. But the achievements of Australian women were impressive. In 1930, for example, Christine Dahm's time of 10.9 for the 100 yards was the third fastest in the world that year, Clarice Kennedy at 12.2 in the 80 metres hurdles was second fastest in the world. In 1931 four Australian women had the second and third fastest times for the 100 yards and in 1932 three women on 11.2 were the second fastest with Edith Robinson, Eileen Wearne and Amy Bremer at 25.5, 25.8 and 25.9, the fifth, eighth and eleventh fastest over 200 metres. The 4 x 100 metres relay team was also the sixth fastest in the world in 1932.

The conclusion from examining the history of these early years might therefore be that women's athletics in Australia was only a little behind the rest of the world in getting going. It suffered the dual tyranny of distance in that essentially six small colonies or states on a large continent were well separated from one another and that Australia as a whole was very distant from the rest of the world. Nevertheless, within four or five years of the beginning of women's athletics in Australia, the standard was of world class. Initial progress would surely have to be considered exceptional. If we compare the women's achievements with those of men, they are certainly as good.

For example, Australian men appear only as 20th fastest and 36th fastest runners over 100 yards in 1932 (Edward Hampson 9.6 and Evan Davidson 9.7). They were first, seventh, thirteenth and fourteenth fastest in the 200 metres that year but were only 15th fastest in the 400 metres, 32nd fastest in the 800 metres and 10th fastest in the mile. Neither men nor women appear to have made any world class performances in any of the field events during these years.

With this background it is to be expected that success in international competition would come for Australian women in due course. It duly did so in the third Empire Games held in Sydney in 1938. There were eight events for women on the program and Decima Norman won five gold medals (100 yards, 220 yards, long jump, 440 yards relay and 660 yards relay).

In addition Australian women won silver medals in the 100 yards, 220 yards and the 80 metre hurdles and bronze medals in the long jump and the 220 yards — a medal haul superior to that of the Australian men from the equivalent events. Decima Norman equalled the world record for the 100 yards at 11.0 in 1939, the first Australian name to appear on any world record list in any event. It is widely speculated that but for the interruption of international athletics during the war, several Australian women would have achieved success in the Olympics and elsewhere in the early 1940s. Australian women's athletics could be said to have arrived by the late 1930s. It would surely be no surprise therefore that in the post war Olympic and Commonwealth Games Australian women should be so successful. In the London Olympics of 1948, Australian women won a silver medal (the 4 x 100m relay), and two bronze medals (100m and 80m hurdles by Shirley Strickland). In the Auckland Empire Games of 1950 the medal haul was golds in the 100 and 220 yards, and 80 metre hurdles, the Javelin and two relays, silvers in the 100 yards, 220 yards and long jump. The 1952 Olympics in far away Finland and the 1954 Commonwealth Games in Vancouver, consolidated the progress. The results and achievements at the 1956 Olympics in Melbourne were simply staggering: 4 gold medals and 3 bronze medals with three world and Olympic records broken or equalled. By 1956 Australian women had broken the world record in the 100m (Marjorie Jackson twice and Betty Cuthbert), the 4 x 100m relay (in 1952 and 1956 twice) the 4 x 200m relay and the now discontinued events over the corresponding imperial distances numerous times.

The medal winning and the record breaking has continued almost unabated until the present day. A simple list of successes in the last three decades makes the point.

World Records

200m	Betty Cuthbert	23.2	1960
	Margaret Burvill	22.9	1964
400m	Marlene Matthews	57.0	1957
	Nancy Boyle	56.3	1957
800m	Dixie Willis	2:01.2	1962
	Judy Pollock	2:01.0	1967
100m hurdles	Pam Ryan	12.5	1972
Javelin	Anna Pazera	57.40m	1958
5,000m walk	Kerry Saxby	20:34	1987
10,000m walk	Sue Cook	46:42.6	1982
	Sue Cook	45:47.0	1983
	Kerry Saxby	42:53	1987

Olympic Medals

Rome 1960
Silver	Brenda Jones	800m

Tokyo 1964
Gold	Betty Cuthbert	400m
Silver	Michelle Mason-Brown	High jump
Bronze	Pam Kilborn	80m hurdles
	Judith Amoore	400m

Mexico City 1968
Gold	Maureen Caird	80m hurdles
Silver	Pam Kilburn	80m hurdles
	Raelene Boyle	200m
Bronze	Jennifer Lamy	200m

Munich 1972			
Silver	Raelene Boyle		100m
	Raelene Boyle		200m
Los Angeles 1984			
Gold	Glynis Nunn		Heptathlon
Bronze	Gael Martin		Shot
Seoul 1988			
Gold	Debbie Flintoff-King		400m
Silver	Lisa Martin		Marathon

In 1928, Australian women obviously thought 220 yards was a long way to run, although the 1933 Australian National Titles had the three throwing events and the two jumps which form the field events program of the Olympics today.

John Daly tells us in **Ours were the Hearts to Dare** that *all the girls in this early team ....trained three nights a week between the hours of 5.00 and 7.00 pm.* Training at this level continued *throughout the season which lasted from October ... until March with competition on Saturdays.* This level of activity continued throughout the 1930s. The usual program for a women's meet, Daly informs us *included a sprint (usually 75 yards) or one or two lap walks (preferably the former), a long jump and as time ensued, two throws — the javelin and the shot put.*

Things have changed drastically today. In 1948 the Olympic Program for women was the 100m, 200m, 80m hurdles, 4 x 100m relay, high jump, long jump, shot put, discus and javelin. By 1988 this 9 event program had exactly doubled with the addition of 400m, 800m, 1500m, 3000m, 10,000m, marathon, 400m hurdles, 4 x 400m relay and heptathlon events. But still there were many events on the men's program which were absent from the women's, namely the triple jump, hammer, pole vault, the two walks and the 3000m steeplechase.

The training schedules adopted by Australian women athletes in the 1980s had changed even more radically. In this book Dick Telford tells us of his belief that women can manage heavier training regimes than men and indicates the number of hours of training and kilometres of running that marathon star Lisa Martin puts in each week. Field event star Gael Martin bronze medallist in the shot at the Los Angeles Olympics and World Champion power lifter trained up to four and a half hours every day of the week — for a lot of the time this was squeezed into a day which included fulltime employment. She would train from 6.00am to 7.30am, noon until 1.30pm and from 5.00pm until at least 6.00pm. Her training involved running and weightlifting as well as practice of her particular events.

Today, standards in world sport are even higher and to have any hope of success, athletes have to train even harder and more effectively. The establishment of the Australian Institute of Sport which provides scholarships to allow the more promising athletes to train free of the need for a job, has been one response to this situation. In 1988, there were 114 sportswomen on scholarships at the AIS.

Attitudes also have changed. I have already referred to the fact that in the 1930s it was considered risqué that men and women should train together. In 1933 the executive of the South Australian Amateur Athletic Association withdrew its patronage of a women's walking team because there was 'not satisfactory control over the training of women athletes' by the Adelaide Harriers Club. By the 1950s, Dawn Fraser was able to train with men — but that may have been because she was so superior to the other women swimmers of her day, she virtually had to in order to have some sort of challenge. By the 1980s most of this sort of petty restriction has disappeared. After her 1984 Olympic gold medal, Glynis Nunn was actually invited to help with the training of an Adelaide League Football Team. As well as the symbolic importance of this particular event, she also quickly showed that she could do anything the footballers could do and was actually fitter than they were!

It can be argued with some validity that performances and achievements today by Australian athletes (both men and women) are less distinguished and successful than they were in the so-called 'golden age' of the 1950s. In reply, it might be stated that this merely reflects the fact that vastly more women around the world now participate in athletics than used to be the case; that as the eastern European countries have emerged from the devastation of war and realised the diplomatic and political advantages to be gained from success in sport; and as African and other developing countries have taken to sport, so women's (and men's) performances around the world have improved enormously. Australian women can still be successful on track and field as Glynis Nunn, Gael Martin, Sue Cook, Kerry Saxby, Debbie Flintoff King and Lisa Martin among others show.

The different nature of international sport today and the need to be more professional and thorough in training, coaching and overall preparation has been recognised by the Australian Government through its establishment of the Australian Institute of Sport in 1981. This provides the best of facilities, the best of coaching, the best of scientific support for promising men and women in a range of sports including athletics. Equal opportunity in most sports clubs and those sports where 'strength, physique and stamina' are not of major significance is now largely secured by various state and Commonwealth legislation. Sport and physical education in the primary school has gone a long way towards becoming either integrated or organised so that no girl can be stopped from playing in what have previously been regarded as boys sports if she is good enough.

The Commonwealth Schools Commission's recent Girls and Physical Activity project (Dyer 1986, Oldenhove and Emmel this volume) shows that the importance of opportunity and encouragement and skill training for young girls is recognised. In most State Departments of Sport and Recreation there are now women's advisers to the Minister whose job it is to promote the interests of women's sport and ensure that financial and other resources are allocated as equally as possible between men's and women's organisations. The establishment of the Women's Sport Promotion Unit to try and rectify the pronounced media inequalities in the coverage of men's and women's sport can be seen as the final link in the chain of government support. The rest, it might be said, is up to women themselves. And judging by the successes of Australian sportswomen in 1988 they are capitalising as almost never before on the opportunities open to them.

The foregoing is a reasonably clear statement of what might be termed the internalist view of women's sports history. Reading that, however, would not prepare anyone for the sort of history which Anne Summers writes in chapter 3 of her **Damned Whores and God's Police** nor Brian Stoddart in chapter 6 of his book **Saturday Afternoon Fever** nor the sort of article which Helen King wrote in 1979 entitled **The Sexual Politics of Sport: An Australian Perspective**. Nor, indeed, would it explain the need for and particular structure of the conference which this book reports and comments on.

In 1962 the Australian News and Information Bureau produced 'Sport: a Reference Paper' designed to give detailed information on the subject and a general review of the place of sport in Australia's culture. It was reproduced in 1976 in a volume entitled **Sport in Australia** (Jaques and Pavia 1976) at which time the editors of the volume observed that it was the only available statement on sport available from the Australian government and that it represented a viewpoint pertaining to sport much of which was as relevant in 1976 as when it was written in 1962!

There were 19 or so pages of this paper reproduced by Jaques and Pavia. Among other things, it mentioned most of the men and some of the women who had won had won medals, broken records and set standards in several of the more popular sports in Australia. Among these nineteen pages there are but three paragraphs devoted to women's sport; they begin with the following sentence:

> As elsewhere, **girls** in Australia had to work hard to be accepted as senior sporting personalities.

The penultimate paragraph of this chapter reads:

> **Girls** will continue to come, like Betty Cuthbert, from among the flower pots of her father's nursery to smash world records. **Men** like Herb Elliott will continue to lay their study books aside to run tirelessly up and down the sand dunes of Portsea until their muscles are toned sufficiently to take them to Olympian heights of sport.

The emphasis is mine. Other chapters in the book, including those headed *Sport in Australian Society: A Perspective; The Reasons Why: Young Men in a Hurry; Sport and the Australian Identity;* and *The Australian Government and Sport* simply make no mention of women's sport at all. One wonders which sort of treatment is preferable: trivialisation or total omission.

But that was 1976. The conference which this book records was held and this book was written in 1988 — Australia's Bicentenary year. Things surely have changed. Well, as some of the papers in this conference make clear some things have changed, but some things stay depressingly the same. The Australian Bicentennial Authority organised a Sport 88 Program to celebrate the Bicentennial and produced a bimonthly newspaper to report on events of significance.

An analysis of the first four issues of this quasi official view of Australian sport after 200 years of development is instructive. The four issues comprise 32 pages. On these pages there are a total of 120 photographs; of these 96 are of sportsmen, 90 being action photographs and 6 non-action portraits.

There are, on the same 32 pages, only 12 photographs of sportswomen in action and 2 non-action portraits. There are only 3 photographs involving both men and women (skating pairs etc) and there are 7 photographs of racing cars, yachts, etc in which the sex of the human participant is not mentioned and/or cannot be directly determined.

These four issues contained a total of 81 separate stories, articles or news items. Of these, 47 (or 58%) involved men only. Thirty-five separate sports were covered and there were four stories on recreational or fun events including such things as wheelbarrow racing, boomerang throwing and shearing. In comparison there were only 6 stories, involving 6 separate sports, exclusively concerned with women. This was just seven and a half per cent of all stories. There was a total of 21 stories, covering 17 separate sports, 2 recreational/fun events and 2 stories about sports Halls of Fame, in which both men and women were mentioned. Sometimes, the coverage of men's and women's aspects in these stories involving both sexes was about equal; very often, however, women were relegated to a brief mention in the last paragraph or two. Finally, there were 17 stories in which neither sex was explicitly or directly mentioned. These included 7 stories on sports for the disabled, on sports medicine, on sports sponsorship and two on recreational/fun events — namely earthworm racing and sheepdog trials.

So far as the Bicentennial authority is concerned, women have still hardly made it onto the sportsfield. Why is this?

Helen King concludes that in the early days of women's participation in sport, the particular sports in which women just participated:

assumed first a curative and then a preventive function to ward off sterility and ill-health, and then to maintain physical well-being. With sport relegated to this level, it was impossible for the efforts of sportswomen to be taken seriously. They were also to be encumbered by unpractical costumes and by customs which decreed that women's role in society was first and foremost as wives and mothers; anything else was of secondary importance. Such concepts were introduced at the school level and were reinforced by society at large in newspapers and journals. Where sports such as bicycling and tennis did become popular, it was due to the patronage of the rich and famous that made the pastime socially acceptable and fashionable to follow. Occasionally, the sport was taken over and organized by the 'ladies' of the middle and elite classes, as with cricket. However, serious competition was to be avoided, as it did not conform to ladylike behaviour and the cultural image of women, factors which continued to hamper the development and acceptance of sportswomen in 1920's and 1930's, and hampers their recognition today.

It accounts also for the exclusion of women from the more robust games of football, introduced for boys at school and later as a game to be played professionally. These games taught boys leadership, courage, and lessons in life; the lesson in life for girls was how to be a woman. Consequently, professional sportswomen were not to be found. When they did emerge, it was in the favoured and popular sports, and it is only these women who have so far achieved widespread recognition. It is only on intermittent occasions that sportswomen in Australia attract great attention, when their efforts are associated with the image of Australia at the international level. The great efforts of Australian women in team and other less-well-known sports are ignored in the rush to concentrate upon the efforts of Australian sportsmen. That such sportswomen for the most part remain anonymous is due to the nineteenth-century legacy which saw sport for women as a separate affair of little use beyond physical fitness and a mechanism to maintain the femininity of women.

(King 1979)

The explanation for the lack of recognition of women's sporting endeavour in the 1980s and their continued exclusion from many sports has to lie outside sport itself. Sport and physical activity is widely seen as a 'good thing' for both men and women in terms of improved self-esteem, health, quality of life and better performance at almost everything from academic work to sex. It is true that there are still some myths about sportswomen concerning greater vulnerability to injury, that they are the weaker sex in some non-specific way, and that sport will develop in them unsightly unfeminine muscles. But these myths are being dispelled, if slowly (Dyer 1982; Mitchell and Dyer 1985).

It is true, also, that there is still much prejudice and discrimination against women. But they cannot now be stopped from joining tennis, golf, bowls and other sporting clubs and they must be given equal access to facilities in these clubs once they have joined.

Sport in the 1980s is as much a part of Australian society and culture as it has ever been. But its place and function within that society is undoubtedly different today to what it was 80 or 100 years ago. In the first place it is a much more commercial operation. It is a market for the sale of millions of running shoes, tennis racquets, football jerseys and so on. It is also an advertising vehicle for hundreds of millions of dollars, through sponsorship, endorsements and above all television (Lawrence and Rowe 1986). Sport is both a marketable commodity and an incredibly effective outlet for advertising revenue.

Top level sport at present is in a positive feedback situation. The more it is marketed through the media, the more 'popular' it becomes and hence a better target for advertising. This in turn provides more money for marketing sport and so on.

Even though the evidence at club level and school level is that Australian sport is not that healthy eg the poorly supported Sheffield Shield cricket competition and the struggles of several of the less fashionable football teams (see also Jackie Byrne's, Rosemary Crowley's and Libby Darlison's papers in this volume), at elite and international level many sports are enormously affluent but very much beholden to advertisers and corporate sponsors. Hence sport is very much a general part of the sexist patriarchal society of western industrialised nations. Gender stereotypes are very much a part of that society; partly because as consumers distinctive males and distinctive females will spend money to maintain and enhance their differences. The differences will therefore be emphasised by advertisers, amongst others. All the Equal Opportunity Legislation and Affirmative Action programs will therefore find it very difficult to make progress against these sort of pressures.

Women's sport is therefore faced with two difficult and on the face of it equally unacceptable choices. If women participate in sport as it is at present largely constructed, with its emphasis on strength and stamina, they are conforming to the male view of sport. In their attempts to be successful they are likely to depart, to a greater or lesser extent, from the model of femininity currently adhered to in our society, which emphasises gentleness, submission, weakness and a body shape not always appropriate for sporting endeavours. Even though this view of women is largely created by men, it is a very powerful one not easily challenged — particularly by teenage girls. In the early years of women's sport it was the genteel sports of tennis and golf in particular which were socially acceptable for women. Today the range of sports in which women can participate without too much social sanction is much wider. But football (in its various codes), weightlifting, baseball, even cricket, although all played by women, are looked on with some suspicion. And other sports deemed appropriate for men are simply forbidden women — notably boxing and wrestling. And if women are too successful, for example some of the Eastern European swimmers, runners and throwers, then dark aspersions are made regarding their femininity.

Despite the enormous improvements in women's sports over the last few decades, it is likely that the advantages of strength physically and physiologically at least will always lie with men (ie the tallest and strongest men and those with the largest cardiovascular capacity will always exceed the top women in these areas). Hence if all sports became totally open or integrated, women would be unlikely to make the top teams or win the medals in those sports where such attributes are important and opportunities for them would undoubtedly diminish. But too much of an emphasis on records and achievements will reinforce the view of women as second best and always slightly inferior in most sports.

On the other hand a greater emphasis on those sports in which control, grace, skill, co-ordination and so on are of prime importance can very easily serve merely to re-emphasise those very feminine stereotypes which many women are trying to escape. The introduction of rhythm gymnastics and synchronised swimming into the 1984 Olympics gave us images of light, gentle, artistic women floating gracefully in the water or twirling ribbons to music. Such images do little to challenge male power and are taken by many as accepting the biological inferiority of women and their ornamental function. This in turn has repercussions both inside and outside sport. Within sport it severely hinders women's attempts to attain anything like equality of opportunity in other sporting areas. Are they ever likely to be taken seriously as pole vaulters, hammer throwers, racing car drivers, water polo players, ski jumpers and so on with these images of ultra gentility and ultra femininity seized on by the world's media? And if they are cast in this particular mould in sport they are likely to be similarly assumed to belong to the world of caring professions in and out of the home when they are off the sportsfield. The consequences of this are found at the top levels of sport and at the bottom. For example at the elite level the Australian Institute of Sport awarded 302 scholarships between 1981 and 1986 to promising young sports stars. One hundred and eighty two, or 60 per cent were to men and only 120 (40 per cent) were to women. In athletics there were exactly twice as many scholarships awarded to men (26) as to women (13). In 1988 there were 211 male scholarship holders and only 114 female. A total of 16 sports were supported in 10 of which scholarships were available to both men and women, in 5 of which scholarships were only available to males and only one of which (netball) was an exclusively female sport.

In school sports there are significant differences between girls and boys in terms of participation which appear to influence very strongly attitudes to sport in later life. In 1984 a health survey was undertaken by the Australian Capital Territory Health Commission. This found that while the percentage of boys and girls who had exercised three times or more a week was comparable up to year 10, the figures showed a marked discrepancy after that. In year 11, 81.3 per cent of the boys were in that category compared to 62.8 per cent of girls.

Wendy Ey found in 1982 that the decline of girls playing school sport began even before age 14. By that age only 22 per cent of girls participated in sports compared with 44 per cent of boys. The higher rate of dropping out among girls at all ages among high school students led to a much lower number of girls actively involved in sports in the senior school. The reasons boys and girls gave for dropping out of sport were similar: pressure of homework, lack of interest, part-time job taking all available spare time. There was, however, one significant reason given by girls only: ten per cent of the girls felt they were not good enough. This is a reflection of the poor self-image of adolescent girls. It reflects, among other things, the influence of cultural expectations on girls and earlier lack of opportunities for girls in the area of physical activities. MacIntosh and King (1976) found similar trends with students in Ontario, Canada. Two-thirds of the non-participants were female and they considered the main reason for not playing was that they were not good enough.

Less than than two decades ago a major survey was carried out in 13 government high schools in NSW and Victoria (Hawkes et al 1975). At both the girls' schools and all the coeducational schools they found that teachers complained of the fact that many girls weren't interested in participating. They quoted one physical education teacher as follows:

In form 1 they are usually interested, their skills depend on the quality of the program at the primary school they came from and how much sport they play outside school. By about halfway through form 2, a lot of them are beginning to think girls should be dainty and they are worrying about breaking their fingernails. By form 3, lots of them are turned off it altogether. As they get older, they're just less interested and well . . . it's hopeless.

The girls said things like: 'It just doesn't appeal to me', 'I just don't like it', 'There's nothing interesting to do', 'I prefer mucking around', 'It's too schoolish', 'It's too organised', 'I don't like changing or wearing uniforms', 'If you're tied down with a team you can't go out with boys', 'It's just not much fun', and 'I'm just not any good at it', etc.'

What we do not know is the extent to which this is the cause or the result of the disparity in sports offered to boys and girls in these and, presumably, most other schools. Hawkes et al found that in 1975 the largest of the boys' high schools with 1010 students offered 29 separate physical activities. The largest of the girls' high schools with 950 students offered only 9. Among all 13 schools there were 12 sports offered to boys only on a regular basis: aikido, baseball, fencing, flag rugby, lacrosse, rowing, rugby, rifle shooting, sailing, scuba diving, water polo, weight lifting. Only three sports were offered to girls only: judo, rounders and dance, including jazz ballet.

The authors also noted that men's sporting codes — football, soccer, rugby —

offered what they called 'bribes'. These were donations of equipment and uniforms to encourage the establishment of their particular sporting codes in schools. They came across no comparable donations to girls' sports. It is these very children who are now the parents of children just beginning school and sporting careers and who should be forming the nucleus of sports teams and sports clubs in Australia today. Not surprisingly in view of these facts, by the time they become adults, far fewer women participate in sport and physically orientated leisure activities than men. Not only are there fewer women participants, but there are fewer coaches, trainers, managers, announcers, owners, agents, umpires, and the like. Those who participate do so in a narrower range of activities. Women also watch sport, both live and on television, less than men, read about it less and talk about it less to their friends.

The reasons which women give for their low participation include lack of time, largely because of family responsibility; lack of transport, particularly difficult for those with young children; lack of money; and problems of safety and security in travelling about towns alone and at night. They might also have mentioned that there are more sports clubs with better facilities for men to join. And even in many of those clubs they can join they have until recently not been allowed to play at times which would be most convenient for them.

It will take some time before the full effects of the recent Anti-Discrimination legislation in this area becomes really apparent. It will take even longer before the discrimination, lack of encouragement and negative attitudes they received at school will cease to influence how mothers respond to their own children's attitudes to sport.

Both of the views of the development of women's sport which I have set out above, are valid and true. They have very different implications though. One of the most important things for would be young sportswomen is the presence of role models — successful women who youngsters can emulate and look up to for inspiration. But role models such as Dawn Fraser, Marlene Mathews, Shirley Strickland, Glynis Nunn, Lisa Martin and so on are women who made it despite the system — despite the lack of encouragement, the discrimination and so on. They are hardly the most appropriate people to talk about such difficulties. Their very successes, their records and medals suggest that the internalist view of sport as I have called it is of most significance. This in fact has repercussions regarding where the major efforts should be made — at school, at institutes for the elite, in the law courts, in economics or in the political arena. There is no one resolution to this dilemma, but much to be gained by exploring it further as various papers later in this volume in fact do.

Left: North Adelaide Rockets v Noarlunga City Tigers, District Women's Basketball Final, Adelaide, September 1986.
Photo: Doug Nicholas. Thanks to the Girls and Physical Activity Project.

Netball is one of the most popular participant sports in the world. It is gradually beginning to get the media coverage it deserves as a skilful, fast moving, exciting game. For long it was almost the only team game of it's type played by women. No longer; basketball and volleyball are now also very popular.

Right: A moment of high action in volleyball.
Photo: TAS Photographics. Thanks to the Australian Institute of Sport.

Left: An interstate netball game.
Photo: Cliff Rossel, Australian Institute of Sport.

Almost all athletics events are now practised by women. Famous Australian star Betty Cuthbert (below) is seen here in a typical shot during a 4 x 100m relay. When she ran the 400m at the 1964 Tokyo Olympics, however, it was the first time the distance had been run by women in the Olympic Games. Women marathon runners, such as Australia's Lisa Martin shown here (right) finishing a road race, had to wait until 1984 for their event to get on the program.

SECTION ONE
THE POLITICS OF WOMEN'S SPORT

AN INTRODUCTION

Ken Dyer

The papers in this section present a picture which is both depressing and optimistic and tell a story which is both recent and very old. Discrimination against women in sport at all levels from recreational to elite international is virtually universal and profound. It begins at school — or even earlier — and it continues throughout life. It concerns the opportunities for participation, encouragement to do so, facilities provided for women's sport, the support of clubs and international bodies and the nature and extent of coverage to women's sport provided by the media. The story is a long one, in that this sort of discrimination has been recognised and fought against for a long time in social, political and economic levels of life. It is a short one in that so far as sport is concerned it has really only been on the agenda of the women's movement for twenty years or so.

The questions raised by this discrimination, highlighted by the papers in this section, are many and varied. Perhaps first, we might ask why sport was so long in coming to the forefront of issues of concern — particularly since as we saw in the General Introduction, sport has been so central to the way of life and personal identity in Australia and women **have** been so successful.

There are many reasons — some of which the papers in this section allude to. In the first place, while sport is undoubtedly important, there has been disagreement among the women's movement as to whether it is as important as economic or political opportunities and equality. Is it right to argue about sport, some argue, when jobs, child care, family support, educational opportunities, health and so much else, seem very much more central to women's struggle. Secondly, there is some doubt as to whether sport, at least as it is presently structured and played by men, is such a good thing. Do women want to be part of a system which emphasises violence, competition, aggression and physical attributes so much.

Physical activity and skill mastery are undoubtedly good things for both men and women in terms of health, self-esteem, pleasure and so forth. But that doesn't mean that women should accept the agenda of sport largely designed by and for men which are currently available. In this vein, Lois Bryson argues that much of the problem is with men's sport not with women's sport. it emphasises the values of aggression and competition and devalues artistry, skill and co-operation. This point is also made by Abby Hoffman in her paper through some striking examples. Nevertheless, there is a dichotomy of views here and by no means all women would agree with Lois Bryson on this. This emphasises that it is indeed difficult to arrive at a convincing and universally held general philosophy on a set of practices concerned with advancing women's sport. Abby Hoffman refers to a conference on women in sport held in Canada in 1974 which produced many recommendations but no set of principles or general philosophy underlying them. She describes the emergence of a general view in Canada in which a change was gradually effected such that women were no longer treated as an isolated special target group. The whole sport system became the target. Libby Darlison in her paper implies that such a view is indeed the correct one to follow. But she suggests that in Australia we are some way from adopting that viewpoint — at least so far as the Australian Sports Commission and other official bodies are concerned.

Undoubtedly, one of the reasons why it has taken such a depressingly long time for women's sport to be recognised as important and the subject of gross discrimination is that it has in Abby Hoffman's words 'a silent unwritten history'. The reasons why its history is silent is made clear anecdotally by Abby Hoffman herself and with overwhelming statistical backup by Helen Menzies. A one time practising journalist, Helen demonstrates the appalling record of the Australian media even in the 1980s in covering women's sport. It may have been obvious when pointed out, but documenting conclusively the very low coverage of women's sport, both in terms of the number of column centimetres and range of sports covered, has affected a lot of people in a lot of ways. It played a large part in the setting up of the Commonwealth Government's Working Group on Women in Sport and in the production of its report **Women, Sport and the Media**. And this in turn led to the setting up of the Women's Sport Promotion Unit that Margaret Pewtress describes in Section 7. Inadequately funded as that organisation may be, it is still a big step forward — and shows that small individual acts can have significant cumulative consequences. Progress within the media concerning improved coverage of women's sport is, however, regrettably slow. Helen Menzies' original 1980 survey was repeated by her in 1984 and again in 1988. Little seems to have changed as her paper in Section 7 makes depressingly clear. (Sandy Gordon in his paper in Section 4 also reports on a 1988 media survey with similar findings.)

The phenomenon is worldwide, as Abby Hoffman's examples attest. Among the other problems which the papers in Section 7 raise, is how to translate these insights and demonstrated inequalities into positive and fruitful action. The attitudes which regard women's sport as minor, inferior, less interesting and less skilful are deeply entrenched. There is no absolute agreement as to whether the main attempt to change things should be at the political, legal, financial or behavioural level. Nor, indeed, as these papers show, is there any unanimity over what should be the long-term objectives. What would sport in which men and women played equal roles actually look like? And what sort of effort should be put into actually trying to achieve this equality. In this regard, sport is much like any other major area about which women are concerned. And all are agreed on at least one thing: debate of the issues will positively inform and help the sort of action which is needed.

WOMEN'S SPORT: SOCIOLOGY AND POLITICS

Libby Darlison

Much of what I will say in this paper has been said by myself and many others many, many times before. Nevertheless because things change so slowly, they may be worth saying again. Changes there have been, but they need maintaining and consolidating.

To illustrate some of the changes we have yet to achieve, I will first present some statistics on women in our society generally. These statistics are not about sport but they may help to put our concerns about sport into perspective. Two out of three of the world's illiterates are women; one half of women over the age of 15 in the developing world are already mothers; only one third of the world's women have any access to contraceptive information or devices; and more than half do not have any access to trained help during pregnancy or childbirth. In industrialised countries, women receive only half to two thirds of the rate of pay that men receive for doing the same jobs.

Women are relatively well-off in Australia — although the above statistics still probably apply to Aboriginal women in this country. But we still have to ensure that such gains as we have achieved are maintained.

Women's sport is therefore only one issue among many with which we should be concerned. But women's sport at any and all levels often involves the myths, inequities, the stereotypes and the sex discrimination which women generally experience. Quite often, there is a lot of effort put in to ensure that the connections that women might make between sport and the rest of life are not made. It is made easier to separate sport from the rest of life — as if the idiosyncratic issues of sport are different from and less important than those which arise elsewhere.

Sport and war, it is said, are the last bastions of male chauvinism. Women's sport is much more than the provision of better resources, better facilities, more opportunity. What we are talking about is resisting and revolutionising some very conservative attitudes to women and some very entrenched power bases, deeply entrenched in historical precedent and practice. Many men and many women too, regard these practices as both immutable and natural. In this country particularly, the relationship between sport and male power, prestige and status has evidenced itself in all areas of our life. Sport has always played an important part in presenting our country on the international stage and more intimately in the relationship between the sexes. Our political leaders are very conscious of the power of sporting associations and if they do not play sport themselves are keen to be present at major sporting events, to be No. 1 ticketholders, to present the medals and so on.

Historical precedents have to be overcome. Whatever their occupational background, class, status and power, prowess in sport, especially those sports involving overt displays of strength, aggression and dominance, has always been seen as enhancing a male's maleness. And unfortunately, they have also often been seen as enhancing a women's maleness too. This is a real problem for sportswomen. They have to play down the very qualities that are so highly regarded by and so prominent in their male peers, lest they be seen on and off the sporting field as strong, confident, determined or competitive or assertive. There are now increasing numbers of women who are not prepared to adhere to that double standard. They are saying they wish to determine for themselves their own sexuality, their own concept of being female and that they will in fact do so.

I think that this aspect of the sexual politics of women's sport is very persuasive. And unless women athletes are so good that they simply cannot be ignored by press, sponsors, or audience, then they tend just to conform to an imposed concept of femininity. They feel they have to emphasise that they are still women and spend as much time putting on their make-up as preparing for their events.

Women have to define for themselves what it is to be female. I want to emphasise that point because it is not restricted to sport. In whatever field of endeavour you choose to identify, those women who are prepared to flaunt convention, stand up for what they believe in, particularly if that involves challenging the beliefs of the dominant group, have always been marginalised. They have always been told that they are not real women, that they have a problem. And of course in a way, they do have a problem just dealing with these sort of accusations. We have to be prepared for these criticisms, we have got to be prepared to be vocal, we have got to be prepared to stand up for what we believe in and believe in our goals, our talents and our achievements. We have got to be much more visible and much more vocal or we are not going to have any say in the decisions which affect our lives.

Now it is one thing to say this and another thing to do it. We know all about our under-representation at decision making points in our society. The under-representation is greater at higher levels than lower. For example, there are ten men and two women on the Australian Sports Commission. Among Australian Institute of Sport Head Coaches, there are fifteen males and two females. At the level of the Olympic Committee — international representation — the situation is even more disastrous. There are forty-five men representatives and only three women. At that level, women are virtually invisible. Women do have to be better at promoting themselves and making themselves visible. There is really no shortage of able women who can do the sort of jobs required.

The other major area of the politics of women's sport in which women are deficient is the area of lobbying. It is one thing to have the policies developed and quite another to get them implemented. The Women's Sport Promotion Unit is a big advance. It's birth was slow and difficult and it does not have all the features many of us feel it ought to have, but at least it does exist and is starting to do things. Remember though, we must keep it there and keep it alive. Women must get together as a lobby and support, criticise and help the Unit. We must ensure that they are kept honest: that they are doing the sort of things that sportwomen really want them to do.

So, let us define our priorities; let each of us use the undoubted skills we do have and let us get on and do something. So far as the Women's Sport Promotion Unit is concerned, I believe that the ultimate judgement of its success will be when it doesn't exist anymore. When all sports treat all people as equal, when discrimination is a thing of the past, when the Unit no longer has a need to be in existence, then we can say it has finally succeeded.

SPORT: A FEMINIST PERSPECTIVE

Lois Bryson

The title of my paper as it originally appeared in the program was 'Women's Sport — A Feminist Perspective'. On reflection, however it becomes clear that this is not an appropriate way to frame the issue. Fundamentally the major problem for women's sport is men's sport. Thus to achieve a feminist perspective we must consider sport generally, not just women's sport, and sport must also be considered within the wider social context.

There are two major dilemmas facing a feminist perspective on sport. First, sport is so essentially a masculine domain that even as women participate they are in danger of reinforcing masculine values and men's power. This has the effect of tacitly devaluing things that women do and making their achievements seem inferior. Sport thus plays a significant part in maintaining male domination.

A second dilemma concerns what sort of equality should women seek. If we claim equality in everything regardless of how desirable, then there really is no fundamental dilemma. All we need to do is work out strategies and tactics to gain a half share. Not that wrestling away currently held advantages proves an easy exercise in practice; nonetheless it is not difficult to sketch out the agenda. If, however, at the same time as achieving what we might call simple distributive equality, we wish also to work towards a generally more equal and just society, then the problem is much more complex. We must ask whether we want women to share equally in all things including, for example, acts of violence, the waging of wars and the maintenance of class relationships? In promoting dominant sport as it is constituted today, we are inevitably giving tacit support to the competitiveness, aggressiveness, hierarchy, conflict and discrimination that are embedded in it.

In terms of feminist approaches, what I am posing is the classic tension between a liberal feminist approach to equality and a more radical one. A liberal approach takes the general framework of society as quite acceptable, except for a few blemishes here and there. Gender inequality is seen as one such imperfection. A more radical approach, be it socialist feminist, radical feminist or whatever, sees more things wrong than that. There is concern to do away with all forms of inequality and it is accepted that achieving gender equality should not be at the expense of perpetuating other major forms of inequality, such as race and class inequality.

Taking up the first dilemma — the masculine nature of sport — it is evident that sport as we know it, was actually developed to enhance masculinity and the power of the upper class and it deliberately excluded women. Thus it is small wonder that the task of reclaiming sport as a non-sexist activity is likely to be a difficult and long term process.

While the historical bases of sport can be traced much further back, the origins of modern sport are generally located in nineteenth century Britain. At the time Social Darwinism, with its tenet of survival of the fittest in the human social context as well as the biological, was widely subscribed to. There was extensive segregation of the sexes and a belief that they possessed, innately and inevitably, very different biological and intellectual capacities. Those who promoted 'muscular Christianity' in Britain were concerned to promote sport for its effects on male identity, solidarity and the exercise of power. Of course their mission could have failed: it is abundantly clear that it did not. Baron Pierre de Coubertin was certainly highly impressed by 'muscular Christianity' and was spurred by this doctrine to establish the modern Olympics (Dyer and Dwyer 1984). Today, boys are still taught in a quite straightforward way that sport is a significant part of manliness. At the same time as boys are taught various skills and a sense of superiority, they are taught the need to be tough and bear pain. In this manner sport provides a direct training in a sense of power and forcefulness as well as promoting male solidarity. This has profound effects. Sociologist Bob Connell has pointed to the way in which *concern with force and skill becomes a statement embedded in the body* which is translated *into muscle tensions, posture, the feel and texture of the body.*

In this way, he suggests, power *becomes naturalised* and *important in allowing a belief in the superiority of men . . . to be sustained* [even] *by men who in other respects have little power* (Connell 1987: 85). This co-option by males of power, strength, aggression and forcefulness through sport, is particularly significant in dominance and domination. Radical feminists such as Brownmiller (1976), Anthea Dworkin (1981) and Mary Daly (1978) actually see this physical coercion as **the** major source of male dominance. Other feminist theorists propose rather more complex and compounded causation, but nonetheless coercion remains a central and an irreducible dimension of power.

Socialisation and psychoanalytic theories have long told us that gender formation for males is more problematic than it is for females. Boys are expected to break their early identification with the mother, yet there are not many men around on a day-to-day basis on whom to model their behaviour. The distancing of males from females is posed for boys as an urgent and emphasised reaction which can create an uncertainty and even anxiety about their personal development (Dinnerstein, 1977). This explanation helps account for the fact that many men learn stereotypical masculine behaviour too well and exhibit aggressive and violent behaviour which extends beyond the bounds of the socially approved. In virtually all advanced capitalist societies it is men who fill the gaols, assault both women and men and who generally commit acts of violence. It is significant that this virtual monopolisation of violence by men is rarely publicly remarked on. If any other sub-group was pin-pointed as the perpetrator of all the more serious crimes in our society, it seems certain that they would be identified and the subject of some direct action.

The message which sport conveys is powerful not only because it contributes to personality formation; it is also an immediate mass reality, a reality which forms part of our daily lives. With the increasing commercialisation of sport, and an associated increase in media exposure, the ever-present nature of this reality is likely to be magnified. Thus we are constantly exposed to the promotion through sport of a stereotypical form of masculinity or what has been called hegemonic masculinity (Tim Carrigan, Bob Connell and John Lee 1985: 590).

The effect is the stronger because of the implicit and at times explicit (football coaches routinely accuse their teams of playing like a pack of girls) message which suggests that everything that falls outside the stereotypic frame is inferior. In this way sport contributes to the oppression of women and some men, notably gay men and men with physical disabilities.

Despite its strongly masculine flavour, sport is not a monolithic institution. Sport is claimed as a masculine activity in the face of increasing opposition from women and some men. The areas of overt challenge have gradually expanded as women have extended their participation and their range of sporting activities. Participation itself, however, is just the tip of the iceberg. The processes that disadvantage women are often submerged and even now may be maintained even in the teeth of women's participation (Bryson 1987). In addition, as the challenges strengthen, we must be alert to the possibility (probability?) of new counter-strategies which protect the traditional terrain.

Valued characteristics are attributed to males through their virtual monopoly on the definition of what is important in sport. It has been pointed out that an ideology which claims to be based on biological differences is very powerful as it denies all challenge (Willis 1982: 117). A fixed view of biology is of course itself ideological, since biology is actually mutable (Birke and Vines 1987: 337). The use to which physical capacity can be put is malleable, as even the most cursory glance at the evolution of world sporting records demonstrates (Hargreaves, 1983; Dyer 1982 Dyer and Dwyer 1984). [Dyer summarises some of this evidence in his paper in Section Three of this volume and discusses how even this obvious biological malleability has been interpreted in a way which undervalues, misinterprets or denigrates women's obvious achievements in physical performance *Ed.*]. On top of this and more importantly, even if biology were fixed and differences between women and men were immutable, so that men inevitably and irrevocably did have an edge in sport as we know it, the hierarchy of values which places speed, power, or goal kicking capacity above grace, gentleness, endurance or intuition, is itself clearly socially constructed and can be changed. Jan Wright, commenting on physical education, demonstrates the way in which dominant definitions make people blind to the realities of situations. She notes that physical education teachers, particularly male teachers, often see girls as 'really hopeless', while not acknowledging their superiority to boys in dance, rhythm and spatial skills (1987:20).

Dominant definitions present problems not only for women but also for men who do not wish, or are not able to emulate or even admire the dominant values. This includes men who are non-competitive, cerebral, artistic, gentle, disabled or just not physically skillful. To achieve equality for all, we need to work strenuously to change dominant definitions of sport to something inclusive, something congenial to all people.

As well as suffering because of men's appropriation of the definition of sport and the solidarity that this fosters among men, sport clearly results in discrimination against women in a straightforward sense. They are denied equal access to the benefits that sport's participation brings. Women certainly do not have access to half of the economic resources that are poured into and come out of the sporting enterprise. Men benefit infinitely more than women from the financial rewards that cluster around employment in sport and its allied fields; and as the level of commercialisation increases, the inequity increases. Men also benefit far more from the distribution of resources from government and elsewhere that are made available to make participation in sport possible. To the extent that social status is associated with material criteria, the achievement of recognised status is facilitated by access to resources. Thus unequal access to resources has a direct effect on personal well-being, in addition to the straightforward health benefits associated with participation in sport.

Men overwhelmingly have direct control of sports' organisations and there is an overwhelming majority of men among politicians who are responsible for decisions of direct relevance to sport, and among business people who are responsible for decisions about promotion and sponsorship. Thus with few exceptions, men are making critical decisions that frame the environment in which both men's and women's sport exists. Men fill most of the positions in the media, both as commentator and administrators and this gives power in the arena of image making and projection. The effects of this direct control of virtually all sport by men are too extensive to document, but range from better funding for male sports, through superior access to grounds, equipment, times for matches and for practice, infinitely better access to the media, sponsorship, training facilities and coaches, and so on and so on. Thus while women as tax payers and consumers are significant contributors to the costs of sport, it is clear they do not reap proportional benefits.

Perhaps even more fundamental is the power men maintain over the social construction and projection of the social phenomena we call sport.

Clearly women have always challenged the dominant conception. The question we must confront is how can the challenge be continued and made more effective? Challenge in sport must be seen in the total context of overcoming gender oppression. We have to approach the task through its component parts rather than treat it as a whole, as this tends to support the dominant definitions. The methods for attacking discrimination in employment apply equally to employment in sport. Equality in education must be made to embrace equality in physical education and sport. We need to get the biology, physical education, sport's medicine and human kinetics books rewritten to correct the myths and make good the omissions. Media bias must be treated in terms of general rules about discrimination, as must club membership, the use of facilities and the distribution of resources. We need to develop and foster general principles which address inequality in sport but are not exclusive to the one area.

With resources it is important that women gain genuine power over decision-making, because we may wish our 'half share' to be expended on something other than sport itself (child care is a pressing issue) at least initially. If we are successful in moving away from the hierarchical, elite model of sport for women, this may prove less costly in the long run. In fairness women should decide how any such 'savings' are to be spent.

If policies are to bite at all, we need strong watchdog organisations with appropriate government and community support. The recently formed Women's Sport Promotion Unit is a promising start, but it remains to be seen how extensive and serious is the support it receives. Certainly its initial funding is inadequate. Thus it is not surprising that many of us feel a bit doubtful — but we must hope, advocate and agitate as this is a start of considerable potential. [See Chairperson Margaret Pewtress's contribution to this volume which introduces and describes this Unit *Ed.*].

To achieve genuine equality we need systematic redistribution. This is the nub of the matter. It means that women need to get more of the resources than men until things are evened up. This is the part of the equation that is largely overlooked when politicians espouse equal opportunity policies. This is not surprising since most are men and their own interests and those of just under half of their electorate is inevitably involved — the rather more powerful group to boot. Male sport has taken on something of a sacred status which politicians are keen to make use of (think of Prime Ministers and the America's Cup, Grand Finals, Test matches, golf championships etc.), but are loathe to challenge.

STRATEGIES FOR CHANGE: SOME THOUGHTS FROM THE CANADIAN EXPERIENCE

Abby Hoffmann

Introduction

The purpose of this paper is to make some contribution based on the Canadian experience of strategies for change to improve sport for females. I am not presuming that the Canadian experience is directly applicable to the Australian situation, but my general view is that the general approach now used in Canada may prove useful at least to highlight certain aspects of the debate on strategies for change in women's sport in the Australian context.

As I prepared this paper, I asked myself again *what is the situation we are trying to change; the problems we are endeavouring to overcome*. There are many limiting factors and barriers — both attitudinal and material — but several have arisen in recent weeks — almost as reminders about the status of sport for women — and I thought they might be worth examining in a little detail, since they are so typical of the situations with which women are constantly being confronted in the sports world.

The Calgary Winter Olympics

Just as in the summer Olympics, in the winter Olympics women are severely disadvantaged in terms of the number of sports and the number of events open to them. There are 10 sports on the Olympic program, in only 5 of which do women compete. It is true that the rules don't actually prohibit entries from women in bobsleigh and ski jumping — but the lack of opportunities for women to compete in these sports does effectively bar them. Within these 10 sports there are 46 distinct events of which 28 (61%) are available to men, 18 (35%) are available to women (two are mixed). The proportion of female competitors has certainly increased in recent years from about 12.5 per cent in 1948 to about 23 per cent in 1988, but there is obviously still a long way to go.

There is obviously a complementary relationship between the demonstrated interest of females to compete in specific sports and the availability of opportunities to do so. Changes do occur, women do take up new sports, but in the absence of formal mechanisms and institutional and possibly legislative support the process is long and hard. [Doris Brown in her contribution to this volume describes some of the problems faced by pioneer women long distance runners. And that sport might be described as having been relatively easily conquered. It certainly seems far easier than women's soccer, judo and most other sports *Ed.*].

On the subject of the Olympic Program, it doesn't help matters when the only female member of the IOC's Program Commission, from Bulgaria as it happens, says that to strive for complete equality among women and men in the Olympic Games is not realistic, considering that men's popular sports happen to be more numerous.

Yes, it may be unrealistic to accomplish now; but it is surely not unrealistic to strive for. To say that men's popular sports happen to be more numerous makes it sound as though this state of affairs just occurred through some act of God or nature. On the contrary, gender-based inequality has logical explanations, in terms of male actions, choices and decisions. It is these we must understand if we are to make changes.

There is another aspect of the Winter Olympics which is different for women and men but just as significant in terms of its effects. I refer to the trivial and highly sexist treatment of the female competitors by the media. Katarina Witt, the East German figure skater, defending Olympic Champion and World Champion, was surely one of the most outstanding athletes in the Games. And yet at her opening press conference her sporting skills and achievements were largely ignored in favour of trivial, irrelevant, largely sexist questions about boyfriends, clothes, femininity and so forth. Her enormous sporting ability was totally ignored. Male athletes were usually given a much more serious treatment. The macho image of male athleticism was communicated by the media when they emphasised reports that the father of Italian ski champion Alberto Tomba would buy his son a red Ferrari if he won an Olympic gold medal and by their reporting of Tomba's alleged boastful assertion that he was so good that he could ski down a slalom course, take time to make love to a woman and still win!

The sports media

The quantity and standard of reporting of women's sport in the daily print and electronic media is terrible, as Helen Menzies confirms in her paper in this volume. But the specialist sports press is little better; much of what it has to report makes depressing reading. I support this assertion not by any systematic survey, but by a casual perusal of some recent sports magazines and their content.

Sports Intern Magazine from West Germany for January 1988 had an article on 1987 World Rankings. Not this time the top performers — but the world's most influential sport leaders. The top 12 included the Presidents of the International Olympic Committee, the IOC Board, FIFA President, IAAF President, FINA President and the Presidents of the Olympic Committees of the major nations. Among these there was not a single woman. Nor was there a woman amongst the next tier — presidents of International Federations of slightly less prominent sports or National Olympic Committees of the second rank of sports nations. In fact among all countries there is only one whose National Olympic Committee has a female president and only three International Federations of significant sports have a female as Secretary-General.

Continental Sports Magazine for Autumn 1987 had a special feature on women in the Olympic movement and in the International Sports Federations. Two of the articles in this special feature were in fact on the wives of the International Olympic Commission President and the President of the world soccer federation FIFA. This in itself says a lot about the view of 'women in sport'. But in fact 25 per cent of the article on the wife of Antonio Samaranch, the president of the IOC, was taken up with a description of how her cooking skills are not taxed by Mr Samaranch's frugal eating habits. My response to all this is who cares about Mr. Samaranch's eating habits. What I want to know from him is when women's judo is going to get into the Olympic program; why has baseball been allowed into the Olympics but not women's softball. This sort of article illustrates a major problem which women face. They are still defined by virtue of their connections to men. Would we expect to see similar articles on the husbands of famous female sport personalities?

I next report a purely Canadian example, and one which is not even from the mainstream sports media but from a book published by the Canadian Curling Association — **The Curling Fact Book 1988**. Curling is to my mind a boring sport. It is a sort of bowls on ice, but one which happens to be very popular in Canada. In the first place there are two sections in the book, 'Curling' and 'Women's Curling', as if somehow women do something different. Within these sections there are two photos, the captions of which convey a great deal. The first is of an incident in a men's game. It is captioned 'Intensity at the World Championships' The second, a few pages later is captioned 'Pretty Girls Curl Too'.

Finally I wish to comment on two sentences from the Presidential Speech which Primo Nebiolo gave at the IAAF 75th Anniversary celebrations held at the 1987 World Track and Field Championships in Rome. Among other things he said that:

> Seventy-five years ago women were not a part of the sports world. Today they play an equal role in track and field athletics, bringing to our sport the qualities of grace and beauty.

First, his definition of equality is not mine. How can a competition program in the Olympics and World Championships that lacks 2 walk events, 2 jumping events, 1 throwing event and 1 track event (the steeplechase) be said to be equal? Or how can the fact that there are only 2 female representatives on IAAF Committees (other than the Women's Committee!) and there are no female Councillors or Executive members be said to indicate that women 'play an equal role'.

Second I turn to the notions of grace and beauty which are inevitably and exclusively, it seems, associated with women. Two of my childhood heroes in athletics were Australian Sprinters Betty Cuthbert and Brazilian male triple jumper Adhemar Ferreira da Silva. For me Betty Cuthbert brought power and immense effort to sport — typified by those famous photos of her at the finish of her races, mouth open, body straining, lunging for the tape [see photo on p.16 *Ed.*]. On the other hand it was da Silva who brought seemingly effortless grace and beauty to athletics.

At its anniversary celebration in Rome in 1987, the IAAF introduced a wonderful book and film featuring 100 great moments in the history of the sport. The fact that these 100 moments included only 24 females might be understandable, given the somewhat abbreviated history of women's athletics. But between 1912 and 1960 only two females were recognised (Fanny Blankers-Koen and Wilma Rudolph) and from 1960 still only about one third of the moments (22/65) featured women. Based on these few random but recent examples what are some of the problems which emerge?

— There is a general trivialisation of women and their achievements.
— There are inadequacies in the competitive program — throughout the system not just in the Olympics.
— There is a general lack of understanding of the relationship between participation in and popularity of sports and the availability of opportunities to participate in them.
— There is blatant sexism in much of the reporting of sport.
— There is an almost total lack, or at best severe deficiency, of women in key leadership positions in sport.
— There are widespread stereotypic notions of female athleticism inevitably and exclusively meaning grace and beauty.
— There are problems with the definition of equality.

Any strategies for change must address these problems (and others), and while confronting them head on, must attack also their origins. In many instances the problem as we in Canada see it in sport is simply the manifestation of some more fundamental forces operating in the general society. Where, then, can we look for guidance both to help us to understand these problems for women in sport, and direct us to strategies which will rectify them?

The history of the movement for change in Canada

Quite a few people have been working hard in this area for many years. In 1967 a Royal Commission on the Status of Women was established which reported in 1970. Sport featured in its report in only a minor way, but one of its major findings was that there was a much lower participation rate in sport among school age girls compared to boys. [As Henny Oldenhove shows in her paper in this volume, the same thing is true in Australia and has remained true nearly twenty years after the work of this Canadian Royal Commission *Ed.*]. In 1973 the Federal Department of Sport created the first program related to women in sport and initiated various promotional activities. The first National Conference on Women in Sport was held in 1974 at which virtually every woman significantly involved in organising, coaching, leading and administering sport in Canada was represented.

Many recommendations resulted from this conference, but they were indiscriminately directed to all and sundry without regard to jurisdiction, contradiction among recommendations, priorities, costs, realism etc. There was, in other words, no organising principle or philosophy underlying the recommendations.

No systematic research or data gathering was carried out and consequently when the first Sport Minister ever in Canada, who happened to be a woman, concluded the development of a National Sport Policy for Canada after several years work, women barely rated a mention. The attempt to hit every target had obviously been counterproductive. During the late 1970s even the promotional programs dwindled to nothing.

In 1980 the Federal Government initiated a new women's program. It was without any coherent policy framework, nor was it based on any research data but it had nevertheless some reasonably sound program elements. It contained, for

— a leadership survey

— a planning workshop which eventually led to the creation of a national advocacy organisation CAAWS

— an internship program for women athletes

— various promotional projects including biographies of notable female Canadian athletes

— the provision of special project seed money for projects devised by National Sports Organisations aimed at increasing female participation.

This program was implemented for 3 to 4 years and achieved a number of positive things. But there were still some clear limitations. In retrospect, the biggest single shortcoming in my view, was that women were treated as a special population (a target population as the bureaucrats like to call women) almost outside of the existing sport system. We took the approach that the problem was women as a group, and that we needed to 'do some repair work on women' and then things would be OK — this would bring about equality. Actually we knew that this approach wasn't really going to work, but we really didn't know what was wrong with it, and we weren't sure which way to go.

What evolved over several years, was a movement away from treating females as a target population, to a better understanding that we must deal with the inherent sex inequality of the sport system in Canada, and that the gender-based inequality in sport was closely related to social, economic and political inequality in the general society. These conclusions were arrived at in 1982/3. But it took several years to devise a policy based on them. From the vantage point of 1988, this is hardly earth-shattering news.

But it is worthy of a reminder because while I think we may be more conscious of the societal roots of inequality today, that does not necessarily mean that we act on the basis of that knowledge.

And, it is understandable why we don't. If we look at the literature on women and sport we can see why. This is not the place for an exhaustive critique of the academic contributions to the field of women in sport, but a quick overview of some key areas might be helpful, if only as a reminder as to what we should avoid.

The contribution of previous research planning for change

Regardless of the subject area, previous research tends to be descriptive, perhaps analytical, but almost never prescriptive in any meaningful way. I will consider some aspects of prevous research under three headings. Firstly History.

The historical record highlights the nature of female involvement in antiquity; it describes the early revival of the Olympic movement and the international sport movement. There are also numerous national studies. But:

  (i) The history is incomplete; one generally finds that there was a great deal more going on than the literature suggests — we have a silent unwritten history

 (ii) There is almost no social analysis which would connect periods of advance and regression in women's sport to different social, economic and political conditions. There is, for example, said to be a golden age for women's sport in Australia in the 1950s and 1960s. Why? There seems to have been little analysis carried out with a view to explaining why.

(iii) Previous research or its analysis contains few, if any, prescriptive recommendations. It was as if merely pointing out the deficiencies was sufficient.

The second main heading for considering earlier research is that of psychosocial meanings.

This field looks at the impact of sport involvement on females in terms of both the psychological development of the female athlete herself, and on the perceptions of society of the female athlete. The researchers in this discipline seem to suffer from a pervasive, perverse, persistent obsession with the femininity (and masculinity) of the female athletes.

We have suffered decades of alleged 'sex role conflict' as a causal explanation for lower levels of female sport involvement. Are we any further ahead as a result? While there are clearly some aspects of sport which make it unattractive to females, my suggestion would be that lack of opportunity to participate in sport, lack of adequate introductory programs for girls in schools, lower expectation when it comes to physical performance among girls (itself a product of some abstruse link in the minds of educators, instructors and parents about the natural ability and proclivity of boys for vigorous activity, by contrast with the more passive and less capable young female) etc. are far more influential in deterring young females from active involvement in sport than are all sex role conflict theories.

The point is that there are clearly questions of motivation which require study and which would be helpful in planning programs which would attract female participants. But little work of real value has been done in this field. And, to make matters worse, psychologists have helped perpetuate the bi-polar notions of masculinity and femininity which can be extremely oppressive for women; and simply serve to maintain the social sanction on sport involvement by females.

Thirdly and finally there are the biological issues. Previous research, particularly in the last two decades, has dealt quite thoroughly with many of the so-called medical and physiological problems and limitations which females might encounter as a consequence of involvement in vigorous sports and games.

There are indeed two or three papers in this volume which summarise them and I need only cite the volumes by Dyer (1982) and Wells (1985) to support the assertion. Compared with two decades ago, scientists are now very interested in women's physiology and performance. But some things don't change. Scientists today show an inordinate interest in those aspects of female athleticism which might affect reproductive capacity and fertility. In this they are no more than reproducing the less focussed concerns and more extravagant claims of the past concerning the likelihood of inducing permanent sterility or less severe damage as a result of sporting exertion (Lenskyj 1986).

A recent example is the pre-occupation with amenorrheic female distance runners and the impact that reduced body fat percentages and certain hormones (notably oestrogen) might have on fertility. The pre-occupation with fertility has prevented investigation on other matters of interest to epidemiologists and females themselves: namely that the reduced fat and oestrogen levels of the female athlete may be one of the best defences against the major cancer killers among women — breast and uterine cancer — as well as against diabetes.

The physiological and bio-medical research literature is filled with articles which document differences among males and females on various physical parameters and tests. But, it is apparent that research which failed to document differences or indeed confirmed similarities among males and females was not considered to be significant research at all, and hence was often not published or seriously pursued. As Felshin and Oglesby (1986) have said *almost every girl who has played sport knows she is as good as some boy.* Yet the formal literature until very recently has led us only to consider differences in capacity/strength, physique, stamina etc. between the sexes. The underlying problem is the bias which infuses the questions which are asked in the first place. The point is that the answers we might seek on such questions as the suitability of mixed sex sport, simply aren't there because the researchers are victims of their own biases.

And their biases do not run only to assumptions of male physical superiority, but include presumptions about the social role implications of women which are derived from their biological functions. Once the medical community got over the psychological hurdle of believing that pregnant women might be also interested in exercise, they were prepared to entertain the notion that exercise might have a salutory effect on pregnancy, and proceeded to study and prescribe exercise for pregnant women. (One might add that they have contributed little to this field that anecdotal information from any of our mothers would not also have provided.) But such are the pre-occupations and priorities of the medical profession that while they have studied the influence of exercise on pregnancy, we can find almost nothing in the literature which documents the impact of pregnancy on the female athlete. After all, as we all know, the priority task of females is having children, not sport! So we are, presumably, to be interested in how exercise enhances pregnancy but not how pregnancy may affect the serious athlete.

If historical analyses, the work of mainstream psychologists and sociologists and the bio-medical experts and physiologists, have been of little help to us, who can be of help in formulating policy? In terms of our policies we have turned increasingly to what can generally be described as feminist modes of analysis. It is this therefore which forms the final segment of my paper.

Feminist modes of analysis

There are many definitions of feminism, and it is not my intention or desire to describe any of them in any depth. For the purpose of this paper and as far as relevance to Canadian policies on women in sport is concerned, we mean by feminism the definition which Janet Radcliffe Richards adopted in her book **The Sceptical Feminist**

> feminism is intended to mean only that there are excellent reasons for thinking that women suffer from systematic social injustice because of their sex.

To that we would add some other elements: the notion of patriarchy; the need for some significant economic and political transformation in the gender-based arrangements in society if radical change in any specific area is to occur; a commitment to social action; and a healthy scepticism about the traditional explanations as to how and why things got to be the way they are.

Doubtless we would be accused in Canada of pursuing very liberal, as opposed to radical, solutions to the women in sport questions, because on the one hand we have chosen government policy as a viable vehicle for change, and on the other because we do not see society as so monolithically patriarchal that at least worthwhile incremental change is impossible.

In fact I will go a step further in arguing the case for a liberal approach by noting the fact that sport not only takes place in the public domain, but is largely supported in almost all industrialised countries (be they socialist, capitalist or something in between) by public resources — either governmental resources, or non-taxed based funding schemes which operate in the public domain. It is eminently reasonable, in our view, to ensure that organised sport operates in accord with the legal conventions of the society on such matters as sex equality and anti-discrimination. Sport is the pre-eminent form of popular culture in our society. Our objective in sport policy is quite simply equality.

It became clear to us by the mid-1980s that we needed a clear policy statement if we were to cross over from a series of programs which focused on particular aspects and problems facing women in sport, to an approach which addressed the basic issue: that is, that the Canadian sport system is fundamentally one which contributes through its very nature to sex inequality in sport. We had to move our target group from females as an isolated group to the overall sport system. Further, we had to acknowledge as well, that much of what we sought to change in sport, had its root cause outside of the sport system and that there were (and are) a number of basic gender equality issues which are bigger than sport which we would have to address in our policy and in the related programs.

After several years of work the policy was finally released in 1986. The overall goal of the policy is simply to attain equality for women in sports. In the words of the policy

> Equality implies that women at all levels of the sport system should have an equal opportunity to participate. Equality is not necessarily meant to imply that women wish to participate in the same activities as men, but rather to indicate that activities of their choice should be provided and administered in a fair and unbiased environment. At all levels of the sport system, equal opportunities must exist for women and men to compete, coach, officiate or administer sport.

Sports organisations are monopolies and publicly funded. There exists one and one only Track and Field organisation, for example, and there is room for no other. Such organisations should therefore have both responsibility and public trust. They should have equality forced on them.

The policy also identified a number of major issues which it was felt needed to be addressed. These included the following six major areas.

Systemic Injustices/Discrimination

Arrangements of sport organisations may be highly discriminatory toward girls or women in their net effect, even though they are not intended to be directed at any particular female, or indeed in an adverse way toward females in general. For example, Canadian sport bodies support the events of the Olympic program. They thereby support twice as many sports and events for males as for females. A league or sport organisation which denies playing rights to a girl on the basis that the governing body of the sport prohibits integrated play is as guilty of discrimination as if it formulated the rule itself.

Structural Injustices/Discrimination

This refers to the overall arrangements (economic, political, social) within the society generally which influence the nature and quality of female sport opportunities. The principle examples here include employment opportunities for females in sport, the costs and social arrangements for sports clubs and facilities.

Resource Allocation

For various historical reasons, and because sport funding tends to be driven by demonstrated demand (rather than the need to create opportunities for those who have historically been under-represented), less funding has been directed to sport for females.

The Need to Create New Opportunities for Females

We proceed on the premise that the biggest single influence on increasing female participation in sport would be through the provision of new opportunities for girls and women to play.

Stratification

We used this term instead of integrated sport, co-ed etc. We agreed that sport must be stratified to create fair and equal competition, but we also insisted that the basis for stratification should not arbitrarily be established as the gender of the participant; rather it should be demonstrated ability and experience. We decided that for one sport there should be one sport organisation. In other words we proposed the amalgamation of existing sex-specific sport organisations (men's and women's organisations in hockey, bowls, curling, golf and so forth). And we impressed on sport bodies that the existing organisational infrastructure now serving primarily male participants must in future also serve female participants, and indeed, must direct its energies in a pro-active way to enlisting new female participation. In ice hockey for example, the community resources (volunteers, facilities etc.) are largely taken up with boys' hockey. There are insufficient resources to crease a parallel system for girls' hockey, so we insisted that the existing structures take on the responsibility for organising the sport for girls as well.

Responsibilities of National Sports Organisations

National sports organisations have a responsibility to the public at large; they have a monopoly status with legal authority to convey or deny the right to compete and stage competition and in return they have a responsibility to act in a non-discriminatory manner.

Policy Statements

In addition to these specific issues which we expected the policy to address, there are 13 policy statements — each with its own programmatic aspects. [These are reproduced here and should be compared with the policy statements to the Australian Sport's Commission's National Policy and Plan for Women in Sport reproduced on pages 238-246 of this volume *Ed.*]

1. *Policy and Program Development*
Within the federal government's own program structure, we will ensure that the needs of females are taken into account, that no programs will be initiated or retained which embody any form of sex discrimination.

2. *Sport Stratification*
Integration as a matter of course up to the age of puberty.

3. *Infrastructure*
One sport/one sport organisation.

4. *Leadership Development*
Positive efforts should be made to increase the number of women training for technical, administrative and coaching positions.

5. *High Performance Sport*
Equality objective — including support for lobbying for expansion of major Games and World Championships programs for women.

6. *Participation Development*
Attempts to identify specific needs for women and rectify existing reasons why women participate at lower levels than men.

7. *Resource Allocation*
'... in cases where inequities are demonstrated, Sport Canada contributions will be made conditional on guarantees from the NSO that funds will be distributed more equitably among males and females ...'

8. *Liaison*
Provincial governments etc.

9. *Research*
In high performance, leadership and participation development

10.*Education*
Level of awareness (analysis) especially within NSOs

11. *Promotion*
Encourage the promotion of women's sport as much as men's.

12. *Advocacy*
Assistance to advocacy organisations

13. *Monitoring and Evaluation*
Keep the whole program under review

There are some other aspects of our whole approach which are worth mentioning. Much of our work is carried out through existing methods of interaction with National Sports Organisations. This certainly true for our major planning activities for high performance and domestic development. The plans which are developed must address the status of females in the sport and consider gender specific issues and means for their resolution within the normal planning processes of the sport. This emphasis on the National Sports Organisations had some disadvantages. The schools, for example, did not have very close or good relationships with the National Sports Organisations. They therefore tended to be missed out in applying the policy.

In the early 1980s a number of women's committees were created within many of the National Sports Organisations. However the plans they produced were often unrealistic and the program delivery structure wasn't in place. We are now seeking a higher degree of integration of women's committees and their plans within the entire National Sports Organisation structure. We are also still encouraging the formation of these committees because they can act as internal watchdogs, develop policy and do more detailed planning on women and sport matters than would otherwise occur.

One of the major focusses of the whole policy is on leadership. We have increased the number of women among lower and middle level managers significantly, but the number of female technical directors and coaches remains very low. We are now addressing this issue through scholarships to the National Coaches Institute for special three-year coaching apprenticeships.

This area of leadership is one where an analysis and solution beyond the usual boundaries of sport is required. We start with the premise that while sex is an explanatory variable, it is not a causal variable — ie sex is a significant variable when it comes to explaining who is involved in coaching and who is not — that males are and females are not. But what requires further analysis is why it is that females comprise only 10 per cent of national level coaches. Is it biology, social role, lack of role models or some other unknown? Depending on the answer to this question, certain types of program are required.

We might, for instance, adopt a repair model approach, ie give females comparable training to that which males have usually had. But if the major factor lacking among would be female coaches is simply practical experience, then no amount of training will compensate. Alternatively we might decide that the most fruitful thing to do is to review the actual hiring processes and the career opportunities open to women. But before long we run into one of the most important distinctions in our society — it is that where there is a two person parental group with one career, that career is usually for males. On the other hand where the two person unit has two paid careers, it too often means that the female has two careers — one inside and one outside the home.

Outcomes of the policy

The policy — as far as the sport bodies is concerned — works on a voluntary basis. But to the extent that the whole nature of the government's funding programs, planning interactions with NSOs, and specific programs are aimed at creating a non-sexist sport system, the reach is considerably greater than if we simply said there are opportunities available to NSOs to develop special programs for women if they want to. Relatively little money is being spent on the program — three staff and under $500K per year directly on the program — but our main avenue is not through special programs but rather by seeking major change in the overall system. The entire Sport Canada budget is $55 million per year — more change through that means more change than through specific programs.

Our overall objective is to stop treating women strictly as a disadvantaged target group whose condition can be improved exclusively by programs aimed at females. We have taken the tack instead that a re-orientation of the whole system is necessary. We are reasonably confident that changes can be brought about within the Canadian sport system, although we think those changes will take place over a long period of time. Those changes for women in sport which are dependent on the changes in the larger social system will take even longer, but we think there is some complementarity between what we are doing in sport and what others are doing on broader social issues.

SECTION TWO
WOMEN'S SPORT AND THE LAW

AN INTRODUCTION

Ken Dyer

The objective of legislation involving women and sport is to achieve equality of opportunity. This equality of opportunity has to be both on and off the field, at junior and senior levels if it is to have any meaning and any effect. Equality itself is probably impossible to achieve on the sports field, partly because very often the whole object of sport is to maximise inequality, ie to find winners and losers. Furthermore, males and females are anatomically and physiologically different in ways that are relevant to their performances in many but by no means all sports (and not all of the advantages favour males either).

There are at least three ways to interpret 'equal opportunity'. First, we could decide to ignore an ascribed characteristic such as sex. If we did this, women would in fact have even less opportunity to participate in many sports, because sex differences in size and strength cannot be removed. A policy of non-discrimination in sport, therefore, would actually decrease equal opportunity for females (except for prepubertal girls, who may be equal in size and strength to young boys).

Second, we could equate equal opportunity with an equal chance to participate. Everyone, male and female alike, has an equal right to what could be called the 'basic benefits' of sports (eg, health, fitness, fun, skill development). Therefore, equal opportunity exists in sport if everyone has an equal chance to play. If a girl is less adept than a boy at some sport, because she has never had an opportunity to learn, this is not sufficient reason to deny her these basic benefits by refusing to allow her to participate. Nonetheless, and particularly in sports involving strength directly, the very real problems of differing size and strength may still be present.

The third interpretation of equal opportunity is more complex: it calls for equal achievement for the 'major social groups'. Therefore, women are said to have an equal opportunity to be doctors, for instance, when there are approximately the same numbers of female and male doctors in the population. However, this interpretation of equal opportunity is difficult to apply to sport. Is it unfair, for example, that far less than half of all professional cricketers say, are women? No, because physical differences prevent most women from playing top-level cricket with men; moreover, women do have their own league in which to play. It is unfair, however, that sports women do not have equal access to the 'scarce benefits' of sport, which include such tangible aspects as salary and prize money and the less tangible aspects of status and publicity.

Unfortunately, therefore, equal opportunity in sport seems an elusive goal whichever interpretation we adopt. While it might be agreed that everyone has an equal right to the basic benefits of sport, we are still faced with the problem of how to make certain that physically different individuals always have the same access to these advantages. Presumably it might also be agreed that women must have the same access to sport's scarce benefits, although we cannot expect to see equal numbers of women and men in all sports. Again, physical differences prevent this.

Many people believe that since neither equality nor equal opportunity seem to be entirely possible, what we really must settle for is equity, which has been defined as 'fairness, impartiality, justice'. What, then, is the fair and just way to treat physiologically different groups? One suggestion is to have individuals compete on the basis of some clear-cut physiological characteristic such as weight or age. This is done in boxing and wrestling, for instance, or in age-group swimming. However, sex is a frequent justification for establishing separate competition groups: the rationale is usually that females need protection due to their assumed physical inferiority.

Females can sometimes move 'up' to compete with males, but the reverse rarely happens, which may in itself seem discriminatory. Where sex is not relevant to performance, the sport probably could be integrated; often, unfortunately, this is not the case. As we better understand whether existing sex differences in performance are due to physiological characteristics or to cultural and social inequalities, more and more sports will become integrated. Therefore, although there is some justification for segregating teams and competitions on the basis of sex, there are some obvious difficulties.

Another way to treat physiologically different groups in order to ensure equal opportunity or equity to group individuals is by ability. Even if this principle were applied across the sexes, women would still probably be relegated to the second or third grade leagues because of a lack of ability due to differential socialisation as well, perhaps, as the same physical 'disadvantages' discussed previously.

Where does this leave us? There is simply no way out of this problem unless sports particularly suited to women's distinctive attributes (for example, smaller size, flexibility, lower centre of gravity, better insulation) are considered absolutely equal to sports in which speed, size and strength are essential. Most women are at a physiological disadvantage when participating in such sports. As long as our society believes that only such sports as football, cricket and basketball have spectator appeal, sex equality in sport is unattainable. If our primary emphasis is on participation, there is no justification for the 'swifter, higher, stronger' ethos as the only conception of sport. The tremendous popular appeal of women's gymnastics and figure skating, and the inclusion of rhythmic gymnastics in the 1984 Olympics, are signs that our tastes in sport are broadening. Sex equality in sport will have been reached only when women's sport is evaluated as something worthwhile in its own right, without the illegitimate and irrelevant comparisons to the different sporting achievements of males.

In sum, it is not easy to answer the question 'What is the meaning of sex equality in sport?' Just asking the question poses more questions. The nature of sex equality in sport and the question of whether it can ever be achieved, turn out to be difficult problems. The eradication of sex discrimination in sport by obliterating all sex differences is clearly unwise if not impossible.

'To the extent that equality is a good thing, what it calls for is justice rather than identical treatment. In this sense, the sexes could be 'equal' without becoming indistinguishable' (English 1977).

Faced with these problems it is not surprising that legislative approaches in the

UK, Canada and Australia, as described in the papers in this section, have run into practical difficulties and have failed to solve adequately the problems intended to be solved. Furthermore the very objectives of the legislation, as well as the administrative policies meant to achieve them, are often dismissed as social engineering or belittled by the media. Again the papers in this section have examples of each of these tendencies. Fortunately there do appear to be some grounds for hope and some slow improvements in attitude, as each of these papers describes.

As Josephine Tiddy predicts, however, a period of backlash often follows one of major advance in which significant improvements occur. Two articles which appeared in South Australian newspapers during September 1988 and which are reproduced here as Figures 1 and 2, show how right she was. Legislation is a necessary, but by no means sufficient, requirement for improving women's performances in sport.

Figure 1: A front page headline story for mixed junior sport from the Adelaide Advertiser, September 1, 1988

The Advertiser, September 1, 1988

Mixed sport policy puts schoolgirls out of the race—

By Education Reporter
MARK BATISTICH

Girls are losing out from a school sports policy that is supposed to help them, according to a leaked report by a key sports group.

The SA Primary Schools Amateur Sports Association says the State Government's mixed sport policy in primary schools has been "counterproductive and clearly disadvantaging to girls".

The policy — which allows only "mixed sex" and "girls only" categories — was introduced earlier this year to encourage girls' skills and fitness so they could compete on more equal terms with boys.

But the report says that, instead, the policy has led to a dramatic fall in girls' participation rates in some sports.

The Opposition yesterday described the policy as an "unmitigated disaster".

And the SA Primary Principals' Association president, Mr Alec Talbot, said it was "social engineering" and girls were losing out.

The report, leaked yesterday by the Opposition spokesman on education, Mr Lucas, says this year SAPSASA had sought feedback on the policy from parents, staff, sporting and educational groups.

"Without fail all groups have continually and repeatedly expressed grave concerns about the current emerging decline in girls' participa-

tion in sport — the group this policy was specifically set up to assist," the report says.

It says data gathered over the past 10 months shows that:

● Basketball was conducted as an "open" or mixed sport, but only 28 p.c. of the competitors were girls. The figure had been "far higher" in the past.

● In tennis, if teams were picked on ability, only 15 p.c. of competitors would be girls.

● In "open" cross country events, "girls were mistaken for boys (and vice versa) and they were humiliated and embarrassed when asked by caring officials and parents to identify their gender".

Girls who would in the past have finished first or second in such an event when it was "girls only" were "finishing 73rd, 91st and 106th". As a

result, girls did not receive the "accolades and recognition" they deserved, the public was "indignant" and the event received media criticism.

"In nearly every case the parents of girls are those who are most vocal in their criticisms," the report says. "Some of the concerns expressed are that girls are actually dropping out of sport rather than competing against boys."

Mr Lucas said the report showed that the mixed sport policy had been an "unmitigated disaster" but the Government had "persisted with a political and ideological policy devoid of common sense".

Mr Lucas said the report calls for the policy to be changed to allow separate girls and boys event in athletics, swimming, hockey, netball, softball, basketball, table tennis and cross country.

Mr Crafter said the policy was an interim one. It was being closely monitored and "any necessary modifications will be incorporated" when the interim period ended this year. It was "aimed at improving access and skills among primary school children".

The Commissioner for Equal Opportunity, Mrs Josephine Tiddy, said school sport would be "going back centuries" if it returned to separate events for boys and girls.

Mrs Tiddy said if girls were being discouraged, it was the job of SAPSASA to encourage their skills, fitness and participation rate to ensure this was no longer a problem.

Figure 2: A story on mixed junior sport from the Adelaide Sunday Mail, September 4, 1988.

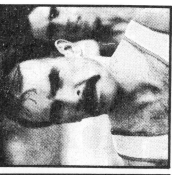

Adelaide Sunday Mail, September 4, 1988

Girls are girls and boys are . . .

Lisa Martin

Mrs Josephine Tiddy

Robert de Castella

□ GIRLS have been the losers under a controversial State Government mixed sport policy for primary schools, it was claimed last week.

□ The policy, which allows only "mixed sex" and "girls only" categories, has been "counter-productive and clearly disadvantaging to girls," says the SA Primary Schools Amateur Sports Association.

□ The SAPSASA report claimed girls were dropping out of mixed sporting events and some had been humiliated and embarrassed when asked to identify their gender.

□ Parents of girls were critical. The Opposition education spokesman, Mr Lucas, described the policy as an "unmitigated disaster". The SA Primary Principals' Association president, Mr Alec Talbot, said it was "social engineering."

□ But the Commissioner for Equal Opportunity, Mrs Josephine Tiddy, said school sport would be "going back centuries" if it returned to separate events for boys and girls. Sports editor PETER HURT puts his point.

An open letter to Mrs Josephine Tiddy, Commissioner for Equal Opportunity:

Dear Mrs Tiddy,

I have two young children. One is a girl, one is a boy.

I saw them in the bath last night. They are different.

I play netball, cricket and football with them in the backyard. Other boys and girls join in. Good, clean, healthy fun.

But that's as far as it goes. When it comes to almost every organised sport, the girls should play with the girls and the boys with the boys.

If my daughter wants to play in an organised game of football, fair enough. But not with the boys, thank you. I don't want her complaining the boys were too rough and hurt her and she didn't get a kick. Neither would I want my son playing football and getting into trouble because he hurt a girl in the other side.

If my daughter wants to play basketball or compete in athletic events, fair enough I will give her every encouragement, but not with the boys, thank you. I don't want her complaining etc etc.

Of course, here we're talking about that nasty word, competition. We can't have that in our lives can we? I mean if we did that we'd have a lot of losers and, worse still, winners. You know the sort of people . . . like Glynis Nunn, Raelene Boyle, Lisa Martin.

And that's the point I'm trying to make. In two weeks all Australia will be glued to the TV, day after day, watching the Olympics, the greatest feast of sport in the world.

And the funny thing is, we will see men against men, women against women in almost every sport and every discipline.

Lisa Martin wouldn't stand much of a chance against Robert de Castella in the marathon. Her best time is 2hr 26min 7sec, set at the 1986 Commonwealth Games in Edinburgh.

Lisa, as we all know, won gold that day. She would have finished nowhere in the men's event.

Deek's best time is 2: 07.51, set in the Boston Marathon the same year.

It was pointed out the other day, Lisa can now run the marathon faster than Emil Zatopek did in the 1950s.

Terrific, and full credit to Lisa. She is a champion. But has anyone noticed Deek can run a lot faster than Zatopek too?

The astonishing and continuing improvement in athletics performances has come about for a variety of reasons — improved physical fitness, diet, training methods, sports psychology etc etc.

But does anyone seriously believe the Lisa Martins 50, 100 or 200 years from now will run as fast as the Deeks of the future?

There will still be a difference between the best woman and the best man just as there is now in every athletic event, track or field, every swimming event, every team sport.

Can you imagine the Aussie women's hockey team defeating their male counterparts, or the same happening in basketball or cricket?

Please don't try to tell me it's all a matter of lack of opportunity in the past, that centuries of depression have left women lagging in the sporting arena. And don't try to tell me the State Government's mixed sport policy will miraculously overcome these deficiencies and we will soon produce a race of superwomen able to conquer the world. Even the East German women, though some of them may look like men, have never caught up with their male counterparts.

Equality of opportunity is free, very laudable, long overdue. But it doesn't mean the boys should play basketball with the girls or bowl with their weaker arm to give the girls a chance in cricket. That won't help anybody.

We're not going to produce a Lillian Thomson able to compete on equal terms with a Malcolm Marshall any more than we'll produce a Gabriela McIntosh, a Roberta de Castella, Philippa Smyth or a Joanna Sieben.

There are certain mixed sports which work well and are very popular, such as korfball and touch football. My children played teeball — but even at the age of seven the differences in ability between the boys and girls were obvious.

This is the greatest country in the world for kids, for sport. This is the country that produced Dawn Fraser, Shane Gould, Betty Cuthbert, Heather McKay, Raelene Boyle, Glynis Nunn, Margaret Court, Evonne Goolagong, Debbie Flintoff-King, Tracey Wickham and Janelle Elford.

It's great to watch them defeat the best women in the world.

They are all women, great competitors, champions, wonderful ambassadors.

But they are women, not girls who want to be boys.

THE LAWS: LEAD US OR LEAVE US ALONE

Josephine Tiddy

In 1888 the American feminist Elizabeth Cady Stanton wrote *Many a woman is riding to Suffrage on a bicycle*. There have always been women, like Stanton, who have recognised the link between fitness and freedom, between sport and power. I assume that is why women have struggled, in the face of continual or recurrent male determination, to take equal place in Olympic Games and in other major sporting events.

When women in Greece were banned from the Ancient Games, they held their own equivalent, the Heraean Games (named after Hera, the Goddess of Women), every four years in Olympia. Gradually, the competence and the persistence of the women ground down the opposition and in 741 BC, women's events were included in the Olympic Games.

But when the Modern Olympics began in 1896, the battle had to be fought again. The founder of the Games wanted them to be all male. A Greek woman Melpomene asked to run in the highlight event, the marathon, and was refused permission so she ran anyway, and finished (an achievement, incidentally, which eight of Australia's twenty-five male runners in thirteen Olympics have not matched). So when Joan Benoit crossed the line to win the inaugural women's Olympic marathon in Los Angeles in 1984, she was finishing a journey begun about two thousand, seven hundred and twenty-five years before.

I think there is no question that this journey was speeded up towards the end because of the existence of equal opportunity and anti-discrimination laws. You will probably all remember how Greta Waitz, Mary Decker, Ingrid Kristiansen and 79 other women athletes took out a Federal Court action in 1984 against the IOC for not including a women's 10,000 metre event in the Los Angeles Olympic Games when there was a men's event of that distance. That suit was unsuccessful, but only in the short term — there was a women's 10,000 metres in the 1988 Seoul Olympics. And anyway, and perhaps more importantly, the action of Greta Waitz and the others showed women that there **are** laws, and that those laws can be used, by sportswomen as much as by anyone else.

That sounds so obvious as not to need saying — but in fact, it marks a key change, and a change that is at the heart of what I want to say. The fact is, there had not in the past been that link between women, sport and the law.

Elizabeth Cady Stanton may have ridden to suffrage on her bicycle, but she and the other brave feminists of that generation did not pedal beyond suffrage and into the dazzling new world they planned. One reason was that the law, instead of leading, left alone. We can follow this process in practice, and learn the lessons we need from it, by looking at the history of women in my own State, South Australia, in this century. The century began with high hopes following the granting of the vote to South Australian women in 1894 (second in the world only to New Zealand). But then, after gaining the vote it took 65 years for South Australian women to actually break into State Parliament. What had gone wrong? Why had it taken so long to move from winning political rights to exercising real political power?

One reason was probably that the Labor Party, traditionally the agitator for change, was fiercely male dominated; as was the workforce, and thus the trade unions. So even women who had filled 'men's jobs' during the second World War, and had shown that gender need not matter at work, were shunted as soon as possible back into the home and ignored. Clearly if things were to change for women, women themselves were going to have to force it to happen.

The basis for this change was the expansion of secondary education for girls, followed by scholarships to tertiary studies, in the 1950s and 1960s. This produced a generation of educated girls who developed a political awareness that, along with other factors, was the foundation of the so-called 'second wave of Australian feminism'. Those other factors included the freedom of choice that came with the Pill, movement of married women into the paid workforce, publicity given to overseas feminists, and to Australia's own Germaine Greer, and the coincidence of Gough Whitlam and International Women's Year.

With Gough Whitlam, the Australian Labor Party at last took up the cause of 51 per cent of the country's population — at the very vocal urging of groups like Women's Electoral Lobby which surveyed every candidate for the 1972 federal election, and published an often embarrassing 'form guide on women's issues'. The Australian Labor Party Government recognised 1975 as the first year of the United Nations Decade of Women and this seal of approval turned 'women's lib' respectable for vast numbers of non-radicals. And this time, with such wide-ranging support, there would be no erasing the progress that was being made.

To make certain of permanence, women's groups and the men who saw their cause as just, lobbied for the changes to be entrenched in law. And once again, as with the first wave of feminism at the turn of the century, South Australia led the way.

The South Australian Sex Discrimination Act, introduced as a Private Members Bill in 1973 by Liberal Member of Parliament Mr David Tonkin, was the first such legislation in Australia. It was followed in 1976 by the establishment by the Labor Premier, Mr Don Dunstan, of the Office of the Commissioner for Equal Opportunity.

Now there are those who say that you cannot change the way people think and act by bringing in laws. But as we learnt from those early Suffragettes, unless rights are guaranteed in law, they will be lost as soon as good times turn tougher. And also, as Martin Luther King once said *morality cannot be legislated but behaviour can be regulated. Judicial decrees may not change the heart, but they can restrain the heartless.*

I am firmly of the school of thought which holds that it is worth forcing changes in behaviour because these eventually lead to changes in attitude. We have certainly seen evidence of this in South Australia in relation to sport and I will illustrate it with two examples from the files of my own Office.

In 1978 the Sex Discrimination Board refused an application from the Trotting Control Board which would have banned women from gaining licences to drive in the same races as men. The way that decision was reported in Adelaide's daily newspaper **The Advertiser** is shown in Figure 3.

I will highlight two quotations from members of the Trotting Control Board giving reasons for their application. The first reads *the public like to have everything going for them and when someone of a lesser ability is driving they are not going to support a race.* The second reads *a male driver or trainer driver is used to knocks and bumps from boyhood through sporting activities, a race fall happens very quickly and the track is very hard, I think it is fair say a woman has not the same reflex in that sort of instance.*

Figure 3: A story from the Adelaide Advertiser reporting an early case on sex discrimination in sport in 1978

The Advertiser, February 2, 1978

SA trotting board in battle of the sexes

Women trotting drivers would have a detrimental effect on the industry in SA, the Sex Discrimination Board was told yesterday.

Mr. W. Adams, a member of the Trotting Control Board said:

"Everything depends on public confidence.

"The public like to have everything going for them and when someone of a lesser ability is driving they are not going to support a race.

"We want the fairest possible deal for the public."

The TCB asked the board for a 12-month exemption to study the effects of introducing women drivers in other States before licensing them in SA.

Mr. Adams said a great fall in TAB returns in recent years was affecting clubs adversely.

"The anticipated profit of the TAB in the 78-79 season, on current figures, will be about $635,000—barely enough to cover costs," he said.

The TCB chairman (Mr. R. G. Rees) told the board that in the past ladies' races had resulted in a poor turnover in the betting rings —even with top women drivers.

"The SA trotting industry cannot afford at the present time to conduct races which do not give the opportunity to get maximum benefit financially for the clubs," Mr. Rees said.

The TCB secretary (Mr. K. W. Porter) said he did not dispute that skill played a great part in driving trotters, but strength often played a big part.

"A male driver or trainer-driver is used to knocks and bumps from boyhood through sporting activities," he said.

"A race fall happens very quickly and the track is very hard. I think it is fair to say a woman has not the same reflex in that sort of instance."

He said women had shown themselves to be more cautious in the past.

But the vice-president of the SA R e i n s w o m e n 's Association, Gail Ramage of Balaklava, told the board the TCB could not judge wo-

Mr. Rees . . . "ladies' races have resulted in poor turnover."

men's abilities from one race a year — the present quota for women drivers in SA.

"Before a woman could get a licence to drive she would have to go through the same processes as men and be passed fit to drive by the stewards so there would be no risk to the betting public or other drivers," she said.

There would be four or five women in SA who would immediately apply for a licence to drive in races if the rules were changed.

Mrs. S. Noble, a stablehand of Port Augusta, said that in Queensland and NSW, where women had licences to drive, they had proven to be of high ability.

"Here women do not get the same opportunity as men, especially women trainers who, unlike the male trainers, do not have the opportunity to drive their own horses," she said.

The chairman of the Sex Discrimination Board (Mrs. E. Johnston) told Mr. Rees the TCB could confer authority and qualifications by desire.

Its desire not to do so in this case had given rise to the discrimination. She reserved decision.

And now let's look at another newspaper report of that same decision of the Sex Discrimination Board shown in Figure 4. The first thing to notice in this article is the headline 'Hobbles off girls in the sex stakes'. The second thing to notice is that the picture of the young lady in the trotting uniform is actually of a model not of a trotting driver. And the third thing is the response from a woman who was an official with the South Australian Reinswomen's Association at the time. She said she was happy for the girls, but she and many other women trainers were content with segregated races. *I'm a mother of five and I don't want to be treated like an equal. I don't want to drive against the men.*

That was in February 1978. I want now to move forward exactly ten years to look at coverage that was given to an item on sex discrimination in sport in February 1988. In 1986 the State Equal Opportunity Act came into operation, replacing the Sex Discrimination Act. This Act, as did the previous State Sex Discrimination Act, makes it unlawful to discriminate on the grounds of sex (being a girl or boy, woman or man) except in competitions where strength, stamina or physique is relevant. In 1984, the Federal Sex Discrimination Act also made it unlawful to discriminate on the grounds of sex in the provision of recreation and sporting activities, including the administration of sport, coaching, umpiring and for children under 12 years of age; except again, in competitions where strength, stamina or physique is relevant.

The Federal Act therefore deems strength, stamina and physique not to be relevant for children under 12 years of age. This, in essence, means that children of primary school age, girls and boys, must be offered the same range of sporting activities and the same level of coaching and facilities, and more than that, the chance to play in mixed sex teams, or as some have euphemistically said, integrated sport. Such an interpretation caused a furore in 1986: girls would be disadvantaged, girls and boys should not play together they might touch each other's erogenous zones! Competitions would be ruined, and so on. Despite the furore, the Education Department, in order to comply with the Equal Opportunity legislation, has worked long and hard to devise and implement policies which will over the next six years lead to demonstrable equality of opportunity for girls and boys in school sport.

Publication of the policy inspired an article in one of our papers outlining objections held by the Opposition Spokesperson on sport. This response was not, I think you could safely say, unpredictable — 'Dump school policy call' (See Figure 5). But it is what came after this article that shows, I think, how far we have come in the last ten years.

First, when the report was picked up by a radio station in its news, a firm statement in favour of the policy came from the Minister of Education. Then, when a radio sports program decided to make an issue of the question, the defenders of the policy were the President of the organisation which controls high level competition for school children, and a representative from the Education Department — both men, which I think the radio announcer found somewhat deflating. 'School chief defends SA sports plan' was the headline on the story written about this debate (see Figure 6). Finally, the follow-up of the article appeared in the same newspaper, giving the positive arguments for the policy, again from the President of the organisation which drew it up in conjunction with my Office, and from the Women's Adviser to the Department of Recreation and Sport.

In all of that, there are several things to note: first, that it was a woman sports journalist, Margaret Ralston, who introduced and balanced the reporting; that there were no joking headlines; that there was no trivialisation of the issue; and

Figure 4: A story from the Adelaide Advertiser discussing the outcome of the 1978 case of sex discrimination in sport

The Advertiser, February 18, 1978

Hobbles off girls in the sex stakes

The South Australian Sex Discrimination Board yesterday gave women trotting drivers the all-clear to compete against men, but not many of them appear to be keen starters.

Reaction to the decision indicates that most of the State's 80 reinswomen were happy with the status quo which harnessed them to women-only races, and they are reluctant to try the rough and tumble of competing against men.

The board ruled in favor of two women drivers, GAYLE RAMAGE and SHIRLEY NOBLE, who charged the SA Trotting Control Board with discrimination for refusing them licences to race against men.

The two were not in court for the judgment.

The Sex Discrimination Board supported their argument, the SA Trotting Control Board expressed disappointment with the decision, and the president of the Reinswomen's Association of SA, MARLENE WEIDEN-BACH, said she was happy for the girls, but she and many other women trainers were content with segregated races.

"The girls wanted to be treated as equals on the track," she said. "I'm a mother of five, and I don't want to be treated like an equal. I don't want to drive against men. All I would like to do is trial against them."

The Sex Discrimination Board said in its judgment: "The women interested in driving do not seek any special considerations. They recognise that they must undertake the required tests and compete with male applicants on the basis of merit.

"In determining whether an applicant should receive a licence, the Trotting Control Board should have regard to the applicant's ability to drive, not his or her sex."

SANDRA Hutchinson kitted out for a women driver's exhibition race in Adelaide . . . now able to race against men.

Figure 5: A story from The News of Adelaide reporting the controversy over mixed primary school sport in February 1988

The News, February 1, 1988

Dump school policy call

'It's out of step with community'

By Marg Ralston

The State Liberal Party today called on the Education Department to withdraw a policy to operate in 1988 on equal opportunity in school sport.

And Opposition Recreation and Sport Minister, Mr Ingerson, said the Government should stop wasting time, money and effort on a policy which was completely out of step with community thinking.

"For example, the policy will require the establishment of quotas for boys and girls playing softball and netball," Mr Ingerson said.

"But surely we should not be hung up about how many of each gender play a certain sport.

"What we should be doing is giving the highest priority to encouraging as many girls and boys as possible to become actively involved in physical education programs. All should be encouraged to improve their skill levels at primary school so they can excel in their chosen traditional sports at high school and in later life."

The proposal submitted to the Education Department by the SA Primary Schools Amateur Sports Association is an interim policy to allow the organisation to conduct competitions in 1988.

To span a six-year period, it has been prepared "on a belief in equal opportunity for all children" and also to comply with enacted legis-

● Ingerson: Nonsense

lation and Education Department requirements.

Mr Ingerson said its contents were contradictory.

"In one part it states the aim of the policy is to work toward a situation whereby all sporting competition will be open with selection based on merit," he said.

"But it then goes on to propose quotas for various sports, the need to give recognition to both boys and girls in term of placegetters, and the employment of efficient managerial skills to assess the performances of boys and girls.

"This talk of quotas, special management and timing systems is nonsense."

Research and documented evidence support a

widespread belief there is little or no physiological difference between girls and boys at primary school level. And the commonly held theory is that eventual selection into primary school sports' team should be made on the merit of ability alone.

The interim policy clearly states that all children will play in competitions appropriate to their level of ability regardless of their sex, physical impairment or race. It further claims for this to occur, "special measures" will be invoked according to the needs of each sport.

Special measures as defined in section 47 of the Equal Opportunity Act make allowance for programs which redress any recognised imbalance of previously disadvantaged groups. SAPSASA says successful implementation of the policy will rely heavily on constant review.

It also will continually monitor the special measures programs, in particular the number of teams and also the number of girls and boys participating.

Mr Ingerson said such "heroics" were completely unnecessary.

"What the community wants is more girls and boys participating and more encouragement in the pursuit of achievement and excellence," he said.

44

Figure 6: An article from The News of Adelaide commenting on the controversy over mixed primary school sport in February, 1988

The News, February 11, 1988

School chief defends SA sports plan

SA Primary School Amateur Sports Association (SAPSASA) president, Mr Peter Burgan today defended his organisation's equal opportunity policy against attack from the State Liberal Party.

In a recent article in *The News*, Opposition Recreation and Sport spokesman, Mr Ingerson said the Government should stop wasting time, money and effort on a policy that was out of step with community thinking.

Mr Burgan disagrees.

"We are required by legislation to have a policy," said Mr Burgan.

"And, over the past eighteen months, we have sought community views even on the draft, interim policy, which is the document referred to by Mr Ingerson."

Mr Burgan said the policy would be phased in over the next six years and care was being taken to ensure the community at large had the opportunity to comment on its contents.

In his criticism of the policy, Mr Ingerson slammed the establishment of quotas for boys and girls playing softball and netball.

He said: "We should not be hung up about how many of each gender play a certain sport.

"What we should be doing is giving the highest priority to encouraging as many girls and boys as possible to become actively involved in physical education programs.

"All should be encouraged to improve their skill levels at primary school so they can excel in their chosen traditional sports at high school and in later life."

In reply, Mr Burgan said: "That's exactly what we (SAPSASA) are about.

"We agree that competition can help children appreciate and value effort and excellence in

MARG RALSTON

themselves, their team-mates and opponents and because of our close contact with people in the community, we know this is what they want.

"We know at a secondary school level there is a participation drop-out. This applies in particular to girls. To help overcome it we have introduced more sports and more teams.

"This year there will be twice the number of netball and softball teams participating at district and intra-school level.

"Because we are tackling the introduction of equal opportunity with care and sensitivity for a couple of years we will include quota systems in netball and softball, not because of 'hang-ups' and 'against community thinking' as has been suggested by Mr Ingerson but because parents have asked for it to be done.

"There is total flexibility in the policy. Change can be negotiated if it is believed either girls or boys ae being disadvantaged."

Women's Adviser to the SA Department of Recreation and Sport Wendy Ey said that, while comment on the policy was outside her jurisdiction, she supported Mr Burgan's statements as they applied to sport.

"Because the values of sport are identical for girls and boys and because fewer girls than boys are taking part, we need to do something about it," she said.

"And I think that always has to be the premise upon which we operate, particularly in my pos-

● Mr Ingerson: Criticism

ition of looking after the needs of women."

Ey said reasearch clearly had proven that, up to the age of 12, girls and boys should be able to compete on equal terms.

"There are no significant physiological differences, its well documented and scientifically proven," she said.

"Now that is the long term aim for sport, in the short term it is necessary to take special measures because of the disadvantages girls have suffered.

"Boys get far more exposure to sport from the age of two or three onwards and much more practice in developing skills.

"So, it becomes an unfair competition between girls and boys because of the social factors that are involved rather than the biological reasons. We need to address this.

"In the meantime, it's no good putting girls and boys together in open competition, because it would not be fair."

that there was no quibble from either women or men with the claim that girls need and deserve sport as much as boys.

So there we have it. The law, given enough pushes, will lead us — us being the community as a whole. But I finish with a word of warning: the pushes must continue. We must learn from the past. This history is reflected in the title of this paper: lead us is followed by leave us alone.

Periods of the granting of equal rights, which are seen as the making of concessions are followed by periods of backlash, when the claim is 'they're going too far'. Then, what has been gained so slowly and painfully is consolidated or dissipated depending on the ability of the following generations to exercise their power.

We are now that following generation. It is up to us to exercise our power to act on the rights enshrined in the laws. We can, if we don't lose heart or get lazy, go even further than riding on our bikes to Suffrage. We can swim and hit and throw and leap and kick and run our way into the Nirvana of real equality.

[A further article on the workings of the Commonwealth Sex Discrimination Act and junior sport by Henny Oldenhove, appears in Section Six. It gives a more national perspective and draws out some of the policy implications *Ed*.].

INTEGRATING SPORT:
THE CANADIAN EXPERIENCE

Abby Hoffman

We have had an interesting ten years in Canada regarding the integration of sport. There have been very many court cases especially within the province of Ontario. But thinking back over the very many often acrimonious debates before the legislation was enacted — there has really only been progress specifically within sex integrated sports. If we ask whether legislation generally can bring equality overall in women's sport, the answer would be very guarded.

Human rights legislation has been used to advance sex integrated sport in Canada and we believe it is one area where progress has been made. Included in the new Canadian Constitution (which as an Act of the Canadian Parliament dates only to 1982) is a Charter of Rights and Freedoms. It provides a far-reaching and wide-ranging protection under the law for women and other groups, but nobody has yet tried to use it to ensure that there should be, for example, equal government funding for men's and women's sports organisations, even though the public sector tax based distribution of funds to men and women are not in any sense equal. In fact this Charter has not so far been used in any comprehensive way in sport.

One of the positive things which the Charter of Rights and Freedom does allow at both the Federal and Provincial level is the initiation of Affirmative Action Programs. Temporary positive discrimination is allowed in order to put right historical wrongs.

Sex integrated sport has been on the agenda for many years. When I was an

8-year-old, I wanted to participate in the National Religion — Ice Hockey. I joined the local league and on registration night, among hundreds of screaming youngsters, I was accepted for a particular team. I managed to make the all-star team for my league and was eventually chosen to play against the champion team from another league. Again I had to turn in my birth certificate, only this time there were not hundreds of screaming youngsters around — only 14 birth certificates in an envelope. This time there could be no overlooking my sex.

I was told officially I would not be able to play in the championship match. There followed a huge public controversy. Although not allowed to play in the interleague match, I was allowed to play out the rest of the season in my league — with my own private dressing room. My league had not previously had a rule which prevented females from playing. They had then to draft one to forbid me to play thereafter.

By the early 1970s the frequency of girls wanting to play in what was usually the only available game in town — a game for boys only which now had by-laws forbidding girls to play, was steadily increasing. And despite the by-laws many girls were allowed to play initially.

The local convenors of the various sports leagues were usually not perturbed; the provincial administrators were generally extremely disturbed; the national bodies were distraught and the international federations were almost catatonic about the whole thing. Ultimately, most of the girls were told that they could not play on the only available league in baseball, softball, lacrosse, ice hockey, etc.

By this time there was human rights legislation in Canada in several provinces. When girls, their parents or coaches tried to assert their rights, ie insisted on playing in the league and turned to the legislation to support them, they found that the legislation stated that discrimination on the grounds of sex was not allowed in the case of services generally available to the public. This seemed to support their case and when the cases came before the Human Rights Commissions, they, the Commissions, generally found in favour of the plaintiffs — that after all was their brief. But in most cases the decisions of the Human Rights Tribunals were appealable to the Provincial Supreme Courts. In most cases, the original decisions of these tribunals, when appealed, were overturned and the girls were forbidden to play. The usual argument given was that the services provided by the sports associations were not available to the general public. In other words, the sports associations argued that since they offered softball or baseball or hockey or whatever only to boys, it was not available to the general public and therefore the girls had no argument to be allowed to participate — a classic catch 22.

The kind of information and testimony which was brought forward by these league managers was often both offensive and absurd. They found doctors and physical educators who would testify that girls aged 8, 9 and 10 were either physically inadequate to play with boys or that they were incapable of playing to the same standard as boys. They marshalled all the so-called public decency arguments, including the notion that it was immoral for boys and girls to have to share dressing rooms (at age 8 for softball games!) They argued in effect that because the games were run by volunteers, these volunteers should be allowed to vent their own prejudices. 'I just know in my heart that it's the wrong thing to do' said one administrator, when asked why girls and boys should not be allowed to play together.

All this legislative activity caused some difficulty for women activists. Many feminists argued strongly for separate but equal facilities for boys and girls. Others, of whom I was one, said that all the financial, physical and human resource inputs into one sports league, the boys league, could not be duplicated. The administrators, the pitches, the coaches, the drivers of children to and from matches could not be made available for boys and girls separately. The provision of separate but equal facilities simply made no sort of sense; it had to be integrated sport or nothing. Clearly what many women in the sport community were concerned about regarding integrated sport was that such girls teams and leagues as existed would be overrun by boys, and that girls would never get a chance in mixed sport.

When the Charter of Rights and Freedoms came in, basically there could be no exceptions to its provisions. The situation now in Canada is that any person of one sex can try out for and be allowed to play on any team irrespective of the sex composition of the team before they join it. This has only recently been clarified as the situation, but it is likely before long that at the junior levels there will be both boys, girls and mixed teams and that gradually mixed teams will come to be seen as the norm.

Sports organisations are public organisations, operating in the public domain. There is an expectation therefore that they will conform to certain social norms and expectations. That fact, and the implications of sex equality legislation in sport, are now much more clearly understood in Canada. It cannot be said that the situation is finally resolved but we definitely have made some progress.

SPORT AND EQUALITY: SOME ISSUES, PROBLEMS AND POSSIBILITIES IN THE INTERPRETATION OF CURRENT LEGISLATION

Ken Dyer

Introduction

In her paper in this volume, the South Australian Commissioner for Equal Opportunity presented some background material on why the laws on sex discrimination in sport needed to be changed and some of the general consequences which have resulted from the change. The purpose of this paper is to examine in some detail the workings of one of the particular pieces of Australian legislation to which she referred on opportunities and outcomes in girls and women's sport. The legislation is the Commonwealth Sex Discrimination Act of 1984. This makes it unlawful to discriminate against people in certain circumstances on the grounds of sex, marital status and pregnancy.

This Act covers clubs, including sports clubs and, in conjunction with various pieces of State legislation, renders it unlawful for any educational authority to discriminate against a person on the grounds of sex, marital status, pregnancy, sexuality, physical impairment or race:

— by refusing admission as a student
— in the conditions offered to the student

— by denying or limiting access to any of the available benefits

— by expelling or subjecting the student to any other detriment.

I present below the relevant sections of the Commonwealth Act. I intend to analyse in particular section 42 (1) of this Act and Section 47 of the South Australian Equal Opportunity Act which allows *measures intended to achieve equality.*

The whole thrust of both Acts is to achieve equality of opportunity so far as is possible. Why, then, is one of the major exceptions to both Acts that of sport — an activity which is so central to life today, nowhere more so than in Australia?

I reproduce two clauses of the Commonwealth Sex Discrimination Act, namely Section 25 which refers to clubs including sports clubs and Section 42 which shows how much of sport is excluded from the ambit of the Act.

COMMONWEALTH SEX DISCRIMINATION ACT 1984

Clubs

25 (1) *It is unlawful for a club, the committee of management of a club or a member of the committee of management of a club to discriminate against a person who is not a member of the club on the ground of the person's sex, marital status or pregnancy*

    (a) *by refusing or failing to accept the person's application for membership, or*

    (b) *in the terms or conditions on which the club is prepared to admit the person to membership*

(2) *It is unlawful for a club, the committee of management of a club or a member of the committee of management of a club to discriminate against a person who is a member of the club on the ground of the member's sex, marital status or pregnancy*

    (a) *in the terms or conditions of membership that are afforded to the member*

    (b) *by refusing or failing to accept the member's application for a particular class or type of membership*

    (c) *by denying the member access, or limiting the member's access to any benefit provided by the club*

    (d) *by depriving the member of membership or varying the terms of membership; or*

    (e) *by subjecting the member to any other detriment.*

(3) *Nothing in sub-section (1) or (2) renders it unlawful to discriminate against a person on the ground of the person's sex if membership of the club is available to persons of the opposite sex only.*

(4) *Nothing in sub-section (1), other than paragraph (1) (a), or sub-section (2) renders it unlawful to discriminate against a person on the ground of the person's sex if the discrimination occurs in relation to the use or enjoyment of any benefit provided by the club where*

    (a) *it is not practicable for the benefit to be used or enjoyed*

        (i) *simultaneously; or*

        (ii) *to the same extent, by both men and women; and*

    (b) *either*

        (i) *the same, or an equivalent, benefit is provided for the use of men and women separately from each other; or*

        (ii) *men and women are each entitled to a fair and reasonable proportion of the use and enjoyment of the benefit.*

(5) In determining any matter relating to the application of sub-section (4), regard shall be had to

(a) the purposes for which the club is established;

(b) the membership of the club, including any class or type of membership;

(c) the nature of the benefits provided by the club;

(d) the opportunities for the use and enjoyment of those benefits by men and women; and

(e) any other relevant circumstances.

Sport

42 (1) Nothing in Division 1 or 2 renders it unlawful to exclude persons of one sex from participation in any competitive sporting activity in which the strength, stamina or physique of competitors is relevant.

(2) Sub-section (1) does not apply in relation to the exclusion of persons from participation in

(a) the coaching of persons engaged in any sporting activity;

(b) the umpiring or refereeing of any sporting activity;

(c) the administration of any sporting activity;

(d) any prescribed sporting activity; or

(e) sporting activities by children who have not yet attained the age of 12 years.

The unity of sport as a concept

Sport or sporting activity is not defined in the Act. In the absence of a statutory definition the commonsense ordinary meaning of the term should be used. The Concise Oxford Dictionary includes *amusements, pastimes and games* among its definitions of sport. But this still leaves some issues unresolved. For example, the Board of the Australian Institute of Sport voted only by a majority of one to exclude chess from its list of approved sports. What we might ask would be the fate of such activities as hang gliding, darts, mountaineering and so forth should the Australian Institute be asked to vote on whether they should be considered as sports.

More importantly, the whole concept of sport includes activities which have so little in common with one another that we may be misled in dealing with them in a uniform way. There are individual and team sports; sports with balls, balls and implements, implements to be thrown, used as weapons, jumped with; combat sports; sports involving animals, boats, bikes; and so on. It is hardly to be expected that any uniform or universal set of principles will emerge which can be applied to such a variety of activities.

In addition there exist totally amateur and fully professional sports, traditional and 'new' sports; sports specially modified for young people, to be non-contact, for indoors and so on. Finally, there is fully competitive sport, and 'recreational' or social sport which may have some competitive content. The definition of competition, incidentally, is absent from the Act which may be considered surprising given the centrality of this in Section 42 (1).

The Act may set a general philosophy and from this, very general principles may be adduced. But specific guidelines are likely to be required for groups of cognate sports and sometimes for specific sports. So the Act in this respect is just a beginning.

At the school level (and beyond), sport and physical education or leisure activities are inextricably linked. Competitive sport does not involve all school children and certainly does not involve all adults. But physical education does involve 100 per cent of children, at least in all except the most senior years and it is this which, if conducted in the spirit of the equal opportunity laws, gives children the options and opportunities that they need in order to be able to make sound decisions about future sporting and related activities. In other words, the intention of the Act is to increase choices and participation, for women in particular. It is important, therefore, that any impacts of the law in the area of competitive sport are not at the cost of the non-competitive physical education programs which concentrate on skill and attitude development. If that were the case, the overall effect would be detrimental not helpful to women's chances and opportunities.

The exemptions

There are, it appears, 3 possible reasons why Clause 42 (1) was included in the Act.

    a) That sports where strength, physique or stamina are relevant are inherently dangerous for women, or rather, more dangerous for women than men. This apparent greater danger may result from vigorous physical contact, the use of dangerous implements, possibilities of injury or exhaustion. In other words, women are being protected.

    b) That men will be inhibited in their play because of fear of injuring women or taking unfair advantage through their greater strength. In other words, the current form of the sport and the way that men play it is being protected.

    c) That women will be at an inevitable and ineradicable disadvantage because of their lesser strength, physique or stamina. Hence they will win fewer contests, fewer prizes, will receive less publicity and that therefore women's sport will suffer overall.

The first two possible reasons can easily be shown to be either spurious or easily overcome: specific empirical evidence is referred to elsewhere in this volume and is dealt with specifically in various books including Hall and Richardson (1982) and Wells (1985). The third has wide support among both sportsmen and sportswomen. But there are a number of questions which must be asked which make it obvious that the situation is by no means so clear as it at first seems.

— What do the terms 'strength', 'physique' and 'stamina' mean?

— In which sports (and when and in which circumstances) are they 'relevant'?

— Under what circumstances can skill, training and commitment, compensate for their alleged deficiencies?

— How can the fact that we are dealing with normally distributed populations (in the statistical sense) be dealt with in law? (In other words a high proportion of women are 'stonger', have 'more stamina' and a more appropriate 'physique' than the majority of men?

— Is it not possible in individual sports to allow mixed competition but award separate prizes or titles to women?

— Is it not possible in team sports to regulate height and weight of team members irrespective of sex?

— Who is to decide the above questions and in what way?

British legislation avoids these questions to some extent by making the sports to which this exception applies those in which *the average woman would be at a disadvantage in competition with the average man.* But the whole point is that the average woman at the moment may have less strength and stamina simply **because** she has had fewer opportunities — a lack of equal opportunity. And in any event men and women seeking to excel at the top levels of competitive sport

Table 1: A comparison of the world freestyle swimming records for men and women showing percentage difference in performance in 1958 and 1988.

Event	Men's record		Women's record		Percent difference	
	1958	1988	1958	1988	1958	1988
100m	54.6	48.74	1:01.2	54.73	10.9	10.96
200m	2:03.0	1:47.44	2:14.7	1:57.55	8.7	8.62
400m	4:21.8	3:47.80	4:47.2	4:06.28	8.8	7.51
800m	9:14.6	7:50.64	10:11.8	8:22.44	9.3	6.35
1500m	17:28.7	14:54.76	20:03.1	16:00.73	12.8	6.86
4 x 100m relay	3:46.3	3:17.08	4:17.1	3:40.57	12.0	10.68

are hardly average. What should we make of the sport of swimming (and possibly endurance events in other sports)? Certainly in most Olympic and Championship events women's performances, despite having improved dramatically in recent years, still lag behind men's by several percent (Table 1). But how do we answer the contention that women's body shape is more streamlined than men's, that their higher fat content gives them better insulation and buoyancy than men and their stamina is really greater? In other words, how should we respond to the claim that if only opportunities were equal, women's performances would exceed those of men? We might ask in the first place on what basis is such a claim made. The evidence is there in abundance.

On September 4, 1981, 157cm 55kg Jocelyn Muir, a fifteen-year-old Toronto high school student, became the youngest swimmer ever to conquer the 49km stretch across Lake Ontario. She did it in 15 hours, 35 minutes. Marilyn Bell was sixteen when she swam the lake in 1954 and so was Cindy Nicholas, who conquered it twenty years later. In 1977, then nineteen, Cindy swam the English Channel both ways without stopping. She reduced the previously established fastest time of 30 hours, set by a man, to just 19 hours and 55 minutes. A year later she knocked another 40 minutes off the record. By 1977 the three fastest times for England to France Channel swimming and eight of the ten fastest in either direction were held by women swimmers. The record, by English swimmer Wendy Brooks was 1½ hours faster than any man.

Wendy Brooks set her Channel swimming record in 1976. Four days after doing so she beat forty-three opponents, including thirty-three men, over a distance of 10½ miles in the annual long distance championships at Lake Windermere, with a time of 4 hours 25 minutes 47 seconds. This was thirty-five minutes ahead of her nearest rival. The following weekend she won the women's three mile race in Trentham Lake in 1 hour 3 minutes 42 seconds, which was four minutes faster than the winner of the men's event. Two of the four fastest swims ever recorded in Lake Windermere have been completed by women.

The equivalent in America of swimming the English Channel is swimming the twenty-eight kilometre Catalina Channel in California. The record from the mainland to Catalina is held by Penny Dean who in 1976 swam the distance in 7 hours 15 minutes 50 seconds. In 1977 she shattered Greta Anderson's two-way non-stop swim record by recording 20 hours 3 minutes 17 seconds. On the way she set a new record from Catalina to the mainland of 8 hours 33 minutes and 15 seconds.

Early in 1988 in Australia, a 57 kilogram female primary school teacher blitzed the field at the 1988 Ironman of Mallacoota event. Twenty-year-old Yvonne Geerts proved the event to be a misnomer, beating home a field of 14 he-men including All Australian Amateur football champion Philip Kingston, the hot favourite. She used her stamina and skill as a swimmer over the two-kilometre course to glide ahead of competitors who had ploughed past her in shallow water where they could run. Yvonne made up about 25 metres on the tiring Kingston over the last 75 metres, then dashed up the town boat ramp to a historic victory. Yvonne had warmed up by earlier winning the women's event. The swimming course for the 'fairer sex' was only 400 metres.

In 1979, women competed for the first time in the unbelievable triathlon — a 2.5km ocean swim, followed immediately by a 180km cycle race, and ending with a 42km marathon. Lyn Lemaire, a 26-year-old New England physiologist, finished the non-stop triathlon in 12 hours, 55 minutes and 38 seconds. The only female participant, she was fifth in a field of 15.

To all intents and purposes, therefore, equality between the sexes has already been attained in long distance swimming and endurance events. The winners and place getters in any event cannot be predicted on the basis of sex alone: it is no longer the case that the fastest performers for any course or distance are invariably men. The evidence from Table 1 is that it may not be long before the same is true for standard Championship events in the pool.

And yet neither in international, national nor major club competitions is there equality for women in swimming. There is no 1500m for women in major championships, there are fewer events for women on most programs and mixed competitions in diving or water polo are unheard of. Women might have expected that the law would aid them in their search for equality. In fact, it does no such thing because of the exceptions where 'strength, physique or stamina' might be relevant.

The terms themselves are problematic. They also have to be considered in a social context. They are the outcome of biological development. This itself occurs in a series of socially defined environments of which such things as diet, activity levels and encouragement are a part and which are known to differ for boys and girls. Measurements cannot be done in socially neutral environments. Differences between men and women might therefore themselves change as social inputs change. Indeed, everything we know about sporting performances and participation rates demonstrates just that, as several papers in this volume clearly demonstrate.

The term 'relevant' is not defined. Is, say, a mean difference of 10 per cent in leg strength relevant in swimming or a mean difference of 5cm in height relevant for basketball? (Remember that we are dealing with normal distributions of variables such as these, which means that people are going to vary a good deal anyway.) Or are we concerned with much more detailed and specialist differences such as upper leg length, forearm length and the like? It is not practicable to carry out the large number of investigations which would be required to answer such very detailed questions for every sport, but it is also difficult to arrive at adequate generalisations without them.

Furthermore, in some sports, strength may be important in one phase of play or in one position in the team but not elsewhere. Strength may not be a relevant factor in the selection of a cox in rowing or a goalkeeper in soccer, even though it may be relevant in other positions in teams in these sports. Strength may be necessary to bowl fast in cricket but it is not necessary to bowl slowly effectively.

While there are some sports in which strength, stamina and physique are clearly relevant (eg the martial sports, weight lifting) and others where they are virtually irrelevant (eg lawn bowls), there are others in which their relevance is quite uncertain (eg table tennis, badminton). There seems no alternative to obtaining opinions and empirical data for a range of such sports.

There are also a number of sports, notably equestrian sports, which are integrated (even if women's opportunities are hardly the equal of men's in some areas) despite the fact that strength, physique and stamina are undoubtedly relevant. Any general guidelines introduced to cover all sports will have to be carefully drafted to cover these situations and to ensure that women's current opportunities in these sports are not prejudiced and in fact, continue to improve.

Discrimination and competitive sport

Competitive sport is in essence discriminatory; its whole purpose is to reward the strongest, most skilfull, fastest etc. To attempt to incorporate any policy on sport within an anti-discrimination Act seems almost inevitably contradictory. This in part explains the paradox of exempting a rather large part of modern life — much competitive sport — from the provisions of the Act.

Sport itself is full of mechanisms by which some of the grosser forms of advantage/disadvantage are reduced in order to promote greater equality of competition. These include:

Age division	(juniors, masters, veterans, etc)
Weight division	(fly weight to heavy weight in combat sports and some performance sports)
Competence division	(A grade, B grade, handicap systems etc)

Most argue that the division of sporting competitions into male and female should be maintained for analogous reasons, viz that women are systematically disadvantaged in many sports.

Just as there are 'open' divisions in most sports which are divided according to the criteria listed above to which those deemed disadvantaged are not prohibited entry if they can demonstrate competitive competence, so it might be argued that there should be 'open' events for men and women and also events restricted for women.

With the possible exception of contact sports, such a model could be adapted for most sports (ie individual sports, interacting team sports and co-operating team sports). I believe that approaches along these lines should be the ultimate objective and command the widest support amongst both men and women.

This is quite definitely not an argument that all sports for all age groups should eventually be integrated. After all, it has been argued that unequal attainments lead to a lessening of self-respect among all women, and sportswomen have certainly had much less access to the rewards of success in their field than have men. Maintaining segregated competition in some sports could enable women athletes to become recognised as heroes in their own right and to receive an equal share of the rewards and benefits of success, something that would probably not happen if the sport were integrated.

More and more talented young female athletes are demanding the right to compete in boys' teams where there is no equivalent competition for girls. The equality position is surely that where females do not have the opportunity to participate in a particular sport except through an all-male team or league, they should be permitted to play with the male athletes if they have the necessary skills.

What then of the male who cannot make the boys' team? Should he be prohibited from trying out for the girls' team? In my view, yes. I argue this on the basis that it is the 'disadvantaged' individual who should be allowed to move 'up' and the 'advantaged' should not be allowed to move 'down'. In sports where divisions are based on weight, for instance, it is always possible to move up and box, wrestle or whatever in the next weight category, but it is impossible to move down to a lower one without losing weight. As more and more sports become integrated, including the 'contact' sports, factors other than sex, such as weight, size and ability will become the criteria for participation.

Finally, we would add the caveat that common sense must prevail. Obviously as boys and girls mature, the strength factor becomes more important even if height and weight remain the same. Therefore, we cannot insist on totally integrated sports competition, because if we did, it would have the unfortunate effect of producing predominantly male teams. This would further perpetuate a lack of opportunity for adequate participation by women. The answer has been to provide the same number of opportunities for males and females although the sports available may vary. We could then say that the opportunities are comparable.

Difficulties do arise, however, with this approach. For instance, the two most popular sports for men and women in Australia are football and netball. Unfortunately, the two sports are not valued equally: more time, effort and money are poured into men's football than are ever devoted to women's netball. Women athletes are denied equal access to scarce resources, and this is surely unacceptable.

Perspectives for the present or the future?

While it is accepted that in most sports women would currently be disadvantaged to greater or lesser extents if they were compelled to compete with men, many argue that this is because they have had fewer opportunities, had much less encouragement to compete and have had hitherto on average much less adequate coaching and skill training than men. [The sort of information and suggested strategies in Henny Oldenhove's first paper in this volume shows that much of this systemic disadvantage goes right back to primary schools *Ed.*] If this is indeed the case, then, I would argue, guidelines should be set to attempt to rectify these deficiencies so that in a few years 'strength', 'physique' and 'stamina' would be much less relevant in fewer sports than at present. Any guidelines which are developed to implement this legislation should at least be sufficiently flexible or varied to allow this possibility where practicable.

Both the State and the Commonwealth laws recognise the need for temporary special measures that allow the backlog of certain disadvantages, either social or cultural, to be gradually lessened and eventually erased. Special measures are programs aimed at bringing a previously disadvantaged group, as quickly as possible up to the level of the previously advantaged group so that, from then on, both groups can be treated equally.

For example, some girls might need separate instruction and practice in cricket before competing for a place on a mixed team. This would help to offset the head start of very many boys in the skills and tactics of the game. Or there may be a need for a special measures program for boys in dance, or gymnastics, or netball. 'Catch-up time' and 'gradually' cannot be given a strict definition in relation to the existence of special measures.

Each local area or school will have to assess its own particular needs in a commonsense and fair way, and the period of existence of any special measure will depend on that context. What is important is that any special measure must be discontinued as soon as the desired result has been achieved. So schools and clubs ought to keep any special measure they take under constant review to make sure that the need for it still remains.

Legal and policy precedents

Legislation with related objectives to the Sex Discrimination Act 1984 exists in the USA, Canada and the UK. Several Eastern European countries have entrenched similar objectives into their constitutions. While most of these countries have been markedly successful in women's sport, it is not clear that this policy is the main or even a minor contributor. In Canada and the United States, there has been considerable litigation, but not a great deal has been achieved formally.

Perhaps the cases are useful more because they draw attention to the issues surrounding sex discrimination in amateur sport than because they assist in promoting justice. Most of the complaints have been submitted because no opportunities existed for very talented young female athletes to play the team sport of their choice. They therefore seek to play on a boys' team.

In many cases they have been playing on the boys' team without controversy for some time. Their participation becomes an issue only when they wish to play on a team under the jurisdiction of a provincial or national sports governing organisation that restricts its membership to males.In countries other than Australia the sports associations have in general argued that they are private organisations and that they do not have to abide by human rights legislation designed to protect us against discrimination in those facilities and services considered public. By and large, at least the higher courts have agreed and have refused to consider a wider interpretation of the words 'services and facilities' which would include sports organisations. Further litigation might change their minds but it seems unlikely.

This line of argument has not been so readily available to Sports Associations and clubs in Australia, because the Australian legislation specifically includes clubs within its ambit (see Section 25 of the 1984 Act reproduced earlier in this paper).

During some of the legal hearings overseas, the respondents have argued that if the legislation were meant to prohibit sex discrimination by amateur sport associations, such a prohibition would have been made explicit. It has to be said that there is no such specific prohibition in the Australian legislation. Another way in which legislation can protect such associations is by providing them with an exemption. Unfortunately, this is precisely what was done in Great Britain and Australia. For instance, the terms of the British Sex Discrimination Act make it unlawful to discriminate 'on grounds of sex in employment in sport, or training facilities offered, or in the general sporting facilities available'. Written into the Act, however, are two important qualifications.

First, sex-segregated competition where *the physical strength, stamina or physique puts the average woman at a disadvantage to the average man* does not contravene the Act and is within the law (Section 44). Second, non-profit, private, voluntary organisations can legally restrict their membership and facilities to one sex. These exceptions, according to the Equal Opportunities Commission in England *seriously hamper our attempts to counter sex discrimination in sport*.

The way in which this exemption was interpreted in England is in the Court of Appeal judgement in **Theresa Bennett v The Football Association Ltd and the Nottinghamshire Football Association**.

Theresa Bennett was a girl aged eleven who *used to play football at school with the boys. She ran rings round the boys.* She applied to be registered as a member of the Muskham United Football team, which competed in the Newark Youth Football League, itself a member of the Nottinghamshire Football Association, which, in turn, is a member of the Football Association Limited. The Nottingham-shire FA and the FA Limited did not (and still do not) permit mixed teams to participate in league matches and did not permit a male to play a female team. So, despite the eagerness of Muskham United to include Theresa in their team, she was denied the opportunity to compete, such rejection being by reason of her sex.

Lord Denning said that in the absence of section 44 there would have been no answer to the complaint that the defendants were in breach of the 1975 Act by sex discrimination in the provision of recreational facilities. All three members of the Court of Appeal agreed that section 44 prevented Theresa Bennett from claiming a legal entitlement to be granted the recreational facilities without less favourable treatment on the ground of her sex. Lord Denning said that *'Just reading that section, it seems to me that football is a game which is excepted from this statute. It is a game (in) which on all the evidence here the average woman is at a disadvantage to the average man because she has not got the stamina or physique to stand up to men in regard to it.*

He observed that women *have many other qualities superior to those of men, but they have not got the strength or the stamina to run, to kick or tackle, and so forth.* The other two judges agreed. They all dismissed the contention put forward on behalf of Theresa Bennett that section 44 requires consideration of the physical strength, stamina or physique of the average woman and the average man who were of the age of the complainant. Hence they rejected as irrelevant the evidence produced before the Country Court to show that below the age of puberty a girl's strength, stamina and physique is not markedly different from that of a boy.

Lord Justice Eveleigh emphasised that section 44 *is describing classes of competitive activity generally where the physical attributes of womankind put them at a disadvantage and I can see no justification for reading into the section after the words 'average man' the words 'of a similar age to the complainant' or such words as 'who have not reached puberty'.*

The Court of Appeal therefore adopted a wide construction of section 44. It is evident that, as Sir David Cairns noted *It was the relationship of the average man and the average woman in connection with the sport and not the position of the particular individual that was relevant.* But section 44 is equivocal on the question whether the average strength, stamina or physique should be measured by reference to all women, to women of the age of the complainant or to women who play the sport in question. In reality, 'the average man' and 'the average woman' are spectators, not competitors. In view of the construction adopted by their Lordships, it becomes even more important to consider the rationale behind section 44. Why should Theresa Bennett have been denied the recreational facilities available to boys when she, considered as an individual irrespective of her gender, was qualified to make use of them? Lord Denning, alone of the three judges, made reference to what he saw as the social policy of section 44:

> *It is as plain as can be, I should have thought, that football is not within the Sex Discrimination Act, and I think most people would agree with that. If the law should bring football within it, it would be exposing itself to absurdity. Everyone would say with Mr. Bumble: 'If the law supposes that, the law is a ass — a idiot'. The statute would be 'a ass — a idiot' if it tried to make girls into boys so that they could play in a football league.*

In Australia children below 12 are not covered by the exemption of S42(1). This does not mean, in my view, that there are no differences in 'strength', 'physique' and 'stamina' at these ages, only that if they exist they are presumed not likely to be relevant for sporting participation and outcome.

The age of 12 is arbitrary, but the intent of the law, that there be equality for children in sport, is clear. The South Australian Commissioner for Equal Opportunity has therefore concluded, with the agreement of the Primary School Sports Association that the terms of the equal opportunity legislation will apply to all primary school children even if they are older than 12.

Over a period of time, children in primary schools will be developing skills in a wide range of sports. As part of this educational process, girls will become as experienced and skilful in traditionally 'boys' sports', as will boys in traditionally 'girls' sports'. One result of this is likely to be a change in attitude of many children, teachers and parents about what sports and recreational acitivities are appropriate to each sex.

These changes in the development of skills and experience and in attitude, will mean that girls and boys may want to play 'non-traditional' sports in their out-of-school hours as well. The equal opportunity legislation says that if this need develops, it must be met. If, for example, a girl wants to play in a football team — and she can win a place in that team on merit (and where the criterion for selection is merit) — she cannot be banned from that team, nor can the team be banned from its association. Or if, for example, a boy wants to play softball or netball, and those sports are offered at the school, he should either be allowed to, or he should be catered for in some other way, such as in a mixed team, or an all-boys team.

There has been no litigation in Australia either involving under- or over-12s. The development of detailed guidelines regarding the relevance of stamina, physique and strength for each and every sport (or even each group of similar sports) and procedures about implementing them might be fairly time-consuming but seems both justified and necessary, given the inhibiting effect that certain judgements may have if matters ever do reach litigation. [Unfortunately, as Henny Oldenhove discusses in her paper on this topic, which has been included in Section Six on junior sport, the response by the various Australian states has been far from uniform and considerable confusion and sometimes lack of progress has resulted *Ed.*]

The international dimension

In many sports sex segregation is written into the constitutions and procedures of international sports bodies, for example, the IOC, IAAF, FINA, ISU etc. This strongly influences the selection of National and State Teams, the format of national championships etc. The validity of records achieved in mixed competition might not be accepted by such bodies and in some cases registration of club or player might be threatened, if teams or competitors are mixed.

This international dimension has in fact been invoked by the New South Wales Government, newly elected in 1988 and bent, it seems, on turning the clock back as quickly and as far as possible in this area. The Premier said that regulations requiring schools to allow girls to play in boys' sporting teams were *a case of anti-discrimination gone mad*. And the Minister of Education said he would try to have the anti-sexism rules scrapped. He would seek legal advice on whether the laws were binding on the States. If there was any way around the regulations NSW would return to separate sporting events for boys and girls. And, invoking the international dimension, the Minister said the laws had even sparked threats from some countries to boycott selected events in the Pacific School Games to be held in NSW in 1988. He said some Islamic countries would not allow girls who had reached puberty to mix in sport with boys. *So the laws have already created an international problem in school sport* he claimed.

The NSW Government's plan to de-zone schools might give it a loophole around the laws. Parents could be given a choice of whether to send their children to schools which offered mixed sports or single-sex sports. The Education Minister had no doubt that most parents would opt for schools where boys and girls had separate sporting teams. *The fact is very few girls enter the open events anyway,* he said. *So the policy is an absolute charade. All it has done is make an ass of the important areas of equal opportunity which prevail. I have no doubt the majority of schools would prefer to go back to the old system.* The president of the NSW Federation of Parents and Citizens' Associations, said she understood the laws were under review by the Federal Government. *As far as I understand, the laws allowing primary school girls to play in open events were under a 12-month trial which should be completed soon. Until the trial is completed and the laws reviewed, I don't think it is fair to comment.*

At the level of international competition this is a formidable difficulty. It might be difficult to envisage at the moment a situation in which a woman soccer player or tennis player would qualify on merit for the national World Cup or Davis Cup squads. But it **is** conceivable that a woman would be good enough for a place in a shooting or archery team or would merit selection as a cox on a rowing crew. Arguably this international dimension is an area to which Australians should give some attention in at least some sports if they are serious about removing discrimination in sport.

Conclusions

In the conclusion to his booklet **Sex Discrimination in Sport** Pannick (1983) concludes that *all classification by gender is offensive and unjustifiable in the context of sport.* He allows but one exception, *the provision of separate sporting programs from which men are excluded (while talented women are permitted to compete in events hitherto confined to men).* He further concludes that section 44 of the British Sex Discrimination Act of 1975, and by implication therefore the equivalent section 42 (1) of the Australian legislation, *serves no valid purpose whatsoever.* As I have already pointed out, to enact sex discrimination legislation which then exempts one of the most important sectors of modern society from its provisions does seem absurd. On the other hand, there are some powerful arguments which oppose going any further with this legislation or its enforcement.

— Significant sections of the general population and politicians are opposed. Recall that one of the early actions of the newly elected Liberal (= Conservative) government of New South Wales was to call for the reversal of the guidelines for primary school sport developed in response to the Act.

— At the present time women would be severely disadvantaged in terms of both participation and achievement if all sporting events became 'open'.

— Many feminists argue that the values of sport today are inherently masculine — overly aggressive, competitive and elitist (see Lois Bryson's paper in this volume).

— Most international sport is sex segregated, which almost inevitably means that national teams, state teams and other top level organisations will be also.

The issue is a structural one in our society. As such the solutions will provide for radical change. The law can and should help — but the very nature of the issue dictates that change will be gradual. Skills cannot be attained overnight. The changes at international level sport will proceed at the pace of the slowest nation. Parental influences on children's behaviour will diminish only slowly.

The fact that Australian legislation has ensured that primary school children will have essentially integrated sport and that it has included sports clubs within its jurisidiction is most important. Change will be slow but is likely to be certain.

*Photo: Doug Nicholas. Thanks to the
Girls and Physical Activity Project.*

*Sport is just as valuable and
possible for the not so young
and the disabled. Shown here
are some not so young distance runners, a handicapped
rider and Karina Gawlik of
South Australia who finished
the women's wheelchair 100
metres in 20:45 sec.*

Photo: TAS Photographics.

Sport is not necessarily confined to a pitch, court, pool or track. But opportunities for women in these wider areas have if anything, been even more limited in the past than in more formal sports. Nevertheless, as these photos show, this too is changing.

Photo: Australian Bicentennial Authority

Photo: Catriona Owens

Photo: Christine Marshall

SECTION THREE
SCIENCE, MEDICINE AND WOMEN IN SPORT

AN INTRODUCTION

Ken Dyer

Scientists take pride in their neutrality and objectivity. The findings of science tell it like it is, so goes received wisdom. If science finds that women are less capable of performing arduous intensive sport, if they are likely to be at greater risk of injury or damage, if they perform less well in performance sports, if they have less strength or stamina for sport, then so be it.

Less than two decades ago most sports scientists were saying these things and believing them. The curious thing is that these sort of conclusions were based largely on ignorance with a good dash of prejudice. Almost all of the physiological studies and sports medicine were carried out on men. It was simply 'assumed' that what men's physiology and anatomy allowed them to do, women would, if they could do it at all, be able to do at some lower level. Women might, 'on average' be less strong, have lower maximal oxygen intake and be generally smaller and slighter. But, the differences were rarely accurately measured; the significance of such differences as existed for various sports was rarely considered; and the fact that women had previously had very different lifestyles, had done much less training and had been actively discouraged from undertaking hard physical exercise was rarely considered. Furthermore the undoubted advantages for many sports which women do have were rarely mentioned, let alone scientifically investigated. Women are more flexible, they are more agile and have better balance than men (in part because their centre of gravity is lower). They have on average more body fat, which provides a definite advantage in swimming: it provides buoyancy, reduces body drag in water and gives extra insulation important in long distance events. Women sweat less than men and their bodies probably convert fat to energy faster than do men, which may be important in marathons.

It is curious that until fairly recently physiologists on the basis of their scientific investigations of energy reserves, oxygen transport and so forth, usually concluded that men ought not to be able to run marathons at the speed which in fact they were running them. They were even more convinced that women could not run marathons at all. Their conclusions inevitably affected women. In the 1920s as we saw in the historical introduction, Australian women felt that 220 yards was a long way to run. The distressed condition in which some of the runners finished the 1928 Olympic 800 metres seemed to confirm women's problems over longer distances.

For women to attempt to run marathons was considered dangerous and impossible folly. In 1967 even after Kathy Switzer had, by a mixture of subterfuge and brute force, successfully run in and completed the Boston Marathon, American athletic officialdom, supported by scientific and medical opinion, banned women from running marathons for the next five years.

Scientific research on sportswomen, then, was just not done until recently. Even now, as Julie Draper points out in her article in this section, *research on elite female athletes shows big gaps in important areas* and *research into women's team sports has been lacking in this country to date, as has research in the medical, nutritional and sociological areas*. The situation is improving today as many of the papers in this section and in Section 5 make clear. Part of the reason for the deficiency of research on sportswomen was the assumption that they were essentially similar to men, differing only in being smaller, weaker, of lesser capacity and so forth. There is a danger that much of today's research is still essentially comparative in nature.

There is some virtue in showing that women are indeed much less 'the weaker sex' than used to be thought the case. There is also some virtue in showing that women can run, jump, throw, swim, cycle and so on, much closer to the levels that men can do those things than was formerly believed. This is one way in which myths about biological inferiority and disadvantage of women can be destroyed.

Dyer's paper in this section is in this tradition. But some argue that to present data and arguments in this way merely perpetuates the idea of male superiority and that maleness and male sports are the norm against which women must be matched. Indeed some of the assertions about the dubious femininity, even femaleness, of some successful sportswomen referred to in Dyer's article underline this very point. For further information and some of the arguments on this point see Chapter 4 of Adrianne Blue's **Grace Under Pressure**. The reader will just have to make up her or his mind on this point.

Meantime there can be little doubt that further research into every aspect of sportswomen's potential and the conditions needed to realise that potential is very necessary. And it should be done for its own sake and on its own terms not just, and definitely not **solely** just, to effect comparison with men.

EATING FOR HEALTH AND PERFORMANCE

Angela Hehir

The application of the principles of sound nutrition should be a priority for people participating in sport at all levels of involvement. As it is for the whole population, diet is integral to an athlete's health both in the short term and the long term. Sixty per cent of Australians die of diet related disease (eg cardiovascular disease, bowel disease and certain cancers). In addition poor diet is a contributory factor in disability and reduced quality of life (Better Health Commission 1987). If we are to encourage increased levels of activity and participation throughout life, then maintaining good nutritional health is imperative.

In addition to the obvious relationship between diet and health, nutrition also plays a very important role in sporting performance. It is clear that eating appropriately can allow an individual to train and perform to their full potential. While diet is on the agenda of many athletes and coaches, health considerations are often incidental to the main priority — improved performance. Fortunately the basis for a sound baseline sporting diet reflects the principles of eating for good health.

Given the influence of the current Australian diet on the health of Australians, the Commonwealth Department of Health produced in 1986 a set of Dietary Guidelines as a basis for developing strategies aimed at improving the health of the population. A glance at these recommendations highlights the similarity between the type of advice that is given to athletes and the type of dietary change encouraged for the population as a whole.

Studies carried out on groups of athletes suggest that while dependent to an extent upon the sport (diet can more directly and noticeably affect some sports than others) and upon the individual, many athletes are not making significant dietary change from the current population average (Brotherhood 1984; Perron and Endres 1985).

Contrary to popular belief, humans do not have an instinct for choosing an adequate diet. A number of factors work against making appropriate choices such as dramatic increases in the numbers of 'new' and 'different' foods from which to select, the heavy impact of advertising and promotion and the often confusing and misleading nature of 'information' that is proliferated about foods (Gussow and Contento 1984).

So, the fact that many athletes may not be achieving stated goals should not perhaps surprise us. (Being an athlete does not automatically make choosing appropriate foods any easier.) It does illustrate though the need for education with regard to making wise food choices.

Nutrient adequacy

The first guideline that an athlete should follow is to ensure that they eat a variety of foods; that is, to include each day, foods from the five food groups. Eliminating or avoiding a particular group, without ensuring adequate alternatives, will place an individual at risk of nutrient deficiency. In general, an individual who is eating a variety of foods should be receiving all the nutrients they require. Because of their increased levels of activity, individuals participating in sport will have a greater requirement for some nutrients (for example, the B group vitamins). However, the increased intake of food which results from the greater energy requirement, will provide the extra requirements as long as the diet is varied.

Routine supplementation with vitamin and mineral preparations is not generally recommended (American Dietetic Association 1987). In some cases it can be dangerous; for example where toxic levels can be reached with megadoses. The supplementation often masks other dietary problems ('as long as I take my tablet I am OK'), to say nothing of the added expense of purchasing nutrients already provided in sufficient quantities by foods eaten.

There are two nutrients that should be of particular interest to sportswomen however — iron and calcium. The occurrence of iron depletion, with or without the obvious anaemia is a risk factor for some athletes — particularly women, adolescents and endurance athletes. There may be a number of reasons for this, which may include increased losses in sweat, urine and gut during endurance exercise, increased destruction of haemoglobin, decreased absorption from food, or poor iron intake (Van Swearingen 1986; Eichner 1986). The depletion of iron results in an impairment of work performance, generally proportional to the degree of the deficiency.

Table 2: Recommended dietary intake of iron for women, compared with available survey data

Age (years)	Recommended dietary intake (mg)	Dietary survey data (mg) (from 1983)
8-11	6-18	—
12-15	10-13	—
16-18	10-13	—
19-54	12-16	10.6
55+	5- 7	10.1

Women, whether athletes or not, need to be aware of levels of iron intake due to regular losses of iron during menstruation. The potential problem is compounded when an athlete is on a restricted kilojoule diet to control body weight, or is avoiding meat and meat products [see for example Peter Brukner's paper in this section *Ed.*].

Comparison of the **Recommended Dietary Intake for Australian Women** with the 1983 national dietary survey of adults carried out by the Commonwealth Department of Health is shown in Table 2.

This comparison suggests that many women may be at risk of iron deficiency. The risk for women athletes is clearly increased due to the reasons mentioned above. Data for children are not yet available (results of the 1985 Commonwealth Department of Health survey of children's eating habits were not published when this paper was prepared), but the picture is unlikely to be any better for girls.

There are a number of food sources of iron, but not all are equally efficient. Haem iron is the most easily absorbed by the body and is found in foods such as liver, kidney, meat, poultry and fish (approximately 30 per cent of haem iron is absorbed). Non-haem iron is not as efficiently absorbed (approximately 2-10 per cent), but its absorption can be enhanced by combining it with vitamin C or a source of haem iron and avoiding coffee and tea at the same meal. Sources of non-haem iron include dried peas and beans, nuts, bread and cereals, green leafy vegetables, and eggs. While ensuring an adequate intake is easier if meat is a regular part of the diet, vegetarian diets can provide sufficient iron provided care is taken in food selection.

It is important that athletes at risk have periodic iron status evaluations. A review of the diet should be carried out to determine the cause of the depletion, and if necessary appropriate dietary modifications should be made. Supplementation may be necessary where anaemia is present, or where dietary sources cannot provide sufficient iron for the individual's requirements. This should, however, be carried out under medical supervision.

Ensuring sufficient calcium in the diet may also be a concern for some women. Osteoporosis is a condition characterised by a decreased bone mass and an increased susceptibility to fractures. Due to its association with decreased oestrogen levels, it affects mostly post-menopausal women. An inadequate dietary intake of calcium at any age, however, can place the body in negative calcium balance which accelerates the rate of calcium loss from bones. Younger women and girls can be at risk, especially the amenorrheic athletes who can develop osteoporosis in a manner similar to post-menopausal women (Deakin 1987). Compounding this, many women and girls may restrict calcium rich food sources because of their perceived association with weight gain. Table 3

Table 3: Recommended dietary intake of calcium for women, compared with available survey data

Age (years)	Recommended dietary intake (mg)	Dietary survey data (mg) (from 1983)
8-11	900	—
12-15	1,000	—
16-18	800	—
19-54	800	740
55+	1,000	718

compares the Recommended Dietary Intake for women with the 1983 dietary survey data.

This comparison suggests that, as for iron, many women in the population are at risk of deficiency. While activity is a beneficial factor in preventing osteoporosis, it does not make up for an inadequate intake. Maintaining an adequate intake of calcium is important for women at all ages. For children and adolescents it is critical to establish adequate bone density. Even when growth has ceased, the calcium levels should be maintained to achieve calcium balance.

It is possible to meet calcium requirements with an appropriate diet. Some sources are much richer than others though, and avoiding milk products can place a woman at risk of deficiency. Adequate calcium can be obtained without a high fat intake by selecting low fat products such as reduced fat or skim milk, low fat cheeses such as cottage or ricotta and low fat yoghurts. If dairy products are avoided, much more attention must be paid to careful food selection in order to optimise calcium intake. A calcium supplement may be necessary, where dietary intake cannot match requirements. Amenorrheic athletes, who may have a requirement of up to 1,500 mg (Deakin 1987), may need to supplement their diets with alternative sources such as calcium lactate, calcium gluconate or calcium carbonate tablets.

Meeting energy requirements

Meeting energy requirements is also important for women participating in sport. As mentioned earlier, increased levels of activity will result in increased energy requirements along with increased requirement for some nutrients. The require-ments can be met with extra servings representative of the five food groups. However, it is not only the amount of energy that is important, but the contributing sources of the energy. In order to optimise training and performance potential it is generally recommended that 55-60 per cent of the total energy intake comes from carbohydrate sources, with 25-30 per cent contributed by fat and 10-15 per cent from protein (Inge and Brukner 1986). Energy derived from alcohol should be kept to a minimum or avoided completely. Currently Australians obtain approximately 44 per cent of their energy from carbohydrate, 38 per cent from fat, 12 per cent from protein and 6 per cent from alcohol (Better Health Commission 1987). This suggests that the type of diet recommended for athletes requires a shift from the 'typical' Australian diet. In simple terms, it involves moving away from a diet based on foods high in fat, such as fried foods, pastry, fatty meats and snack foods and added fats, and increasing intake of foods high in complex carbohydrates such as cereals, bread and fruits and vegetables (this shift in food choices reflects the recommendations made for all Australians in the Dietary Guidelines).

Energy balance and weight control is an issue for many individuals participating in sport (as for the general population), and this is particularly so for women. A recent survey of working women's participation in exercise in South Australia emphasises that a major reason for women starting to exercise is primarily to lose weight (Clarke and Haag 1988).

Weight control can be particularly important for some athletes where carrying excess body weight can impede performance or even restrict entry into competition. While weight loss may be important, it should be remembered that health (and subsequently performance) may be compromised with severe dietary restriction. It is important to remember that reducing energy intake also reduces nutrient intake and fad diets which severely restrict energy intake, or which avoid certain food groups, are unlikely to provide adequate nutrients. Weight control should always be approached on a long-term basis with average weight loss of approximately 1 kg per week generally recommended.

Dispelling myths

Clearly there is much misinformation in the market place regarding the 'ideal' diet for athletes. There are numerous supplements, drinks and 'special' foods that are on offer to athletes to improve their performance. The heavy endorsement and advertising of these products make it very difficult to know what and who to believe. In 1987 the American Dietetic Association acknowledging the confusing situation in the market place, published a position paper summarising their recommendations based on evidence currently available. They concluded that while extended physical activity may increase the need for some vitamins and minerals, this can be met by consuming a varied diet which meets the extra energy requirement. The position paper states that there is no conclusive evidence that intakes of vitamins and minerals in excess of levels recommended for the general population actually enhance performance. Similarly, ergogenic aids (for example, bee pollen, kelp, lecithin and amino acids) are in most cases without validation, producing no measurable physiological effect. The individual psychological effect may however influence performance for some individuals.

Even though the protein requirements of an athlete may increase with levels of physical activity, the American Dietetic Association concludes that a diet where 12-15 per cent of energy is derived from protein will be sufficient for women who are consuming at least 5,000kJ. Excessive protein consumption (either by consuming large amounts of high protein foods or using special supplement powders and drinks), is not necessary and in some cases may be dangerous to the athlete's health.

In summary

Women at all levels of sporting involvement can optimise their performance potential with appropriate food choices. Eating to optimise training and competition performance should follow the same principles as those laid down for the healthy diet. This paper has endeavoured only to present general nutrition information which can provide a basis for women involved in sport across a range of activities, ages and participation levels. Clearly many individuals will have their own dietary needs dependent on the demands of their special requirements. However, ensuring all nutrients are adequately supplied, meeting energy requirements and following the recommendations outlined in the dietary guidelines will provide women with a sound basis for making the most of their health and performance potential.

SECTION HEADING: 734027. Track and field - Marathon and ultramarathon - Biomechanics.
Extensive study has been done on male subjects dealing with gait analysis, but similar investigations of women runners are limited. The purpose of this study was to quantify the essential characteristics and alterations in gait mechanics of women marathoners. Forty elite women marathoners were filmed at four camera locations during the first US Olympic Women's Marathon Trial. Data were quantified with a microcomputer and digitising system. Quantification of 11 kinematic and temporal variables of gait were obtained. Five variables were examined bilaterally to determine degree of symmetry. Results showed remarkably consistent characteristics of gait across the four camera locations. However, substantial changes did occur between the third and fourth camera locations in stride length and horizontal velocity. All subjects displayed little asymmetry throughout the race. Minimal differences between the top and bottom 10 finishers were noted.

There are differences between the gait patterns of men and women distance runners. Stride length, support/nonsupport time ratio, and percent overstride appear to be important factors for success of women distance runners. Most alterations in gait mechanics appear to occur between the 20- and 24-mile marks of the marathon.
KEYWORDS: elite athlete; woman; marathon; biomechanics; gait cinematography; kinematics; stride length; speed; centre of gravity; stride frequency.

0185432
Kinematic analysis of elite javelin throwers
Rich, R.G.: Gregor, R.J.: Whiting, W.C.: McCoy, R.W.: Ward, P.
In, Terauds, J. (ed.) at a., **Sports Biomechanics.**
Proceedings of the 2nd International Symposium of Biomechanics in Sports 1984, Del Mar. Calif..
Research Center for Sports, c1984, p. 53-60.
NO. REFERENCES: 12
LANGUAGE(S): English
DOCUMENT TYPE: Book analytic
COUNTRY OF PUBL: United States
CLASSIFICATION NO: QP302 SIRC BOOK NO: 20774
LEVEL: Advanced
SUBFILE: v.14
SECTION HEADING: 750027. Track and field - javelin throw - Biomechanics
KEYWORDS: track and field; javelin throw; kinematics; elite athlete; man; woman; comparative study; release.

0185409
Specificity in plyometric training for the discus throw.
Calder, S.E.: Zebas, C.J.
In, Terauds, J. and Barham, J.N. (eds.) Biomechanics in Sports II. **3rd International Symposium of Biomechanics in sports**
Proceedings of 1985, Del Mar. Calif.
 Research Center for Sports c1985, p.285-291.
NO. REFERENCES: 16
LANGUAGE(S): English
DOCUMENT TYPE: Book analytic
COUNTRY OF PUBL: United States
CLASSIFICATION NO: QP302 SIRC BOOK NO: 20775
LEVEL: Advanced
SUBFILE: v.14
SECTION HEADING: 746312. Track and field - Discus throw - Training and conditioning: 902910. Training methods - Plyometric training.
KEYWORDS: discus throw; plyometric training; biomechanics; elite athlete; woman; case study; track and field.

EXERCISE AND PREGNANCY

Rosslyn Carbon

Until recently pregnancy usually heralded retirement from sport for most women. A pregnant body was not to be flaunted for social reasons and after delivery it was not feasible for the mother to leave her child to indulge in sporting pursuits. For physical reasons it was considered that once pregnant a woman was in a delicate state and could not exercise and once a mother she was irreparably damaged or unable to reach the physical fitness or strength needed to play sport.

Certainly there have been more misconceptions about pregnancy than about almost any other human experience. Depending upon your place in the socio-economic hierarchy of your society, you may be expected to continue working in the fields until your delivery, when you will have to labour even harder — or you will be put to bed for the duration of your pregnancy until your confinement.

However there is a growing feeling in athletics that pregnancy and childbirth are endurance events which prepare the body in an excellent way for future excellence in sporting performance. Many women have shown that exercise during pregnancy and high sporting achievement once a mother are not only possible but should be expected.

Ingrid Kristiansen is but one example. She was 5 months pregnant and wondering why her marathon times were declining before her condition was diagnosed. Just 4 months after delivery she won the Houston Marathon and a year later set a world record. Tatanya Kazankina improved with successive babies. In 1976 she won gold in the 800m and 1500m. In 1978 she had her first baby. In 1980 she won gold and broke the world record in the 1500m. She had her second baby and subsequently went on to set a world record in the 3000m.

Many other women have had significant sporting achievements while pregnant. Margaret Court and Evonne Cawley have played championship tennis. Evelyn Ashford broke the 100m world record in 1984 while pregnant, and at the other end of the distance spectrum Michelle Davis ran the 1984 US Marathon Olympic Trial when six months pregnant — quite amazing. In the 1956 Olympics, 10 of the 12 Russian women medal winners were pregnant.

Of course not all women can or want to be world beaters when they are pregnant. For every champion there are women who, for reasons of morning sickness, fatigue, backache or discomfort, particularly urinary frequency, find it too difficult to keep up any very vigorous or frequent exercise. For them swimming, walking or gentle callisthenics are much more important.

All pregnant women should see their doctor first. All women and all pregnancies are different. One of the most important concepts to grasp is that the whole woman is pregnant not just her uterus. There are enormous changes in a woman almost from the moment of conception. In particular, changes in the skeletal muscle system are significant. There are weight gains of up to 10 kilograms — half of which are in the uterus, the amniotic fluid and the baby itself; there are also general fat depositions and increases in breast tissue. Most of this increase occurs in the front of the centre of gravity of the body, so that there is a change of posture; there is an increased curve in the lumbar spine and a tilt in the pelvis. Furthermore there is increased ligament laxity towards the time of delivery. The ligaments around the pelvis become more lax so that it can move during pregnancy. But this looseness contributes to the waddling gait of late pregnancy which is not conducive to weight bearing activities.

However the uterus and the baby are very well protected. In the early stages of pregnancy it is well protected within the bony framework of the pelvis. Even when the uterus expands into the abdomen the baby is protected by up to a litre of amniotic fluid and the spongy tissue of the uterus itself. Damage to the baby by direct contact during sport is almost unheard of. Only in such things as car accidents where the pelvis itself is crushed is there any record of damage to the baby and it is probably more dangerous for a pregnant woman to drive a car than to play tennis, netball etc.

Cardiorespiratory changes are also enormously important in pregnancy. From the baby's point of view the most important thing is the blood flow to the uterus which increases early on and must be maintained throughout pregnancy. The placenta is that part of the uterus where the circulation of mother and baby meet and where exchange of nutrients and oxygen takes place, where heat is dissipated and where waste products from the baby are got rid of.

For the mother the resting pulse increases. By the time of the first missed period it is up by about 10 beats per minute — by the end of pregnancy it is up by about 20 beats above normal at rest. There is a massive increase in blood volume during pregnancy — up to 40 or 50 per cent for a 10 to 15 per cent increase in baby mass. So all the blood vessels and the heart are dilated during pregnancy. There is more plasma, that is fluid blood, rather than red blood cells, so there is a dilutional effect. But there is an increase in iron requirements, even though haemoglobin concentration declines. During pregnancy a woman hyperventilates, that is she breathes more deeply and there is therefore more oxygen in the blood — up to 40 per cent. This helps an exercising woman because there is more which can be delivered to the muscles **and** the baby. Respiratory function of a woman in pregnancy is not a problem. However cardiac output which is the amount of blood pumped by the heart per minute increases by up to 40 per cent during pregnancy, reaching a maximum by about mid-pregnancy and then declines. This is thought to be because there is not so much blood getting back to the heart, largely because of blood pooling in the legs and extra blood flow to the skin.

There are many studies of the effects of exercise during pregnancy. What is obvious is that both the pregnant woman and the foetus tolerate exercise very well. There is always the theoretical risk of decreased blood flow to the foetus during exercise. This is because during exercise blood goes to the working muscles and there is a fear that blood flow to the uterus might drop. However all studies which have measured this show that there are no adverse outcomes of pregnancy, provided that exercise levels gradually decrease as pregnancy progresses. Trained women have clearly been found to tolerate exercise better; they respond better to exercise during the first six months of pregnancy. By the last three months, however, there is little difference between those women who were initially fit and those who were not. It is not generally wise to cease exercise suddenly during late pregnancy. There is a very dramatic fall in cardiac output then, largely because of pooling of the blood in the legs, which is not a good thing for either woman or foetus.

Of importance to athletes, however, is that fitness parameters are measurable again after delivery. Those women who were fit before pregnancy quickly show up and are able to resume training again very shortly after delivery and quickly improve on that fitness. Animal studies are important in this area because of the difficulty of carrying out studies on human foetuses and uteruses. It seems as if there is some reduction in blood flow to the uterus during exercise from studies in goats, but the developing foetus seems particularly well adapted at extracting oxygen efficiently even from a slightly reduced blood supply. Studies on human babies show that there is an increase in pulse rate of the baby for 10 to 20 minutes after exercise but not outside the normal range.

It must be stressed that although measurements of foetal heart rate and other parameters are unreliable in humans, simply because of the practical difficulties involved, no adverse effects have ever been demonstrated.

Only those women who continue endurance training during late pregnancy show any significant detrimental effects in the outcome of their pregnancy. Endurance training is defined as exercise at 50 to 70 per cent maximal heart rate for an hour or more every day up to delivery. Such women show a significantly lower than normal weight gain, they have significantly higher numbers of pre-term births and their babies have a significantly lower average weight at birth — some below the tenth percentile. This is only one study however and no account was taken of maternal nutrition. Another study of women who exercised at 70 per cent of maximal heart rate three times a week for 30 minutes showed no detectable effects on foetal growth.

Another possible risk revised recently is that of hypothermia — elevated body temperature. There have been reports in the literature of heated pregnant women with febrile illnesses early in their pregnancies, who produced children with severe neurological defects. However in these cases body temperature was over 40°C for 3 or 4 days. Clearly this is above anything likely to be experienced from exercise. Also pregnant women do not store heat — they dissipate it well and their core temperature does not rise above 39°C. Furthermore there are no reports whatsoever of elevated temperature nor birth defects among women who do exercise in pregnancy.

Dehydration is a theoretical risk; it would lead to decreased blood flow and elevated temperature, but virtually all athletes are aware of this risk and pregnant women are really little more vulnerable than any other athlete.

There has been a long debate about the capability of women to conceive and bear children if they are regular exercisers. There seems in fact to be no difference between athletes and non-athletes in this regard. Some studies of Olympic athletes show they have shorter and less painful deliveries than non-athletes although measures of pain are very subjective.

Some recommendations put out by the American College of Obstetrics and Gynaecology in 1988 have generated considerable controversy. One of the recommendations is that competition should be avoided. This is not accurate —what should be avoided is dehydration or letting the pulse rate rise too high. The third recommendation is that ballistic movement — jumping up and down — should be avoided. There is just no evidence for this. You may be too uncomfortable to do it but you are not going to hurt anything by doing it. The recommendation that a pulse rate of 140 should not be exceeded is quite arbitrary and has no basis in terms of available evidence.

The most fundamental advice is that exercise during pregnancy should be in line with your pre-existing fitness level. You should always warm up and cool down. You should avoid dehydration and overheating and you should maintain adequate weight gain. Don't set goals and be prepared for bodily changes. To sum up: if it feels good, do it — if it doesn't, don't. And after pregnancy be prepared for wonderful achievements in sport — even if we can't all emulate the achievements of Debbie Brill who set a world high jump record just three months after the birth of her baby.

STRIVING FOR SUCCESS: THE ROLE AND SIGNIFICANCE OF PERSONALITY DEVELOPMENT FOR THE ACCOMPLISHMENT OF HIGH ATHLETIC ACHIEVEMENT

Ruth Fuchs

Introduction

In his book **Handlungstheorie und Sportswissenschaft** (Action theory and sport science) (Koln 1978) the sport scientist Weinberg defines sporting activity as an athlete's purposive, conscious and volitionally goal-oriented contest with the environment. It is determined socially, and the contest with the environment takes place in collectively and individually determined forms of learning. The sporting activity exists in the form of ideal and non-material results as well as in the formation and development of the subject (ie personality development) (1978, pp.135-136).

If one agrees with this definition, one can see competitive sporting activity as a linked together sequence of actions that make possible and necessary the realisation of two goals that determine each other:

1) the development of high athletic achievement, ie the level of aspects concerning motoric sport activities.

2) aspects concerning cognitive emotion-motivational actions, ie the personality itself.

Only the combination and influence of achievement and personality on each other makes the development of athletic mastery possible in an extended process of instruction and education in competitive sport activities. I shall now consider each of these briefly.

Achievement

At international congresses and seminars when the development of forms and methods of training and competition are discussed, questions and discussion complexes concerning new insights into training methodology dominate. In other words there is a concentration on the realm of physical development, ie athletic performance. This is to be expected since the production of top achievements is the declared aim of competitive sport activities.

Achievement is what we need and want to develop in training so that it can be counted on at just the right time and place, ie during competition, in order to achieve victory. Hardly any other result of cultural activity depends so much on immediate acknowledgement and resonance of the consumer than athletic top achievement, due to its relatively ephemeral character. It lacks the tangibility of a material or mental product like a work of art or a book. Its resonance therefore, depends primarily on the level of achievement, in victory or defeat, in competition. My own past victories would nowadays hardly be noticed anymore; every achievement has its historical framework and focus.

At present, we athletes can be proud of the fact that records in our kind of sport, be they achieved by men or women, receive high international acclaim, representation and positive valuation by the producing athletes and above all by the consuming public. The President of the IAAF, P. Niebolo, was able to announce at the 1987 Congress in Rome that the total membership of IAAF, namely 182 countries, makes us the largest sports federation in the world. The track and field world championships in Rome received enormous media coverage and therefore had a strong effect on the spectators of many countries and nations.

Athletes are idols in many places: they are above all examples for the young generation. Even if athletic achievement remains the main criterion for this, it becomes increasingly evident that the total view of personality, ie the manner and behaviour of the athlete during competition and surrounding it, become part of an evaluation process. They all contribute to the overall effect and importance of the achievement.

The fact that the record achieved is tied in directly with the achiever means that the person of the athlete increasingly gains in importance. The achievement exists, after all, only through him/her, and the immediacy of the connection with the person creates a cultural factor. The effect of athletic achievement in public thus depends more and more on how much the athlete represents the ethical-moral ideals and values of sport in general — and those of the organisations running it, in our case those of the IAAF.

Personality

Apart from the right to personal presentation and that of subjective striving for athletic fame, it has, in my opinion, become necessary to pay more attention to personality development in coaching for competitive sports. The level of achievement and behaviour of the athlete not only influences the extent to which the consumer of sport, the spectator, values, perceives and enjoys what the athlete is doing, but the spectators themselves, be it in the stadium or via television, radio, or newspaper confront the natural and social qualities of sport achievements according to their own pre-existing orientation and interests.

By the nature of their achievements and their overall behaviour, ie sticking to the rules of fair play during competition, respect and acceptance of the other competitors, or being able to win or lose with dignity, the athletes essentially determine the identification process of the public, both with them as individuals and in the particular sport in which they are performing. The athlete determines the degree of valuation, recognition and acclaim of her national association as well as the reputation of the international federation. Resulting from this there is, in my opinion, a social responsibility that, if properly recognised and experienced by the athlete, can become a stimulus for achievement and motivation.

Team work

The induction of ethical-moral values into the educational process for competitive sports has also allowed an achievement-motivation to grow in our national team-collectives that we call identification with society and social responsibility.

In a number of surveys I conducted in connection with my doctoral thesis on 'problems and motivation development in sports activity', around 80 of our top track and field athletes during the 1980s expressed the view that membership of the national team and the method of training and competition accepted by the team had a positive influence on their collective and individual degree of achievement. They also realised the extent to which their individual athletic achievement and success was partly the product of team-work.

The coach

Apart from the experience of team support, the person of the coach as leader of the educational and training process has a dominant position in motivating athletes at all levels of the long-term building process of achievement and stress endurance. He/she is, according to my research, of unparalleled importance for the realisation of a successful career in competitive sports. The dominance of the coach is undoubtedly due to the fact, that he/she is not only the active organiser of the educational process in competitive sports, but that he/she as a person, through his/her actions, leadership qualities and social connections with the athlete, becomes a determining factor for the motivational development of the latter.

This becomes all the more significant as the coach through her/his dominating position can become a creator of many other motivating factors. The direction and strength of the coaches motivating influence are determined by the subjective recognition given to it by the athlete and the position the athlete develops in regard to it. Important in this identification process, concerning the coach's worth and role for the athlete's personal development in competitive sport, is the fact that both are united by a common goal, and in attaining it feel the need to depend on each other.

Today's high level of athletic achievement gives rise to the thesis (for which there are of course always exceptions) that the talented athlete will never attain his/her highest level of performance unless he/she has a coach who is prepared and capable of leading him/her to top achievements. On the other hand, practice proves that the best coach can lead only those athletes to world records who are prepared to put the coach's ideas into practice.

Of particular importance, therefore, are the coach's style of leadership, depth of knowledge and level of pedagogical abilities coupled with their psychological empathy with their athletes.

Experience shows that athlete-coach relationships which are conflict free, productive and mutually stimulating, in other words real partnerships, are a determining factor in successfully shaping and developing athletic mastery. Such partnerships on the basis of mutual respect and acknowledgement as well as absolute mutual trust, depend also on long-term development. They need the athlete's acknowledgement of the coach's leading role concerning education and training during its formation.

The mention of the athlete-coach relationship is really already part of my explanation of the second reason why more significance ought to be attributed to personality development in its complex effect on sport achievement.

In competitive sports the athlete from the start is confronted, during the long-term build-up of his/her achievement, with ever new and higher challenges. This perpetually recurring discrepancy between the actual level of achievement and stress endurance and the prognostic aims of his/her development also demand an increasingly higher level of personality development. This process, however, is not linear, since it is determined by factors like age, development and training. There is evidence, particularly in young athletes, that personality development takes place intermittently with achievement development. Overestimation of personal abilities, unwillingness to train and lack of stress endurance as well as lack of discipline, is often the result. On the other hand, the opponent is often underestimated. Successes diminish while failures increase and the lack of strong personality qualities often sees a promising athletic career discontinued.

Consciously working through experiences of success, and even more, failure, and above all in a way that fosters achievement, is one of the dominant pedagogical tasks of the coach. It should be he/she who consciously points out to the athlete the individual discrepancies between her/his achievement and personality development.

Athletic achievement is developed as a result of the training process and becomes evident in competition. These two principal aspects of competitive sport activity have goals that need to be regarded separately.

In training, stress endurance is the chief objective and training achievements are provisional goals to attain the achievement structure. In competition, however, the attainment of high athletic achievement and success are the goals of action. At the beginning of my arguments I mentioned that the level of sport achievement depends on the strength and efficiency of both physical and psychological capacity. The closer the physical levels of achievement of the athletic competitors are, the more the degree to which the level of psychological achievement components have been developed become the decisive factor for winning. The cognitive-emotional-motivational activity aspects that are necessary for high athletic achievement become continuously available with great certainty if they are stable and firmly established psychological personality traits.

They have to be present in talented young athletes as psychological prerequisites, but they can be strengthened and developed through competitive sport activity. It is therefore true that trainers forego important possibilities to develop athletic top achievement for themselves and their proteges if they do not pay sufficient attention to the enhancement and formation of their athlete's personality — in its totality and complexity.

This might occur if, through a failure of pedagogical guidance they:
— do not use the potential to exhaust all internal and external possibilities to develop the individuality of the competitive athlete
— fail to allow the individual subjectivity and self-reliance of the athlete to become active in a relatively self contained way
— do not demand discipline, readiness to endure stress, consciousness, consequence and willpower from these athletes
— put little importance on the potential of athletes to put knowledge and experience to use and take up and use information of all kinds and do not bother about the development of the educational level overall
— leave the educational development of any progress towards self motivation entirely up to the athlete.

In relation to my subject, the striving for success can thus be learned and trained, ie infuenced pedagogically!

Conclusions

An athlete who has the best and most able partner in this learning process, ie their coach, will find that the risks and imponderabilities of optimal achievement development diminish. At the same time he/she will be put in a position to develop personality traits that are of high significance for the coping with and mastering of so-called everyday problems during, and above all after his/her career in competitive sport.

I believe and I wish that all of us sports officials, coaches and athletes should consider this possibility for personality development, despite the justifiability and necessity of striving for even higher achievement.

Apart from the striving for victory and success — without which competitive sport cannot exist — this competitive sport activity offers, above all to young people, the chance to open up an important social realm of life where, in unity with others, they can attain self-development.

PREDICTIONS OF RECORDS AND ELITE PERFORMANCES

Ken Dyer

Biological and social variables

In one sense each event of a performance sport is a biological experiment. The conditions, ie distance, rules of the event and so forth, are accurately specified. Achievement, as measured by time, distance, height etc. should therefore accurately reflect the workings of underlying biological processes. We also know, however, that social variables in the shape of opportunities, rewards, encouragement, markedly influence performance. The ready availability of data in the shape of world records, the best 50 or 100 performances in each event each year, national records and so forth for both men and women allows detailed analysis of the interplay of these biological and social variables.

There are difficulties, though, both statistical and intrinsic in analysing the data. For example, one of the consequences of the workings of both of these sets of variables is that the biological experiments are carried out not on a total population (eg all able-bodied adults), nor even on a random sample of the total, but on those who have been both socially and biologically advantaged with respect to that event. In any one year we may have, let us say, 1000 athletes returning accurately measured performances for the 100m or the high jump or whatever. But we do not know whether any or all of the 'best' athletes competed in that year, since they may have been injured, have preferred to play football or did not even have the opportunity to compete. These facts raise some problems about the meaning of the data we use — be they world records, the top 10 or whatever —and the way we can analyse them statistically. It also means that in predicting the future we are not actually making predictions about the same populations; our predictions are therefore more sociological than biological. This is a most important point to remember, particularly with respect to predictions about women's future achievements when sceptics deny the likelihood of continued improvements in sporting performance.

For example as the years pass we know that:

— Training regimes change — probably for the better, as knowledge of human physiology catches up with the reality of achievement.

— Technique changes — also probably for the better, as video cameras, computers and so forth supplement the human eye in analysing performance.

— The population sampled changes. In most cases it increases in size and hence for this reason alone we might assume that the likelihood of 'better' athletes participating is increased. The fame and fortune to be made from sport these days no doubt also increases this likelihood.

— Conditions in fact do change — track surfaces improve, running shoes, starting blocks and everything else likely to influence performance also improve.

It is the consequence of the operation of these four factors among other things that world records and other reputable best performances have improved to extraordinary extents over the last few decades and are continuing to improve — in all sports and in all events. It is my assertion, based on the analysis of the data with all the shortcomings and difficulties I have hinted at, that women's performances are improving faster than men's in virtually all events in all sports and will continue to do so for the foreseeable future.

The increases for both men and women are far from uniform and regular; years, decades sometimes, pass without a record being improved. This, and an apparently commonsense approach to sporting achievement — there has to be some limit on how fast humans can run or how far they can jump or throw something — has led numerous commentators in the past (scientists, statisticians, competitors) to suggest that the limit has, in fact, been reached in this or that event. Without exception, all predictions made in the past have been shown to be false. Records which were claimed to represent ultimate performances have been equalled and exceeded. Physiologists used to say that men could not run marathons in 2 hours 20 minutes — there weren't enough energy reserves in the body. Women can now run close to this time and it was not so long ago that medical scientists said they couldn't and shouldn't run marathons at all! I have no doubt that even the longest standing records on the books today — Bob Beamon's 8.91m long jump from 1968, Beryl Burton's 446.2km in 12 hours cycling from 1968, and others, will be exceeded in due course. There may well be limits on sporting achievement. I assert that we don't know what they are and whatever they are, they have not yet been reached.

Prediction is therefore fun; it is also difficult; any particular prediction is certainly doomed to failure; but, for both scientific and sporting reasons, it is of some importance.

Hypotheses

The likelihood of setting a world record depends so much on the constellation of a multitude of chance events that predicting any particular record breaking event is futile. But with data on the top 10, 50, 100 performances from each year available, it is possible to assess on a reasonably secure statistical basis the likelihood of the range of top performances continuing to improve in the future in the same way that they have in the past. And by the very nature of things this means that world records are likely to improve. Using a selection of the readily available data on women's athletic performances I shall try to demonstrate very briefly the following four points:

1. In most athletics events (the same is true probably for most other performance sports but I won't consider them) the performances are improving as fast as ever.

2. This improvement is not just because women have taken up the events recently.

3. The improvements are not just due to a few outstanding women (or women of doubtful sex, gender or sexuality).

4. The improvements are **not** due primarily to drug taking.

1. Women's performances are improving as fast as ever.
I present in Figures 7-10 data on the top 10 performances each year for as long as the data are available from a sprint event, a middle distance event, a jump and a throw. In each case the year by year data are plotted and a regression function which accurately describes the changes occurring. These curves speak for themselves, no limits for future performance are currently in sight. The data and the analysis come from Lames and Letzelter (1983) and Dyer (1985, 1986).

It is worth pointing out, however, that the regression curves, and therefore predictions derived from them, are very sensitive to the dates chosen for analysis. For example, analysis between 1960 and about 1976 or 1977 in the long jump, 400m and javelin would have suggested that limits were being reached. Such is clearly not the case when analysis is continued up until 1986. The increases in performance **may** come to an end in 1989, but all the evidence we have suggests this will not be the case.

2. The phenomena of improvement is not just because the events are recent.
It is widely claimed that since women have only relatively recently taken up most performance sports with any seriousness, their rate of improvement in them will be rapid at the moment but will soon level off. [Note that this claim has already been partly refuted in Section 1 *Ed.*].

Those who have asserted that women have only recently taken up Track and Field have relied on official International Amateur Athletic Federation (IAAF) and International Olympic Committee (IOC) publications and are obviously unfamiliar with the history of the Federation Sportive Feminine International (FSFI) formed in 1921, and the major series of women's meets that it sponsored between then and 1936, when it handed over full control of international women's athletics to the IAAF. Typical in this regard is one of the earliest studies of the changing performance differential between men and women athletes (Furlong and Szreter 1975) who, while collecting a substantial body of data and subjecting it to careful statistical analysis, could still write *Since women came comparatively late on the scene for the 800m, the large slope (ie a fairly rapid convergence of performances) is to be expected.* In fact, women have been running 800m since before the First World War!

Women have been running, jumping and throwing in most of the regular events, apart from the longer track events and those field events from which they are still excluded, since the 1920s. Well-authenticated best performances were known long before official IAAF recognition for world record purposes. These earlier best performances are collected together in my **Challenging the Men** (Dyer 1982) and later supplementary papers (Dyer 1985, 1986). The performance differentials (strictly seeking a percentage proportional performance differential, since what is being calculated is the difference in average speed, or distance thrown etc. expressed as a percentage of the male performance) between men's and women's records for these events from 1921 to 1984 are summarised in Figure 11. Also shown in this figure are linear regression curves which are significantly better fits than any other regression curve. This should not be taken as ruling out an eventual levelling off of the performance differential, only that any levelling off is not really yet detectable.

In other words simple statistics suggest that women's best performances in these events may one day equal those of men. It is clear that for the track events, the

Figure 7: The improvement in the average of the top 10 performers in the women's 100 metres 1952-86

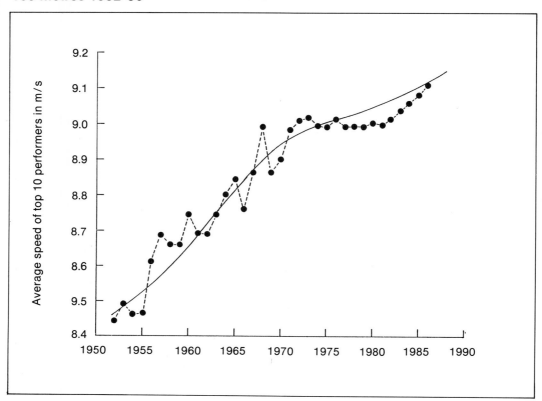

Figure 8: The improvement in average speed of the top 10 performers in the women's 3000 metres 1972-86

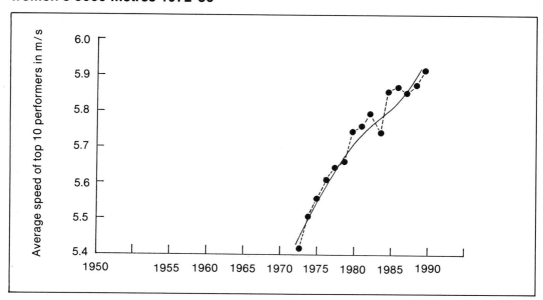

Figure 9: The improvement of performance of javelin throwing from 1960 to 1982 based on the average of the top 20 performers for each year

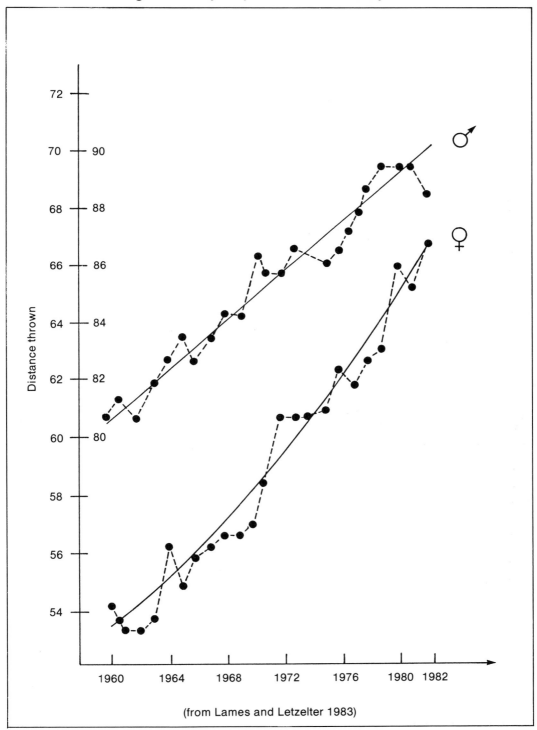

(from Lames and Letzelter 1983)

Figure 10: The improvement of performance in the long jump from 1960 to 1982 based on the average of the top 20 performers for each year

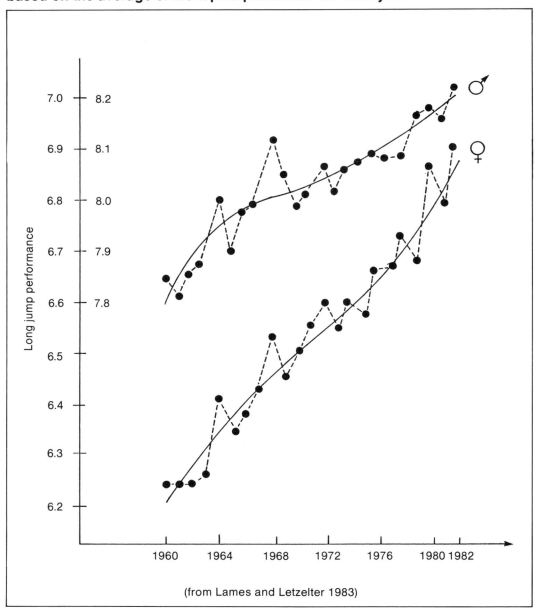

(from Lames and Letzelter 1983)

jumps and the throws, the rate of decline in the sex differential is virtually as great now as it has ever been at any time in the sixty odd years that women have been competing.

Extrapolation of linear regression curves is notoriously unreliable. The estimates for the year 2000 are therefore indicative only. In addition to the statistical uncertainty of the predicted figures for each group of events, it has to be remembered that each group is heterogeneous and any predictions may conceal

Figure 11: The change in the performance differential between the sexes for three throwing events (discus, shot, javelin), two jumps (high jump and long jump) and eight track events (100m, 200m, 400m, 800m, 1000m, 1500m, 4 x 100m relay and 4 x 200m relay), 1921 to 1984. The data plotted are the average differences in the world records or unofficial best performances at the end of each year. Also shown are the linear regressions calculated from these data with their predictions for the year 2000.

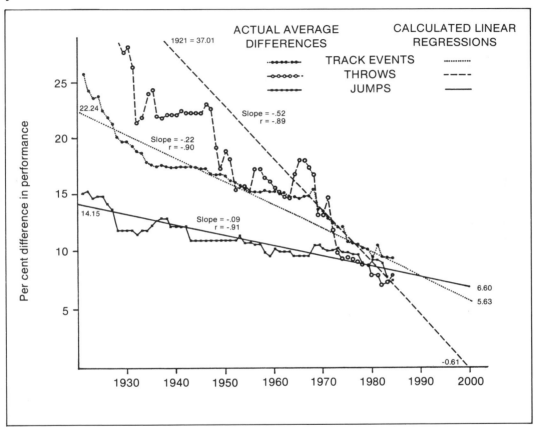

important differences between events. For example, the shot put and discus events currently show approximate 'equality', while the javelin does not and before the change of implement thrown by men, seems unlikely ever to have done so.

Women first began to run marathons and other long distance races in the mid-1960s and it is the astonishing improvement in their times which has prompted much of the speculation about women's likely future achievements. It is, in fact, salutary to compare recent improvements in the eight '1920s' events (100m, 200m, 400m, 800m, 1000m, 1500m, 4 x 100m and 4 x 200m) with those which were taken up later. These later events with the date of the earliest authenticated best time are as follows: mile (1936), 2000m (1978), 3000m (1966), 5000m (1966), 10000m (1967), marathon (1963), 4 x 400m (1954) and 4 x 800m (1969). The decline in the average performance differential for each of these two groups of events calculated using world records or best performances for each event in them are shown in Figure

Figure 12: A comparison of the change in sex differential in performance in eight track events run by women since the 1920s (100m, 200m, 400m, 800m, 1000m, 1500m, 4 x 100m relay and 4 x 200m relay) with those in events introduced more recently into the women's program (mile, 2000m, 3000m, 5000m, 10,000m marathon, 4 x 440m, 4 x 800m).

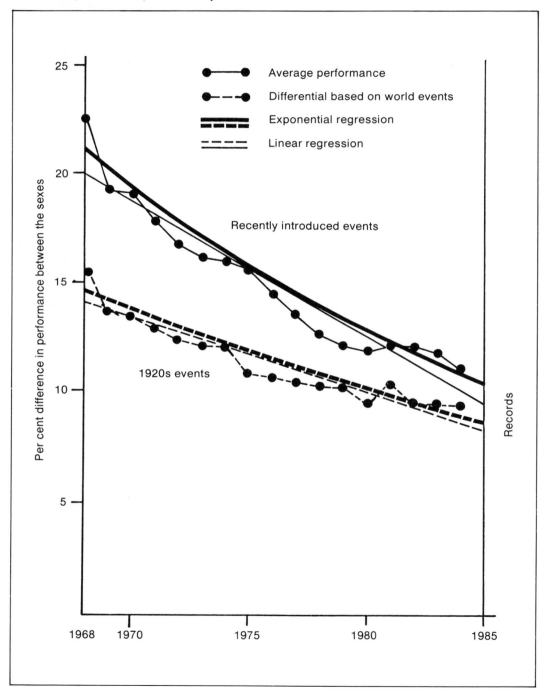

12. Also shown are the linear and exponential regression curves. In each case, the exponential curves are a slightly better fit to the data, suggesting that the rate of women's improvements is declining slowly. Since 1968, the difference in performance between the sexes in the eight 1920s events has declined from 15.55 per cent to 9.39 per cent. This is a 39.6 per cent reduction in performance differential. The eight '1960s' events, by contrast, have declined from 22.22 per cent difference to 11.1 per cent — a reduction of just 50 per cent in performance differential. This comparison between '1920s' events and '1960s' events is certainly not one which supports to any substantial extent the hypothesis that it is the recently introduced events which are the principal or only contributors to women's athletic improvement. Substantial women's improvements are still expected in both groups of events. Indeed, it is interesting that the 'best' predictions given by the exponential regression figure for the year 2000 are almost identical at around 5.6 per cent average difference between the sexes! (And remember in all this that men's events are improving as fast, if as irregularly, as ever (Dyer and Dwyer 1984)!)

3. Are women's improvements simply due to a few exceptional women?

There are two sources of data which provide evidence on this question. First, there are the number of different women who have broken or equalled world records since their inception. If the exceptional women hypothesis is correct, then there should be significantly fewer women than men so involved. Table 4 shows that for all of the regular running events there were 163 women who have broken or equalled recognised records or best performances since the event was first regularly run or officially recognised and over the same periods of time for these events 147 men broke or equalled the records. This is hardly a major difference, particularly when the fact that there have always been far more men athletes than

Table 4: Numbers of individuals breaking or equalling world best performances and official world records

	Women	Men
100m[2] [3]	24	32
200m[3] [4]	13	10
400m[2] [3]	20	17
800m[2]	21	16
1000m[2]	9	21
1500m[2]	16	26
Mile[5]	11	6
3000m[5]	8	3
5000m[5]	11	7
10,000m[5]	12	5
Marathon[5]	18	4
Total	163[6]	147[6]

1. The men's events have had official world records recognised since 1921. For women's events well-established world bests are utilised prior to official IAAF recognition.
2. 1921-1986 inclusive.
3. Hand timing prior to 1968; electronic timing thereafter.
4. 1951-1986 inclusive. (Prior to that, most of the men's best performances were on straight tracks and difficulties of comparability are too great.)
5. 1966-1986 inclusive.
6. If those individuals who appear in more than one event are counted only once, the figures are 118 women and 113 men.

Table 5: Number of individuals breaking or equalling world best performances and official world records in jumping and throwing events 1921-84

	Women	Men
High jump	27	17
Long jump	18	11
Shot[1]	18	19
Discus[1]	21	24
Javelin	20	20
	104	91

[1]. 1923-1984.

Table 6: Mean performance ratios of the top 10 performers in the regular track events compared with the 1981 world record performance ratios

	1951	1956	1961	1966	1971	1976	1981	1981 world records
100m	87.32	88.87	89.20	89.26	90.30	90.39	90.82	91.45
200m	85.30	86.82	86.11	87.18	88.49	89.26	90.92	90.83
400m		83.78	84.12	85.14	85.90	89.37	88.70	90.25
800m	82.37	83.43	83.91	84.90	87.20	90.00	88.65	89.68
1000m						88.41	86.90	87.77
1500m				79.80	86.40	89.30	89.05	90.92
1609m							86.60	87.40
3000m						87.80	88.53	89.15
5000m							84.89	86.51
10,000m							84.54	86.20
Marathon						79.97	86.31	88.13

women in all events is taken into account. Furthermore, if those athletes who featured in two or more events (eg 100m and 200m or 5000m and 10000m) are counted only once, we find that 118 different women are involved in record breaking or equalling, and only 113 men. This is the reverse of the situation which the exceptional women hypothesis predicts. It therefore must be rejected. A similar conclusion follows from examining the same data from the field events shown in Table 5.

There is a second possible test of this exceptional woman hypothesis. Since 1951, the Association of Track and Field Statisticians has produced at the end of each year lists of the 20 or more best performers for that year. If it is exceptional women who are responsible for setting world records, then the mean of the top 10 men performers each year should be much further ahead of the top 10 women performers year by year than is likely to be the case for irregularly set world records.

Data bearing on this point are presented in Table 6. Those events for which there are data over a number of years show significant increases in performance ratio; the top women, not just the occasional exceptional women, are, year by year, getting closer to men's performances. In most cases, the performance ratio of the top 10 in 1981 is a little less than the performance ratio of the world record at that time. The exception is the 200m in which the top 10 women performed better vis-a-vis the top 10 men than the level indicated by the world record. The depth of talent in women runners may, in general, be a little less than among men, but the difference is not large and the notion that it is rare exceptional women who are setting world records cannot be sustained. Data from the throwing and jumping events support this conclusion, although they are not presented here.

4. Is it primarily the taking of drugs, especially steroids, which has brought about women's improvements?

It is regrettable, but almost certainly the case, that drug taking is widespread amongst top men and women athletes. Despite attempts by the IAAF and IOC to control drug taking, the tests to detect usage have not been widespread enough, nor have the penalties imposed on those caught been severe enough to deter athletes.

The following points are relevant. First the benefits which drugs, in particular the steroids, confer are not accurately known. No athlete can admit to taking them and no official doctor or accredited scientist would publicly prescribe them. They have not, therefore, been subject to the careful double blind trials needed to evaluate their effects on performance, or to determine what are the optimum dosages or possible side effects. Second, we don't know just which, if any, record breakers and top performers have taken drugs, for how long and in what doses. Therefore, even if some drugs do have significant effects, we don't know what the effects have actually been on athletic performances.

Steroids were first available in the 1960s. One test of their impact is therefore to compare the rates of improvement before and after their introduction. A substantial increase in the rates of improvement since 1960 would be compatible with the hypothesis that drugs have been responsible for much of the improvement. It would not be conclusive, of course, since better facilities, greater incentives, more numerous opportunities and much wider participation must also contribute. If there has been no great increase in improvement rates over those occurring before 1960, then this would suggest that drugs cannot be the predominant reason for improvement. It would not, of course, rule out any effect. It could always be argued that women had achieved close to their potential before drugs appeared on the scene or, at least, that their rates of increase would have been much lower without drugs. Table 7 shows the results of comparing improvement in records before and after the introduction of drugs onto the athletic scene. The events represented include speed (an anaerobic) and moderate endurance (or largely aerobic) track events, the three throws, which are heavily dependent on strength, and the explosive jumps. They lend little support to the idea that drugs are the main cause of improving performances. The average improvement 1941-61 is only a little less than 1961-81. In five cases the improvements are greater 1961-81 than 1941-61 and in three cases they are less. None of the differences are very large. In every case the 1961-81 improvements are less than the improvements 1921-41. In the last two decades, as already mentioned, there have been undoubted improvements in facilities, coaching opportunities and incentives. Drugs have no doubt played their part in the overall improvements in women's performances recently witnessed, but to attribute to drugs an overriding role is to do a serious disservice to the cause of women's sport in general.

Conclusions

The four hypotheses in this paper have been widely canvassed; they have now been tested and found wanting. In fact, they never had much validity. It is curious that those with an apparent high regard for scientific accuracy and a concern to make judgements only in accordance with facts should have so casually accepted the assertion that women have had a very short history in athletics. Their

Table 7: Comparative improvement of world records before and after the introduction of steroids

	1921	1941		1961		1981	
	Record	Record	% im-provement	Record	% im-provement	Record	% im-provement
100m	12.8 (13.04)[1]	11.5 (11.74)[1]	11.07	11.2 (11.44)[1]	2.62	10.88	5.15
800m	2:30.2	2:16.8	9.80	2:04.3	10.05	1:53.43	9.59
1500m	5:44.0	4:41.8	22.09	4:22.2	7.48	3:52.47	12.78
Shot	9.41m[2]	14.38	52.82	17.78m	23.64	22.45m	26.27
Discus	27.39m[2]	48.31m	76.38	58.98m	22.09	71.80m	21.74
Javelin	30.45m	46.74m	53.50	57.49m	23.00	71.68m	24.68
High jump	1.45m	1.66m	14.48	1.91m	15.06	2.01m	5.24
Long jump	5.54m	6.12m	10.47	6.48m	5.88	7.09m	9.41
		Mean improvt.	31.33	Mean improvt.	15.69	Mean improvt.	16.41

[1] Hand timing is thought to give a time about 0.24 seconds faster than electronic timing. This adjusted figure is therefore used for calculating improvements.

[2] 1923 record.

achievements may not have been widely known, but they have been documented in the press and the scientific literature. For example, the great A.V. Hill, who started so much work in this area, cites a woman's world record for 1000m in his oft quoted 1925 paper. While his conclusions are often cited, his data are not.

The exceptional woman hypothesis derives partly from the veiled assertion which often used to be made that any women sporting champions were not women at all, but were in whole or part chromosomal males. The introduction of the chromosome sex tests in the late 1960s silenced that objection, but it reappears today in the claim that many women athletes, although undoubtedly female, are certainly not feminine.

> There are very many men and women around the world who would be delighted if the IOC would eliminate the shot put and discus from the field events for women in the Olympic Games because often the feminine self-image is badly mutilated when women perform in these two sports.
>
> (Jernigan 1966, cited in Dyer 1982)

These insinuations have been extended to most of the events in which women are currently improving their performances. In one sense, of course, both men and women world record breakers are exceptional people. But those men who develop their body and push themselves to the limit are hailed as pioneers and used as role models. Women who do the same are said to be destroying something essential of themselves and labelled as deviant for doing so.

Both men and women athletes have undoubtedly been taking drugs. But, equally, both men and women have had to train for long wearisome years and push themselves to the limit in their events to achieve world records or gold medals. Drugs are no substitute for the hard work, dedication, determination, courage, self-confidence and the supreme effort which all record breakers must bring to their events. To ascribe the extra improvements which one sex is making compared to the other as largely due to drugs, even though both sexes are taking the same drugs, is scandalously dismissive of women's achievements, even were it to be true.

It is now widely accepted that our current knowledge of physiology is not sufficient to make accurate predictions of future performances, nor indeed to explain past improvements. Maximum Aerobic Power is the parameter most widely cited as best predictor of performance in middle and distance events. Yet top men athletes beteen 1935 and 1945 had maximum oxygen uptakes of between 60 to 81 mL/kg/min (Dill 1967), figures which are no less than those measured today. Running records, however, have increased by as much as 10 per cent since then (Dyer and Dwyer 1984). These improvements cannot therefore be due to changes in aerobic power; they have been attributed variously to improved running efficiency, increased anaerobic capacity, and improved facilities (Faulkner 1968; Lloyd 1966, 1980).

In a review entitled **Future Performance in Footracing** (restricted to men's events only), Ryder, Carr and Herget (1977) wrote:

> ... a highly competitive situation brings out in the finest of athletes a level of performance of which even they are incapable under less challenging circumstances ... What is needed is not better runners but bigger challenges ... At present, the factor limiting record performance may be pathological or psychological, but it is not physiological.

Interviews which Terry Dwyer and I included in our book **Running Out of Time**, notably with Herb Elliott, confirm that this is what top men athletes themselves believe.

I would say the same about women athletes, emphasising that sociological factors are also of considerable importance. While they have shared, to some extent, in many of the improvements in facilities and training which have characterised men's sport, and are now beginning to enjoy a similar range of opportunities in terms of numbers of events and range of meetings open to them, it could hardly be said that women's opportunities are yet equal to those of men. Sportswomen themselves still identify many areas of disadvantage, discrimination and prejudice (Mitchell and Dyer 1985). The reason why women are improving their athletic performances are therefore largely understandable. Indeed, it would have been surprising if they had not been improving fairly rapidly. But it is also clear that we can expect them to continue to improve rapidly for some time yet.

Many women athletes have maximum oxygen uptake values higher than all but a handful of men. And in other important parameters such as strength, endurance and amount of body fat, their greater levels of training are bringing benefits. Physiological differences are undoubtedly responsible for some of the per-formance differential between the sexes but it is simply flying in the face of the evidence to label physiology the sole cause. To do that directs attention from what those other causes might be. It is a similar strategy to that of adopting one of the four hypotheses discussed earlier, which largely dismiss the need for serious scientific discussion of women's current sporting improvements.

Women's athletic performances today are better known than once they were; academic analysis, popular journalism and television have seen to that. It is a matter of some sociological interest that denial of continued improvements of women's performance and the three spurious explanations for the recent improvements which demonstrably have occurred and which I discussed above, have gained such wide currency. They are clearly, however, no more valid than were such assertions that women were incapable of running track events longer than 200m, or running road races, swimming further than 800m, and so on, which were put forward and, it seems, widely believed not so very long ago [as is recounted in the historical introductory section to this book using, in part, primary data gathered by John Daly who contributes elsewhere *Ed.*]. What has changed is that it used to be men who were making up the difference. Today it is women.

There are many so called non-traditional sports which are still enormously popular with women and which have established world championships, international and national competitions. They involve strength, skill, speed and concentration — everything in fact which characterises sport. Why do they not get the publicity and media attention they deserve?

Top: Marilyn Waller at the Women's World Championship Powerlifting Championships, Brussels 1988.

Centre: Skiing. Women now have downhill, slalom, and cross country events on their program; but why no ski-jumping?

Bottom: Australia's Wendy McGuigan at the 1988 World fullbore rifle championships.
Reproduced with permission of the Bicentennial Authority.

Top right: Kerri Tepper a table tennis representative at the 1988 Seoul Olympics.
Reproduced with permission of the Bicentennial Authority.

Top left: The Biathlon, a combination of cross country skiing and shooting. Gillian Croudwell competing at Mt. Hotham, Victoria.
Photo: Katrina Bridgeford. An entrant in the 1988 ACHPER/Bicentennial Authority Photographic Competition.

Right: The women's 3000 metres at the World Speed Rollerskating Championships, Adelaide, September 1986.
Photo: Doug Nicholas. Thanks to the Girls and Physical Activity Project.

SECTION FOUR
RECRUITMENT AND PARTICIPATION OF FEMALE ATHLETES

AN INTRODUCTION
Ken Dyer

One of the most significant and best documented aspects of women and sport is that far fewer women participate in sport and physically orientated leisure activities than men. Not only are there fewer women participants, but there are fewer coaches, trainers, managers, announcers, owners, agents, umpires, and the like. Those who participate do so in a narrower range of activities. Women also watch sport, both live and on television, less than men, read about it less and talk about it less to their friends.

The reasons given for their low participation include lack of time, largely because of family responsibilities, lack of transport, particularly difficult for those with young children, lack of money and problems of safety and security in travelling about towns alone and at night. There are also many more sports clubs with better facilities for men to join than for women. And even in many of those clubs they can join they have until recently not been allowed to play at times which would be most convenient for them. (The Equal Opportunity legislation applies to sports clubs in Australia; in many other countries, notably the UK, it still does not, which is a very powerful source of disadvantage to sportswomen.)

Two questions arise. When do girls begin to be less interested and begin to drop out and what reasons do they give at that stage or are likely to be relevant for them discontinuing sport? The reasons why adult women do not participate are valid enough (if only part of the story) but are not likely to be the overriding reason why teenagers give up sport.

As Simone de Beauvoir (1960) pointed out, puberty takes on a radically different significance in the two sexes because it does not portend the same future to them. Among other things parental control becomes more restrictive and society demands that the girl behaves in a way that conforms to a feminine sexrole stereotype. Her social acceptance as a woman and hence her self-esteem depend on the manifestations of her femininity.

Although a young girl may be unclear about what to do in order to be a woman, she does respond to a simple, clear directive which is to withdraw from what is obviously designated masculine. Sport, as Lois Bryson showed in her paper in an earlier section, clearly falls into this category. Hence, unless an adolescent girl has the supportive family and social environment to counteract these cultural influences, she will probably choose to opt out of sport at school and drop out of sport when she leaves school. Perhaps, most importantly, avoiding sport is

101

considered normal in teenage girls and the collaboration that they receive from their parents is testimony to the widespread social attitudes that prevail concerning women's sporting participation. Conversely, those who carry on and become high achievers usually have strong support from their parents, as Sandy Gordon shows in his paper in this section of the book.

In some earlier research carried out in Australia, Wendy Ey found the decline of girls playing school sport began even before age 14, by which time only 22 per cent of girls participated in sports compared with 44 per cent of boys. The higher rate of dropping out among girls at all ages among high school students led to a much lower number of girls actively involved in sports in the senior school. The reasons boys and girls gave for dropping out of sport were, she found, similar: pressure of homework, lack of interest, part-time job taking all available spare time. There was one significant reason given by girls only. Ten per cent of the girls felt they were not good enough. This is a reflection of the poor self image of adolescent girls. It reflects among other things, the influence of cultural expectations on girls and earlier lack of opportunities for girls in the area of physical activities (Ey 1982).

Nevertheless, despite the high drop-out rate amongst adolescent girls, there are still many girls who remain actively involved in sport and other physical activities until they are adults. And there are some impressive statistics to show that, in Australia at least, some sports are of immense and rapidly growing popularity among women. There are, for example, in Australia about 350 000 women netball players, 150 000 women lawn bowlers, 120 000 women golfers, 110 000 women hockey players as well as, in what are regarded as less typically womens sports, 7500 women soccer players, 4000 women cricketers and 2500 women lacrosse players. It might be more instructive to study girls and women who continue to participate in sport than to study the drop outs. What motivates them? Do they find themselves in role conflict situations? What benefits do they get? This is precisely what Sandy Gordon and his team from Western Australia set out to do. The work reported in his paper, although still incomplete, is a valuable contribution to our knowledge in this area.

Tony Sedgwick in his paper in this section points out the enormous change he has experienced in the last two decades regarding the participation of women. The Institute for Fitness, Research and Training in Adelaide dealt only with men when it was founded in 1969. Today at his institute there are 55 per cent women and only 45 per cent men. As he shows, the women's programs are offered in a non-threatening, non-competitive supportive environment. We should consider the implications of this carefully.

One conclusion which emerges from several studies is that girls may be involved to quite a significant extent in community sports and physical activity programs as well as in school programs. This was certainly found to be the case in two recent Australian studies. Ey (1982) found 31.5 per cent of high school girls involved in school sport and 43.5 per cent involved in community sport. Poole (1983) found 24.5 per cent involved in school sport whereas about twice as many, 50.6 per cent, were involved in community sports. Perhaps this is an area which should be more emphasised.

Thus it seems that, in general, those adolescent girls who do continue to play sport prefer to play for the fun and enjoyment it provides. They like sports activities to be of a social and recreational rather than of a competitive nature, although competition is not unimportant. While being a member of a sports team is not the way to achieve peer group status for girls, as it is for boys, many girls do remain involved in some form of physical activity, particularly if they can participate in a socially conducive environment. Jackie Byrnes in her presentation in this section, points to many of the practical difficulties women face. Are they fighting social and psychological obstacles as well?

These empirical findings and the conclusions based on them have been arrived at from the sociological perspective. There has also been a great deal of work done from the psychological perspective, one aspect of which Sandy Gordon explores in his paper. He and his colleagues are conducting a major inquiry including careful evaluation of features in common among elite sportswomen who did not drop out.

The end product of the talent development process, he writes, *is an intrinsically motivated high achiever who has a holistic world view of her goals related to her capabilities. Such individuals appear to be well equipped to tackle any of lifes challenges — a proud and fitting tribute to the socialisation process through organised sport.* We may not yet know how best to ensure that girls and women participate and continue to participate in sport. But for those who do persist the rewards are rich indeed.

RECRUITING FEMALE ATHLETES AND KEEPING THEM

Jackie Byrnes

Introduction

When I was first given this topic to present I wasn't sure whether to discuss the structure and process of recruiting women athletes in NSW or to plead for help from you to give me direction on how to:

— Get female athletes into the sport.

— Once you've got them how to keep them.

Asking for the direction and ideas seems to be the better alternative but I will first discuss what I am doing in my state.

Firstly I would like to outline my role as NSW coaching Director. It is important to make you aware that my area of responsibility with coaching programs is directed towards both the male and female athletes. I am employed by the NSW AAA with my salary provided by Streets Ice Cream and my expenses covered by a grant from the NSW Government, which also covers expenses incurred by the 13 Honorary Regional coaching directors working throughout the state. My areas of responsibility include:

Camps	Junior development
Clinics	Coach development
State Squads	Coach education (in conjunction with the Australian Track and Field Coaches Association)
State Teams	Recruitment
Country development	School liaison

Table 8: Female registrations in NSW athletics

	1967/68	1977/78 (amalgamation)	1982/3	1986/7
Metropolitan	1032	1255	1100	871
Country	690	1477	1280	1282
Total	1722	2732	2380	2153

With an area of 801,428 square km to cover and a population of approximately 5.8 million, it is an enormous job for one person.

The current state of athletics in NSW

Some statistics on registration for female athletes over several years are shown in Table 8.

Both Metropolitan and Country registration show a decline from the peak of 1977/78, but Metropolitan registrations have declined further. The 1282 Country registrations for 1986/87 include an unbelievable 484 under 12s; in 1982/83 there were only 70. Many of the 86/87 Under 12s hold joint registration with the Little Athletics Association of NSW and the senior body. For comparison, male registrations for 86/87 were Metropolitan 1779 and Country 1277, giving a total of 3056. Currently in NSW there are 41 Metropolitan clubs and 70 country clubs. There were 363 registered coaches in 1980 of whom 102 were females.

There were 15 state event coaches in 1986/87, of whom 5 were women, and there was 13 Regional Coaching Directors, of whom 3 were women.

My trip to the UK in 1986 and my work with several coaches from the USA, South Africa and various European countries has confirmed my impression that the drop in number of competing athletes in our sport is a general trend throughout the world. We have less people competing in track and field but ever increasing numbers in the 'fun runs', both male and female. I believe this is one of the areas where we could recruit for track events.

Unfortunately the managers of athletics in this country, both at state and national level, see falling numbers as signs of failure. They fail to consider the improvement in performances across the board. In NSW when our numbers were highest, our performances at National championships were at an all time low. I believe it is important to measure success by performance at all levels, and enthusiasm of those participating rather than simply playing the numbers game. But numbers of course means revenue, hence the management attitudes towards large numbers. Surely performance, international success and media coverage will attract sponsorship more than numbers!

Nowadays we have to compete for new members with many diversified and exciting sports in which women are competing and participating. Many of these sports are well-presented by the media without the 'tom boy' tag that athletics sometimes unfairly and unnecessarily receives, instead of highlighting the achievements and skill of the individual.

Current initiatives in NSW

Over the last 8 years I have made more than 500 school visits. During this time I have come across a disturbingly large number of male PE staff who show very little enthusiasm towards any sport which doesn't involve playing with a ball, and who do little to encourage their female students to do anything physical other than supporting their (male) football teams!

It seems to me that achievement in, and more importantly acknowledgement of team sport, has a much higher priority at school assemblies than has the individual achiever, such as those in track and field and cross country athletics. In my experience this has been especially so for females.

Over the last 3 1/2 years I have implemented a number of programs designed especially for our females both at elite and beginner levels. Such programs have not received any specific funding recently.

Unfortunately women's issues are no longer seen as important by the Managers of Athletics in NSW, I therefore approach planning for the year with the knowledge that any specific women's activities that I may wish to set up to try and encourage performance improvement or to try and increase women's registration, may be seen as 'no benefit' operations and not receive the level of approval that they have in the past.

On the positive side there is no doubt in my mind that the best way to recruit and keep female athletes generally is by conducting camps and clinics. I have found such camps are the very best way to communicate with the athletes: for me and the other coaches involved in the camp to get to know the athletes and for the athletes to get to know us. Through the camps we also make contact with the teachers, parents, coaches of the athletes both through face-to-face meeting and through questionnnaires that we hand out at camp. This establishes a system whereby I can keep in contact with individual athletes by adding their address to mailing lists for future camps and clinics and for sending special articles etc.

Clinics have also proved a useful communication tool and these perhaps more so than camps bring me in contact with 'new' athletes. During 1987 we were able to achieve some 30 new registrations at our clinics in various areas. In 1986 four athletes from clinics made finals at the national U/16 and U/18 championships. This year a young lady introduced to athletics in 1986 won the U/18 Javelin.

I am fortunate in NSW in having a good working relationship with the Little Athletics coaching staff. We have jointly established a junior development plan which the Little Athletics Management have fully supported. They have in fact appointed one of their staff as junior development officer, the main task of this officer being to recruit and ensure that as many little athletes in the U/15 age group register and compete in senior athletics. It will be some 2-3 years before we can properly evaluate this project.

Perhaps the single biggest problem I have as Coaching Director in both recruiting and keeping athletes both male and female is the vastness of the state and in the country the long distances between clubs, athletes and coaches. I don't know what the answer is and can only keep working towards the directions that I have taken, though I am open to new ideas from you.

Conclusions

It is vitally important, I believe, that we all work towards making athletics an exciting and great place to be. This not only has to come from the coaching arm of the sport but also the administrative side. At times there seems very little flexibility from our administrators and often demonstrations of absurd inconsistencies and gross insensitivity which are enormously frustrating and annoying for the athletes. Inconsistencies such as an athlete not being able to compete because they have forgotten their number, or signed in late for a championship after having been involved in a car accident on the way, are known to occur from my personal experience. At the same time there are many cases of athletes who need to polish up their act.

One word keeps coming into our conversations about coaching and competing. We must function as a 'professional' body. This is often, unfortunately, not the case at the present time. The quicker the word 'amateur' disappears from my association's name the better I will feel. I doubt that the traditionalists will allow it to happen without heated debate. We must be seen from the outside as an interesting and exciting sport that is well-administered and offers sound and progressive coaching programs for all levels of athletes and coaches.

AVOIDING THE 'DROP OUT' SYNDROME

Christina Lee and Neville Owen

Introduction

Sports and physical activities of all kinds have numerous well-documented benefits for the participant. Physiological benefits, particularly from aerobic exercise, include a reduced risk of coronary heart disease, improved blood lipid balance, reduction of body fat, and increased strength and flexibility (Powell, Thompson, Caspersen, Kendrick, 1987). Exercise improves sleeping patterns and increases recovery rate from minor illnesses and injuries, as well as being associated with safer, shorter, childbirth and fewer complications (Thomas 1979).

The psychological benefits of exercise are well documented. Exercise has been shown to alleviate depression and anxiety, both problems which are commoner in women than in men. Reductions in stress levels, improved ability to cope with everyday problems, and subjective feelings of greater energy and higher self-esteem are commonly reported. Although the mechanisms by which these improvements occur are not clear, there is consistent evidence that sport or exercise involvement does have these benefits (Hughes 1984).

There also may be social benefits, in providing companionship and social networks for people who might otherwise be socially isolated, a particular problem for the mother of young children, the supporting mother, and the non-employed woman. Despite the many benefits, however, rates of exercise and sporting involvement are low for both sexes in Australia, with women's involvement much lower than men's. A National Heart Foundation (1983) survey showed that 10 per cent of adult males and 5 per cent of adult females exercised regularly at a vigorous level; a further 25 per cent of men and 21 per cent of women exercised vigorously on occasion. Regular participation in less vigorous exercise was also reported by 27 per cent of men and 24 per cent of women. Similar findings have emerged from surveys in Canada and the USA (Stephens, Jacobs, and White, 1985). School children also have low levels of sporting involvement, with approximately 48 per cent of adolescent boys and 41 per cent of girls engaging in competitive sport, and 42 per cent and 37 per cent respectively in non-competitive sports.

For those children involved in organised sports, dropout rates are high for both boys and girls; Lee and Owen (1984) found a 52 per cent dropout rate over 6 months in girls' competitive gymnastics, while Sands and Ekberg (1983) found a 73 per cent dropout rate in mixed Little Athletics in the course of one season.

Clearly, sport and exercise are valuable for all members of the community, and increasing the physical activities of a particular group benefits the community at large as well as that group in particular. Girls and women have lower participation rates than boys and men, and a case may be made that females are sufficiently different, socially, physically and psychologically, from males to be considered as a special group who may need special attention. This paper draws upon work conducted for the Sport and Recreation Ministers Council (Owen and Lee, 1984), which involved the development of principles and guidelines for the promotion of physical activity in Australia. From a review of relevant theory and research, we developed a set of eleven principles which appeared to characterise successful interventions to instate or maintain exercising (Lee and Owen, 1985). Our approach has also been used recently to develop a set of guidelines for the National Heart Foundation's community exercise strategies (Owen and Dwyer, in press). In this paper we describe the principles which we have used in this work, and consider ways in which these might be applied specifically to the promotion of exercise for girls and women.

Principles for promoting exercise and sporting participation

Principle 1 — Appropriateness and convenience of settings
The lower the travelling time, expenditure, and disruption of other activities required, the more likely it is that a person will continue with an activity. Convenience is an important factor in people's decisions to take up exercise (Teraslinna, Partanen, Koskela, and Oja, 1969). While this is a general principle, the implications for women are important. Women make up the majority of low income earners and welfare recipients. In Australia single-parent families are most likely to be headed by a woman (Better Health Commission, 1986). This means that facilities for exercise must be made accessible by public transport, that more facilities must be developed in less affluent areas (particularly the outer suburbs of major cities), and that facilities must be made available at low cost. Outdoor facilities which require little expense to use, such as cycle paths and running/walking trails, may be more appropriate than expensive indoor facilities. The provision of child care in or near exercise centres, or the organisation of child care groups within sporting clubs, is essential.

Principle 2 — Stages of behaviour change
A change in behaviour to a more active lifestyle is not an event but a process. Behaviour change requires a process of producing awareness of an issue, then motivation to change, followed by instruction on how to change, the initial adoption of the new behaviour, and a final stage involving the maintenance of the new behaviour (Maccoby and Alexander, 1980). Different behaviour-change techniques are effective at different stages in the change process, and for this reason it is important to know what level of knowledge and motivation already exists in a target group so that interventions can be appropriately focussed. It is also necessary to be aware that a change in knowledge or attitude will not automatically lead to a change in behaviour, and that this must be planned for.

Principle 3 — Setting of realistic targets
Since most women and girls take very little exercise, the first step towards a more active lifestyle may be small for many people. It is argued that the main benefit in

terms of community health will come from instating at least some exercise among the habitually sedentary, rather than focussing entirely on those already active (Thomas 1979). An image of vigorous, competitive, activity as unfeminine acts against involvement, as does the fact that many women in stringent financial circumstances and/or with dependents have difficulties in finding time to exercise. These factors make it unrealistic to aim for high levels of sporting involvement for at least some groups of women, in the short term. Programs which promote a small amount of activity and suggest ways in which this activity can be integrated into work and/or child care are needed.

Principle 4 — Specificity
The more specific the aim of a campaign, program, or message, the more likely it is to be successful (Olson and Zanna, 1981). Thus, interventions need to be orientated specifically at sub-groups of the community. Even a focus on female participation may be too broad: programs might usefully focus only on particular groups of women. For example: mothers of young children; women with arthritis; female students; migrant women from cultures which discourage independence and activity among women. The needs, interests, and concerns of such specific groups will differ.

Principle 5 — Variety
The greater the variety of specific messages and programs presented, the more likely it will be that people will be affected. Promoting a variety of specific activities, without excessive complexity or confusion, will provide appropriate choices for a variety of women in Australian society and will also suggest that there is an even greater range of alternatives available (Bandura 1977).

Principle 6 — Multiple levels
Intervention at many levels (individual, family group, community) is likely to be more effective than at a single level. Women in particular are limited by their relationships (both home and work) in the choices they can make. Therefore, it is necessary to target employers and other family members in order to gain their support for women's increased involvement in sport. For many women to take time for sport or exercise, or indeed for any personal interest, it may be necessary for family members to adapt and share roles such as cook and child minder. It is important, therefore, to convince other family members that this is a worthwhile enterprise.

Principle 7 — Use of social networks
The use of existing social networks to disseminate information, and the reorganisation of existing community groups to provide sporting activities, is likely to be more effective and less expensive than the development of new structures and organisations. The social networks targetted will depend on characteristics of the group of women who are the focus for the campaign. Church groups, school parent groups, employee associations, and special interest groups are all potential avenues for reaching groups of women. If exercise leaders are drawn from the existing social group, effectiveness may also be enhanced. Learning is often most effective if the leader shares some characteristics with the trainees (Bandura 1977: Lee and Owen, 1986).

Principle 8 — Choice
If people feel they have chosen a course of action for themselves, they are more likely to persist than if they feel it has been forced upon them or that it was the only option available. For example, women members of a health club were twice as

likely to persist with a program if they were given an opportunity to reach a reasoned, personal, choice concerning their involvement (Thompson and Wankel, 1982). Therefore, provision of information to allow a reasoned choice will be more effective than simple 'you should' messages. Alternatives should be made clear, so that choices may be made on the basis of accurate knowledge. Choice, however, is constrained by environmental and social factors, and cannot be seen as simply a matter of individual decision-making.

Principle 9 — Intrinsic value

Activities which are interesting because they provide enjoyment, skill develop-ment, competition, feedback on ability, and variety, or which offer opportunities for socialising or are in attractive surroundings, are preferred to other activities and thus people are more likely to persist with them. It seems that programs emphasising physical conditioning only (generally jogging and calisthenics) may have the highest dropout rates (Fitness Ontario, 1981). There is of course enormous variation in what women find personally rewarding, which implies that a range of activities must be made available. Fitness leaders and sports coaches need to orientate their activities to the provision of fun, not just training. If potentially boring repetitive exercises are considered essential (for example, in rehabilitation or in pre-natal exercise classes), their interest may be enhanced in a variety of ways, for example by the addition of music.

Principle 10 — Sound information and instruction

Instructors and exercise leaders can combine their knowledge of exercise and the principles outlined here to enhance the quality of their exercise programs and to make them more appropriate for the particular group they are dealing with. Sound information should also be readily available to independent exercisers (for example, see Egger and Champion, 1986; Owen, Lee and Gilbert, 1987). While this is a general principle, there are particular concerns which may be more relevant to women than to men. Education specifically about the effects of exercise on women and girls (eg recreational levels of exercise won't develop huge bulging muscles, won't damage fertility, and will make women more attractive and self-confident) needs to be made generally available.

Principle 11 — Independence

Training people in the skills required for independent activity will increase the likelihood that they will continue with that activity. Such instruction must provide the requisite skills and knowledge, and direct training on dealing with barriers to exercise is highly desirable.

Information on how to train must be readily available, and fitness instructors can profitably orient their approach towards teaching independent exercises rather than towards 'converting disciples' (Owen, Lee and Sedgwick, 1987). Women in Australian society often have fewer opportunities for independent choice than men, and are more constrained by family obligations. Women need to be helped specifically to deal with these barriers to independent exercise.

Conclusion

Women and girls have in general, lower levels of participation in physical activity than men and boys, despite the fact that there are health and social benefits for all people who exercise regularly. In promoting exercise for women, the principles outlined above may be useful in designing interventions which are successful. It is also important to bear in mind that individuals act in a social context, and that social context may also need to be a focus for change (Winkler 1986). A number of the principles we have described can equally be applied to changing attitudes and behaviours throughout the community to promote an environment which encourages women, and men, to exercise.

WOMEN'S PARTICIPATION IN EXERCISE PROGRAMS

Tony Sedgwick

The aim of this paper is to review briefly what has happened, what is happening, and to recommend what (perhaps) should happen to women's exercise programs based on my experience in Adelaide in the last twenty-five years. The exercise programs to which I refer are courses specially designed to increase physical fitness.

Changes in the last 25 years

In 1960, when I started working in South Australia, there was little interest in women's exercise, fitness and health, compared to the level of interest in men's exercise. There were very few exercise programs for women; women were rarely seen doing strenuous things; a female jogger was a bit of a joke, even to other females.

The Institute for Fitness which started in 1969, dealt at first with men only. Now, 20 years later, all that has changed. There are probably more programs in SA for women than for men, female joggers are everywhere, women pump iron in gymnasia, and at the Institute for Fitness Research and Training there are 55 per cent female and 45 per cent male participants.

These changes must be seen, on the whole, as very encouraging. What has caused them? Perhaps some or all of the following:

— Exercise has become widely accepted as essential to good health for everyone at all stages of life, and sedentary living is seen as a health hazard.
— A wider role in all features of life has been accepted for women, including a physical role.
— Exercise and fitness have been recognised by women as important in exploiting their wider role in life (eg fitness to fulfill a double role as mother and wage earner).
— The media have spread the word in various ways, to good and bad effect, but they have, in general, undoubtedly popularised the concept of exercise being right for women.
— Commercial interests have pushed the exercise movement in order to make a profit from the sale of running shoes, head-bands, leotards, trendy gear, deodorants, medicaments etc.
— Worship of the body beautiful, associated with commerce, the media, and fashion has kept exercise to the fore — it is pictorial, dramatic, sexy, etc.
— Men support the idea of the body beautiful; exercise is one aspect of the

wider role of females which men encourage because they sense it is in their own sexual self-interest.

— Schools are encouraging physical education and sport exercise for girls and women because of the academic and psychological benefits it brings.
— Governments support it, for health and economic reasons.
— The medical and para-medical professions, sporting organisations, and many others support it.

Surely all this represents an important step in social anthropology. In 25 years women have become physically released from the strait-jacket concept of female fragility. It is recognised that life for women is as much a matter of muscle work and training as it is for men.

How does this relate to the future, if at all? Perhaps it will help us plan future developments based on recognition of the advantages and disadvantages of what has happened so far.

The current system

This has good and less good features.

The Good Features
There is acceptance, as just described, of the need for females to exercise; there are some progressive exercise programs; there is strong governmental support (eg the South Australian Health Commission, the Department of Recreation and Sport); there is private sector support (eg the health insurance organisation Mutual Community); there is education system support; there is work-place support; and there is good instructor training run by the Department of Technical and Further Education. No doubt there is support by corresponding organisations in other states.

The Less Good Features
Some programs are poorly managed and staffed, leading to high drop-out rates and de-motivation of participants; unsuitable exercise is widely applied with inadequate objectives; little consideration is given to group dynamics as a vital feature of motivation; certain social groups are poorly catered for such as blue collar workers and many ethnic groups. Unfortunately women are still in general in this category of being poorly catered for; there is inadequate provision for individual differences — biological, social, and psychological; media coverage is varied and ambiguous; the effects of exercise are misrepresented by commercial groups and some professional organisations; commercialisation has distorted the marketing of exercise to favour the young and trendy and to disadvantage the older, less lovely, and fat; little thought has been given to the educational and motivational components of exercise programs. There is clearly a lot to be done.

What, perhaps, should happen?

A priority is surely to develop a sound knowledge about current trends in fitness participation, the problems which people experience and of the programs they take. Research and evaluation have not figured prominently in the 25 year fitness boom so there is much to learn. It would seem important, however, to examine questions such as:

— Why the large drop-out rate from exercise programs?
— What will attract the interest of blue collar and ethnic groups?

— Does reasonable exercise really influence body-shape, bone density etc.?

— And above all, in the present context, how might women's interests best be served?

It would seem essential to evaluate programs to identify important issues for research, the findings of which may then be used to provide a rational basis for program development. Hitherto much has been based on tradition, guesswork, or what on the surface appears to please women, at least in the short-term.

Seek honest promotion

This calls for a different sort of participation; in leadership, in politics, and in lobbying as distinct from in exercise per se.

It would seem essential for women to demand unambiguous, realistic information from public health authorities and the media alike so that current confusion can be avoided and women can feel confident that advice presented to them about exercise is worth following. Advertising in particular calls for careful and vigorous attention, because much of what is currently presented about exercise is

Figure 13: The research system: women's health and fitness program

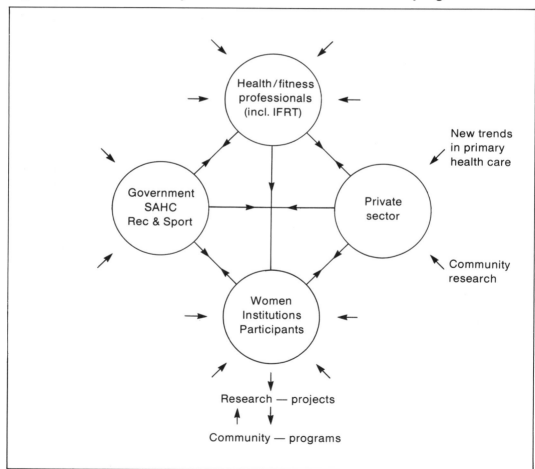

112

absolutely outrageous (eg 'you can strengthen your stomach muscles quickly, without tiring exercise, by electrical stimulation'; 'you can lose weight simply and permanently'; etc).

As with food advertising and labelling there would seem to be an urgent need for legislation about what is presented to the public; there is room here for public anger in the face of attempted (and probably successful) exploitation of women (as well as men). If health and fitness are truly important then we should not accept the rubbish fed to us by the media. We should question it and demand good sense. Similarly, we should demand equal opportunities for disadvantaged females, and educational programs (which give us the ability to manage our own exercise) in place of 'follow my leader' programs which in the long-term change the exercise habits of very few women.

Research and development at the Institute for Fitness Research and Training

With the foregoing in mind, the Institute is establishing in the near future a women's health and fitness research system illustrated in Figure 13. It is hoped the system will involve four crucial components.

- Government instrumentalities such as the Health Commission and the Department of Recreation and Sport.
- Private sector organisations, notably health insurance companies such as Mutual Community.
- Health Professionals, that is IFRT personnel and collaborators from several SA Institutions (University of Adelaide, Flinders University, IMVS, CSIRO, Daw Park Repatriation Hospital).
- Representatives of Women's Organisations, and female consumers relevant to specific projects.

The plan is to integrate expertise, skills and ideas necessary to tackle research effectively in a number of areas, eg on pregnant women, young mothers, on the effects of menopause, the ageing woman and so forth. The findings of these research projects can then be applied to the development of appropriate fitness programs and the improvement of health generally.

TALENT DEVELOPMENT OF ELITE SPORTSWOMEN: A RETROSPECTIVE PICTURE OF THE PROCESS

Sandy Gordon

Introduction

The research reported in this paper is part of a larger 2 year project entitled 'Drop-Out Phenomenon in Organised Sport' which has been funded by the Western Australian Sport Council's Women in Sport Committee. The whole project involves 9 sub-projects which are illustrated in Figure 14. In addition to this paper which reports one of these sub-projects, some of the results from the

Figure 14: The research project 'Drop-out phenomenon in organised sport'

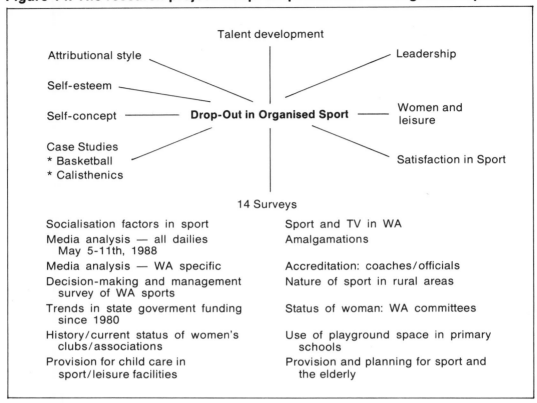

14 Surveys

Socialisation factors in sport	Sport and TV in WA
Media analysis — all dailies May 5-11th, 1988	Amalgamations
Media analysis — WA specific	Accreditation: coaches/officials
Decision-making and management survey of WA sports	Nature of sport in rural areas
Trends in state goverment funding since 1980	Status of woman: WA committees
History/current status of women's clubs/associations	Use of playground space in primary schools
Provision for child care in sport/leisure facilities	Provision and planning for sport and the elderly

media analysis survey, one of the 14 surveys which comprise another of these sub-projects are reported in the paper by Helen Menzies in this volume. That particular survey was designed as a precise replication of her earlier work.

Purpose and methodology

The purpose of this particular sub-project is to describe the characteristic and common features of the process of talent development as related retrospectively by elite athletes themselves. These well-known national and international Western Australian athletes did **not** drop out of organised sport: instead they have become leaders in their chosen talent field. Both team and individual athletes identified for interview are listed in Table 9.

Thirteen female undergraduate and graduate students from the Department of Human Movement and Recreation Studies, University of Western Australia were assigned to one or more of the athletes listed in Table 9. Athlete interviews lasted 2-3 hours, were taped with consent, and were followed up with interviews of the athlete's parents or siblings or, in some cases, coaches. The second interview enabled interviewers to elicit elaboration and/or confirmation on salient features of the athlete's background and development through different stages in her chosen sport(s).

Strict confidentiality at all times to conceal identities ensured free and uninhibited responses to all questions which resulted in both candid comment and firm

Table 9: Athletes interviewed in the 'drop-out project' listed by sport

Cricket	Jenny Owens, Debby Wilson, Zoe Goss, Peta Verco.
Netball	Sally Ironmonger, Diane McDonald, Jill McIntosh
Archery	Sandra Thompson
Diving	Raelene Lyon
Rhythmic Gymnastics	Karen Ho
Swimming	Lyn Bates
Track	Lyn Foreman, Shirley de la Hunty
Hockey	Pam Glossop, Elspeth Clements, Lee Capes, Sharon Patmore, Adele Boyce, Colleen Pearce.
Volleyball	Mandy Coombes
Badminton	Karen Perham, Audrey Tuckey
Squash	Robyn Lambourne
Tennis	Margaret Court, Elizabeth Smylie
Triathlon	Carol Pickard
Cross Country	Sue Malaxos

opinions on various issues in sport. A pleasant, relaxed, and comfortable interview was reported by both interviewers and interviewees. Parents and athletes appeared to enjoy the experience of reliving previous years and significant events and also indicated a strong interest both in this study and in the larger research project. The minimum criteria used for selection of athletes was national representative for more than one year and/or world ranking at a consistently high level. No age limit was imposed in spite of concern with memory lapses.

Table 10: The sample: Personal details

Age Distribution	10 — 19-25 years 8 — 26-30 years 7 — 31-35 years 2 over 36 years
Sporting Activity	21 active (currently competing)* 6 retired — 'naturally'
Marital Status	15 married, 7 w/children * 12 single (* 9 retired/returned: all married, 6 w/children)
Current Occupations	Administrative Officer Full-time coach (2) Laboratory technician Part-time coach (2) Professional athlete (3) Secretary Student (3) Clerical typist (2) Full-time mother (3) National Heart Foundation Officer Physical education teacher (5) Receptionist Sport administration officer University lecturer

Table 10 summarises data from 27 completed interviews concerning age, current sports activity, marital status and occupation.

Two features of Table 10 merit further clarification. First, 9 of the active athletes had retired/returned and were all married, 7 with children. These athletes had temporarily retired from elite competition either to get married, have children, have a break or to sulk for a while. Second, the retired (non-active) athletes did not consider themselves drop-outs. Two each reported old age, coaching job, or achieved all that was desired from the sport as reasons for discontinuing their elite involvement. All 6 athletes however, were still physically active in sport at club or social levels.

The interviewing style made use of open-ended funnel-type questioning which allowed free but not casual responses. The framework for interview questions was similar to that of Bloom (1985) and his associates who listed seven major areas of enquiry. These same seven areas will be used to summarise findings in this study and to delineate some tentative generalisations about the talent development process. Where possible, direct quotes from both athletes and parents are used in the text to punctuate certain points of interest. The origin of each quote is identified but concealed by a letter and number, eg (H-4) represents one of the Hockey players, but number 4 on the list. (F of B-1) represents the father of a Badminton player. Individuals from sports with only one representative are listed and numbered as (I).

Discussion of the findings

1. Special physical, intellectual, or other relevant characteristics evident in the individual at an early age.
With only one possible exception all athletes seemed to be **born** with 'natural talent' and physical 'gifts'.

> . . . at a party once, her reactions were uncanny . . . a bottle fell off a table and she not only caught it before it hit the ground but righted it to prevent any spilling! (F of B-1)
>
> . . . seemed that I was always taller and stronger than others . . . and naturally I've always had a good jump. (I-1)

Reaction time, co-ordination, hand-eye skills were all there at an early age and all athletes soon realised their superiority over their peers. Some walked at 10 months, others attended ballet at 4 years. Everything physical seemed to come easily for them and hence their parents, teachers, and coaches referred to them as 'naturals' and 'fast or quick learners'. Their early success in sport however, was not restricted to one activity. Indeed, all athletes seemed to be proficient in many sports in their early years, which contributed to a forced choice dilemma later in their careers. Sport and physical activity definitely dominated the early years and childhood experiences were unanimously described as 'very, very happy'.

2. Role of the home in guidance and support of talent from early years to later stages in development.
With only two exceptions the athletes emphasised both the quality and quantity of support and encouragement they received from parents. Others, eg relatives, neighbours and friends of the family, were also significant but parents received special mention.

> We always knew that he was . . . well both my parents . . . were there to support us. I think that is important. You can lead your children into many areas, but unless the children feel that the parents care, I don't think their interest is going to be maintained. It didn't matter what I was doing, my parents were always there. Always. As long as I can remember — for all of us, not just me. (T-2)

The involvement of parents went beyond 'taxi-service' status. They took an active interest in the athlete's activities. They watched, looked on, monitored progress and gave encouragement throughout. They did not knit, read the newspaper or fall asleep in the car — like some parents apparently did.

The emotional contribution of all significant people to the child cannot be overemphasised. With approval and encouragement these athletes somehow got the feeling that it (sport activity) was worth trying — so they did.

Parents took the kids everywhere and the talent field provided opportunities for the whole family to enjoy activities together. Meets, tournaments, and competitions became family affairs.

> Dad went to train for water-polo so we went too . . . and mum. It was natural for the whole family to be swimming. I can't remember not being able to swim . . . from there it was just a progression. (I-2)

> . . . it was mass involvement of the whole family; we even have home movies of Lizzie (youngest sister) doing long jump at age two! (H-2)

The majority of families had 'strong' or 'very strong' sporting backgrounds, however there were two cases where the resources, models of encouragement and support **and** initial instructional opportunities, were made available outside the family. These individuals were able to 'achieve' without any parental support whatsoever which made the process 'a little harder'. Generally speaking however, it was parents who made the sport or talent field accessible and desirable.

The childhood environment was most often in small rural communities and farms where athletes as children played for long hours outdoors, even after dark, which is less common in larger urban centres. Parents clearly did not live their children's lives; they did not push their children into, or at, any activities or force them to make choices. All the athletes were quite clear on this, ie they remember quite vividly how **they** chose whether or not to continue or drop-out of an activity.

> . . . we always made a point about the kids feeling happy with themselves and with what they did as long as they did their best . . . we never put her down for anything she did and always tried to encourage her to do better . . . but never to be the best. (M of N-1)

> I don't think we pushed them into anything or at anything. I just wanted them to enjoy what they did. Except I did have a rule — once you start something, you finish it. It's a little bit of discipline. (M of I-3)

Parents, however, did emphasise and promote self-discipline, the importance of doing one's best and the satisfaction of accomplishment in all activities — sport, school and domestic chores — and this work ethic is what Bloom (1985) refers to as the 'value of achievement', which perhaps discriminates between those natural talents who do and don't achieve.

For example, some parents reported other siblings who were 'more naturally talented' than the elite athlete; however the characteristics that distinguished between the high achiever and her more naturally talented brother or sister seemed to be a strong desire to excel, persistence, and an indomitable work ethic. Perhaps the fact that the more naturally talented individuals did not continue in sport further highlights the hands-off, non-pushy parent and positive characteristic of good parenting.

Parents clearly sacrificed a lot for their children, for example money for travel, and time to transport children to and from training and meets.

> It's a lot of money. Every year they would fork out more than a thousand dollars — probably two thousand for away trips. They never said anything about it. They've always supported me and mum and dad are poor now as a result. They've spent at least twenty grand on my sport. (I-1)

> . . . you don't want to hold your kids back when they get to that level . . . they deserve every chance they can get. (M of I-4)

Travel time and costs are excessive in WA, which is one of the most geographically isolated outposts of humanity in the world. Six athletes actually commented that as far as the 'Eastern staters' are concerned 'you would think that in the sport world no life existed beyond the Nullarbor'. Parents however, did not complain about these sacrifices for their children, even in hard economic times. They believed the children deserved every chance they could give them. All athletes commented on their tomboy image and status.

> I was a real tomboy when I was a kid, because I only had my brothers and his mates to muck around with. (I-1)
>
> I was a tomboy. I did everything . . . played cricket, swam, kicked footy around, did netball at school — anything that was active and outdoors — I did it! (T-1)
>
> Oh certainly she was a real tomboy; she could bat and bowl as well as any of the local boys. (M of C-1)

It is interesting that almost all the athletes reported playing 'mostly with boys' when younger. Only two played 'mostly with boys and girls'; and only one played 'mostly alone'. None of these female athletes played 'mostly with girls'. These data support the evidence of Mitchell and Dyer (1985) and similar data in the Miller-Lite Report (1985).

Finally, parents remembered children out practising at 'all hours' and for 'hours at a time'. The games the children played were largely improvised from the facilities available. Rules were made up or invented and skill development, which became increasingly more formal, was always **fun**. These athletes were evidently not born with convictions to practise or to work hard — but they seemed to develop these habits in a context of supportive and encouraging adults who exuded confidence in them both as athletes and as individuals.

3. Type and quality of instruction and guidance in the talent field available to the individual at different stages of development.
It was evident that the availability and access to facilities was important both for play and for formal organised activity.

> We didn't have a backyard and the school didn't have any grass, so I wasn't allowed to run or do any activity at all like that. Then we moved up to Queensland when I was about eight and . . . the school there had grass, and I was allowed to run, so I went a bit crazy for a while. (H-4)

Ironically, those who had to travel a lot to Perth for representative team trials and meets seemed to benefit most earlier on by living in rural areas where open space and networks of friends in the neighbourhood encouraged their adventurous spirit. Very few of these athletes grew up in city environments and urban conditions, which brings into question whether urban centres do indeed host the best levels of competition at certain age levels.

Bloom (1985) has noted certain stages in learning:

— In age ranges 2-7 years the child needs a mother type and less a teacher type. Most of the early teachers and coaches of the athletes were mums.

> Everybody loved her, she was my phys. ed. teacher at school, she probably didn't know much about hockey but she promoted all things that should be promoted in junior sport. (H-2)
>
> I always loved my coaches . . . I felt closer to them than my parents in a way. (Tr-2)

— From 8-14 years discipline, devotion to drills and habituation become important. The teacher here becomes stricter, less tolerant of shoddy work and is relentless and rigorous in her or his exactions.

— From 14 years the teacher must teach more, know more and be a living fountain of knowledge, not a stagnant pool.

I learned so much from her, not only about netball but as a person. She took time to get to know you as an individual . . . I've got the greatest respect for that woman. (N-2)

These characteristics indeed appeared to be the major qualities of teachers in the 'early', 'middle', and 'later years', although, in general, the athletes were unimpressed with the quality and quantity of coaches. They seemed to respect coaches more as people than as coaches.

These data may reflect a rather ad hoc, confused system of coaching, and coach education in Australia as compared to North America where Bloom's (1985) work was carried out. Coaching as a profession in North America is possibly more clearly valued and respected by athletes of all ages and competitive levels and by society in general than it is in Australia.

It is interesting to note the similarities between these data and the present authors' (Gordon and Smith, 1986) findings from a survey of coaches in Alberta, Canada. This survey involved 227 Level 1-3 coaches in the sports of Gymnastics (49: 32 female, 17 male), Ice Hockey (103 all male) and Soccer (75: 6 female, 69 male). From a list of eighteen important ingredients of effective youth coach characteristics, these Canadian youth coaches listed *making the sport/game fun* and *creating a good learning environment* as the two most important coaching characteristics. (NB 'Concern for gymnast's welfare and safety' was actually ranked No. 1 by gymnastic coaches; 'communication skills' and 'planning and organisation skills' were ranked No. 3 by soccer and ice hockey coaches respectively). Being accredited, being 'qualified', having certificates of attendance at coaching courses **was** important, but clearly not so important for these coaches of younger aged athletes.

There is another type of coach represented in our sample who seemed to be a lot stricter but still fair. This coach was a 'benevolent autocrat' who clearly demanded greater attention from the athlete.

. . jeez scream! . . . a very loud coach . . . but it was motivating and you know she never screamed at you when you did something wrong. (H-1)

She wasn't in it for fun. She was in it to win, and she did win, every year . . . Swearing, shouting, screaming, extra practices, having kids running out crying. But everybody loved her! She produced results. She was a very good teacher. (I-3)

The athlete in turn realised that a more serious application to what they were about paid off, and also that these types of coaches were helping them achieve skill improvement, skill development and success.

He was pretty strict. He'd make us do things a certain way. He was a good basics coach. That's why I think the foundations to my game are pretty solid — because I had a pretty good teacher when I was young. (T-2)

If these 'middle years teachers' (Bloom, 1985 terminology) and coaches had been first teachers, many of these talented individuals might have dropped out of sport after a few years. On the other hand if these teachers had not come along, the athletes would definitely not have reached the levels of talent development that they ultimately achieved. Both parents and athletes realised this.

It was because of her that she probably went further at that stage. She knew so much about netball and was a fairly easy person to get along with. (My daughter) got along with her very well. (M of N-1)

It is apparent that different levels of coaching expertise are required at different age and competitive levels. The increment in knowledge and expertise required to handle top level athletes is probably better understood than the approach, expectations, and demeanor of coaches who work with less able adults, and especially boys and girls. The motives of coaches working with children should ideally match the motives of their athletes. This is often not so. There are exceptions of course, but clearly this motive-mismatch can significantly affect athlete participation rates in youth sports and, in particular, their overall enjoyment of the sport experience.

A number of athletes remarked how well they responded to the coaching of former players, who had played at the same level in the same sport. Perhaps accrediting bodies in both coaching and official education programs should consider making better use of retired elite athletes who have already 'been there' and 'done that'. Their potential in coaching would not only assist their younger peers, it would also maintain a longer term veteran's interest in the sport beyond competitive years.

These data bear out very clearly the wisdom of a developmental approach to coaching combined with support, encouragement and acceptance of the child; and also the folly of assuming matching rates of learning and human development. Athletes do not necessarily learn as quickly as they develop physically and emotionally; in general the athletes in this study did, but there were notable exceptions — 'late bloomers.'

Finally, these data also highlight the folly of using technical instruction with young children with the inevitable punishment and discouragement that it brings down on immature body systems struggling so hard to learn.

4. Sources and types of motivation and reward and special circumstances that gave encouragement and support to the individual at different stages in talent development.

A number of athletes reported serendipitous activity at often critical periods in their lives.

> *Everything that happened to me I just fell into ... State and Australian teams. I was there at the right place at the right time ... which gives me the 'guilts' sometimes when I realise how hard others have to work to make it. (H-3)*

Some believed that fate took over in some circumstances and rationalised steps forward in their sporting career by 'just happening to be there, in the right place at the right time'. Others believed they were caught up in the sports development at both state and national level. In these cases however it was success, advancement and notoriety that strengthened their resolve and appetite for 'more of the same'.

> *I've been very lucky. Unless you start with a sport when it is new, there is no way you can become national champion after only one year. But that's how it happened — I went straight to the top. No fighting my way through grades or levels. (I-3)*

Most athletes again reported the support of parents as important. Their parents typically had begun to use their child's talent field as a hobby, eg spectating or in some cases voluntary administrative positions and even formal officiating roles. Some athletes in early adolescence mentioned a 'forced choice' situation between careers in certain sports as an area of specialisation as a motivator.

Such a dilemma became a significant motivation to aim even higher and higher in their chosen talent field. While one athlete chose a certain sport to spite her mother, most of the athletes chose sports at which they were best at the time or sports that represented 'most variety'.

Finally, the lure of travel opportunities was an extremely important 'carrot', dangled at just the right time, for some other athletes who had been considering their input/output balance in sport.

5. Amount of active learning time, practice, and other learning effort invested by the individual at each stage of development.

The amount of active learning time, practice and learning effort increased exponentially over time, although the playful activity and adventurousness of the athlete as a child had reached similar proportions. In other words, athletes realised how much longer they had trained in formal session as they grew older but estimated similar voluntary 'commitments' in time to informal play and physical activity when much younger.

The athlete's sport life became less and less like play and more an avocation. No complaints were registered about this, even for those who were training up to 4 hours a day, 5 days a week. However, there were comments to the effect that although 'they would do it all over again' these athletes meant 'their way' rather than the way national level athletes are expected to train and prepare for elite competition today.

6. Other factors the individual regarded as relevant to 'discovering' potential, subsequent development, and ongoing encouragement in a particular sport.

While the discovery of potential was attributable to luck in some cases, the means of nurturing that potential seemed to involve close networks of support which included romantic companions who were either 'sporty' themselves or 'simply supportive', or both. The family however was again especially important as **the** critical factor in the athlete's support network.

What was also apparent was the positive reinforcement athletes received from achieving improvement — which, for them, was significantly more important than achieving success.

I think because you know you are good at it, and because you get that positive reaction and positive feedback, you keep going back and doing it. If you are just ordinary — like I am at golf — you won't keep at it so long. So I think that is very important, I knew I was good . . . knew I wanted to improve. (H-4)

However positive reinforcement or feedback from efforts wasn't everything to some athletes either.

. . . positive reinforcement was there but that didn't really affect me. I was playing for enjoyment and getting success at the same time. And if you have success you do it more and you enjoy it more and so on . . . like a big snowball. (C-1)

Enjoyment was always a critical factor in all that athletes did and this seemed true both in and out of sport and especially in careers. Campbell's (1974) excellent book written for a high school/university age readership seems to encapsulate the implied relationship between work and enjoyment. His advice for young school leavers choosing careers includes a reference to talents and skills.

In a crude way talents are naturally given; skills are something you work to acquire . . . In selecting a skill to develop, pick something that you like to do, because if you don't like it you're never going to be really good at it.

(Campbell, 1974, p58)

The final relevant factor in ongoing encouragement for these athletes, was 'husbands'. The nine married athletes were unanimous in their acknowledgement and praise of their spouses who clearly offered both emotional and moral support.

My husband has been great. He'd play his game, I'd play mine and we'd come home and talk about both games. It's been great . . . we helped and coached each other. (H-5)

He has to do some of the work around the house, mind the baby, change nappies . . . that gets to be a huge pain for some men. But a married woman with children needs that sort of support as well as the moral support. (Tr-4)

> *I couldn't survive without him. I'm still always tired and can't sleep well. Sometimes I sit down and quietly have a 'nervous breakdown' . . . and then get going again!* (Tr-1)

One athlete, who has since re-married, partially blamed sport for her divorce but, in general, an understanding spouse who shared the ups and downs, trials and tribulations, and especially household duties and responsibilities was a significant if not critical means of support to married athletes.

7. Ways in which these individuals developed habits, interest, and values that increasingly committed them to their sport and brought them to the limits of learning.

This last question area was perhaps the most difficult to address, however three 'factors' emerge from these data.

First, role models, which were predominantly male, seemed to be important for athletes in times of distress — when they needed 'something' or someone else to look to for inspiration. Martina Navratilova, Shane Gould, Marion Alemore and 'mothers' were frequently mentioned along with Mark Spitz, Daley Thomson, Michael Goodwin, Greg Browning, Bjorn Borg and Dennis Lillee.

Second, a determination to emulate someone who was admired 'generally' for qualities such as 'killer instinct', 'will to win', 'determination', and 'perseverance'.

And third, most important of all, an 'inner drive' was reported by all athletes which they 'developed' themselves over time. This yearning for achievement was the most frequently reported reason for realising the limits of learning. Requests to inspire others were made of these athletes, who undoubtedly 'lived the creed' others would like to aspire to.

> *I've been asked to talk to footy teams about motivation . . . I can't motivate them, it's got to come from within . . . anything else is temporary. It always gets hard but you've got to find the right answer within yourself.* (Tr-1)

Finally, four brief unrelated points of interest from the data should be noted before an attempt is made to summarise the talent development process. First, the development of talented females in individual sports did not appear to differ that markedly from talent development in team sports.

> *. . . early success couldn't have been that important to me because I was never on a successful team! As an individual I knew I was successful myself and came off the court saying I played well even if they didn't.* (N-2)

In spite of Bloom's (1985) assumption therefore, that group activity and team involvement might somehow advantage successful team athletes, the team and individual athletes in this study were more similar than different in background experiences and opinions on significant events in their development.

Second, at no stage in their lives did these athletes worry about their self-image or, more accurately, their body image.

> *. . . adolescent body image was a problem for many of my friends. Me, I prefer to feel comfortable with myself than look pretty.* (N-1)

All these athletes seemed satisfied and content with themselves, what they looked like, who they were, and who they represented.

Third, there appeared to be some positive spin-offs, in hockey at least, from amalgamated club situations that involve forms of occasional child care.

> *The facilities for top grade hockey players (at the stadium) are almost perfect for all of us with children. Lots of fences to stop kids climbing all over goal posts . . . and plenty of kids around for playmates. The only problem is they (club stewards) don't like us changing nappies in the bar area . . . but we don't have anywhere else to go . . . so we do it anyway!* (H-5)

Provision of occasional child care is an important inclusion in our list of surveys and sub-projects, which will collectively investigate important factors that might influence drop-out in organised sports. The provision of child care is of particular significance for older sportswomen with young children. We believe sport associations in WA and elsewhere see a need for child care but, like dealing with the media and attracting sponsors, they don't know how to go about it. For example, what are the physical and human resources required to provide adequate and legal (licensed?) occasional child care units in sports centres and clubs? Does local, municipal, or state policy consider provision for such supervision at sport and health clubs? If not, why not? etc.

Fourth, and finally, there was some good (almost relieving) news about whether or not 'it' (participation in elite organised sport) was a good experience and whether or not all the effort and sacrifice was worthwhile.

> I'm a very one-track, obsessive type of person. At times I regretted not going to parties and things, but I just kept on with what I was doing, just got more and more into it. Now, when I look back, I'm glad I did that because all those people that had nothing better to do than go the beach, hang-out, and go to parties, have very little to show for their lives. I've been very fortunate to have had lots of opportunities. So definitely, yes it's all been worth it. (I-3)

Twenty-seven athletes were unanimous in their opinion that elite sport had been good for them. They had few if any regrets and would 'do it all over again' their way, if given a second chance. This conclusion, from successful achievers, is perhaps not surprising. However, it is still a welcome boost for organised sport which occasionally comes under attack from various internally dissatisfied sections of society and groups who sometimes criticise sport in the same way they criticise the education system as the repository of every societal ill imaginable!

Conclusions

Rather than summarise the experience of 27 individual case histories — a dangerous and highly presumptuous operation — I would prefer to illustrate some key ingredients in the talent development process which I believe emerge from this study. These are listed in Table 11 under individual and environmental categories. The end product of this process, in which social and environmental engineering can obviously play critical roles, is an intrinsically motivated high achiever who has a holistic world view of her goals related to her capabilities.

Table 11: Talent development of elite female sportswomen: Summary of 'ingredients'

INDIVIDUAL	physical talent perceived ability socialised work ethic/ discipline driven by competence motivation	fast learner early success
ENVIRONMENT	opportunity for play access to facilities encouraging attitude from significant others parental interest and/or support different types of coaches	boys fun/enjoyment
END PRODUCT	INTRINSICALLY MOTIVATED HIGH ACHIEVER REALIST AND GOAL SETTER '. . . life is a do-it-yourself project . . .'	

Such individuals appear to be well equipped to tackle any of life's challenges — a proud and fitting tribute to the socialisation process through organised sport.

Acknowledgements

The author gratefully acknowledges the research assistance of the following undergraduate and graduate students from the Department of Human Movement and Recreation Studies.

Their interviewing and report writing skills, and interest and enthusiasm in this particular research are sincerely appreciated.

Megan Armitage	Lisa Fitzpatick
Jenny Banks	Stephanie Hanrahan
Leslie Bremner	Debbie Hoare
Lisa Chivers	Nicola Mussell
Ann Clarke	Connie Nelson
Anne Coffey	Ingrid Nussbaumer
Danae Collins	

TALENT SELECTION:
THE SELECTION AND DEVELOPMENT OF
GIFTED CHILDREN IN THE GDR

Ruth Fuchs

Introduction

The speed with which records have developed at world level during the last few years makes us realise quite clearly that today, and even more so in the future, only athletes who possess certain qualities will achieve important performances and successes at highlight events in sport. They have to be particularly suited for their respective discipline, need to have distinct personality traits, have exceptional condition and technical-tactical prerequisites and capabilities on call, and need to have achieved a high level of consistency in competition within their particular sport.

To develop and form all that in the quality objectively required, and to translate it into top performances would seem possible today only if the necessary foundations are laid in childhood and adolescence. The long term, systematic and goal-oriented preparation of athletes for their top achievements as seniors has thus become a focal point.

Procedures of talent selection and suitability grow in importance together with the long-term creation of advancement and development programs in competitive sport activity of children and adolescents.

In my arguments, that are intended to serve as a basis for further discussion, I would like to convey experiences that are applied in practice by our athletics association in the GDR, in training the coming generation, ie the field of little and junior athletics.

In this paper, I will concentrate on the following major points:

a. Sketching the system for long-term performance and stress endurance building in the GDR.

b. Aspects of sifting, selecting and talent recognition.

c. Exposition of the fundamental content of training the coming generation of track and field competitors in the GDR.

d. Comprehensive social framework conditions, ie the conditional structure for successful translation of long-term performance and stress endurance building in practice.

Long term programs in performance development and stress endurance

We generally assume that the development of athletic mastery, or in other words, the achievement of a pinnacle of athletic performance, is a process which occurs in two stages. On the basis of the development of individual world class athletes of our republic and also of international athletics, two typical stages in development emerge:

— Preparation for specialisation in athletics in general.

— Perfection (or specialisation) in a discipline within athletics.

The aim of the first stage, which is often called training of the coming generation because of its location in the biological development of the athlete, has as its goal, the achievement of a specific preparedness for further training and competition stress. It is characterised above all by the fact that:

— speed and power capabilities as essential prerequisites for all track and field events show a high state of development;

— the co-ordinating motor abilities required as a basis for stable mastery of athletic technique are highly pronounced;

— the raw form of the technical sequence of the future special discipline is grasped; and

— means and methods of training are applied that have a small degree of specificity in relation to the later specialisation and thus keep open opportunities for the application of special means within the second stage.

The second stage within the long-term building of performance and stress endurance is oriented towards the formation of achievement factors in a special discipline, ie the development and perfection of all components that essentially determine and underpin sport achievement.

In our system of long-term performance building we differentiate further within these two stages and subdivide the developmental process of athletic mastership into four training stages. Included in the training of the coming generation are the stages of basic and build-up training. The stage of specialisation includes subsequent and competitive training.

I would like to describe briefly the principal objectives of these four stages.

Basic Training
This involves the development of general athletic prerequisites for achievement including also track and field disciplines with particular attention to faculties of co-ordination and speed.

Build-Up-Training
Concentration on the development of essential foundations for a group of track and field disciplines (divided into sprint, run, jump, throw).

125

Subsequent Training
The development of foundations for high level achievement in one track and field discipline with the aim of winning medals and places in such international competitions as the European Youth Championships, World Youth Championships or the Youth Championships of Friendship. These are a highlight of sport competition of the socialist countries at this level but they allow at the same time a joining up with the world's elite.

Competition Training
The development of an optimal situation in which there is regularly a simultaneous expression of particular abilities needed for high achievement together with maximum possible effort from the individual, with the aim of reaching the highest athletic performance capability in the special discipline.

The time sequence of long-term performance and stress-endurance building can be characterised within our system in the following way:
GLT (basic training) — age group 10-year-olds to 13/14-year-olds.
ABT (build-up training) — age group 13/14-year-olds to 15-year-olds.
End of training for the coming generation.
ANT (subsequent training) — 16-year-olds Junioren (juniors) to 18/19-year-olds.
HLT (competitive training) from age 18/19.

These divisions into age groups are based, on the one hand, on longstanding experience in training practice and, on the other hand, on the biological development stages of children and adolescents, a point to which I shall return again later.

This system in its complexity and totality is the obligatory basis for the trainer working within the individual stages. (It may be noteworthy in this context that we aim for a specialisation of trainers for each stage and have partly achieved it.) It is, however, no dogma, but offers the opportunity for trainer and athlete to work through and translate it creatively.

Sifting, selecting and recognising talent

The basic prerequisite for the success of GDR athletes at Olympic Games, World and European Championships is the generous promotion and support of competitive sport by our socialist state, an aspect which also decisively influences the process of winning talented boys and girls for athletics.

A further important basis is the rule in the curricula of our polytechnical high schools, that regular and varied sport activities for all children and adolescents of our country take place both in and out of regular school hours.

Through close co-operation of trainers, exercise leaders and the leadership of centres for competitive sport, like training centres and sport clubs as well as sport teachers and school principals, it becomes possible to locate and register all children who are suited for the individual kinds of sport. At the same time it is not always possible to persuade the children most gifted in sport to undertake training in training centres or sport clubs. Free will and personal or family oriented ideas about development and the desired perspectives are for us also inviolable basic premises.

Due, however, to the great importance and esteem enjoyed by competitive sport in our country, it is possible in most cases to receive the talents into the training groups of the training centres by age 10.

What are the criteria for taking up competitive training in athletics? (And the order in which I present them is of immense importance in our opinion.)

— The joy of athletic activity in a track and field discipline.
— Height and weight, that become of ever greater importance in certain athletic disciplines like jumping and throwing, but also in recent years in disciplines like sprinting and middle distance running.
— Speed, as one of the faculties that are already fairly pronounced and differentiated at age 9 and 10.
— Agility and movement co-ordination, as an essential basis for motor learning ability and success in many sports.
— Versatility in capacity, not only in track and field disciplines, but in the whole range of sport activity.

Before I can turn to some supplementary remarks to these parameters for suitability identification, I would briefly like to mention the forms through which the exercise leaders, trainers and sport teachers identify talented boys and girls.

As you certainly already know, the Spartakiad movement plays a great part in our country. The central Spartakiad for children and adolescents is a cornerstone of our system of physical education and sport where the best up and coming athletes go at the start of their careers. In particular the school Spartakiads and the regional Spartakiads for children and adolescents are the contests where talented children are spotted and present themselves for competitive sport training.

Apart from that, there is regular competition for the individual age groups on a school basis in such things as school sport days and interschool competitions among athletic work groups and individual schools etc. As already mentioned, obligatory physical education also helps to spot athletic children and to further their development.

Despite this relatively tight system, the selection from the population of suitable children is not always an easy process and the erroneous decisions of individual trainers and exercise leaders cannot always be ruled out. We may, for example, consider the biological age differences within one age group, the different qualifications created by more or less athletic activities during leisure hours or the very different sport interests of the children.

Building on that insight, we regard it particularly important to make a selection on the basis of assessing as comprehensively as possible the level of development and the developmental possibilities. For that reason we test a wide range of faculties and abilities if we make a decision, eg for acceptance into a sport club.

We start by demanding basic exercises in bar gymnastics, in particular floor gymnastics and ballsports. We continue with sprints over 60m and basic techniques in the disciplines of long jump and shot put; and we end with an 800m run to establish qualities of willpower. Of primary importance is versatility, which is expressed in this sort of pentathlon.

I do not think it is anything new, but I will stress it anyway: the trainer's eye and the objective and subjective assessment of given capabilities and skills, but also the noting of training already received, play an immensely important role in these processes, together with an evaluation of the athletic achievement.

The second stage of the long-term stress endurance and performance building, the build-up training, already briefly sketched, is known as the stage of talent spotting and further selection. Since athletic suitability can only be established in training for a particular kind of sport, further suitability testing has to take place in a way that makes demands on the individual that are specific for a particular kind of sport or discipline.

The diagnosis of suitability is oriented towards analysing the developmental process of the young athletes in the factors that determine performance on which training centres, and to draw conclusions from that as to the degree of suitability.

After an almost uniform training we find four factors which allow an assessment of athletic suitability with a relatively high degree of probability. These are indicators:

— of the level of overall achievement through the expression of the specific factors that determine achievement (competitive achievement, contributive achievements);

— of the speed with which performance can be enhanced as evidence for the fact that in uniform training talented athletes enhance their performance faster than less talented ones and that the athlete works through the stress demands effectively;

— of performance stability and enhancement potential as measures for psychological competition faculties;

— for stress endurance, as an expression of present and future potential to cope with ever increasing pressure in a positive way that furthers performance development.

The indicators mentioned are valid particularly during the stages of build-up and subsequent training, but are to be used analogously to the complex faculty tests and development potential tests at the inception of the competitive sport training already mentioned.

In practical training, performance achieved will always be the primary objective in this process; but indiviual specifics, in particular of the biological development of the adolescent, have also to be regarded. For example, we found recently in a male training group of our sports club, biological age differences of as much as 7 years. Chronologically, the boys were all 14 years old; however, the biologically youngest athlete of the group was 11, while the biologically oldest was 18.

Even the trained eye of an experienced coach and knowledge of these biological age differences sometimes do not prevent the situation occurring in which athletes who perform strongly are given the better long-term chances, despite the fact that their rate of performance enhancement and their stress endurance are inferior to that of the biologically retarded ones.

The fundamental content of training

The basic training has two central aims:

— to prepare the young athlete for future training stages, in particular for that of the build-up training;

— to determine the prospective achievement potential.

These aims we realise through the system of versatility and consistency of training. It is relatively easy to ensure the versatility within the many disciplines of athletics which have a rather different character (eg long distance running and the throws), but can also provide a partial basis for one another. We use in this, apart from competitive training, also exercises which are suited to fundamental conditioning and technical co-ordination training. This complex of training methods we call special versatile instructions.

This means in practice that each athlete in the age group 10-12 learns the basic techniques of all track and field disciplines and simultaneously masters the basics of the most important sequences of such means of training which are important for condition development (eg in the development of horizontal jumping power, this is the triple jump, and for specialised throwing skills this is the shot put forwards and backwards).

The second important part of the basic training is the general versatile instruction. In it we use physical exercises from other sports and general exercises respectively. Versatility does not mean aimlessness; quite the contrary. All the components of that stage possess either a recognisable identity with athletic exercises or constitute a recuperative counter-stress strategy. This general versatility is thus goal oriented.

Ball games, for example, are used for the development of jumping power (basketball), of speed and stamina (soccer, handball, basketball). Training exercises like swimming, bar gymnastics, general gymnastics, little team games, skiing etc., are used to further develop the co-ordinative skills and to simultaneously attain a high emotional effect.

The consistency of training I need not mention further. The most important facts have already been mentioned in the section about suitability and talent recognition.

The condition for translating training potential into practice

It is significant for basic training that performance building is chiefly steered by continuously raising stress demands whereby the increase in the frequency of training, or in other words the number of training units per week, constitutes the most important criterion. Thus an athlete, during his/her first year of membership in a training centre, trains on average three times per week for $1^1/_4$ hours. That is raised during the third year to between four and five training units of $1^1/_2$ hours each. Increasing the length of each training unit is not the most important aim during this stage. Concentration and enjoyment of training would be influenced negatively by an extreme increase in the number of hours.

The individual training stages bear the character of a close sequence of preparation periods within the process of stress rhythmics. Since competitions have no direct relevance at this stage, typical competition periods are not included. Within the course of the year an accentuation of training concepts is attempted, ie a non-complex application of all means of training and simultaneous development of several abilities and skills, but a phased concentration on the development of an athletic technique and a condition skill respectively.

The second stage of the long-term competitive sport development, namely build-up training, has the following aims:

— Enhancement and stabilisation of the general foundations (fundamentals) through general goal-oriented training.

— Development of sport performance prerequisites through extensive special training in one of the track and field disciplines eg jump, sprint, throw or run.

— Preparation of further specialisation through extensive development of athletic performance within one group of disciplines. This is achieved by training and competition in several disciplines of the group.

This set of tasks gives a key function to the stage of build-up training for further successful performance development. On one hand a high capacity should already be achieved, particularly during the last year of build-up training for the 15-year-old age group. On the other hand the foundations for the following stress endurance have to be laid.

Focal points in training are thus a further development of speed faculties, co-ordination faculties, general stress tolerance and the individual athletic techniques, especially those of the respective group of disciplines. Under observation of international trends we concentrate on mastery of the refined form during the process of learning the techniques of the later competitive discipline. Beyond that we start specialisation proper in a discipline with the 15-year-old age group.

As already described in basic training, the principle of versatility further dominates during the first two years of build-up training. The attempt is made to definitely determine the suitability of the athlete for a specific discipline and simultaneously to prepare and perfect all factors of the performance structure of a competitive discipline. This is done by creating specific-multilateral and general-multilateral bases. Building on that is the challenge to further train the entire range of track and field disciplines while developing the competitive performance in several disciplines. At the same time capabilities in other kinds of sport should be perfected, multiple kinds of motion be experienced and condition faculties be enhanced to a certain degree and in a very differentiated way. Competitions play a larger part in this training stage compared with basic training. They are, however, not prepared for in a goal-oriented fashion as far as stress dynamics and stress rhythmics are concerned, but form an integral part of the training system.

After they have finished this stage of their competitive sports activity, the most talented and capable boys and girls go through the stage of specialisation with its successive levels of subsequent and competitive training.

The social framework for realisation of sporting potential

In our day and age, it is truer than ever that sports, and in particular competitive sports, (or as it is internationally called vanguard sport) along with their educational, ethical and moral values, their content and ideas, cannot be judged without consideration of their social environment.

Every athletically gifted and interested young person's decision to become a competitive athlete is influenced in no small degree by whether they are socially secure and integrated during and especially after their career in sport. This is particularly so today, when record achievement in track and field can only be attained through many years of performance and stress-endurance building and where the age at which top performances and records can be achieved is calculable from the start for each specific discipline. Likewise, aspects of commercialisation and professionalisation gain an increasing influence on international sport and thus help to determine the norms and values of sport in the personal development of competitive athletics. This seems to make a positive resolution of the social security problem more and more important to them.

In my country, the German Democratic Republic, social security together with appreciation, respect and acknowledgement during, and above all after, the conclusion of a sporting career (successful or less successful), have led to an increased interest and readiness amongst children and their parents to engage in a career in competitive sport. This quantitively secures a methodical sport-specific talent quest and advancement. Our society enables every athlete to maintain the process of his/her education and/or job-training at the same level and the job security available to every other young person who is not hampered in his/her educational pursuits by time and energy consuming training and competing over many years. Job security is similarly guaranteed.

This is one reason for our successful development in competitive athletics. Another is that in contrast to other countries, all state and social institutions, firms and organisations are obliged to promote physical education and sport within their domain in every possible way. This is an obligation which is rooted in our constitution as well as in specific laws and by-laws concerning the right to recreation, sports activity and travel, for people of all ages in the GDR.

These organisations are thus partners of our sports organisation and support it in realising its goals and tasks. This not only means additional financial aid to secure the material and technical bases of physical education and sport, but also support in securing the personnel for the various tasks in sport.

Our sports organisations, including our athletics association, have a certain number of professional officials. They are permanently employed sport specialists such as trainers, sport scientists, club and association officials, sports physicians etc. Even if their number is greater than in other national athletics associations, we too could not perform our extensive tasks without the readiness and assistance of honorary unpaid helpers.

In the little and junior athletics field for example — in which our athletics association caters for almost 145,000 children and adolescents — we have the support of more than 16,000 honorary exercise supervisors with appropriate sports faculty training. This training can be acquired in free qualification courses. If the time spent on exercise supervision exceeds their leisure time — eg during travel to competitions — we have the possibility in our country to attain a legally guaranteed leave for them without loss of pay or holidays. The same kind of support is available to those persons who help to maintain the various competition programs at all levels by honorary umpire and judging work.

Another factor determining the successful development of sport in our country could well be that the DTSB (a German physical education and sports organisation which celebrates its 40th anniversary this year) plays as decisive a role in the promotion of physical education and sport as it has done in the past. As laid down in its statutes, its objective is to unite all athletes and associations on a voluntary basis and to enable all our citizens who are interested to participate actively in sport or its promotion according to their rights as laid down in the constitution. Every citizen of our country can become a member of the DTSB and can participate in the discipline that interests him/her, be it as a competitive athlete or just to engage in a sensible, healthy leisure activity. In 1987, the DTSB had a membership of 3.6 million, that is almost 21.5 per cent of our population. The track and field athletics association had around 190,000 members altogether, which makes it the fourth largest group within DTSB.

Its greatest proportion is the children and adolescent sports sector with 2.3 million members of up to 18 years. The monthly fees are:

Children	0.20 Marks
Adolescents/apprentices/students	0.80 Marks
Adults	1.30 Marks

These fees include the use of all personnel and material DTSB facilities as well as sports medical supervision and insurance in case of sport accidents. Further financial expenditures are not necessary.

Next to the development of popular mass sport, the area of competitive sport receives a lot of attention, above all in advancement and support of children and adolescents who are interested in sport. In a global context, the latter is based on two fundamental ideas. The dominant advancement of sports for children and adolescents leads on the one hand to formation of the necessary cadre pyramid for competitive sport. On the other hand, it makes our young people see physical education and sport as significant aspects of their leisure activities, which not only generate fun and enjoyment, but also enhance health and physical performance. It also satisfies the need for social contact and helps to form positive personality traits.

Not only is the healthy physical and mental development of the human being, his/her universal and harmonious personality development socially desirable, but the greater demand of our citizens to engage in regular sports activities is indicative of a high degree of congruence between social and personal spheres of interest.

In the field of little and junior athletics the DTSB co-operates closely with the ministry for general education [Volksbildung — which corresponds in Australian terms with TAFE *Ed.*] by supporting mainly the organised extracurricular sport conducted by the school sports groups. Four out of five children and adolescents between 6 and 18 years belong to either a school sports group or a sports association of the DTSB.

We assume that enjoyment and love of sport has to be awakened in early childhood, for whoever develops a liking for sport as a child will have desire to keep up sports activity in the later years of his/her life. In the kindergarten that almost all of our children attend between the ages of 3 and 5, we start with age specific sports activities and games as well as simple competitions that relate to the children's natural desire to move. This initiates the children to sports activity. At school it is continued on a higher level.

At the 10-grade secondary school, physical education is obligatory for all children. Like all other subjects it is taught according to uniform government curricula. Physical education teachers are specialist teachers with a tertiary education. Obligatory physical education is taught for 2-3 hours weekly, depending on the age of the children.

At age 7-10 years all children are taught to swim by special teachers. Like all school education, the swimming training is free of charge and a part of the central curriculum of physical education.

Sociological surveys have shown that the 2-3 weekly hours of physical education often do not satisfy a child's natural need for sport and games. So we created further possibilities by founding school-sport societies. These provide the opportunity for children and adolescents who are interested in sport to fulfil their wish for regular sports activity outside school hours, chiefly in the popular and generally prescribed kinds of sport like athletics, physical education and all kinds of ball games. Here too all children are coached and supervised pedagogically and methodically by honorary instructors. The finances needed by the school-sport societies are provided by the government; there are no membership fees.

Around 75 per cent of all students in our country belong to either school-sport societies or the DTSB sections for little and junior athletics. Sports activity has become an integral part of their leisure occupations.

In addition to the school, ward, regional and GDR championships, the national Spartakiades for children and juniors, which take place on a school, ward and regional level, as well as the biennial central children's and junior's Spartakiade on a national level in summer and winter, have become competition highlights for young athletes. The inaugural event was in 1966.

Children with a special interest in sport may join a sport-specific training centre where they engage in organised exercise, training and competition. As already mentioned, the fees are 20 pfennigs and the pedagogical guidance and subject methodical training is partly done by permanently employed staff but chiefly by honorary instructors and sports professionals. The most talented children are delegated to a sports school for children and adolescents where they are coached by experienced and well-trained teachers with a diploma in physical education.

In 1985, 2,700 children and adolescents were admitted to special sport schools for all Olympic disciplines, around 500 of them for track and field disciplines.

After they finish school (class 10 or matriculation), they can become members of a sportsclub which enables them to pursue their interests in competitive sport while otherwise engaged in their further education and job-training. Sportsclubs are our national centres for competitive sport apart from the BSG's (Betriebssport-gruppen) sportsclubs formed at and attached to the workplace, ie factories etc.

I have tried to show the sport-specific aspects and fundamental content of the process of long-term performance and stress endurance building, concentrating on the training stages for the coming generation as was my topic. I believe, however, that the description of more general aspects and tendencies of talent selection and promotion will have helped to demonstrate the reasons why our relatively small country with its limited population has developed into one of the leading sports nations in the world, particularly in track and field.

The internationally known achievements of our competitive athletes have not been brought about by miracles or mystical secrets. They are the result of a collective effort over years to attain records in the field of competitive sport and to make physical education and sport important factors in the lives of our citizens. [This article should be read in conjunction with that by Klaus Schonberger in Section Six on 'Young People in Athletics in the GDR' *Ed*].

The range of sports open to women at the Olympic Games and other major events is slowly increasing. Four of the wide variety of such sports are shown here.

Right: A budding archery champion.
Reproduced with the permission of the Bicentennial Authority.

Below: Amanda Cross and Susi Deterding Adelaide University Boat Club, State Lightweight Crew, South Australian Rowing Association Regatta.
Photo: Doug Nicholas. Thanks to the Girls and Physical Activity Project.

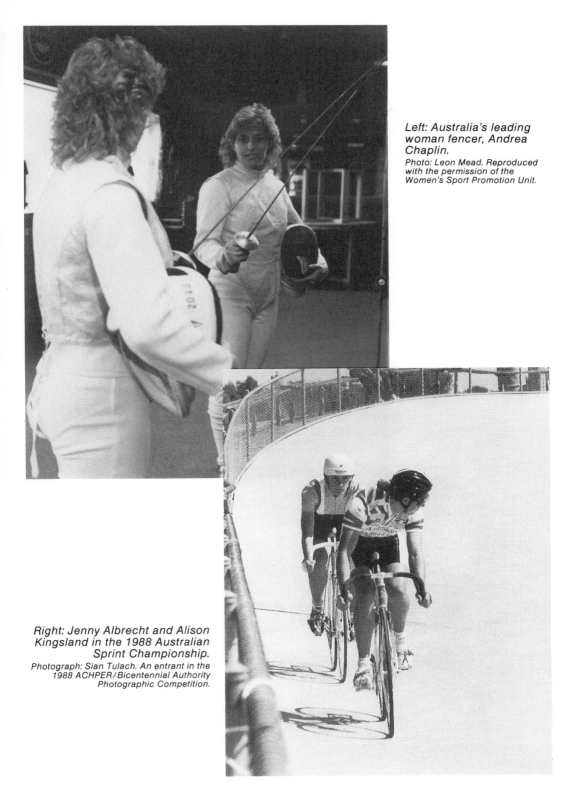

Left: Australia's leading woman fencer, Andrea Chaplin.
Photo: Leon Mead. Reproduced with the permission of the Women's Sport Promotion Unit.

Right: Jenny Albrecht and Alison Kingsland in the 1988 Australian Sprint Championship.
Photograph: Sian Tulach. An entrant in the 1988 ACHPER/Bicentennial Authority Photographic Competition.

Mary Peters in training during her active years. Speed, strength, flexibility and agility were all important for her events.

SECTION FIVE
TRAINING AND COACHING FOR WOMEN ATHLETES

AN INTRODUCTION

Ken Dyer

One of the threads running through this section is the similarity of men and women athletes so far as their abilities and training needs are concerned.

Quality of training is dependent on ability not gender, says athletics coach John Daly in his paper.

Psychologically and physically, women are well equipped for distance running, says AIS Distance event coach Pat Clohessy.

One of the most significant changes for women in recent years has been a downgrading of the importance of differences between the sexes and a recognition that they have more in common than they have differences. These are the words of one-time javelin world record holder and now East German sports scientist Dr. Ruth Fuchs.

What should women do to continue improving? asks medical scientist and athletics writer, Professor Terry Dwyer. *Roughly they should do what men do* he concludes.

There are of course some anatomical and some physiological differences between men and women which have to be taken into account in planning training and preparation schedules for women athletes. These include amounts and distribution of body fat and the particular requirements for iron — two matters to which Dick Telford gives particular attention in his paper. But he goes on to show that women can and do train very intensively — indeed that they can accommodate long gruelling training sessions more comfortably than males, a conclusion remarkably at variance with generally accepted opinions barely two decades ago.

Intensive training for women was said to be impossible/dangerous/damaging/ to be discouraged for women because:

— it would render them sterile

— it would subject them to numerous injuries

— it would put their health at risk

— it would cause them to develop unsightly muscles

— it would destroy their femininity.

Each of these assertions are clearly shown to be a nonsense in this section (and elsewhere in the book).

Less often stated, but perhaps as important for women have been the difficulties of arranging time for training, arranging for child care during training sessions, persuading boyfriends, husbands etc. that they would rather train than watch them play football etc.

The worst of the discrimination against women about using facilities or occupying the court, track, course, pool etc. may now have been removed in Australia and many other countries, but many of the particular difficulties for women attaching to family commitments, transport difficulties and, unfortunately, personal safety still remain.

In the late 1940s and early 1950s the immortal Emil Zatopek revolutionised our ideas of athletic training — running distances and training for periods of time which astonished his contemporaries. In 1952 Zatopek completed a unique triple triumph in the Olympics — winning gold medals in the 5000m, 10000m and Marathon. His marathon time was an Olympic Record of 2:23.04. Three decades or so later women are training at the same intensity as Zatopek did and Lisa Martin, for example, who trains twice a day every day, produced in early 1988 a time to match Zatopek's: 2:23:51. (Included in this section of the book are training schedules carried out by runner Irena Szewinska and swimmer Janelle Elford; the effort and dedication required are clearly displayed.)

Most of the myths about women's training (and participation) have now thankfully been laid to rest. When the attitudes to women athletes that John Daly describes — praising them for their passive compliance and encouraging them to live out roles of dependence and heteronomy — have also changed, then women will undoubtedly improve even more. The successful sportswomen of the past were those who dared to be different; different that is from the conventional stereotype. Our objective for sportswomen 2000 should surely be that they do not have to be different. All women, in other words, should be encouraged to participate to the best of their ability and potential and should be coached and allowed to train with that and only that objective in mind.

COACHING WOMEN ATHLETES

John Daly

It is the spirit we bring to the fight that decides the issue. (George C. Marshall)

Success in sport, any sport, at the highest level needs initial talent but demands as well, commitment, perseverance and competitive drive. The best athletes, researchers inform us (Bierhoff-Alfermann 1983) are independent and self-sufficient, aggressive and self-confident. They exhibit low anxiety and high emotional stability. Terrific. This is what we would expect the academics to say about successful athletes: that they are tough, resolute and singleminded. Why then do they write of women athletes that they are 'emotional', less achievement-orientated, more dependent, 'different'? Because they do. Coaches also say of women athletes that they are loyal (they often mean coach-dependent!) conscientious to an extreme and easy to coach (Treutlein 1983). Why is it that male athletes to be successful must exhibit the traits of aggressive independence and emotional stability, yet women athletes are praised and often preferred by coaches for their passive compliance — usually, I might add, described as their 'coachability' (Hahn 1983)?

I don't have to convince you that this is yet another example of role conflict — the talented woman athlete who wants to succeed in what is deemed a male preserve but has to meet societal expectations and remain feminine. Sport is still widely claimed as a proving ground for masculinity. 'Sport will make a man of you' is the promise. If that is true what does it do for a woman? If she makes a serious commitment to sport she risks being labelled unfeminine.

Gaylene Clews, giving an athlete's view in her paper in this volume, exposes the dilemma: *To win we must be aggressive (like men) . . . but to be allowed to participate we must remain like women are 'supposed' to be — gentle.* It is a brave woman who seeks to overcome this dilemma, to ignore the connotations. It is also a high price to pay for athletic excellence, particularly when success can not be guaranteed despite the sacrifices made.

But having made the choice to be a serious athlete, to risk all in a quest for personal excellence, she has the added burden of continual role conflict and innuendo imposed on her by others, often 'significant others', to deflect her from her mission. Perhaps we should not be so surprised that there are few women seeking to replace the Dawn Frasers and the Shirley Stricklands in the arenas. It would seem that being athletic and female are incompatible.

Or are they? Certainly being considered a serious athlete and female presents some problems for some people — both male and female. Indeed the female athlete is looked on as a special kind of woman because of her interest in sport, but because she is a woman she is often looked on as a special kind of athlete. While I admit that there are differences between male and female athletes, there are more factors in common than there are differences. Social expectations over-emphasise the differences and as a consequence women athletes are often sold short in their quest for excellence. Less is expected of them; they are given training workloads appropriate for children (male children that is!); they are made coach-dependent (male coach-dependent!) rather than encouraged to be autonomous, independent athletes with appropriate workloads. In his paper in this book, Professor Terry Dwyer confirms that *there are no (significant) differences . . . between men and women (athletes) and therefore the balance of training should be similar.* Doris Heritage in her paper makes the point that, training schedules should be individually designed — certainly not decided on the basis of sex. Dick Telford in his paper suggests that some women at least can train at a level, length and intensity which men just cannot match.

My experience with elite women athletes has led me to concentrate on their being 'athletes' rather than their being 'women'. Only where biological parameters justify special consideration do I regard them as 'different'. Their workloads are comparable to men, in fact the better women athletes do more than the lesser talented men, and the quality of their training is dependent on their ability not their gender. More importantly, I encourage their autonomy, their independence, their competitive spirit — all of those traits that the experts tell us are the important characteristics of the champion athlete. Granted I've been fortunate in that I have been privileged to coach Glynis Nunn and Judy Daly — two successful women athletes who have been strong enough to withstand the cultural pressures — but it seems to me that the Australian female athletes that I respect and admire have all exhibited the traits common to successful athletes. Who would deny the spirit of independence of a Dawn Fraser or a Raelene Boyle? The competitive urge of a Pam Kilborn or a Debbie Flintoff? They admit that these traits ensured their success. But perhaps these are the anomalies — those who dared to be 'different' in a sporting world that guarantees success for those who risk and compete aggressively. If we demand these attributes in a male athlete, then why deny their existence in a successful woman athlete? And why encourage women athletes to live out the role of 'dependence and heteronomy'? It is belittling to serious athletes and certainly not appropriate if they are to be successful international performers.

Perhaps it is the male coach who is as much to blame as our social structure for the presence of the dependent, compliant woman athlete in a sporting arena that demands autonomy, aggression and spirit? It is they (or some of them) who praise compliance, feel threatened by independence in women athletes (yet expect it in male athletes!). Where are the women coaches in sport? The successful sportswomen of the past — those who dared to be 'different' — surely should be the ones to teach the next generation how to be athletic and female rather than a female athlete?

Australia has enjoyed a reputation for sporting excellence in world arenas quite out of keeping with its relatively small population. Much of the nation's success has been won by women athletes, although this is not often acknowledged. Names like Marjorie Jackson, Shirley Strickland, Betty Cuthbert, Dawn Fraser, Margaret Court and Heather McKay, to mention just a few, remind us of heroes who have helped win that reputation (Mitchell and Dyer 1985). But why are there so few women coaches? Australian women were successful in sport from the thirties to the sixties because they competed in what was considered elsewhere 'a male domain'. They dared to participate in 'manly' (but selected) activities. Women still dare greatly in the field of sport. But the dare is now to compete with the intensity expected of male athletes — to risk 'femininity' and succeed both as an athlete and as a woman! The question of course is: 'Are the young sportswomen of Australia prepared to take that risk now?' Where are the replacements for Dawn Fraser and Raelene Boyle? And given the radical role many women played via sport in the past, why haven't more women, especially the successful ones, become coaches?

Coaching in Australia is still a male domain, even in the so called women's sports like softball and netball. Indeed in softball in South Australia at present only three of the ten A grade coaches are women. The situation in track and field is comparable, perhaps worse. There are very few women coaches in the sport, especially working with elite athletes. Shirley de la Hunty is a rare exception, but an ideal role model, having been an Olympian and a world record holder. But there are few women athletes who have followed her into coaching. Feminists would argue (and do) that this control of women's sport by men should surprise none. *Competitive sport is an institutionalised aspect of our culture which helps to maintain masculine hegemony* according to Bennett et al (1987), an opinion which Lois Bryson in her paper in this volume also puts forward (see also Bryson 1987). This may be so, but certainly the idealised traits of the successful athlete — dominance, self-assertion, achievement orientation — are not characteristics encouraged in women in our society. So I am not surprised that women athletes, having struggled against the odds to compete seriously, don't engage in yet a second battle and seek to coach 'in a man's world'.

Since I have asked so many questions I should at least suggest some answers even if they are speculative. I believe that the questions and answers are all interrelated. I believe that we have as much talent now as we had when Betty Cuthbert and Dawn Fraser were world champions — no more, no less. However we have to accept the fact that more women compete in more sports now than previously and in countries which previously excluded them; accordingly it is a tough arena. Only the talented who are committed, who persevere, who train hard and compete aggressively will succeed these days. Hence my initial comment: if women athletes are encouraged to role-play the compliant, fragile sportswoman, they will not achieve excellence! Given that some will dare greatly and achieve, they should be encouraged to assume a coaching career when their competitive days are over. They could then be great role models for the young and aspiring, both male and female, but more importantly they would prevent the continuation of the myth that one is either a successful athlete or a woman!

WOMEN COACHES AND COACHING WOMEN

Shirley de la Hunty

This paper will not be concerned with the relative physiological strengths and abilities of men and women. Such comparisons prove nothing in my opinion, and add little to the enhancement and the provision of opportunities for women to participate, and to be involved in the control and coaching of their sport. I have been involved in competition, coaching and administration of sport — the barriers are relatively the same, and are similar to society's barriers in other fields. My two main areas of expertise are Track and Field and Education. Both of these are traditional bastions of male management and dominance, with women seen at most as pale backdrops to male excellence — depended upon, tolerated, offered occasional rewards for obedience, dedication or decoration, but fiercely resisted at the first sign of daring to presume equality or aspiration to positions of power. Even the most 'understanding' male loses understanding and interest when the truism becomes evident that for every woman who achieves in open company with men, a man must miss out.

I believe the most important and enduring gains in the struggle for acceptance as equally capable have been by legislation. Change by social awareness is very slow and uneven — even when tracked across more than half a century — particularly in a world where scientific, commercial and political changes have accelerated at astounding rates.

The manpower needs of two World Wars stimulated limited acceptance of the abilities and capacity of women through their achievements when given a chance. Change mostly follows need, but sport, a peacetime activity, did not receive comparable stimulus for women.

But now there are numerous policies in the area of sport and elsewhere which are supported by legislation and formal established bodies. Among these are the initiatives of the Australian Sports Commission's Task Force: the National Policy and Plan for Women in Sport and the Women's Sport Promotion Unit, and governmental policy and legislation on Affirmative Action and Equal Opportunity. Despite this there are still hurdles to overcome. A seminar on Affirmative Action which I recently attended received vigorous and righteous support from male higher level academics until they discovered that all things being 'equal', a woman would get the job — and that a male consequently **would not.**

Many other writers in this area have referred to the problem of gender identity which has inhibited and discouraged women in sport and Mary Peters and

Gaylene Clews refer to it in this volume. I well remember wearing exotic hairstyles and Chanel No 5 during my competitive days to reassure myself as well as everyone else that I was a female. While it does not seem necessary to go to quite those lengths today, there are still many suspicions and criticism that are laid on sportswomen about their femininity and sexuality. I find it difficult to detach myself from life's continuum — to look both ways — to be objective about the direction of change and its speed — and to use my experience to draw conclusions of benefit. I shall be anecdotal to find some essence that is more intrinsic — to avoid today the temptation of the technicalities of coaching speed and hurdles for or by women, and not to attempt to explain, if it still needs to be explained, why women enjoy physical activity that is not work in the fields, in the factory or the family home. I watched a newly walking toddler at the airport while waiting for my plane, so excited by the sheer sensuous joy and freedom of being able to walk and run! Why do we ever have to explain, be challenged or checked as we grow up?

If men and women are different, how is it so? — or why is it so? A dear male colleague once said in dismay when suspecting my female attitude, *But* **you're** *not a feminist — you think like a* **man***!* and couldn't understand that I was not flattered or totally impressed!

David Hemery in his book **Sporting Excellence** attempted to analyse or isolate the characteristics of top sportspeople around the world, without great success, it has to be said, but a lot of interest. The problem was that the subjects were all totally different in background and environment. While our genes are powerful directors, we are largely products of our environment.

When trying to answer the queries about motivation that are put by people like David Hemery, I realise that somehow I managed to avoid some of the social conditioning in my early youth that girls then and now receive. I was the only daughter of pioneering parents in a remote country area. My father was a big athletic man, a Stawell Gift winner of 1900, a great footballer and cricketer, a man with great confidence in the power of strength and skill to achieve what he needed for himself and his family. He tried to tame a plot in the North Eastern wheatbelt — it took twenty years of agonising labour, climate failure and deep poverty to destroy him and his self-respect. My mother was also a strong woman — physically and mentally — but she survived because we had to survive. I grew up big, strong — wide expanses of bush to physically explore with my two feet or horses, carrying my full share of farm labour, with my four brothers as my only childhood company until I went to a country High School. I only got there because my mother, in defiance of the tyranny of the edict developed by the bank in the midst of the Depression to 'keep the girl on the farm', managed to salvage from dead and rotting sheep killed by the drought, enough wool to pay for my education.

So I left home at twelve, and managed virtually on my own from then on, as so many country children still do. I was inarticulate, shy, inordinately curious about the world beyond the farm fences and keen for learning. I had certainly not identified any barriers to my desired directions. The first I can recall was when I presented for enrolment at the Faculty of Engineering — to the discomfiture of the then Dean, who explained the dilemma I was creating — there was no women's toilet! Being seventeen and very shy, I was suitably deterred and enrolled for Nuclear Physics, again not realising that girls are not supposed to handle Mathematics. Yet even today, National programs are in place to attempt to alter this perception; a perception which may begin in pre-school children.

In my sport, which I only took up in my twenties, the sensuous excitement of fast movement and my curiosity about my physical machinery was powerful motivation for me. Again, not only the social concept of femininity of appearance and personality, but also that of a wifely and motherly role bothered me — my rugby boyfriend slightly disapproved of my absence from the game on Saturdays, and I was bothered by the pretties who fluttered on the touch line in my absence. Finally the spectre of age was drawn to my attention by a coach when I was just twenty-three years old. I went on to hold or co-hold four world records at the age of thirty-one.

I coach more men than women. In coaching women, I draw heavily on my long experience as an adult in world competition to reinforce their self-image, their assessment of themselves and the significance of what they are doing.

I also believe that phases of a woman's life are more clearly identifiable than a man's, and should be better understood and coaching consequently modified to accommodate life support activities. If we are serious about seeking greater female success in world track and field, we must develop support in major ways including child-care. These supports must be provided over at least the decade that I believe is required to achieve maximum physical potential as an adult.

As a coach and administrator, I am aware that the traditional male attitudes and control in sport are still very evident. One only has to do a cursory count of almost any dual sex sporting organisation at coaching or administrative level to find that the numbers tell the story. As an athlete I believe I was popular as long as I was demure, appreciative, decorative, obedient and winning. As soon as I moved out of the competitor ranks and presented myself to the male administrative and coaching heirarchy, I quickly found my attractions diminished. There was a new game to be learned — the rules changed.

Reading recently the story of women in the Olympic Games, I am appalled by the sustained attitude of the 'Father of the Modern Olympic Games', Baron Pierre de Coubertin, who fought to keep women out, describing them as the 'regrettable impurity'! And I am appalled by the repressive role of the IAAF and the Olympic Movement generally. That nothing more than 200 metres was allowed for women from 1928 to 1960 — 32 years — is incredible, but I am full of admiration for that wonderful woman, Madame Alice Milliat of France, who, when the International Olympic Committee refused the request for women's track and field athletics to be put on the Olympic program, formed the Federation Sportive Feminine Inter-national in 1921. This body organised the Women's World Games, initially with just five nations competing. By 1936 the fifth and final Women's World Games had grown to 30 nations and a bigger track and field program than women were to achieve in the Olympics until 1972. The women involved originally sought to use the word 'Olympic', but this was denied them. This organisation was finally laid to rest by the IAAF and the IOC because it was not thought appropriate that women were in charge of international events, the rightful province of males. In spite of the fact that those organisations disapproved of women in the sport and had largely refused their participation, they eventually had allowed them into the Olympics in 1928 and had then been concerned to defend the primacy of the Olympics.

While there is today a degree of lip service to equity, equality and opportunity, I do not believe the changes are fast enough. I regret to say that the signs around Australia in Track and Field are that women, for perhaps a range of reasons, are in a weaker position at all levels than in the immediate post World War 2 decade. At that time, like Madame Milliat after an earlier War, we had to form our own Associations to compete overseas as the male Australian Athletic Union did not register women. I deem it important that women survive in this male environment, hence considerable efforts are still needed.

TRAINING FOR WOMEN

Terry Dwyer

Introduction

In this paper I will concentrate on athletics and within athletics on middle distance and distance running, since that to a large extent is the focus of this conference.

There is a lot written on training in general, most by coaches who tend to try and rationalise in some sort of systematic way the things they have done to bring success for their runners. There has been more emphasis in recent years translating what the physiologists have been saying about what should happen in training. This is likely to increase with the establishment of organisations such as the South Australian Sports Institute and the Australian Institute of Sport in this country and similar ones overseas.

Much, however, is still of a general nature. I shall not discuss this but will focus on the sort of different things that women might have to do in training to achieve success.

Anatomy

Women have wider hips and the angle of the femur is different in women to that of men. There has been a lot of speculation that this might have the consequence of producing more injuries in the hip joint in women at equivalent levels of stress or load and possibly also in the knee joint where the angle of the quadriceps muscle on the knee is a little different in women. This might cause some problem of increased soreness of the kneecap due to rubbing of the patella (the kneecap) on the femur underneath. There has, however, not been a single study of injury rates of men and women at these two sites in competitive athletes. Two studies on joggers suggested that the injury rates were about the same.

The hypotheses for training would therefore be that because of anatomical differences women could not undertake so many kilometres or such vigorous work as men. The epidemiological evidence suggests that this is not so. [And as noted Australian authorities Dick Telford and Pat Clohessy observe in their contributions in this volume, many women do train at levels as high as, if not higher than, most men without any disadvantage Ed.]

Physiology

There are in this area some acknowledged differences between the sexes which suggest that a variety of different training regimes should be tried. Not all have in fact been tried.

As a background to discussion of these physiological differences between the sexes I will present some data from the 1985 Australian Health and Fitness Survey in which 9000 school children were measured — a representative sample of the total population aged between 7 and 15.

Among other things measurements were taken of their body fat and of how strong they were, as well as how fast they could run. One of the most important observed differences between boys and girls is in body fat. As girls go through puberty their body fat increases quickly. The figures, presented in Table 12, show the 95th percentile, because this is most relevant for elite performers and is less influenced

Table 12: Body fat (measured as magnitude in millimetres of skinfold) for boys and girls of various ages. The figures shown are the 95th percentiles, ie the level of body fat which 95 per cent of boys and girls exceed.

		9 years	12 years	15 years
Suprailiac skinfold mm	Boys	3.0	3.4	3.7
	Girls	3.4	4.0	5.5
Mid-abdominal skinfold mm	Boys	4.0	4.4	5.2
	Girls	4.4	5.9	7.6
Biceps skinfold mm	Boys	3.0	3.2	3.0
	Girls	4.0	4.2	4.2
Subscapular skinfold mm	Boys	4.1	4.5	5.2
	Girls	4.6	5.2	7.0
Triceps skinfold mm	Boys	6.0	6.2	5.4
	Girls	8.0	8.0	10.0

Table 13: Strength measurements for boys and girls of various ages. The figures shown are the 95th percentiles, ie the strength which 95 per cent of boys and girls exceed.

		9 years	12 years	15 years
Right grip strength kg	Boys	22.0	31.0	50.0
	Girls	20.0	29.5	35.0
Leg strength kg	Boys	106.0	155.0	264.0
	Girls	89.0	137.0	164.0
Shoulder pull strength kg	Boys	15.5	24.0	45.0
	Girls	14.0	21.0	30.0
Shoulder push strength kg	Boys	15.5	30.0	56.0
	Girls	18.0	28.0	39.0

by lifestyle differences between the sexes. As an aside I might emphasise that as well as sex differences in body fat, there are considerable ethnic differences in body fat. By and large those peoples from the tropical regions carry less body fat. Aborigines, American blacks, Maoris and so on have on average less body fat than their European compatriots. This is as might be expected, since if you live in Scandinavia or Northern Asia extra body fat to keep out the cold would undoubtedly be beneficial.

But it also means that something has to be done to reduce body fat. This can be achieved by reducing calorie intake through diet or by increased calorie output through extra training (although this brings with it an increased likelihood of injury). Either way it may take several years to reduce body fat to a level suitable for optimum performance.

Body fat is one of the most important features of which coaches should be aware in their athletes and skinfold measurements should be taken regularly — but should be emphasised in women.

The second most important difference between the sexes is that of strength. The characteristic male hormone testosterone, and its derivatives the anabolic steroids, certainly influence strength, and after puberty in particular when the

Table 14: The times recorded for a 50m run by boys and girls at various ages. The figures shown are the 95th percentiles, ie the times which are equalled or bettered by 5 per cent of the sample.

Age	Time (sec)	
	Boys	Girls
7	9.03	9.51
9	8.35	8.59
11	7.90	8.10
13	7.48	7.84
15	7.04	7.70

Table 15: The times recorded for a 1.6km run by boys and girls at various ages. The figures shown are the 95th percentiles, ie the times which are equalled or bettered by 5 per cent of the sample.

Age	Time (sec)	
	Boys	Girls
7	7.50	8.51
9	7.01	7.58
11	6.40	7.43
13	6.16	7.29
15	6.05	7.30

hormone differences are maximised, males become on average markedly stronger than females. This is the case more or less whichever muscle system you choose ie whichever measure of strength and whether you look at the 50th or the 95th percentile. Table 13 shows some of the relevant figures.

The implication is that females should spend more time on weight training — even for middle distance and distance running.

Muscle differences

I will now examine some of the differences in fast twitch and slow twitch muscle fibres. The former seem to be at high frequency in those individuals with ability in distance events, although there seem to be differences in the slow twitch muscle group in their ability to work aerobically. All these muscle groups are trainable by different sorts of activity and if it turned out that men and women had different proportions of these muscles, then it might dictate that women should do longer aerobic runs say, or shorter anaerobic work. In fact there seems not to be any difference in the balance of these muscle types between the sexes.

Figures for sprint performances in boys and girls, presented in Table 14, show that girls run very close to boys at the 95th percentile up until puberty. After that as the boys develop muscle power, they do improve relative to girls.

In the 1.6K run, data for which are shown in Table 15, girls do not perform as well as boys even before puberty, although the activity levels even among 9-year-old girls seems to be significantly less than in boys, which may explain much of the performance differences. At the elite Little Athletics level the differences between boys and girls is less than at the 95th percentile. All of which suggests that the balance of fast twitch and slow twitch muscles is very similar in the sexes.

Conclusions

Turning to elite athletes we find that the world records for men and women are coming closer. (World records for the standard track events as they were in 1958 and in 1988, are shown in Table 16.) Women's records are now about 90 per cent of those of men in all distances from 100m to marathon. Although they have been improving most rapidly in the long distance events, they are actually closest in the sprints [and as Florence Griffith-Joyner showed in July 1988, significant improvements are still possible in the sprints to bring women close to 94 per cent of the level of men's performance Ed]. In earlier years women were banned from running

Table 16: A comparison of performance levels of men and women in track athletics as indicated by world records in 1958 and 1988

Event	Men's records		Women's records		Performance levels	
	1958	1988	1958	1988	1958	1988
100m	10.70	9.83	11.30	10.49	90.38	93.7
200m	20.60	19.72	23.20	21.71	89.79	90.8
400m	45.20	43.29	53.40	47.60	83.18	90.9
800m	1:45.70	1:41.73	2:05.00	1:53.28	84.56	89.8
1500m	3:86.00	3:29.46	4:22.20	3:52.47	80.10	90.1
3000m	7:52.80	7:32.10	9:44.00†	8:22.62	78.70	89.9
5000m	13:35.00	12:58.39	16:45.00†	14:37.33	69.26	88.7
10 000m	28:30.40	27:13.81	38:06.40†	30:13.74	75.28	90.1
Marathon	2:15.17	2:06.50	3:19.33†	2:21.06	69.15	89.9

† 1966 records

marathons which is a part, but only a part, of the reason they are further behind men in these events. The predictions in the book **Running Out of Time** which the editor of this volume and myself published in 1984, that women would at some time in the not too distant future equal or better men's times in the marathon and other events were, as we said at the time, by no means a total absurdity, although they did make us feel uncomfortable. [Four years on such predictions still seem improbable, but most of the explanations advanced so far for the continued improvement of women's performances which seek to demonstrate that they are the result of something other than a general improvement through better training and opportunities are false, as I show in my paper in Section 3 of this book *Ed*].

Women have not yet achieved equality in running events but they are still improving and emphasise that the similarities between the sexes are greater than the differences. The question then is what should women do to continue improving. The answer is roughly that they should do what men do.

There are several factors influencing performance. First, co-ordination. This has been recognised and given a lot of attention by sprinters but has so far been under-emphasised by distance runners. Nevertheless neuromuscular co-ordination is of importance for all runners.

Second there is speed — anaerobic power as the physiologists would put it — the ability to use high energy phosphates over 7-10 seconds.

Third is anaerobic capacity — the ability to extract energy from the breakdown of glycogen in the absence of oxygen and the ability to withstand the effects of the breakdown products — lactic acid in particular.

Aerobic capacity — the total amount of oxygen which can be used by the body or a group of muscles in a particular period of time — is among the most frequently measured and used concepts. But what is important is not just the capacity but the proportion of that capacity which can be used over time — aerobic tolerance. Finally there is aerobic efficiency — that is the efficiency with which the oxygen taken in can be used. Two athletes may have similar maximum aerobic capacity but because of differing efficiencies may still have very different running potentials.

All this information has to be used in developing training programs for both men and women. I believe that for women in an average week, every other day should be a 'hard' day in which they either do aerobic capacity or aerobic tolerance work. Once or twice a week they should do anaerobic capacity and anaerobic tolerance work. Add to that a long run once a week to ensure that slow twitch muscle fibres get good training gives a complete week for both males and females.

[As an Appendix to this article I have included a one year training program devised for and used by Irena Szewinska whose story is told in Section Eight *Ed.*].

APPENDIX

ONE YEAR TRAINING PROGRAM FOR SPRINT WOMEN
Devised for Irena Szewinska

One year program divided into five main periods

PREPARATION WINTER PERIOD (10 weeks)
Introduction Training (2 weeks)
Main Preparation Training (6 weeks)
Prestarting Training (2 weeks)

INDOOR COMPETITION PERIOD

SPRING PREPARATION PERIOD (10 weeks)
Main Preparation Training (6 weeks)
Prestarting Training (4 weeks)

SUMMER COMPETITION SEASON (18 weeks)
First Competition Part (6 weeks)
Training Part Period (3 weeks)
Second Competition Part (9 weeks)

POST SEASON PERIOD — ACTIVE RELAXED

PREPARATION WINTER PERIOD
Introduction Training (2 weeks)

Weekly Training Program
mon.   general strength
tue.   endurance
wed.   general strength
thu.   endurance
fri.   general strength
sat.   endurance
sun.   rest

Strength Training
Strength Training includes many exercises of general preparation with special stress on developing weaker muscle parts.
The loads are not higher than 60% of body weight, about 40 kg.
During one strength training unit the athlete does about 10 exercises in 6 series of 10-20 repetitions each. Exercises are selected in order to develop all muscles. For example:

— press the bar in lying position
— exercises of the abdominal
— lifting the bar
— half squat jumps with the 12kg sand bag
— exercises to strengthen the back
— exercises to strengthen the hamstrings
— exercises to strengthen the quadriceps
— exercises with the medicine ball
— squats with the 40kg bar
— easy repetition up to 60-80m stretching exercises including hurdles

Endurance Training
Endurance training is normally done outside.

— warm up part: about 30 min, including frog jumps, squats
— main training part: 10-8 × 2 min, breaks 2-3 min all distances should be run easily following ten minute jogging

Main Preparation Training Phase (6 weeks)
Weekly Training Program (9 units)

mon.	strength		
tue.	speed and technique	general preparation	
wed.	endurance I	strength	
thu.		jumping exercises	
fri.	endurance II	strength - endurance work	
sat.		endurance III	
sun.	rest		

Strength Training
load up to 90% max strength
the number of series, 6-4
the number of repetitions in each series, 3-20
For example:
— press the bar in a lying position
— exercises of the abdominal
— lifting the bar, up to 30kg
— alternate jumps with thte bar, up to 30kg
— half squat jumps with the bar, up to 40kg
— arm technique work with barbells 2.5kg
— squats with the bar 40-60kg
— half squats with the bar 70-100kg
followed by stretching exercises and easy running repetitions

Speed and Technique Training
Special running exercises were used during this training, to develop technique and speed with maximum relaxation of accessory muscles.

— relaxed running with acceleration
— different kinds of starts
— flying running with 3/4 speed
— other exercises to improve running technique

Speed Training
During the last phase of the warm up, power speed exercises were done over the distances of 20m; skip A, skip, B, boundings, high skipping, hopping, high hopping.

— the distance of running repetitions does not exceed 60m
— the breaks between repetitions allow rest
— the repetitions are fast relaxed, with increased intensity but no time taken

General Preparation Training
During this training the athlete executes many exercises for the muscles.
Special flexibility exercises, skill workouts with medicine balls, hurdles, etc.
All exercises should be done in a dynamic and rhythmic way.

Endurance I Training
8 × 250m — making changes in rhythms (100m running, 50m jogging, 100m running), breaks about 3 mins.
The repetitions are easy, no time taken.

Endurance II Training
8 × 1 min (about 300m).
Every 1 min, 2 mins break.
After 4 repetitions, a 4 min break.
After 3 weeks, lasting distances will be changed to 300m, breaks will be the same.

Endurance III Training
8 × (5 × 100m) - interval, breaks 3-4 mins
In this period, in the endurance training, quantity and not quality work is important.
The number of repetitions and not the intensity is important.
The breaks are short and the b.p.m. before the next repetition will not be higher than 120-130.

Jumping Training

— full squat jumps	6 × 10 repetitions
— boundings L-R legs	6 × 20 repetitions

— boundings L leg   6 × 20 repetitions
— boundings R leg   6 × 20 repetitions
— high hopping L-R leg 6 × 30m
— frog jumps   6 × 10 repetitions
Following relaxed running; repetitions and jogging.

Strength - Endurance Training
Skip A on following distances:
2 × 40m; 2 × 60m; 2 × 80m; 2 × 100m; 2 × 120m; 1 × 80m; 1 × 60m; 1 × 40m.
Breaks are short during the walk.
Technique and rhythm are important.

Prestarting Training (2 weeks) - indoor.
The number of training units during a week was reduced to 6.

Weekly Training Program
mon.   strength
tue.   speed
wed.   endurance I
thu.   power-speed
fri.   endurance II
sat.   rest
sun.   test

Strength Training
Load up to 90% of the max. strength.
Each exercise has been done in 4 series.
Number of repetitions in one series 3-10, for example

— exercises for abdominal muscles
— alternate jumps with the bar up to 30kg
— half squat jumps with the bar up to 25kg
— hopping with the bar up to 20kg, L and R legs, distance 20m
— full squat with the bar up to 40-60kg
— half squat with the bar up to 70-100kg
Followed by running repetitions and stretching exercises

Speed Training
This training in comparison to the previous speed training period will be different:

— in the end phase of the warm up, exercises focus on technical speed and power speed form
— there are starts with the gun
— some parts of repetition are run with time taken
— the breaks between repetition are longer, for example

— starts from starting blocks no command 4-6 × 20m
— starts from starting blocks with the gun 6-8 × 40-60m
— flying starts 4-6 × 40-60m

Endurance I
6-8 × (3 × 100m) interval, breaks 3-4 mins

Endurance II
6-4 × 150m with time taken, breaks 8-10 mins

Power Speed Training
4 × 10m skip A; skip B; bounding L-R leg; acceleration up hill, high hopping; acceleration

Test
2-4 × 60m from the starting blocks with timing, breaks 15-20 mins

INDOOR COMPETITION PERIOD (6 WEEKS)
The training cycle during the indoor competition period is similar to the prestarting training.
The quantity of training is reduced. The tests are replaced with participation in competitions.
The indoor competitions are elements in preparation for the outdoor season. There is also a break in intensive training during the winter time. They allow also to improve the technique of the crouch start, running technique and they are excellent speed training.
The indoor competition provides information about the success of the previous training period.

SPRING PREPARATION PERIOD (10 WEEKS)
This period was divided into 2 phases:

Main Preparation Training
During the first 6 weeks special preparation was done with large training quantity.

Prestarting Training
In the next 3 weeks of the prestarting phase the training becomes more specific with smaller quantity and more intensive work. Tests were introduced.

Weekly Training Program

mon.	strength	endurance I
tue.	speed	
wed.	jumping	general preparation
thu.	endurance II	
fri.	strength	strength endurance
sat.	endurance III	
sun.	rest	

After the indoor season the preparation for the other season began.
The training is similar to the one executed in the early winter training period. The main stress was put on the strength and endurance work.
Now the preparation is at a higher level.

Strength Training
This training is similar to the one of the Winter Main Preparation Period training.
The number of series and repetitions were the same but the exercises were done more dynamically. During Prestarting Training (3 weeks) the number of exercises and repetitions decreasd. It is a typical power speed work, but squat and half squat with max. and submax. load are limited to 1-3 repetitions.

Speed Training
During the first 6 weeks running repetitions of 40-6-m with flying starts were done and technical starts from start blocks and 20-40m with no timing.
Technique is specially important. During Prestarting Training, part of the speed work was done with timing.

General Preparation Training
This training includes flexibility, using hurdles, medicine balls, shot put and skill exercises.

Endurance I
6 × (3 × 100m) interval, breaks 3-4 mins.
This training has been used as relaxation running after strength training.

Endurance II
Main Preparation Training
6-8 × 200m with timing, breaks 8-10 mins.
The distances are run with increasing intensity.

Prestarting Training
6-4 × 150m with timing, breaks 8-10 mins.

Endurance III
Main Preparation Training
8-4 × 300m on timing, breaks 10 mins.
8 × 300m, breaks 4 mins
4 × 300m, breaks 10 mins.

Prestarting Training
1st week — test — 2 × 300m, break 30 mins.
2nd week — test — 2 × 200m, break 45 mins

Strength Endurance Training
Main Preparation Training
Training is similar to Winter Preparation Training period.

Prestarting Training
Skip A; 2 × 10m; 2 × 40m; 2 × 60m; 2 × 40m; 2 × 20m.
At the end of the training period 4 × (4 × 40m) interval.

Jumping Training
During the **Main Preparation Training** period 6 series and later 4 series of each exercise. For example:
6-4 × 10 repetitions
— full squat jumps; bounding L-R legs; frog jumps; hopping × 20m
Followed by relax repetitions running.

This spring period is a very important phase in all year training.
Special stress should be put on the endurance work.

The tests and starts begin from longer distances, 300m; 200m; and later 100m. This prevents injuries

SUMMER COMPETITION SEASON (18 WEEKS)
Weekly Training program in 1 and 2 competition part.

mon.	endurance I	endurance I
tue.	strength	strength
wed.	speed	speed
thu.	endurance II	jumping tr.
fri.	rest	endurance II
sat.	competition	rest
sun.	competition	competition

2 days competition   1 day competition

The goal of this training is peak for the top competition.

Endurance I
6-4 × (3 × 100m) interval, breaks 10-15 mins.

Strength Training
Special stress on dynamic exercises.
There are also exercises with a sand bag (12kg); hoppings, jumps etc.
Also exercises to strengthen the back, abdomen and arms; half squats with the bar at submax load, repetition in 4-2 series 5-1.

Speed Training
This training is similar to the training in **Spring Prestarting Training** Period.

— after warm up exercises of power speed
— 6-8 × 20-4-m block starts
4-6 × 20-60m flying starts
Not all repetitions are with timing.

Jumping Training
Each exercise was done with 6-3 series:

— long jump from the spot
— triple jump from the spot
— five jumps from the spot
— ten jumps from the spot
— squat and jump × 10 repetitions
At the end of training 4 × (4 × 50m) interval.

Training Part Season (3 weeks)
Weekly Training Program

mon.	strength; endurance I
tue.	rest; speed
wed.	jumping ex.; strength; endurance
thu.	endurance II; rest
fri.	strength; rest
sat.	rest; endurance III
sun.	rest

Strength, speed, and jumping exercises and strength - endurance training are similar to **SPRING**

PREPARATION PERIOD (10 WEEKS).

Endurance I
6-8 × (3 × 100m) interval breaks 3 mins.

Endurance II
6-2 × 150m with timing, breaks 10; 15; 20 mins.

Endurance III
4-2 × 300m with timing, breaks 15; 20; (30-45mins).

During training camps, which are short, held between the first and the second competition phase, strength and endurance were especially built up.

WOMEN IN SPORT:
SOME SPECIAL CONSIDERATIONS

Richard Telford

Performance differences in young boys and girls

The physiology of women, whilst being similar in many respects to that of men, certainly has its differences which are undoubtedly significant so far as performance in many sports is concerned.

Some of these differences emerge at an early age. Numerous research studies have shown that pre-pubescent girls have advantages in joint flexibility, boys have advantages in running speed, running endurance, and jumping explosive power, and that there seems to be little difference in muscular strength. However, upon closer analysis of results, it is evident that much of the difference lies within the fact that, even at pre-pubescence, girls carry more body fat. This in turn reduces their power to body weight ratio. Hence activities which require body weight to be moved in short bursts (sprinting) or over longer periods (endurance running), girls in general do not perform as well as boys. In swimming, however, body weight is supported by water and the differences in performance between young boys and girls is small. It is important to note that I refer to average values. There are always the cases of the talented and (usually very lean) girls that compete favourably in speed and endurance with the majority, if not all, of the boys.

Figure 15: Sum of 7 skinfold measures in female Australian athletes — means and ranges (from Sports Science and Medicine Quarterly 1(2), 1984)

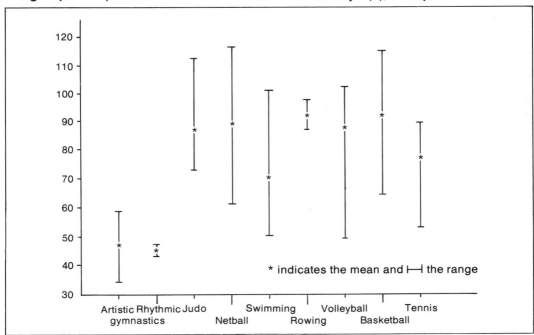

* indicates the mean and ⊢⊣ the range

The body fat issue

During adolescence, the power to body weight factor becomes much more pronounced — in general, boys tend to become relatively more muscular, taller and leaner. Again it is stressed that I refer to trends, and that some females continue to stand out among the best performers in mixed company. Those that do are inevitably lean and muscular. In fact, the very best of female speed and endurance athletes in Australia are always in the lowest skinfold categories (Figure 15). Consequently, there is a continual push by coach and athlete alike toward leanness. Unfortunately, it seems that females must sometimes develop lower levels of body fat than those conducive to their best health. This seems paradoxical, but sometimes peak performance in a specific sport may not necessarily coincide with optimal body function as a whole. For example, an extremely lean distance runner, at 36mm skinfold total, while performing very well on the track may be amenorrhoeic; this may adversely influence other aspects of physiology such as calcium metabolism. Coaches of women distance runners are only too aware of the relationship between extreme leanness and stress fractures of the lower limb and foot.

It is for this reason that regular monitoring of skinfold thickness is recommended. Using a total of 7 sites a 'skinfold sum' can be calculated. When females fall below 40mm in total, then problems with bone and / or joints tend to emerge. In general, it would seem that during intense training it is advisable to maintain a skinfold sum of 45mm or greater. It should be pointed out that the average slim female athlete is probably closer to 80mm, but for highly motivated elite runners and gymnasts, we find them edging down below 40mm.

The iron issue

Another facet of physiology which is of critical importance in which females tend to run increased risks, is iron status. Iron is vital to optimal oxygen transport and to both aerobic and anaerobic capacity. This is because it is critical to red cell production and to biochemical activity in the muscle. It is also important for immune responses. In our laboratory, we have regularly found that iron deficiency causes lethargy in training and general tiredness well before any signs of actual anaemia set in. Consequently we use the measurement of serum ferritin (an iron storage protein) to indicate the status of body stores of iron. Red cell counts or haemoglobin usually begin to fall after iron stores have become extremely low.

Women engaging in heavy endurance training probably turn over red cells more rapidly than inactive women and in so doing require more daily iron. Unfortunately, not all the iron can be 'caught' and reutilised, and this factor, together with iron losses at menstruation and in the sweat, puts the endurance training female at risk of iron deficiency. Furthermore, in the ongoing quest for low body fat, some women make the mistake of removing lean red meat from their diet. Lean meat is the best form of relatively readily absorbable 'haem' iron and also helps in the absorption of non-haem iron from vegetables.

Figures 16a and 16b show the result of just one week of iron supplementation in a group of netballers arriving at the Institute of Sport after summer at home. Not only was there a general increase in blood ferritin (iron stores), but their increase in haemoglobin indicated that iron deficiency had also compromised their oxygen transport and hence endurance fitness. Another example is the case of Suzie Landells, former champion Australian swimmer. Only weeks before leaving for the Commonwealth Games and having arrived back from a two-week training camp in Brisbane, Suzie could not train with anywhere near the quality we had come to expect from an Australian champion. Consequently, it was suggested that after

Figure 16a: Ferritin levels recorded in supplemented (A-E) and unsupplemented netballers (H-K)

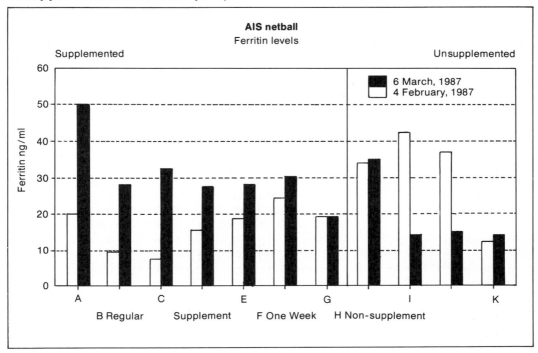

Figure 16b: Haemoglobin levels in supplemented (A-E) and unsupplemented netballers (H-K)

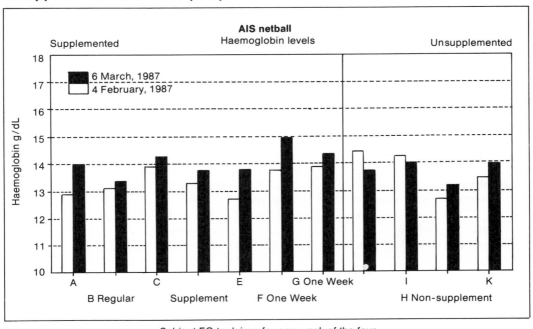

Subject FG took iron for one week of the four

her 1984 Olympic silver medal, she could not maintain adequate motivation and had let her form fall away. Suzie herself began to doubt her ability as well. Withdrawal from the team was discussed. However, a blood check revealed that, in contrast to a check just three weeks prior, her ferritin level was now in the danger zone. An increase in dietary iron through lean meat and iron supplementation resulted in an increase of ferritin to an adequate level in three weeks. During this time, it was obvious that Suzie was picking up with better training performances. History has it that she did go to Edinburgh and brought home two gold medals. A similar story can be told about Australia's greatest ever female marathoner, Lisa Martin, who also suffered from iron deficiency. Following this diagnosis, Lisa's form improved as she introduced more lean meat and other foods of high iron content into her diet. Lisa subseqently ran the 4th fastest marathon by a woman in early 1988 and won a silver medal in the Seoul Olympic Marathon.

Women can and do train very intensively

Whilst sport-related, physiological deficiencies exist between males and females, I sometimes get the impression that females can accommodate long, gruelling training sessions more comfortably than males. My current thinking may be somewhat biased because I regularly observe, amongst other elite women, two champion Australian women train. One is the previously mentioned Lisa Martin, and the other is Janelle Elford, the distance swimmer.

These women are examples of exceptionally gifted athletes, both physically and psychologically. Physically they possess the 'motors' to go fast for long periods and the 'chassis' that are not prone to breaking down. Displaying a remarkable psychological aptitude, Lisa is able to run by herself for 2-3 hours in her long runs and train twice a day, every day. Janelle is able to train intensely 12 sessions a week for $2^1/_2$ hours at a time with nothing to look at except the black line on the bottom of the pool. Figure 17 presents a typical training week for Janelle. They can do this because they are highly motivated to succeed, and do. They also display exceptional ability to back up with successive intense sessions — and seemingly they do this better than their male counterparts. No runner in Canberra can train

Figure 17: Training week — Janelle Elford

	am		pm	
Monday	$2^1/_2$ hours over distance 10 K		Threshold 9 K	
Tuesday	Sprint/drills 60 x 25 distance in 10 K	1 hour gym	Threshold 6 x 400 in 10 K	
Wednesday	Off		5 K threshold in 9 K	
Thursday	4 K time trial in 9 K	1 hour gym	3 x 1500 or 15 x 300 in 10 K	
Friday	Recovery 9 K		1m quality 10 K	1 hour gym
Saturday	Threshold 11 K		Racing 8-9 K	
Sunday		Rest		

Best session 18 x 800 in 10 minutes!
Total K in water — 110

with Lisa's continued intensity and I believe no swimmer in Canberra could match Janelle's training program — male or female.

So whilst I have pointed out a few areas of difference in men and women, which may favour men in speed and shorter term endurance, through lack of participating numbers we have not really had the chance to see whether women can match it in the 'ultraendurance' activities. While writing this paper, a young lady was introduced to me looking for advice regarding her running shoes. I asked her what race she wanted to run next. She told me it was the Sydney to Melbourne ultramarathon. Perhaps this is a sign that the numbers of women will increase in these types of events! Whilst we may get an answer to our question of relative endurance capacity, I must say that I do not recommend anyone trying to run 1,000 kilometres in six days!

THE DEVELOPMENT OF WOMEN'S DISTANCE RUNNING: AN AUSTRALIAN PERSPECTIVE

Pat Clohessy

The past

The year of 1988 is a most historic one in Australian history — our Bicentennial Year — and it is also historic in women's distance running with the eagerly awaited full Olympic recognition after many Olympiads of struggle. In the past, women's distance running has received virtually no international/Olympic recognition (The modern Olympics began with a 'Male Only' policy of the 1896 Olympic Games Committee; there was no women's Track and Field program at all until 1928 and no distance events until the 1500m was introduced in 1960). In addition there was no encouragement — nor even tolerance — of women runners at domestic or international level. Medical opinion opposed women's distance events; indeed society and the community did not encourage women's participation in social or competitive sports in general and certainly not distance running. *The old fashioned, ill-informed medical and sports community tried to protect women from irrevocable damage, or even death, by limiting their running distance to a half mile* (Rhodes 1978).

Women's considerably greater involvement in the wider community in the 1940s and the consequent women's liberation movements after World War II contributed to change in community attitude to women in sport. But progress was slow. Important supportive factors were:

— Medical acceptance and later medical support: *Practice of endurance sports corresponds perfectly with the female psyche* (Jeannotat 1980). Dr Ernst van Aaken and Dr Charlie Robins were among the first from the medical profession to speak out in favour of women distance runners.

— Community awareness of value of exercise: *Running is the fountain of well-being and satisfaction* (Dr Howard, Director of Research Institute of Federal Sports School at Magglingen, Switzerland, quoted by Jeannotat 1980).

— The work and inspiration of activists and advocates such as Joan Ullyott,

Doris Brown and Kathrine Switzer [as Doris Brown Heritage herself describes in the final section of this book *Ed.*].

The United States played a critical role in the development of women's sport towards equality. It was in that country that the current running boom began. The great increase in men's running led to complementary interest in women's jogging and running. Articulate and dedicated activists gradually brought about change in community attitudes and consequent participation in high profile events such as the Boston Marathon.

Constitutional support for women in the US under 'Title IX' (1973) provided Equal Opportunity for US female students in American College System (eg NCAA) and led to the development of an excellent system for the development of women track and field athletes. This was to result in the uprecedented expansion of women's running and the rise of stars like World Champion Mary Decker (1500m and 3000m) and Olympic Marathon Champion Joan Benoit among many others. It also led to the great success of US women in the World Championships of 1983 and the Los Angeles and Seoul Olympics of 1984 and 1988. US women runners won the 1500m, 3000m events at the World Championships in 1983 and the 100m, 200m, 400m and marathon in the 1984 Olympics, as well as the 4 x 100m and 4 x 400m relays. In 1988, with no major boycotts to dilute competition, they won six gold medals, more than either the Soviet Union or East Germany. This historic US legislation also had significant implications around the world.

Although Title IX legislated for equal opportunity, it could hardly have achieved anything like equality in the 15 or so years since its enactment, because the starting points of the sexes were so unequal (Dyer 1982). In fact, in 1984, the power and promise of Title IX was cut short by a Supreme Court decision that narrowed its scope.

Because she is a contributor to this conference, it is worth mentioning the part played by Doris Brown, one of the early enthusiasts, activists and advocates for women's running in the US. Her paper in this volume tells its own story and is an important document. I quote from Raymond Krise and Bill Squires' book **History of Distance Running**:

> *The fabulous Doris Brown inaugurated her succession of World Cross Country Champion-ships in 1967. Incontestably, the greatest woman distance runner of the late 1960s and early 1970s, the 24-year-old native of Gig Harbor, Washington, won the first World Cross Country Championships, held in Wales in 1967. She also won the second, third, fourth and fifth. (Only Norway's Greta Waitz, the heir to Brown's mantle of pre-eminence, has come close to the feat to date).*

(Krise and Squires 1983, p18)

International recognition for women's running quickly followed and comparative equality was complete by 1988 when a range of distance races namely the 1500m, 3000m, 10,000m and marathon were included in the World Championships of 1983 and 1987 and the Olympic programs. In addition international teams races for women have become well established (eg Eikden Relays, World Cross Country and the World 15km Road Race Championship). I say comparative equality because there are as yet no walk events for women on the Olympic program, there is no steeplechase and there is a 3000m event not a 5000m.

Australia has kept pace with international progress in women's distance running and was well-represented in major inaugural events from the Munich Olympic 1500m in 1972, World Championships Marathon 1983, Los Angeles Olympic Marathon and 3000m, as well as the World Cross Country and Women's 10km/15km and the Eikden Relays.

Coaching

In coaching women — elite and non-elite — I have observed in them strong initiative, a range of commitment (from firm in the case of the elite, to relaxed but consistent in the case of the non-elite) and a marked endurance. Dr Charlie Robins in 1962 predicted that since running is primarily a test of heart and circulation, not brute muscular strength, the competition between men and women would become closer as distance increased (quoted in Rhodes 1978). He was among the earliest authorities to make such a prediction, even before women were running long distances in any numbers. In recent years we have seen evidence of this in the case of the marathon. In a comparatively short period, women's marathon times have come down so quickly that elite women are now regularly eclipsing men's Olympic marathon times of greats like Zatopek (2:23:03 in Helsinki, 1952) and Mimoun (2:25:00 in Melbourne, 1956). Ingrid Kristiansen 2:21:06, Joan Benoit-Samuelson 2:21:21 and Rosa Mota 2:23:29 are leading examples. [For a somewhat more rigorous treatment of the relative improvement of women's long distance running in recent years see Dyer's paper in this volume *Ed.*]

I have observed this special aptitude for running distance events among a range of women. Psychologically and physically women are well equipped for distance running. I advocate a balanced training program with some emphasis on long endurance running, while at the same time encouraging racing at a range of shorter distances from 1500m, 3000m as well as cross country. This formula/practice has been followed with significant success by the legends of women's distance running: world champions Doris Brown-Heritage (5 times World Cross Country), Greta Waitz, Ingrid Kristiansen, Rosa Mota, Olympic Champion Joan Benoit and others. I also advocate regular consultations with sports medicine doctors to ensure correct balance of diet and training and to guard against iron deficiency and calcium problems [Ullyott 1984; see also Peter Brukner's contribution to this volume *Ed*].

Coaches of female athletes are aware of the all too prevalent problems in this area. I believe sports medicine specialists and sports scientists have a critical role in the continued development of women's distance running, partly, but not just because of these issues.

The future

Our (women's) glory is not only in our accomplishments but in our bright future (Ullyott 1984).

With an attractive international women's elite distance running program now functioning, women distance running enthusiasts have indeed accomplished a great deal and the future is certainly bright. I now see the need to meet a new challenge, to move in a new but complementary direction. I see the challenge of the future as largely a social one to:

— spread this opportunity of well-being and satisfaction to the less privileged countries

— utilise Sport Science/Medicine to meet the too prevalent problems of injuries

— broaden the appeal to cater for women involved in large participatory sports (eg netball in Australia has 400,000+ adherents) in small running programs

— promote regular corporate social runs and women's only jogalongs in co-operation with community and regional departments of Sport and Recreation.

Tens of thousands run, some in competitive pursuit, some in combat with themselves, some for health, some for company, ... all in their own good form, all of them runners (Krise and Squires 1983, p270).

A case study — women's distance running in Canberra

I now present a case study of a progressive women's running community. My purpose in so doing is that it may well serve as a model for other progressive communities in Australia and elsewhere.

Partisan observers view Canberra as the women's distance capital of the world. Certainly I know of no other location to match the Australian National Capital's physical environment; its easy accessibility to interesting running courses and, in addition, this largely public service city has a range of competent and enthusiastic organisers who are sensitive to the special needs of women runners. Canberra is a city of opportunity and comparative equality for women in the growing field of distance running.

Complementary groups — under the leadership and guidance of the ACT Cross Country Club, including various corporate groups, Government Departments, Summer Series, Veterans and the Women's Jogalong Committee, work harmoniously to encourage women's distance running. They combine to provide an attractive range of social running with emphasis on enjoyment and participation, handicaps and weekly group training runs and lunch time runs.

Over 200 runs are organised each year including weekly pack runs, training (Sunday morning) and weekly races (fun run contests). Most runs are mixed runs but there are several which feature women only, including a monthly jogalong. Some of the organised runs are listed below as an indication of the range of opportunities.

Women's Jogalong
    Monthly Sunday morning handicap race
    Social afterwards
    Attractive, popular venue — Deek Drive Stromlo Forest
    Numbers 100 approx.

Corporate Runs (Mixed)
    Wed lunch time (100+/30+ women)
    Fri lunch time (Customs Dept organiser)
    Tues lunch time (Sri Chimnoy from Parliament House)
    Annual Post Budget Depts Fun Run 1500 (500+ female)
    Convenient Venues — Round the Lake, near Government Offices.

Summer Series (Weekly mid-week Feb-April)
    Distance 4km-10km
    Numbers 150, 50 women
    Tuesdays at 6.00pm, attractive venues ie Round the Lake Deek Drive (Stromlo)

Women's Fun Run
    Annual Womens Only 10km Fun Run 600+

ACT Cross Country Winter Series
    Weekly runs including a variety of distances — relays, road, cross country
    Two distances short (3km+) and longer (8km+)
    Mixed races but scored separately

Parliament House Relays
    Mixed teams of 10 (2 women + 8 men)

50 teams include: clubs, sporting groups, business houses, government
departments, social groups

Veterans
    Sundays 9.00am
    Thursdays (track session)

SOME ASPECTS OF STRENGTH IN WOMEN'S FIELD EVENTS

Ruth Fuchs

Introduction

Almost everything that humans do is connected to some extent with strength. In some cases, simply walking a certain distance, for example, the strength required is very small. A person walking the same distance with a load on their back requires much greater strength expenditure.

Top performances in many sports, and certainly most track and field events, are impossible without highly developed strength. The importance of strength for both men and women is likely to increase in the future. In the past, opportunities to improve sporting achievement through strength training was largely the prerogative of men — who were viewed almost universally as the 'stronger' sex. Today, scientific research has shown that women, the 'weaker' sex, can benefit at least as much if not more than men from a careful program of weight training.

Strength development in women

One of the most significant changes for women in recent years has been a downgrading of the importance of differences between the sexes and a recognition that they have more in common than they have differences. This realisation, even if it has not always been without problems and complications has been part of the reason behind a considerable change of thinking about the place of women in society. But it has also revealed the fact that even now many women all over the world are robbed of an even chance in society and a complete development of their personality.

This change of thinking has led in turn to a change in expectations about the expected limits of performance of women athletes, their physical load capacities and their competitive abilities.

As far as elite women athletes are concerned, to whom strength development plays an important factor in increasing their performance or recognising the likely limits of their improvement, strength training is just as important and necessary as the development of specific skills and abilities. Research results have confirmed that strength training has basic regulating as well as discipline specific functions. Research also shows more and more that not only those events which depend directly on strength benefit from strength training, but so too do sprint, run and walk events which are less obviously so closely related to strength.

Figure 18: The development of power associated with javelin throwing

a) calculation of power index

b) two specific curves for different distances thrown

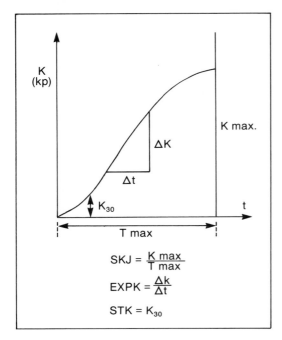

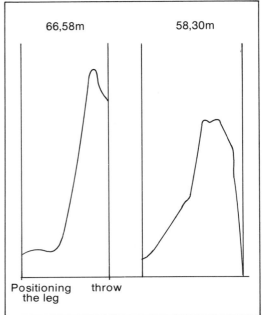

Strength and javelin throwing

In order to understand some of the training regimes which are adopted in javelin training, we should first consider some well known relationships between strength and the time over which is manifested. Figure 18a shows that a power index can be calculated from the maximum strength manifested divided by the minimum time required to attain it. Basic strength is usually calculated as the power which can be generated within 30 milliseconds and the explosive power as the rate of increase of energy generated. Figure 18b shows two different curves for the development of power associated with throwing the javelin two different distances (66.5m and 58.30m). The steepness of the increase in power manifested by the athlete on the left of Figure 18b shows how efficient she is. The variation of slope on the right shows inefficiency in developing power and translating it into throwing speed.

After reaching the deliver position, the process of javelin production starts with an acceleration phase, the characteristic of which depends on the basic strength. The acceleration which follows is decided by the explosive power. The maximum acceleration over the required time reflects the power ability of the thrower.

One of the requirements of success is that maximum acceleration should be reached at the moment the javelin leaves the hand.

Figure 19 shows a structural model of power. Showing the contributions to power in this way, indicates the particular features which should be developed during training. Javelin throwers clearly require both absolute strength and explosive power which in turn depends on the speed of contraction of the muscle fibres.

Figure 19: A structural model for the development of skills and abilities in javelin throwing

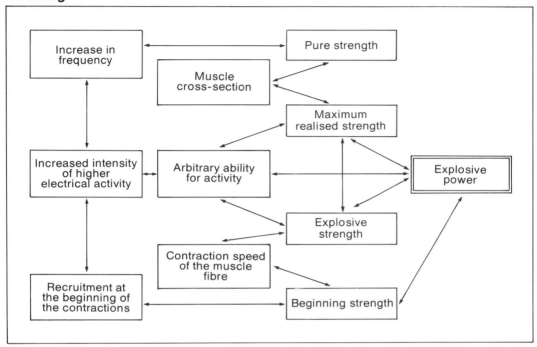

Table 17 shows two different training regimes, both concerned with strength development, but directed to these different aspects of power output.

To improve the speed of contraction of the muscle fibres our javelin throwers carry out special strength training with light implements and general sprint and jump training. The weight of the implements in the throwing exercises as well as the loading in the jumping exercises are so chosen that the exercise can be done in an explosive fashion. Intramuscular co-ordination is also of considerable

Table 17: Two training regimes concerned with strength development

Method	When	Repetitions per week
Muscle Development Training with dumbells and barbells. Weight: 80% to 90% of maximum lift ability. Duration: until complete exhaustion.	In the first three months of training or competition year.	Approximately 180-250.
Specific Ability Training Training with dumbells and barbells — mainly snatching. Loading average from 80% to 100% of maximum lift ability. Single attempts.	At the conclusion of muscle development training.	40-60

importance in the actual usage of basic strength. All the training exercises therefore have to be done in such a way that the maximal number of motor units can be activated in the minimal amount of time.

The present world record holder for the javelin (80.00m set in 1988) is East German Petra Felke. She is of relatively small stature — height 1.71m and weight 63kg. She clearly depends mainly on highly developed strength abilities in order to give the javelin the required acceleration and the highest possible velocity at the actual moment of release. All of the factors which contribute to this have therefore to be developed during training.

When she was 15 years old, Petra Felke could only snatch 40kg and could throw the javelin only about 45m. Today she can snatch 100kg and can throw 80.00m.

But this complex and systematic development has not only to be considered during competition and training immediately beforehand, it must also be the basis for long term planning and/or development of strength in javelin and other throwers.

In East Germany, we have developed some systematic guidelines for strength development in young children and I will conclude by describing them briefly. For children under the age of 15 the only strength development is done by the thrower herself, ie using her own body weight as load in push ups and pull ups. At this age there will be no strength training exercises with weights. Children are in their main growing phase and need a total load chosen in relation to their biological age. Nor is there enough time to allow full muscular response to heavy total training loads.

For advanced athletes between the ages of 15 and 18 we do encourage barbell work as well as the use of special implements to increase throwing strength. The target of weight training at this age is to learn the technique of snatch, bench press and squat.

Only after these techniques have been thoroughly learned will individual bests in these exercises be aimed at.

The targets for each age are shown in Table 18.

Table 18: Strength training with advanced adolescent female athletes.

Age	Repetitions/Year	Snatch	Bench Press	Squat
16	2,400-2,600	50kg	55kg	110kg
17	2,800-3,200	55kg	65kg	120kg
18	3,400-3,800	65kg	70kg	130kg

The team games of hockey, lacrosse, cricket and baseball have much in common. The idea that hockey is a women's game and the others are not is rapidly changing.

Right: Vicki Higham, lacrosse player for the SA team Sturt. Vicki has represented both South Australia and Australia.
Photo: Rosey Boehm. This was the winning entry in the ACHPER/Bicentennial Authority Photographic Competition.

Below: The Grand Final of the South Australian Women's Hockey Association A1 League, September 1986.
Photo: Doug Nicholas. Thanks to the Girls and Physical Activity Project.

Left: A baseball pitcher in action.
Reproduced with permission of the Women's Sport Promotion Unit.

Below: Australia's Belinda Hagget in fine form against England.
Photo: Menna Davies. Reproduced with permission of the Women's Sport Promotion Unit.

SECTION SIX
JUNIOR SPORT

AN INTRODUCTION

Ken Dyer

Children who are at school today will be both the stars and the average sportswomen of the year 2000. However, many, perhaps most, if past history is anything to go by, will unfortunately be non-participants by the year 2000 and well before then probably. The most general issue for junior sport is therefore how to prevent teenagers dropping out. Or, to put it another way, how to capture and maintain the interest of young schoolchildren in physical activity and sport through to adulthood.

In the present context the specific version of this question is how can we particularly ensure that young girls participate in sport and physical activity and continue to do so until womanhood. The converse of recreational sport and the problem of encouraging youngsters to participate is elite sport and its associated physical and social problems of overtraining, over-competition and possible dangers of some events. There are worrying aspects concerning both these sides of the issue among young people of today in Australia as much as anywhere.

The recent Australian Health and Fitness Survey of 1985 involved 8,500 young people aged between 7 and 15. It concluded that half the 15 year olds did not get enough regular exercise. The survey also found that Australian schoolchildren had blood cholesterol levels among the highest in the world, a third were overweight and most risked coronary artery disease later in life. A recent report in the magazine **New Scientist** (Vines 1988) reported similar findings elsewhere. Some of the following findings and quotations of the researchers involved are taken from this report.

Perhaps the most damning evidence for the inactivity of Western youth in general comes from Neil Armstrong, head of the Department of Physical Education at the University of Exeter in England. He and his colleagues are studying 500 children aged 11 to 16 living outside Exeter, as part of a study of the prevention of heart disease in children. They are measuring levels of blood cholesterol, blood pressure, body composition and monitoring stress, smoking and exercise. So far they have analysed the data for exercise just for the 11-year-olds, but the results are startling. *We have shown for the first time that children are nowhere near as active as we thought they were,* says Armstrong.

The researchers strapped electrodes onto each child's chest, with a telemetry system that transmits heart rate to a receiver worn as a watch, for 12 hours at a stretch. The children came back every day for five days to receive a new watch. The study covered 66 11-year-olds, making it the largest accumulation of data for this age in the world. To analyse the data, the researchers divided heart rates into bands, judging less than 120 beats per minute as very low activity and above 160 as high. Children of this age have a maximum heart rate of about 210 beats per minute, so the 'high' rating was deliberately conservative, equivalent to 75 per cent of the maximum work the children are capable of.

Physiologists argue that people need to work at such a high level for at least 20 minutes three times a week to improve their 'health-related fitness'. Not a single child fulfilled this demand. Only 6 per cent of the boys, and none of the girls, even achieved three sessions lasting 10 minutes a week. When the researchers turned to a lower cutoff, of 140 beats per minute, equivalent to walking at a speed of 6 to 8 kilometres an hour, again no-one achieved three sessions lasting 20 minutes of this sustained activity in a week. And only 3 per cent of the girls, and 24 per cent of the boys, had three sessions lasting 10 minutes at this level of exertion. In the 1985 Australian survey, 47 per cent of boys aged 15 claimed to engage in activity three or four times a week which lasted at least 30 minutes and made them huff and puff each time, whereas only 38 per cent of girls claimed the same.

Neil Armstrong argues that schools should promote exercise as part of a healthy lifestyle. *We need not just more competitive sport, for that turns many children off physical activity,* he says. Schools should provide a range of alternative ways to achieve fitness, *to create satisfactory experiences, achievable for everyone. Most school PE is devoted to large-scale competitive games which have little to do with health-related fitness.* The Physical Education Association in Britain is now in favour of promoting health and fitness, but most PE teachers do not realise that team sports do little to enhance fitness. *There is a gap between what the teachers are doing and what they think they are doing,* says Armstrong. PE teachers also need to fight the temptation to concentrate on elite performers who enhance the status of both teacher and school. In August 1988, the Australian Council for Health Physical Education and Recreation (ACHPER) launched an awards scheme for schoolchildren aged between 7 and 15 years, designed to measure, report and improve fitness. So an important first step has been taken in Australia at least.

In the US, the National Children and Youth Fitness Study discovered that a third of the children had a session of physical education only once or twice a week, and lacked certified teachers and gymnasiums. By the time the children are 8 or 9, the emphasis in the US is on competitive team sports, to the exclusion of other types of exercise. *Physical education should help prepare us for being physically active for the rest of our lives,* says the director of the study, James Ross. *As we grow older, it becomes harder to pull together a team. Most people need types of physical education that can be done alone or with one other person.* Paul Dyment, chair of the American Academy of Pediatrics' Committee on Sports Medicine, is worried that physical education in American schools will suffer in the backlash of the 'return to basics' that is sweeping the US as well as Britain.

In the end, we cannot yet say how much activity, and what sort, a growing child should have. The benefits to future health seem substantial, but we may need to worry about the demands made on child athletes. To be sure of these conclusions, researchers and those who fund research must take children seriously.

There are also potential problems for some elite junior performers which are the converse of too little exercise. Too much and too vigorous exercise might harm growing youngsters physically or psychologically. Elite swimmers, gymnasts and tennis players in particular, start very young in sport. They may be world champions by the time they are 20, but they may have spent the preceding 10 years or so doing little else but training hard. The **New Scientist** article already referred to discusses some of the evidence available here also.

A pioneering physical anthropologist, Robert Malina of the University of Texas in Austin, has done much to chart growth and maturation in the 'average' child. The quantity and quality of physical change is enormous. Around the time when children are growing fastest — 11 to 13 for girls, 13 to 15 for boys — their body composition alters radically. Boys double their mass of lean tissue, and put on more subcutaneous fat on the trunk rather than the arms and legs. Girls, on the other hand, gain more muscle and considerably more fat, but show little change in the distribution of that fat.

Changes in physical performance parallel these anatomical ones. A child's aerobic power (its ability to use oxygen to fuel muscles) rises for many years and then levels off at around 13 or 14 in girls, but continues to rise in boys for a time, reflecting their later puberty and greater muscle mass. These generalisations apply to the 'average' Western population, but we have little idea how much the changes reflect habitual levels of physical activity, or how children in different cultures fare. Current differences between the sexes are especially likely to reflect social inequalities, because girls usually have less opportunity to participate in sport.

The anthropometric data may also uncover anomalies in growth and development peculiar to particular sports; for instance, whether tennis players tend to end up with one arm longer than another. Some sports scientists, such as Charles Tipton of the University of Arizona, argue that particular kinds of intensive exercise in childhood might have damaging effects on the growth of the skeleton and joints. Rats and chickens forced to run very vigorously while they are growing develop shorter bones. *Is it not possible that the same applies to children?* he asks. Others deny this possibility. Well-controlled longitudinal studies should clinch the matter.

On the whole, the evidence linking skeletal and muscular injuries to childhood athleticism is shaky. There is one area, however, in which many researchers are agreed — that training from an early age often leads to serious problems in later life; this is gymnastics. *The data on low back problems in girl gymnasts are good*, says Malina. Alf Nachemson of the University of Goteborg in Sweden and a leading back specialist, goes further. *It is an outrage. Active gymnastics by girls between 8 and 10 should not be allowed. They are crippled by back pain by the age of 25. It is too much; the information is known.*

Currently various attempts are being made to chart not just growth — changes in size and composition — but also maturation, the rate of progress towards the 'mature' state. Gymnasts, for instance, tend to be 'delayed' two years, compared with the average, while swimmers are often more 'mature' in their physical development. As a general rule, it has been found, girls who do well at sport are late developers, while boy athletes are the early maturers.

One alleged hazard of competitive sport in childhood has received a great deal of attention: the notion that training can alter the onset of puberty in girls. Several studies comparing gymnasts with their classmates have suggested that girls active in sports tend to begin menstruating later. It could be that the intense training and thin physique of young gymnasts delays menarche. But the finding could be due to 'self-selection' — the tendency for girls with a particular build or rate of maturation to take up certain sports. Studies of identical twins suggest the genetic influences are most important in determining the age of menarche.

There are also considerable social and psychological pressures on elite performers — both boys and girls. In Australia, and indeed throughout the West, most child athletes have to squeeze training into the hours before and after school. A typical 14-year-old competitive swimmer in intensive training, for instance, gets up at five o'clock every weekday to spend two hours training in the pool before school, and often two hours more in the evening. Young swimmers often put in around 60 kilometres a week in training, and then spend the weekend competing.

Such a gruelling schedule may leave little time for socialising with other children, let alone studying. Some of these athletes have few friends and seem to have problems with their peers. Could the competitiveness drilled into them by their coaches or parents make it more difficult for them to make friends? A few of the children also suffer from other emotional problems; they worry excessively about their training and performance, lose their appetite and have trouble sleeping. Such things may be symptoms of 'overtraining', an ill-defined syndrome that can strike adult athletes as well.

A child athlete also puts enormous strain on the parents. The life of the family may become centred on training and competitions, costly in both time and money. Ambitious parents can also intensify the anxiety of a competing child. Many parents unintentionally put great pressure on their athletic child; they don't know how to give the child space within the family. Coaches do scapegoat parents, but parents need help to know what it is to be a young athlete.

Yet no one thinks that sport per se is bad for children. Most believe that athletic endeavours give children many advantages, enhancing their self-esteem and promoting long-term health. Things may be worse for those at the other end of the spectrum, the children who 'fail' at school sports and pursue sedentary lives. The full impact of habitual exercise, or the lack of it, on growing children is far from clear. Does it make them healthier, in the present or future? We have some evidence to suggest that the risk factors for coronary heart disease, the major killer in the West, begin in childhood, and that exercise lowers the risk on several fronts. Exercise in adolescence might even help to prevent some forms of cancer or brittle bones from developing years later. But to find firm evidence for the role of exercise in health requires epidemiological studies on a grand scale — a costly endeavour that would take decades.

The importance of these areas of possible harm and injury to young people and sport is now more widely recognised than used to be the case. This section contains two important statements which, while not part of the original conference, are appropriately reproduced in this volume. These are the Policy Statement of the Australian Sports Medicine Federation Children in Sport Committee on Children and Long Distance Running and the Policy Statement of the Australian National Health and Medical Research Council on Children and Adolescents in Sport. These provide both an authoritative summary of current knowledge in this area and recommendations on safety.

The papers in this section, indeed most of the papers in other sections too, have to be read with all this information as background. Sport and physical activity, in moderation at least, are good for boys and girls. But neither boys and certainly not girls appear to get sufficient to optimise their physical health let alone their psychological and social well-being.

The reason why girls in particular miss out on many of the benefits of sport are a mixture of what might be called 'individual' and 'structural' reasons. The individual reasons include such things as girl gymnasts starving themselves to retain the slim figure which judges of this sport seem to demand and giving up when they either fail to do so or make themselves unhealthy in the attempt; it includes the belief among girls that they will develop muscles if they persist in sport, a belief which is usually enthusiastically reinforced by boys, particularly at about the time

170

of puberty. It includes the notion that some sports such as football are unfeminine. And it includes the notion that girls are inevitably and irretrievably inferior at most sports and therefore might as well not bother.

The structural reasons reinforce each of these but are also quite distinct. These include the financial inequality in the provision of finance and resources to boys' and girls' sport. They include the belief that certain events are unsafe for (or impossible of performance by) girls, and the belief that it is particularly unsafe or immoral or possibly unfair for boys and girls to play together in the same team sports. The greater problems which face girls and women over travelling to and from sporting venues because of their reduced access to private transport compared to males and their undoubtedly greater susceptibility to assault while travelling (either verbal or physical) are also of major importance but difficult to evaluate in their consequences.

Each of these reasons for low participation by girls in sport and physical education must be addressed. As the authors of the very varied papers in this section (and others) explain, it requires general education of parents, teachers and pupils; skill training; the provision of equal resources and opportunities by schools and clubs which sometimes may mean integrated activities and sometimes not; and it means the serious backing of government through the law, special projects, political commitment and so forth.

Most of the attention in this book is on Australian Sportswomen. But Ilse Bechtold, Chairperson of the IAAF Women's Committee provided a fascinating description of the way junior sport is organised in West Germany. Partly for comparison and partly because of the enormous success of East Germany in modern sport, a report by Klaus Schonberger, Deputy Secretary General of the Athletics Association of the German Democratic Republic, is included here. This first appeared in the IAAF journal **New Studies in Athletics**.

Junior sport is arguably the most important topic of all in any consideration of Sportswomen 2000. Hence, it finds considerable emphasis in this volume.

BACK TO BASICS: GETTING OFF TO A GOOD START IN ATHLETICS

Vern Gambetta

The first experience in athletics for the beginning athlete is the most important. Therefore, this experience should emphasise the basics to provide a sound foundation for further progress and development. This experience will serve to maintain interest and raise motivation. It will also serve to promote adult participation in athletics.

Psychological considerations

Fundamental to all other considerations with the beginner are those dealing with psychological issues. Perhaps the most basic of these is the issue of providing an experience that will enhance self-esteem. Without a well developed self-image the athlete will have a difficult time handling success or failure and will not react favourably to correction or criticism.

The most sound method of enhancing self-esteem in the young athlete is to emphasise the intrinsic reward of participation, rather than competing for medals, records, trophies, etc. Extrinsic rewards can give a distorted sense of self-worth and focus attention away from performance. Often, the emphasis placed on extrinsic rewards results in an unhealthy emphasis on winning and records at a young age.

To establish a good system of intrinsic rewards requires much work on the part of the coach/teacher. Much of this work should be directed toward guiding the young athlete toward realistic goals (expectations). It is preferable that these goals be process goals that are appropriate to the age and skill development level of the athlete. For example 'hitting the board', 'finishing the race', 'six fair throws', etc.

The biggest psychological issue the young athlete will have to deal with as success is achieved is that of pressure. Consequently it is important to educate the youngster from the beginning as to what pressure is and how to best cope with it. Most often pressure is the expectations placed on an athlete by others, in most cases the parents and/or the coach. It is important that these people be aware of the effect that their expectations can have on the young beginner. This relates to the issue of intrinsic rewards, encouraging the athlete to participate for the joy of movement and letting the extrinsic rewards come as a by-product of the experience.

Competition

The biggest danger with competition for the beginner is too much formal competition, too soon. Competition for the beginner should consist of informal playdays of relay races, jumping and hopping games, and stone or stick throws. The more variety the better to accommodate the short attention spans, different interests, and competencies. This is also true of the training at this age. The challenge here is for each child to strive to better performance measured against their previous best. They must experience success in order to feel comfortable and maintain motivation.

Competition will assume a large role as skill and conditioning advance. When the young athlete reaches this stage, competition serves as feedback and a learning experience to measure progress. The ratio of training to competition should still remain high, somewhere in the range of three or four to one. A cautionary note must be mentioned: success in age group competition is not a guarantee for results at the national and international levels. In fact it is this author's opinion that early success has little or no relationship to later success. It will be interesting to observe the long-term progress of the young performers from the Junior World Championships and see if this high level competition at a relatively young age accelerates or retards development. Competition in itself is not negative, but it becomes a negative when too much importance is placed upon it and the outcome.

Talent identification and development

The fundamental assumption is that if that talent is identified early, nurtured, and developed to its fullest extent, then those athletes will continue on to the highest levels of competition. The issue is one of nature versus nurture. If a large, healthy, population base is available then a 'Darwinian' process of competition, letting the strong survive, might be acceptable. This system worked well for the US until other nations began a systematic approach to the nurture of the young athlete. The contrast between the two methods is readily apparent on the world list, particularly in events where a high level of skill development is necessary.

The very successful model utilised by the GDR is an example of a gradual progression that continually strives to select and match the young athlete to an event or sport that is suited to their body type and abilities. Their system is closely tied to the educational system through mandatory physical education taught by highly trained specialists. Their philosophy is that training will progress over a six- to ten-year period to achieve top results. Through a planned progression ultimate success will come in the adult years.

It is unrealistic to expect progress at the same rate and same level for all children. A danger of early identification of talent is a narrowing of skills through early tracking. This can easily occur if the initial identification of talent is based on a dominant physical characteristic biased by accelerated growth. This specialisation should be discouraged and general development stressed as a basis for later improvement.

Training

The fundamental goal is to enhance development of the mechanism of force production and to develop motor control. To achieve this at the beginning stages it is necessary to stress fundamental conditioning encompassing the basic biomotor abilities of speed, strength, endurance co-ordination, and mobility/flexibility. Remember, children are not miniature adults, therefore the biomotor abilities must be developed in a manner appropriate to maturation level and stage of development. The more a play element is introduced, utilising natural terrain and obstacles, the more interest will be stimulated and the more progress shown. Also the use of natural terrain and obstacles makes equipment and facilities less of a limitation.

The critical years for motor learning are the years from three to nine. This is when sound fundamental motor skills should be taught to establish basic technical models to provide a foundation for more specialised skills that will follow at an older age. *Optimum motor learning develops in children when skills are taught at the right time (maturation - readiness) and in the proper manner (experience - practice)* (Piscopo and Baley 1981). Big muscle skills should precede fine motor skills. Strength and endurance will increase with growth and maturity. Motor skill and the learning process relate more to maturity than any other single variable. Effective training for the beginner should encompass all of the following:

1) proper conditioning
2) good, competent coaching
3) grouping according to skill, body size, and physical maturation (chronological age is the least accurate means of assessing maturation)
4) safe equipment, and
5) rules and equipment modified to meet the physical limitations and skills.

The periods of sports participation model outlined by Brook is an excellent guide to determine the direction and content of the training process as progression is made through the stages of development. I have adapted this model to include psychological as well as competition objectives for each stage.

FOUNDATION PERIOD
Begins in a range from nine to eleven years.
Three to four years in duration.

173

Games and fun activities, wide variety designed to enhance self-image.
General training, speed development, skill development.
Develop bodyweight strength, mobility, and aerobic endurance.
Develop basic skills and rhythm.
One training session per week increasing to three per week.
Competition should be limited and confined to playful situations.

DEVELOPMENTAL PERIOD

Begins in a range from thirteen to fourteen years.
Four to six years in duration.
Emphasise general training in the first years.
Percentage of specific training should increase gradually over the last two years.
Develop appropriate training and competition behaviour.
Begin goal setting appropriate to level of development.
Teach weight training techniques with 60% maximum loading.
Three training sessions per week increasing to six in later years.
Undertake more formal competition increasing in difficulty as the athlete advances through the developmental period.

PERIOD OF MATURE PARTICIPATION

Begins in a range from seventeen to twenty two years.
Not before seventeen or after twenty two.
Percentage of specific training increases.
The time spent in training increases significantly, especially for the elite athlete.
Frequency and difficulty increases significantly.

Coaching/teaching

Perhaps the most profound influence on the beginner is that of the coach/teacher who provides the introduction to athletics. This person should be the best teacher available because this is the person who will teach the basics of conditioning, technique, self-image, goal setting, and competitive attitude. Unfortunately, in many situations, this is not the case. The coach for the beginner is often the least prepared and competent in terms of coaching/teaching ability. It is thought that working at this level is less prestigious, requiring fewer teaching skills and knowledge. The opposite is the case.

Working with the beginner is very demanding and the enthusiasm and joy of learning is most rewarding. Having coached athletes from twelve years of age up to the elite level I am very concerned about the number who leave athletics because of a poor learning environment, unrealistic expectations placed upon them, or too much intense competition beginning at an early age. Getting the beginner off to the best possible start is the most important job in athletics. The emphasis must be multi-faceted, emphasising psychological consideration, competition, talent identification, training, and proper coaching/teaching. The athlete should be a main focus of a national development scheme and a major emphasis of any national coaching scheme.

(Vern Gambetta is Editor of **Track Technique** *the official technical publication of The Athletic Congress. This article first appeared in* **New Studies in Athletics No.4, 1986** *pp 11-15, reproduced by permission of the IAAF.)*

TURNING ON THE TURNED OFF GIRL

Henny Oldenhove

Introduction

The problem which this paper addresses was one of the central issues of the Commonwealth School's Commission Project **Girls Achievement and Self—Esteem: The Contribution of Physical Education and Sport**. This project operated at state and national levels for three years from 1985-7 and focused on turning on the turned off girl specifically within the educational context by seeking to understand and change many educational practices.

The central feature of the problem was summarised succinctly in one short paragraph by Dr Ken Dyer in his review of research, resources and strategies commissioned by the project.

> *Girls' enthusiasm for and participation in all forms of physical activity, including sport, decline rapidly during their early high school years. Girls' average levels of fitness decline in absolute terms during these years and decline very markedly compared to boys. It is not just in school based activities that girls lose interest during these years. Their interest in all sporting and physical activities decline generally. Current educational practices in this area obviously are doing little to arrest this declining interest and must therefore be changed if they are to meet girls' needs and expectations.*
>
> Dyer 1986:2

The issues have been well-documented and supported by this report and also by comprehensive case studies, teaching resource units and the promotional video **Mirror Mirror**. Information was disseminated through a regular newsletter issued throughout the duration of the project.

But can the process of change be ensured through these endeavours, or will we in years to come still be discussing the same issues and look for ideas to prevent the disinclination of adolescent girls to physical activity? It is our task now to maintain the impetus and support the change process so that it, quite simply, amounts to good educational practice for the benefit of all students.

Let us also reflect on why we believe our actions to be of such importance in a broader context.

Findings

A number of school-based projects initiated by and carried out during the life of the Girls and Physical Activity (GPA) Project have shown the need for the introduction of special measures for girls, and demonstrated some successful interventions which have positively contributed to the sports skills, the participation levels and thereby self-esteem of girls. Several of these projects reinforce and support the findings of the Schools Commission report in relation to socialising influences and especially with respect to 'body image' and self-esteem (Dyer 1986). I propose now to summarise some of these findings as originally reported in the GPA newsletter.

Primary Years
The principal concerns at this stage of schooling are in the following areas:

— *Playgrounds* There is a disproportionate use of play facilities and equipment. Boys dominate the use of oval and asphalt areas. Access to equipment also favours the boys, thus skill acquisition is frequently reinforced by those who can repeatedly practice through the play sessions.

Girls and boys seem to share equitably the amount of time on 'Adventure Playgrounds', however the girls appear to be less active in their use of this equipment.

The structure of many playgrounds, especially for the younger children, does not seem to encourage spontaneous small group play, thus moulding many children to 'major adult games' through the provision of major game facilities. Schools that have broken down this pattern have noticed an increase in informal play by both boys and girls.

— *Skill Learning* The success of structured skill lessons often depends on individual teachers, who generally place greater emphasis on fitness activities. Despite the availability of the Daily Physical Education Program resource, a number of teachers have indicated that their confidence is threatened by the expectation on them to teach a wide range of games skills. Very often primary schools lack adequate equipment to provide for sound skills teaching; often it is inappropriate in size and insufficient in numbers. This can cause teachers to resort to 'games playing' where the skill discrepancies are often reinforced rather than addressed. The different experiences children bring to school are often not recognised, thus boys tend to be poor at skipping and fine motor co-ordination such as balance, and girls are poor kickers and throwers. This imbalance is often not addressed, thus reinforcing the quite stereotypical domains of skill acquisition. This trend becomes more obvious in more senior years where poor exposure to these skills limit students in their performance in a range of activities. Several schools have addressed this issue by conducting some single-sexed lessons at appropriate times where previously unlearned skills are taught in a more non-threatening environment (at Elizabeth Vale Primary School in South Australia for example, a single-sex Friday afternoon program is operated for those students not involved in interschool sport. The girls' group has had measureable success in raising their participation and self-esteem).

— *Fitness* In a three-school fitness survey the level of fitness for girls was markedly poorer than that of boys, especially in the cardio-vascular, strength and power categories with the exception of trunk flexibility. The tests used were standardised through the SA Health Development Unit's '5-Item Test'. The male/female discrepancy occurred at all schools but less significantly at one that placed a high priority on Daily Fitness. Our results tend to support those of the ACHPER Australian Health and Fitness Survey, which were released in 1987.

The indication from one school was that, despite daily PE, the level of fitness for girls remained poorer than that of the boys. In 1986 one of these schools implemented affirmative action strategies for a target group of girls with the specific intention of improving their fitness. Other benefits have also been documented.

In conjunction with the Fitness test, an attitude questionaire was also utilised at two schools. Results indicated that all students were in favour of Daily PE; girls enjoyed the distance running significantly less than boys, but rated aerobics and dance much higher. The socialisation towards involvement in fitness seems to play a significant role and cannot be negated conducting a Daily Fitness Program. In each age group there were outstanding examples of girls in relation to fitness which indicates that the issue is not merely physiological in nature.

If we accept that prior to puberty there should be no physiological reason for not achieving similar levels of fitness for boys and girls, then the trends already evident in these schools are indicative of a real problem for the fitness levels of girls. Using separate norm references for boys and girls prior to puberty does little to encourage a greater push towards equity, as they often reinforce differing standards and an acceptance of poorer performances by girls.

Unfortunately these low levels of fitness are seldom improved in later years of schooling and place many girls at risk in relation to their health and lifestyle.

— *Role Modelling* The effect of role modelling appears to be extremely significant for all students. It is often the lack of appropriate role models in our primary schools that is cause for concern. Sport and physical education seems to be a male domain in primary schools with male sports coaches and often a male PE specialist, yet the majority of primary school teachers are female. It is at the classroom level however, that few girls see their predominantly female teachers taking an active role, either in lessons or in play, with often highly inappropriate attire that tends to reinforce the poor status of activity for girls. One school which addressed this issue had a staff commitment to change and become involved during all lessons and had teachers actively seek play when on 'play duty' in addition to teachers on 'yard duty'. The effect was a much greater participation and involvement of all children in activity.

— *Clothing* Often the greatest encumbrance for girls in primary school is their clothing. Inappropriate footwear and clothing is an inhibiting factor for activity, and one that is not experienced by boys. This often limits the extent and intensity of girls' participation. Lack of changing facilities and school policies in this regard are important issues to address in primary schools.

— *School Organisation* The commitment and enthusiasm for programs of physical education differs markedly in a number of schools. This issue alone causes imbalances between schools and often affects the range of abilities and experiences students take to their high school years.

Schools that emphasise their sporting involvement often reinforce stereotypes of activity when preparing their students for these sports, often neglecting the need for a greater diversity of activities or implementing policies of equal opportunity, where all students have access to the same range of activities. This attitude often reinforces skill development for those already competent at various skills but often fails to develop more appropriate skills for those needing extra help. Thankfully this attitude in schools is declining, but it still exists in some cases.

Most schools have reached somewhat of a crisis by trying to meet the needs of a balanced PE program and a sporting program, and also including all the other curriculum areas into their very tight schedule. Teaching strengths in PE are extremely varied and some schools have committed themselves by allocating staffing time for a specialist noncontact PE teacher. Although schools who have done this have a well-planned PE program, the actual time spent with each class is minimal and often classroom teachers feel that they do not have to supplement this program as it is being addressed. Furthermore, some schools have implemented programs using parent volunteers for poorly co-ordinated children much in the same way as reading programs.

The total school commitment is crucial for the balanced physical development of all children but may be especially so for girls, where poorer skill and fitness levels become evident after about Year 5 due mainly to socialising influences of home, school and community.

It is also strongly contended that the Basic Learning in Primary Schools (BLIPS) program should encompass basic learning through the physical, with the same enthusiasm and commitment as literacy and numeracy. This would help schools present sound programs of physical education.

— *Children in Sport Coaching*
It has been encouraging to monitor the effect of the Children in Sport Coaching Scheme which has actively aimed at teaching skills to both boys and girls through modified games eg tee ball, kanga cricket, sofcrosse, gymfun, minkey, etc. The main target group has been parents and staff. Because they have been predominantly female, some excellent role models will now be operating in our schools, encouraging an integrated approach to sport. The introduction of the AUSSIE SPORTS Program has further promoted integrated modified sports.

— *Equal Opportunity*
The effect of the Commonwealth Sex Discrimination Act has been an issue for primary school sport and has been reinforced with the South Australian Equal Opportunity Act proclaimed on 1 March 1986.

State sporting bodies, the Education Department, the Catholic Education Office, the Independent Schools Board, the South Australian Primary Schools Amateur Sports Association (SAPSASA), and Department of Recreation and Sport have worked in close liaison with the Commissioner of Equal Opportunity to develop guidelines for the implementation of the Act. An important aspect of the Act is the recognition of the need for special measures for girls in order to bring about greater equality of opportunity and access.

In South Australia an agreement has been reached between interested parties regarding a satisfactory time line for implementation. [For some insights and observations on the South Australian and Commonwealth legislation see the papers by the South Australian Commissioner for Equal Opportunity, by Senator Rosemary Crowley and by Ken Dyer in other sections of this volume. In a later paper in this section, this matter is explored in more detail by Henny Oldenhove, and comparisons made with what other states are doing *Ed.*]

— *Conclusions regarding Primary Schools*
Physical activity is still of low priority in primary schools. Where affirmative action strategies have been undertaken there have been measurable improvements in the participation of girls. Most significant however, is the level of awareness raising that has occurred with staff and parents, leading to more thoughtful and balanced teaching methods and organisational structures taking into account the needs of girls.

Secondary Years
Secondary schools by nature are structurally different from our primary schools. They are, however, following on from a primary program and need to take into account students' previous experiences. Based on their primary years these experiences can be highly varied depending on the diversity of their PE/sport program. As previously outlined, if girls are disadvantaged prior to coming to high

school, these disadvantages can either be reinforced or addressed in the secondary years. If the decline of participating Year 10 girls is any indication, then obviously we need to be concerned with, not only primary experiences, but also our Year 8 and 9 programs that may contribute to this marked disinclination.

As the Schools Commission report indicates, we cannot neglect the influence of the major socialising agents of family, community and peers and we must place the role of the school in perspective. However, the dominant effect of peer group usually occurs in the school environment thus they are not exclusive of each other.

A number of issues become evident in the secondary schools and several projects have attempted to redress the imbalances and look towards structures and curricula that aim at meeting the needs of girls at various levels of schooling, especially in the age 'beyond compulsion'.

The following trends are fairly indicative of the areas of concerns:

— *Curriculum*
  Traditionally the curriculum has assumed a sporting background with heavy emphasis on 'ball' activities. Many students, especially girls, who may not have a highly competent level of skill, often feel threatened and uncomfortable in these activities and although they are seeking involvement in a particular form of activity, may find competitive games inappropriate.

  The very nature of curriculum is a major issue and the notion of choice and core are also aspects which need to be addressed. Where major numbers of girls 'opt' out when subjects become choice (usually at Year 10), there is great concern. But what is it about our program that is not attracting these girls? Major study areas of PE at Year 11 and 12 have very few female participants which is also highlighting the issue.

  Schools that have offered a diverse program that meets the needs of various students and activity seekers, have increased the numbers of girls taking the courses. Some specifically designed single-sexed girls' groups have been very successful in meeting the needs of a targetted group of girls and have observable improvement in attitude and self-esteem.

  It has become evident that our curriculum must be more flexible and diverse, taking into account the range of needs and interests of all our students. There is a danger in treating all girls as one within this group; there are a great many needs which must be met differently.

— *Extra Curriculum*
  The number and variety of sports offered can cause an inequality in both range and actual numbers of positions available for girls. The school sports program whether informal, intra- or inter-school, should attempt to balance opportunity of both access and diversity. Lunchtime clubs and structured activities for girls have been a successful method adopted by several schools to encourage girls in activity.

— *Grouping*
  This has been a major issue and involves several distinct concerns.

  The notion of single-sex versus co-ed has been well-discussed but a flexible approach seems to cater for a greater variety of needs.

  Two schools that have trialled an approach of co-ed high ability and single-sex boys and single-sex girls and co-ed low ability groupings of Year 9, have shown interesting results.

  In a co-ed situation with students of high or low skill level, the students appear to accept each other and their level of skill very well with few observations of 'put-downs' or girls withdrawing. The single-sex groups however, seem to have suited the average ability students with the girls especially feeling comfortable and motivated in their 'climate' or environment. The provision of a suitable 'climate' can differ according to the nature of the students and/or the activity which should be flexible to allow movement between groups.

— *Structure/Timetable*
In secondary schools the constraints of structure and timetable can often be the most limiting factor for bringing about change. The number of staff programmed at any time, numbers of students, availability of facilities both in and out of school, length of time of lessons, year levels programmed, and what PE is timetabled against, often restricts and prevents certain initiatives being undertaken.

Schools which maintain flexibility or have a high level of support from administration have been able to initiate changes. Grouping is often dependent on the blocking of students and this has enabled not only a variety of groupings, but also a variety of curriculum options.

— *Role Modelling*
This can become a significant issue when looking at the way a PE faculty deploys its staff. If female teachers are continually teaching the stereotypical 'girls' sports and vice-versa for the men, then little is being done to break these barriers. Consideration should be given towards more shared roles.

A number of schools have used the 'Active Women's Kit' resource and have invited female guest speakers to talk to groups of students in order to raise the awareness of females' achievements.

— *Teacher Methodology*
The question of physical education teaching practices has been raised by several teachers and they have attempted to direct 50% of their time to girls, having modified their language and expectations to make them more equitable. Methodology changes seem to relate to the extent of awareness-raising about issues of girls and physical activity and help to moderate past practices.

— *Facilities/Equipment*
This is a very practical issue and one which several schools have undertaken to consider. The question of who has access when, can be easily assessed and more equitable sharing be brought about. The provision of sports uniforms and similar quality of equipment are questions of equity of which schools are increasingly becoming aware.

— *Parent/Community Influence*
One study of why Year 10 girls opted out of the Year 10 PE program indicated the strong influence of parents when making subject choices, with PE being 'unimportant for career' or an 'unnecessary subject'. This further illustrates our professional need to make parents aware of what we do in PE and its related benefits to students.

It is often out of ignorance or past experiences that students and their parents ignore PE as a viable curriculum option and we must address ourselves to this issue especially with the trend to individualised programs and greater diversity of courses in schools.

One unique project in 1985/86 involved 'Special Education' students at

Mitcham Girls' High School. Having run a PE program with more emphasis on individual growth and development, through such activities as aerobics, dance, self-defence, ten pin bowling, trampolining and ball games, a measurable improvement of self-esteem was gained. Using Coopersmith's Self-Esteem Inventory as a pre- and post-test, an average 25 per cent improvement in all categories was recorded!

The teachers involved remarked how significant the improvements were, certainly more so than with any previously conducted program of PE.

— *Conclusions for Secondary Schools*
The concern in secondary schools about disinclination and students opting out of courses has been significant for girls, challenging many of our PE teachers to question why and come to grips with the various needs of our students. This concern has generated much discussion and action research in a number of South Australian Schools, and as a result many projects have been undertaken in an attempt to improve and maintain the participation of girls. We can therefore claim that a number of school-based initiatives have led to real and measurable changes.

There is also a need for further research into the multitude of variables relevant to self-esteem and its relationship to physical activity and into the influence of school 'climate' and environment in relation to the impact it has on girls' achievement and participation.

The Schools Commission report will reinforce many of the school concerns and should stimulate and motivate change in our future practices. It clarifies many of the complex influences that operate on girls, placing the role of the school into perspective and also the responsibilities of those who operate in them.

An example has been set. Changes can occur. Yet it now depends on us as a profession, to implement and to ensure that this trend continues.

Outcomes

Given that: Girls in general have lower self-esteem and more negative self-concept than boys

and: Girls who are involved in physical activity have a higher level of self-esteem than girls who aren't

Then: What is the cost of dropping out?
— Personally
— Physically
— Socially
— Educationally

Schools and teachers that have taken action have clearly demonstrated that the benefits gained from enjoyable participation in physical education classes have had a lasting and significant influence on their students.

Students themselves often reflect a greater satisfaction with classes when consideration is given to their interests, level of and need for positive class 'climate' that has an empathy and understanding for their physical selves in particular.

This process of course has challenged many teachers to question the appropriateness of curriculum, grouping strategies, teaching methodology, their expectations and also their level of awareness of how they can positively support students and prevent them from 'turning off'.

The results have been not only increasing numbers of girls in PE courses and sport, but greater diversity of opportunities from which to choose and also the provision of a forum in which to discuss the issue of body image, self-esteem and confidence and how it influences the image of a girl being physically active.

As students interviewed in the video film **Mirror, Mirror** commented:

> *. . . in trying this sort of thing (rock climbing) and knowing that I've achieved it makes me more confident about trying other harder things.*

and another:

> *. . . the increased self-confidence I feel now has influenced my school work.*

The GPA project in working with numerous schools, at an age range of 5-17, has clearly demonstrated that effective planning and provisions in schools aimed at redressing the disadvantages girls have experienced in physical activity and sport can enhance the satisfaction of girls in activity. However, in considering the barriers, both structural and attitudinal, we must recognise the complexity and interrelationship of messages received from peers, family, significant others, the media and the community in general. Success in helping parents and the broader school community to understand the reasons for our concerns and why changes are being implemented, has been an essential aspect in maintaining initiatives.

Mirror, Mirror has been a valuable catalyst in developing this dialogue and appreciation of issues.

The project has also been well-timed in that Anti Sex Discrimination legislation at Commonwealth, and in some cases, State level has encouraged a broader examination of issues such as participation in sport, resource provisions, access and range of opportunities.

The level of public awareness and debate of the issues have increased markedly during the time in which the GPA project has been implemented. Certainly some of the basic equity issues in sport have become formalised and institutionalised, placing greater demands on school systems to also reflect this change. The future for women and girls in sport, in addition to legislative support, now also has government assistance through the recently released National Policy and Plan for Women in Sport and an implementation focus in the Women's Sport Promotion Unit. [Details of both of these are included in Section Seven of this volume *Ed.*].

These Australian Sports Commission initiatives will continue to highlight the need for equitable practices and provisions for girls and women in sport, including the education sectors.

Let us, however, refocus on the achievements of the GPA project. The successful strategies, teaching resources, research base, state interest groups and teacher commitment and goodwill are all there. The myths are breaking down and now only the hard work remains.

We need to acknowledge the environment in which we are seeking to continue and influence teachers to implement and assess their programs. Teachers remain our **key** agents of change and we need to assess their levels of awareness and indeed their willingness to implement a range of strategies. Teacher training, staff development, in-service programs and indeed time, are all factors that need to be considered. With decreasing system support in terms of advisory staff and professional development funding, these aspects will increasingly be placed at school levels, thus administrative support and understanding will be essential.

Indeed, the place of Physical Education and Sport in the school curriculum is also being rationalised, with many students now being able to opt out or into courses as early as Year 9, and in some cases Year 8. Of those dropping out, the majority are girls and it is causing many schools to assess their programs and adopt many of the GPA initiatives to arrest this decline. What does being 'physically educated' mean if our systems are enabling the very students who may need it, to drop out? We may not get a chance to 'turn on the turned off' girl if they have already dropped out!

Thus the task still remains. We will all need to become advocates for maintaining the GPA initiatives, whether in our own practices or through lobbying and advocating for change with teachers, parents, departments, in either teacher training institutions or schools, and with administrators.

The benefits are only too clear. The increased self-esteem, confidence and personal growth and the opportunity to enjoy an active lifestyle makes the task worthwhile.

Let us reflect in years to come that the Schools Commission money has been well spent!

FROM RESEARCH TO PRACTICE IN JUNIOR SPORT

Jeff Emmel

The weary old professor's tongue
Too serious to fool
Shouted out that liberty
Was just equality in school
Equality, I define that term
As if a wedding vow
Ah! but I was so much older then
I'm younger than that now.
                                    R Zimmerman

The issue of equal opportunity has never been more alive. When applied to children's (pre-adolescent) sport it engenders our acceptance of the fundamental human right of a child to choose what to play and at what level. It also focuses attention on the real meaning of equality in relation to the participation, achievement and in particular, the selection of children into teams. No longer are sports to be promoted as traditionally male or female. No longer will children be denied access to a sport of their choice on the basis of gender.

The legislation

The Commonwealth Sex Discrimination Act, 1984 and the various State Equal Opportunity Acts in relation to children's sport have caused considerable debate in family kitchens, classrooms, the media and in Parliament. The intention of the legislation is clear: to increase choices and participation, and to allow girls and boys the opportunity to play 'non-traditional' sports. The implications of this of course, are that these children may need to be catered for in new ways — in a mixed football team, or an all boys netball team for example. The legislation makes it clear that as needs develop they must be met.

Fundamentally people accept the legislation and support the need for girls to get a better deal regarding skills coaching, encouragement and participation. Unfortunately attempts to implement the law at the school and community level have resulted in anger, frustration and misunderstanding. There is continuing debate concerning the research on which the legislation is based, viz., that prior to puberty there are no significant physiological differences between boys and girls. The major tenor of disagreement is tied to the very practical strategies required to make it work at every level of primary school sport. It is just too different for some, it seems, to have to work toward a longer term goal of social change that truly results in more equitable outcomes for girls and boys. For others it is anathema to their view that all males are more physically adept than females.

Basically children do not care about this and mostly they are not familiar with the research debate. Unfortunately however, they respond to stereotypical behaviours of adults and they are always the ones to suffer when adult expectations are continually applied to their games and pastimes.

The research

Oldenhove in her following paper in this section of this book has summed up the research dilemma perfectly. *The research is not conclusive but most research indicates that there are greater differences within the sexes than there is between the sexes.* She goes on to point out that much of the research reflects performance indicators which must naturally be influenced by previous experiences, opportunities and encouragement. By constructing research which seeks to find differences between boys and girls we are already making gender assumptions rather than researching similarities of boys and girls prior to puberty. This is a sound argument but try explaining it to the Under-10 Rugby League Coach who never questions the traditional practice of boy/girl divisions in children's sport.

It is predominantly at this level of selecting and organising teams that the debate flairs and the higher the standard of involvement the more 'agro' there is likely to be. Much of it unfortunately stems from a decision of the Directors-General of Education May 1986 in response to the Commonwealth Act which set up 'Open' and 'Girls' divisions for the conduct of interstate primary school sport. While the intention was that the 'Girls' event was a special measure to maintain positions for girls who might be disadvantaged in the open division, it has not provided a satisfactory remedy. Rather it has had limiting effect on both boys and girls and the irrational critics have used this as a basis to denigrate the intention of the legislation in its entirety, or to abuse Equal Opportunity Commissioners. The Directors-General must be given credit for trying to apply a practical interpretation of the legislation with good intention. However the Education Department and Sporting Groups in each Australian State have developed their own interpretations and strategies for dealing with the issue. These range from 'no action' in at least one State to a longer term 'let's look at alternatives' approach adopted in South Australia.

Good practice

Despite some highly emotional and hostile press and the political exploitation of the issue by the Opposition Party, there are clear signs in South Australia that the legislation is working for the overwhelming majority of children. To a large extent this is due to the marked impact of the Commonwealth Schools Commission's **Girls and Physical Activity Project**, which mobilised many schools and parents to bring about changes in policy and practices in Physical Education and Sport at the classroom level. It is also due more recently to the wonderful acceptance of the **AUSSIE SPORTS Program** which has widened the base of involvement in a co-educational context for thousands of girls and boys.

Teacher and parent in-service has been a key plank in bringing about change; when this does not occur intensified opposition to the legislation is more prevalent. Change resulting from formal in-service and so forth has been further enhanced by the goodwill and hard work of the hundreds of volunteer parents and teachers who, once familiar with the legislation, see its scope as being creative rather than restrictive, helping them in the practical way they provide sporting opportunities for children. The number of adults, involved themselves in playing mixed sports, continues to grow and is a fine example for children.

The challenge

There is no simple solution to the challenge of bringing about more equitable outcomes for girls and boys in sport. There may be a need to apply a different reasoning when developing strategies for the elite 12-year-old performers for example, in individual events. The special measure strategies applied to some team games eg, hockey, may not be what is required for Australian Rules Football or Softball. The South Australian Primary School Sports Association Interim Policy has addressed these issues in some depth and is trialling a complex of special measures which allow for catch up time and skill improvement for girls.

The strong base of research regarding the participation of boys and girls in sport provides us with indicators about the way children feel about their sporting involvement. Concepts of body image develop at a very early age and strongly influence the activities in which boys and girls participate (Dyer 1986). Clearly girls have not enjoyed the benefits to the same degree as boys because of lower self-esteem and skill levels. The fact remains that sport continues to provide one of the most powerful socialising contexts in which children live. The Equal Opportunity legislation cannot guarantee better outcomes for children — only well intentioned adults who try to see the world through children's eyes can do that.

The day will come when people do not find the notion of mixed sport for young children incomprehensible. The examples of successful practice are becoming more and more evident. While legislation is in force there is an obligation to do something about it. We should look forward to the day when people see the need to do something about it irrespective of the legislation.

CHILDREN'S SPORT: WHERE TO NOW?

Rosemary Crowley

Perhaps the first question to ask is why does a book such as this need to address the topic of children and sport at all? I believe there are three important reasons. First because discrimination against girls begins at a very early age and the use of the Sex Discrimination legislation, so ably discussed by the Commissioner for Equal Opportunity Josephine Tiddy in her paper, has become quite controversial. Second, because any analysis of sport will show the need for a pool of sportspeople from which we can draw our sporting excellence. Third, participation in sport is important because of the very real benefits it brings in terms of recreation, health and fitness, and participation patterns and skills in sport are established at an early age.

Our lives are increasingly compartmentalised. The changing nature of human behaviour and activity in our world means that most of us no longer get physical exercise from our work or in our travel to and from work or school. Much of our lives is sedentary — so too are our children's lives. Many of them now spend their days with computers, in school desks, and watching television.

Evidence from many and varied sources, shows that humans are healthier, feel better and live longer if they are physically active within their individual limitations. Fitness evidence is undeniable. The psychological dimension is more difficult to prove, but there is strong evidence which suggests that participation in sport increases confidence and learning skills, teaches us how to win and how to lose, and to have respect for the opposition.

Playing is a very important part of children's learning. They learn appropriate skills, feelings and responses which prepare them for adulthood. Much of this is learnt on the playing fields and in and around them, especially as they grow older and go to school.

Some of the direct and intended consequences of the recent Anti-Discrimination legislation are described elsewhere in this book. But this legislation has had two significant indirect effects which I want to mention. The first is the increased participation in sport by our girls and the second is the increased debate in the community about girls and boys and their rights in sport — and that in itself has been a very constructive outcome.

If our children are debating these issues in primary school and hearing their parents and friends and teachers on the topic, they are part of the mainstream debate. And our children **are** deeply into it — 'It's not fair?', 'Why should I?', 'Girls are wimps', 'Boys are too pushy?' — these are the sort of comments we commonly hear from them. Adults, on the other hand, are subtler. They say such sensible things as 'We are turning boys into girls and girls into boys.' (Please note my heavy irony here!) In the meantime, there are lots of two-sex netball, cricket, basketball, soccer and touch football teams happily playing matches all over the place. These are in the recreational league, but they reflect a reality that many in the community seem not to have caught up with, ie that men and women, girls and boys are already playing sport together and enjoying it.

However we are beginning to see a change in perception about children and sport. More people do appreciate that sex stereotyping was — and is — no more than habit and/or prejudice, and that one's sex is not a constraint for most sporting activities. One's skills and talents are, but these are very strongly influenced by opportunities, training, equipment and facilities not biology.

Increased participation by girls and boys in sport is happening in South Australia! Along with AUSSIE SPORTS and the emerging private enterprise provisions of sporting and leisure complexes, people participation with minimal fuss is under way. Girls and boys are playing more sports and more often, together.

Is this reflected in our sporting institutions? In our media? I would say largely no; very little change has taken place and we have a long way to go. Our media is very selective in its coverage of sport. It largely covers football, racing and cricket. It covers tennis now and then, golf when Greg Norman is winning and all other sports scramble for 'a place in the sun'. [For detailed information on the extent of this selectivity and sex bias in the coverage of sport see Helen Menzies' paper in this book *Ed*.].

Why do I address the media question? Because it is very important in shaping attitudes, in reflecting our world back to us, in modelling, in representing role models for people, especially for our children. We all know the damaging effects of heroes or models who fail their followers. We also know it is part of growing up to have our heroes mere mortals. This effect is buffered by having models from across the range. Pop stars who live in the fast lane, mainline drugs and destroy themselves are tragic — for themselves and their followers. Sport can and should provide different and powerful models characterised by discipline, skill, grace, hard work and sacrifice. Sports people who use drugs, or chuck their racquets around, or who punch up people and swear can, however, be very disillusioning for our children.

Our children, through sports, see that men don't lose their manhood when they are beaten in competition and women don't lose their womanhood when they achieve excellence. Often though, men do lose their cool. A wonderful example is the Alaska Dog Sled Race: one of the men contestants, having been beaten by a woman, was asked for his response. He replied that if a woman could win it, it wasn't worth entering!

Unfortunately lots of things women achieve get diminished once they have done them. The attitude seems to be that because 'it was a girl, or it was a woman' who did it, the achievement was therefore not worth anything.

As Helen Menzies and others have convincingly shown, our media still represents that attitude. There is not much evidence that our media seek facts and information about the sporting successes of women, and the extent of coverage of women's sport is still far too small.

[It might be offered in partial defence of the media that there has been, until recently, very little serious academic work on women's sport on which journalists might draw for authoritative facts, theoretical frameworks and considered opinions and very few authorities in Australia to whom they might turn for comment. Most of these are contributors to this volume and most of the significant academic sources to women's sport are referred to in the Introduction Section and elsewhere in the book *Ed*.]. We want for our children and sport what is enshrined the Equal Opportunity legislation — a broad range of prospects and choices — for all of them. The legislation is in place and beginning to have effect. More girls are involved in sport, slowly our media changes.

We now have to consolidate the gains and build on the practices and structures already in place. The task ahead is to ensure these gains and opportunities for primary school girls are extended to our girls and women through secondary school and beyond. Further, we must work with the new Women's Sport Promotion Unit to achieve adequate funding for coaching, training facilities and equipment so that women's sport is properly resourced.

Finally, we must never cease to urge our media to reflect the great achievements of our girls and women in sport.

Our children can ask that of us — we have a watching brief for their future.

THE COMMONWEALTH SEX DISCRIMINATION ACT (1984) AND CHILDREN'S SPORT: POLICY IMPLICATIONS

Henny Oldenhove

Introduction

The reorganisation of children's sporting activities in Australia as a result of the Commonwealth Sex Discrimination Act 1984, and various state Equal Opportunity Acts, has in recent years caused considerable public debate.

The Commonwealth Act states in relation to sport,

(1) Nothing in Division 1 or 2 renders it unlawful to exclude persons of one sex from participation in any competitive sporting activity in which the strength, stamina or physique of competitors is relevant.

(2) Sub-section (1) does not apply in relation to the exclusion of persons from participation in *inter alia*
— (e) sporting activities by children who have not yet attained the age of 12 years.

States which have their own Equal Opportunity Legislation, (South Australia, West Australia, Victoria and New South Wales) do not indicate a particular age for children's participation in sport, thus in their 'silence' the Commonwealth Act is the prevailing Act. The Territories are under the Commonwealth legislation. Understanding and administering these laws is a complex matter, because although they frequently mirror each other, they sometimes do not.

Sex Discrimination legislation is complaints based: that is any individual who feels that they have been discriminated against can lodge a complaint. This complaint is investigated and a process of conciliation is then initiated. Should the conciliation fail, the case is then heard by a Tribunal and action recommended. The majority of complaints are usually resolved during conciliation.

The age of 12 referred to in the Commonwealth Act should be considered as arbitrary, but the intent of the law that there will be equality for children in sport is clear. Some states are applying the legislation to all children in primary school in order that the transition to high school be a logical, practical and viable one.

Additionally, it should be noted that it is unlawful to exclude people on the basis of their sex from sports coaching, umpiring, refereeing or administration. This is clearly important for children's sport since the filling of such roles by women and girls as well as by men and boys emphasises that sport in all its aspects 'belongs' to females as much as to males.

The research dilemma

The legislation is based on the results of much research which indicates that prior to the onset of puberty, there are no significant physiological differences between boys and girls. This research is not conclusive, some differences in physiology and performance can always be found if looked for hard enough, but most research indicates that there are greater differences within the sexes than there are between the sexes. Much of the research also reflects performance indicators which must naturally be strongly influenced by previous experience, opportunities and encouragement. By undertaking research which seeks to find differences between girls and boys, we are already making gender assumptions rather than concentrating on the similarities of boys and girls prior to puberty. The onset of puberty is not always easily identified and can cause concern for elite performers around the age of 12 who may already have gone through the early stages of puberty and may differ markedly from their peers both in physique and performance.

The background argument is that a better way of categorising children's participation should be developed to promote involvement according to ability, regardless of gender as a division. This is a long term objective and in the short term we know and must accept that a significant number of girls will miss out, not because they **are** female but often because of our expectations and their experiences of **being** female. Thus a more sensitive gradual development must occur especially in addressing the previous experiences that children bring to sport. Adrianne Blue in her recent book **Faster, Higher, Further** writes of Dawn Fraser

> In club races, she was often pitted against boys and given a second start because of her sex. 'I was beating them fairly regularly when I was twelve . . . I hated the easy assumption that girls had to be slower than boys.'

This sort of situation demonstrates the weakness in maintaining traditional boy/girl divisions: we build in different expectations based purely on visible and assumed physical differences that may have no bearing on physical performances. Children, especially at this age, differ markedly in height, weight, strength and other physical characteristics, and certainly not in a way that results in all boys being superior in these aspects to all girls! To say that we maintain sex divisions because it has always been this way is not a valid argument; it is merely a reflection of and a reinforcement of our stereotypical attitudes.

It is unlikely that research alone can provide useful and practical solutions to issues of equity and equality of treatment in children's sport. Rather our focus should be on recognising that there are substantial individual differences among children, irrespective of gender, and providing viable solutions that take every individual's ability into account.

Implementation

In May 1986, a meeting of the Directors-General of Education, made a decision regarding the organisation of children's sport as a response to the Commonwealth Act. The result was that instead of having 'boys' and 'girls' events, as had been the tradition, the events were now to be organised as 'open' and 'girls'. The recognition of the need for 'girls' events was as a special measure so as to maintain positions for girls who might initially be disadvantaged in the 'open' category.

In reality, this meant that girls could qualify to participate in the 'open' events but boys could not enter the 'girls' events. Needless to say, this was the basis for a significant media response and outcry.

'Open' and 'girls' is obviously not an adequate solution for all situations. By just one girl participating in the open event on merit, a boy will lose an opportunity and does not have another place to go. This was not the intention of the Directors-General decision, but it is a practical interpretation that is, in reality, limiting.

The Commonwealth Act does not direct or interpret the methods for implementing changes and the States have been left to devise their own strategies. These unfortunately, have been somewhat different and possibly conflicting. This lack of overall co-ordination is causing continued confusion and unrest. The direction and interpretation that various Directors-General took back to their States resulted in different approaches being adopted.

In NSW, the then Director-General implemented this one strategy approach almost immediately, with little consultation or inservicing of the school sport structure. The process of selection for the Pacific School Games held in that state in which some of our most elite talented children competed, made this situation much more acute. The organisers of that event should have sought an exemption from the Commonwealth Act in the early planning stages and would have most likely been successful. This would have allowed a gradual change at school levels to proceed without the whole process being jeopardised as it now is.

The NSW experience presents a far too 'black and white' situation. A one strategy approach is not totally appropriate, but no other avenues have been explored. To resort back to our traditional approach is no longer acceptable as already the positive benefits of change are occurring at least at the mass participation level of the school.

The multi-strategy approach in South Australia also has its teething problems but is a more rational approach. The South Australian model was based on a multi-strategy approach that was to be implemented gradually over a period of time. Lengthy discussion, debate and consultation took place resulting in an Interim Policy that would be in place for 3-5 years with constant monitoring. In conjunction with this policy development, considerable time was devoted to in-servicing the policy directions with school and community groups.

Some of the strategies included:
— holding open events, but rewarding first 3 boy and girl place getters
— having a quota system with divisions 1 and 2 and then reducing the number in the divisions annually eg 6 girls tennis, 6 boys tennis, moving towards a team ranked 1-12 based on ability
— a process of gradual implementation at specific year and age levels
— a process of gradual implementation at different SAPSASA levels (schools, district, interstate and intrastate)
— holding special measure expos and lightning carnivals.

Some States chose to 'wait and see' what the developments would bring and have yet to implement any strategies.

At a national level, the lack of a considered and consistent approach has caused great confusion, uncertainty and anger, especially at National Primary School Championships. Because of this confusion, concern has been understandable. But it also highlights and gives every opportunity for those who wish to do so, to reinforce our very traditional view of children's participation in sport.

Community impact

The legislation has not yet had an effect on clubs and associations to the same extent that it has on education authorities, although the legislation is equally applicable to both. Many clubs are open to the participation of girls in their traditional boys teams but, generally speaking, the move of boys into traditional girls teams has not occurred to the same extent. It is not unusual to see boys and girls co-compete in such games as hockey, T-ball, mini-basketball etc.

As the Acts are complaints-based legislation, many clubs and associations are not confronted with the need to make changes unless one of their participants lodges a complaint. As a result of this process of conciliation, changes may be required, but the acceptance by all children of changes to their sport is often a result of goodwill and commonsense.

It is also quite ironic that there is an increasing number of adults playing in mixed competitions, albeit for predominantly social reasons, yet we find it difficult to accept the same thing for our young children, where physical characteristics are less clearly developed.

Conclusion

There are as yet no clear or definitive answers to this issue; the air has not yet been 'cleared' for the situation to be appraised more rationally. In some team games, the solution is fairly straightforward as children's skills are developed in parallel and children often play in teams according to skill and ability eg hockey, basketball, volleyball etc. Other sports, traditionally recognised as male or female, such as football codes, cricket or netball, will naturally take longer to become integrated due to the different skill exposure girls and boys have had to these games. Individual sports such as athletics and swimming highlight the issue to a more acute degree, because there is often detailed evidence of previous performance results to substantiate arguments in favour of continued segregation. However, achievements of boys and girls are becoming increasingly more similar. Such achievements serve as excellent examples of what is possible; they can no longer be dismissed as 'freakish' or 'tomboyish'. For us to explore what our children can achieve and what they can be, we no longer need to promote an arbitrary division based on physical appearance and gender.

The Acts are 'enabling' legislation that encourage positive change and open doors that have previously been closed. Although change can often be threatening, the increasing number of case studies which describe good practice will benefit other schools, clubs and organisations by showing how it can be done.

In condemning the Acts in such a short period of time, as many people have done, gradual changes of attitude and behaviour have had little chance to develop. Legislation can change behaviour which may lead to a gradual change of attitude. The first step is the hardest one!

Recommendations

In order to provide and promote for our children a quality and enjoyable sporting experience, there is a need for agencies providing sport to formulate a co-operative and co-ordinated approach to implementation of the Commonwealth Sex Discrimination Act, which will ultimately benefit all children. To achieve this the following recommendations are made.

— There should be liaison between the Human Rights Commission, State Commissions and other agencies to explore a multi-strategy approach to bring about a gradual and sensitive change to the participation of children in sport.

— Education authorities should promote sporting opportunities and access for all primary school children through their school physical education and sport curriculums, and they should adopt special measure programs where necessary.

— The Australian School Sports Council should develop a nationally agreed upon plan for primary school sport at state and national levels of competitions.

— State Departments of Sport and Recreation, National and State sporting organisations must understand current legislation and the rights this legislation gives them and the responsibilities it imposes.

— A national awareness and education campaign should be mounted to explain the purpose, intent and strategies of the Act. This should be modelled on the campaign run in South Australia based on the publication 'Child's Play — Sport and Equality', written by Helen Menzies for the Equal Opportunity Commission in that State.

[The papers in Section Two include one by the Commissioner for Equal Opportunity in South Australia and one by Ken Dyer, analysing the possible interpretations and means of implementation of the Commonwealth Act *Ed.*].

THE ROLE OF SPORT IN EDUCATION AND GOVERNMENT IN WEST GERMANY

Ilse Bechtold

Introduction

Instruction in sport and physical education in schools and universities falls within the jurisdiction of the States within the Federation of West Germany. The Permanent Conference of the Ministers of Education provides guidelines and co-ordinates curricula.

Schools in Germany are structured in the following way:

— primary level (6-10 years)
— secondary level I (11-16 years)
— secondary II level (16 and older)

In general, three hours of physical education per week are scheduled for all grades. There are additional opportunities to join non-compulsory school physical activities and take advantage of the well-developed system of Sport Clubs.

The State Ministries of Education agreed in 1972 that sport can be selected as an area of specialisation in grades 11-13, with 6-8 hours per week. This includes also theory of sport and is part of the written examination for the national advanced general certificate of education (Abitur). This demonstrates the trend to greater intellectualisation of sport instruction which can be observed in all German schools — as well as the tendency to introduce co-education for all age groups.

The educational principles of school sport in the Federal Republic are probably not so very different from those of other countries. Let me nevertheless present a few of the fundamental features of our thinking.

Sport in its many and varied forms is recognised as an important sphere in social and cultural life. Those who engage in sport can enrich their life, foster health and well-being, experience more fully their environment and their own body, build up self-confidence as a result of the experience of success, increase social contacts and develop social patterns of behaviour.

In and through sport, individual potentialities and limitations can be experienced in action as a result of exercise and training. And it is precisely to the development of children and young people that these experiences in the spheres already mentioned, and in many others besides, contribute in a wide variety of ways.

But since sport can offer very many more possibilities for people of every age, the school is able to cover only a part of them, although undoubtedly a very important part. So in the sports instruction that pupils are given in school, they ought also to learn how to make good use of the possibilities and chances that sport offers outside school. They should be made receptive to the ideal of a healthy athletic way of life. They should be given access to branches of sport that particularly appeal to them and which can become a lifetime interest, and with or without membership of a club, they can take that sport with them as an accepted component of their pattern of living, that will accompany them into and enrich their adult life.

The aims of school sport in West Germany

I set out in this section some of the aims of school sport in the Federal Republic of Germany. There are, of course, differences between the various states since the states have considerable constitutional independence in educational and cultural matters.

Athletic Performances and Self-Confidence
Sport ought to offer all pupils a wide range of possibilities, appropriate to their individual abilities, for achieving and improving their performance. Sport should also guide them to an understanding of the criteria by which sport is assessed.

Health Way of Life and Preventative Training
By regular training, sport should promote the health of all pupils, particularly of those pupils who have faulty posture or circulatory insufficiency. It should develop knowledge of and insight into the sphere of sport, and create habits of sport. It should foster a health life style.

Fitness to Play and Awareness of Rules
School sport should develop the ability to take an active part in athletic games governed by rules. It should encourage awareness of rules and teach specific role behaviour, even in situations of conflict.

Material and Physical Experience Through Movement
School sport should provide a wide range of material experience (equipment, music, environment, snow, ice, water) and physical experience (motor experience). Particular experiences that are generally inaccessible to the pupils outside school.

Self-Organisation of Athletic Situations
In school sport, the pupils should learn to organise the basic conditions and the actual running of training and competition situations and to take responsibility for them. They should learn that the given branches of sport are capable of being changed, and also how to organise these in accordance with their own expectations.

Attitude to Sport Outside School
School sport should provide an incentive to motivate the pupils to take part in athletic activity with young people of their own age in their free time, and should be the basis of a lifetime participation in some branch of sport.

Satisfaction of the natural urge for movement

School sport should be a compensation for the necessity for remaining seated during instruction, and should provide an opportunity to satisfy the natural urge for movement in young people.

These broad aims are to be realised within three broad learning target areas: a motor learning target area, a cognitive learning target area and a social affective learning target area.

The Motor Learning Target Area
There are many reasons for ensuring that opportunities for acquiring motor qualifications exist. These include:

— the progressive reduction of possibilities for motor development that result from the processes of mechanisation and urbanisation in our society can be responsible for a range of illnesses caused by inadequate bodily movement and exercise

— the right to the pleasure of movement, activity and the enjoyment obtained through sport can be fulfilled

— it is precisely at this age that the potential for developing motor activity is optimal

— a good level of motor ability has high recreational value and so makes a positive contribution to life.

A distinction is often made between a motor minimum capability and a motor optimum capability. The minimum capability is the obligatory teaching target and the optimal capability is an optional target.

In work spheres three distinct components can be distinguished.

— The motor level of characteristic behaviours.
— The motor level of skill.
— The tactical level of action.

The notional target for the minimum level of motor characteristics is that degree of capacity that enables the subject to live without any heightened risk of, for example, those illnesses that are caused by lack of movement, in other words, a good standard of motor fitness.

A minimum level of skill at the tactical level of action should make it possible to carry out motor tasks in constant and variable situations. The motor optimal level should guarantee a higher state of training and is strongly dependent upon the individual interests and needs as well as on the capacity of the pupils.

The Cognitive Target Learning Area
Cognitive elements are an important part of motor performances. Importance should be attached to the principles of consciousness, of knowledge and effect. There should be encouragement for critical observation and reflection and spectator support should be given to sport in school and in leisure time.

In the cognitive target learning area, reproductive goals such as knowledge and use of principles of training, training programs, effects of training, rules, safety regulations, etc. should be pursued.

The productive goals to be realised are, for example, the development of the concept of movements through courses of movement, the development of tactical levels of action, critical detachment from criteria of assessment for motor activities (orientation by individual or social criteria).

The Social/Affective Learning Target Area

Affective (emotional) states can be affected by motor activities and vice versa. The targets to be aimed at in this area include the following: the development of a stable interest (also extending outside school) in athletic activities by positive, conscious experience; the reduction of tension by motor activity; the acquisition of sports-specific role behaviour; co-operation and fairness in dealing with others; the ability to resolve conflict situations; getting on with fringe groups; and, the acceptance of the rules of the referee, and fellow competitors.

[In this context the papers by Doris Heritage Brown and Gaylene Clews in Section 8 of this volume are highly significant. They highlight the importance of the outcomes of early preparation in the affective domain for the self-esteem and successes of athletes later in life *Ed.*].

Application to track and field athletics

I will now indicate how the above concepts are actually translated into practice so far as Track and Field Athletics is concerned in West Germany.

In accordance with the curriculum laid down for sports instruction, training in track and field athletics takes place in three training stages. In them, the pupils acquire abilities, both in the motor and non-motor teaching target sphere, which make it possible for them to have access to the particular branch of sport in which they are primarily interested and, if it is their inclination to do so, for them also to be able to take part in athletic activity outside the school.

In the presentation of the motor learning targets, it should be noted that the sequence used implies no priority or order or rank. The contents are to be looked at as being in the nature of a selection of the most important elements and not as a methodical series. As the yardstick for the assessment of the acquisition of skill and co-ordinated motor increments, the criteria of technique at the 'refined' level of performance is used. The guiding values for assessment of the motor achievements are selected in such a way that they can be achieved by 75 per cent of the pupils. This choice has been arrived at entirely on pragmatic grounds. Because we favour a constant revision of the syllabus, it is desirable that these values should constantly be checked and supplemented by the teacher.

The three stages of training for motor-learning have the following features.

Training stage I

In contrast to the usual idea of basic directives, the learning targets are classified according to class-stages. This classification should show the teacher how far the targets of training stage 1 can be achieved in the individual classes, particularly at the primary stage.

The learning targets in the sphere of skill are equally valid for boys and girls. Differentiation occurs from class 5 onwards only in the sphere of quality, to take into account the differences that occur at this stage in sexual development.The content of teaching given here should be offered with an eye to its use as leisure activity, and in the form of play, bearing in mind the child's natural urge for movement.

Training stage II

In training stage II, on the one hand the level of skill of stage I is developed to reach the 'refined' form, and on the other hand, it is extended by the introduction of new disciplines and techniques (Triple Jump, Javelin and Discus, the 'soaring' technique and the running technique in Long Jump). In these skills, the aim is to acquire the basic 'rough' form. The characteristics level is adapted to the state of skill. With the exception of the Pole Vault and the Triple Jump, teaching targets are the same for both boys and girls. In the sphere of characteristics, sex-specific differentiation is retained.

In the optional sphere (non-compulsory participation and performance groups) the specialisation that has begun in the compulsory instruction is intensified and the individual talents of the pupils for particular disciplines of athletics are taken into account. Over and above that, it is important that those disciplines should be offered which, because of the specific conditions that exist, cannot be offered or can only partially be covered in the compulsory instruction. This applies particularly to the disciplines of Pole Vault, Discus and Javelin.

General motor capability is developed in the optional branch of sport of athletics, as a compensatory activity (eg through ball games, gymnastics etc).

Training stage III
Instruction in stage III develops the level of skill, quality and tactical action to the sports-motor performance under competition conditions. Here the tactical level of action in track and field athletics is important only in so far as in competition the athlete's own capacity is placed in relation to the competitive situation (eg the distribution of the distances in running, the selection of starting heights and observation of the multiple-try rule in High Jump and Pole Vault).

Taking into account and fully integrating the knowledge they have acquired in the non-motor teaching sphere, the pupils should now be in a position to work independently in class.

As in training stage II, the general motor capability is further developed. In achieving the learning targets — particularly in the level of skill — attention is to be given to the provision of exercise in the optional sphere.

Learning targets in the cognitive/affective domain are similarly organised into three stages.

Stage I	Stage II	Stage III
Ability to participate individually and in groups to organise instruction (eg independent warm-up, setting up and clearing away equipment)	Ability to work individually and in groups in accordance with a given program of exercises	Ability to work individually and in groups to a self-arranged program of exercises
Knowledge of competition rules and safety regulations for the disciplines of Stage I and ability to comply	Knowledge of competition rules and safety regulations for the disciplines of Stage II, and ability to comply with them	Act as referee in class and school competitions
Ability to make proper use of the exercises and equipment	Familiarity with technical terms for athletic actions and exercises	Familiarity with phase structure of movements and ability to describe their significance
Ability to make correct assessment of own capacity to perform motor tasks (eg covering set distances in endurance running at a uniform pace	Ability to make correct assessment of own capacity in competition (eg to time the different sections in medium and long distance races)	To adapt to competition situations (eg choice of starting heights for High Jump and Pole Vault, use of multiple try rule, sensible warm-up before competition)

Stage I	Stage II	Stage III
Ability to state the main effects of endurance training on the circulatory system	Ability to state the effects of the Endurance Interval and Repetition forms of training on the human body	Ability to set up independent program of exercises giving attention to the effects of specific forms of training
	Familiarity with the practice forms of running, jumping and throwing as forms of leisure and as ways of promoting health	Ability to set up criteria of assessment for individual athletic disciplines from aspect of health promotion
		Testing self in the role of individual and team person knowing the behaviour patterns required and examining their social function.

Higher education and the administration of sport

In the Federal Republic of Germany, Sport Science is an interdisciplinary science. It investigates the phenomenon of Sport and makes use of both pure and social scientific methods. The orientation of this science has a dual relationship to practice; the sources of sport scientific problems are located in the practical work and the scientific findings have to meet the requirements of the practice.

So a general consensus has been reached that the future development of sport depends to a great extent on the quality of scientific research. During recent years, therefore, structural, personal and material changes have been initiated and executed at Universities and other institutions of higher education. As one consequence it is now possible to obtain a doctorate (promotion) as well as a tenure (habilitation) in sport science disciplines at many Sport Science Institutes or Universities.

The Federal Institute for Sport Science was founded 1970. It is a federal institution dependent on the Ministry of the Interior. It works closely together with the Sport Federations and the Scientific Institutions and with those public facilities and authorities which are involved in Sport and its promotion. The work priorities include the following:

— Promoting scientific research in Sport, particularly in the areas of medicine-pedagogy-psychology-sociology as well as coaching, movement theory, by planning, co-ordinating and financially supporting research projects and the application of research results.

— Counselling the Federal Government scientifically in technical sport co-operation projects in developing countries.

— Co-operating in the planning, improvement and maintenance of federal owned central sport facilities. Helping with concepts for the construction of modern sport installations. Initiating, co-ordinating and promoting relevant research programs, as well as evaluating research results and practical findings.

— Operating a national Centre for documentation and information of sport.

Thus the Federal Institute for Sport Science has a predominantly supportive role and attempts to co-ordinate research programs both nationally and internationally. This involves inititiating and conducting conferences and meetings of working parties and specialist groups and assisting in the organisation of national and international congresses.

Just as one example, the Federal Institute for Sport Science, together with the IAAF and the German Athletic Federation, organised and ran the 1983 Congress on Women's Athletics in Mainz. The 1987 Congress on Junior Athletics was also to a great extent financially and with manpower supported by the Federal Institute.

Another example of the very good support for overcoming some of the short-comings in women's athletics in West Germany, is that the Federal Institute, at the request of and with assistance of the German Athletic Federation, help with finance and manpower for several research projects such as those on anorexia nervosa, gynaecological problems, strength training and others. The Federal Institute for Sport publishes regular achievement reports at two-year intervals, an information pamphlet. Important research results are published in the **Monographic Series of the Institute** as well as in the journal **Sport Science**.

The German Association for Sport Science represents the union of Professors and other academic staff within the various sport science university institutes. The aim is to promote the development of sport science and its prime objectives are to:

— stimulate and support sport science research. initiate and organise scientific co-operation between diverse sport science disciplines

— make pronouncements on issues of training and teaching of sport science

— support the structural development of sport science institutions

— promoting junior staff in sport science

— further a scientifically adequate and efficient staff structure within sport science institutes

— represent issues of sport science both nationally and internationally.

This Association is fulfilling its tasks through sections such as: History of Sport, Sport Sociology, Motor Learning and Training as well as through temporary committees. The Association arranges regular sport science conventions dealing primarily with general issues of sport science.

Sports in Institutions of higher learning is organised and promoted both for recreation and through intercollegiate athletics. It is available for all student and Staff members and it is generally without athletic requirement. The General German University Sport Association is an associate member of the German Sports Federation and a member of FISU, the International Federation of College-level Sport.

There is an Association of Physical Education Teachers which is characterised by a wide range of occupational pursuits and demands. It is not surprising that in addition to academic training programs at university level, there are many non-academic courses available for sport teachers, coaches, instructors and youth leaders in public institutes, private schools and the Coaches Academy, all offering officially recognised qualifications. Also, the national Federations provide courses as well as the State Sport Confederations, all leading to a licence to practice as an instructor, coach or specialist teacher.

The Committee of German Physical Education Teachers (ADL) was founded in 1953 as the governing organisation for all categories (5) of sports teachers and scientists. One of its prime objectives today is to ensure the continuation of the traditional Conferences, which deal with basic issues and problems in the field of physical education. This organisation is also responsible for the series **Contri-**

bution to Teaching and Research in Sport; Texts, Sources and Documents in Sport Science and **Sports Science**. The aims of the German Association of Physical Education Teachers (DSLV) are mainly the further education of teachers and dissemination of information about new trends in physical education. It includes such professional societies as those of fencing instructors, soccer coaches, golf instructors, ski, dancing, tennis and diving instructors. They have a monthly journal called **Sportlesson**.

The Sport-Clubs and Federations in the Federal Republic of Germany act as autonomous units. Governmental support is aimed at furthering self-reliance of the autonomous system, and is of subsidiary function. In accordance to the federal structure of the West German Republic, the Federal Government, the States (Provinces) and the Communities are the primary agents of public sports administration.

The Federal Government is, in regard to Sport, chiefly responsible for those tasks which are of central importance for Germany and which cannot be accomplished simply by any of the eleven states. It must be seen in connection with the representation of the nation in sport, especially in the field of top level competition.

There are eleven departments dealing with issues of sport within the Federal Government. They are co-ordinated by the Minister of Interior who is also responsible for top-level sport, sport for disabled and international sport policies. A central aspect of the promotion of the top-level competitive sport is the support offered to the national Federations such as advancement of training and competitive programs, salaries for full-time Managers, national and honorary coaches and for health-care programs for athletes.

The German Sport Confederation receives project funds for fundamental measures such as coaching seminars or biomechanical investigations. The National Olympic Committee receives federal support for sending teams to represent the FRG at the Olympic Games. The Federal Government also offers support for building sport facilities, mainly for permanent training centres and Olympic training centres, for recreational sport programs and sport facilities for institutions of higher learning.

In addition to this, the Minister for Youth, Family, Women and Health supports youth activities in sport and the Minister for Labour and Social Order offers help for disabled people. An important area of public sponsorship is the field of technical co-operation in sport for developing countries. This is carried out by the Ministry of foreign affairs in co-operation with the Minister for Economic Co-operation.

As mentioned earlier the Minister of the Interior is responsible for top level sport and its necessities in all respects, so, in conjunction with the German Sports Federation and the Olympic Committee, the above-mentioned Ministries have formed an Interministerial Committee to co-ordinate all programs.The German Parliament has its own sport committee, in which representatives from the major political parties are involved in important political questions related to Sport. Also the political parties each have a sport committee and issue a policy on sport.

The German Sport Conference was established in 1970 and comprises twelve members from the private sector of Sport and twelve members of the public sector. It is an instrument of co-operation for governmental bodies, political parties with sport and so helps to develop and promote sport activities at all levels.

In accordance with the constitution of the FRG many aspects of sport are the sole responsibility of the States. One of their important aims is to promote recreational sport within and outside the sport federations. Sports facilities at community and club levels are also a responsibility. The States provide financial support, offer services in planning and construction of these facilities. They construct and maintain regional training centres and sport schools, as well as subsidising payment of instructors and administrators.

Each State has within its Ministry of Education a 'State Director for Sport in Schools' They are responsible for advising on all questions related to school sports, physical education curriculum, standards for examinations, experimental models and with questions on training and tests in sport.

There is also one person, in most cases in the Ministry of Social Affairs, who assists community bodies and sport federations at State level with financial or other supportive measures in areas of such as the planning of sport facilities, support for top events, training, youth work, continuing education, medical assistance and so on.

The support of sport by the districts and local communities is mainly directed towards 'Sport for All' and recreational sport. They are responsible for local sport and recreational facilities, youth centres, supporting the sport clubs, building and maintaining swimming pools and so on. There is also a sports administrative office and a responsible person in each local community.

The private sector

The German Sports Federation was founded in 1950. It acts as an umbrella organisation for the free sports movements in West Germany. At the moment it comprises the membership of 11 regional (State) Confederations (including West Berlin) and more than 50 national Sport Federations. Under this umbrella also belong 6 Associations for Science and Education and 11 special sport federations such as University sport. Altogether in West Germany there are approximately 20 million members in about 60,000 Sports Clubs out of a total population of approximately 60 million. The various Sports Federations, such as swimming, soccer, athletics and others which were either founded or re-established after 1949, are responsible for their rules and regulations. They represent the discipline internationally, organise their championships and meetings, are responsible for forming their top athletes, choose the teams for international meetings and so on. The individual Federations have national training centres and national Coaches hired by the German Sports Federation.

Parallel to the division of German sport into individual sport federations by discipline, there is the division into State sport Confederations in which all sports clubs of the State are organised, regardless of the discipline. The main tasks of these organisations are representing the interest of the clubs at State level, promoting the training, financial support for coaches etc. building sport facilities, carrying out cultural programs, medical care and providing insurance.

Membership of the German Sports Federation has increased at the rate of about 8 per cent annually since 1960. Women and older men are over-represented among new members; they are attracted, apparently, by jogging and other physical fitness programs.

The National Olympic Committee, re-founded 1949, is an independent, autonomous and private organisation. It carries out the functions entrusted to it by the IOC, especially nominating and sending the West German participants to the Olympic Games. Alongside this is the German Olympic Society which was formed in 1951 as a non-profit organisation whose objectives are to offer support to Sport in FRG and to promote and further the Olympic Idea.

The German Sport Aid Foundation, founded in 1967 by the German Sports Federation and the German Olympic Society, acts to provide moral and material support to athletes in recompense for the services they render to society. Up to now approximately 2800 top-level athletes, classified in three performance groups, have been provided with financial or other forms of support. The Foundation relies upon individual and corporate donations, advertising profits, funds raised through the sale of special postage stamps etc.

The Coaches Academy is responsible for qualifying coaches in the area of competitive sport. It serves as a professional academy to the German Sports Federation and is administered by a Board of Trustees, which co-operates with the Ministry of Education of the State of Northrhein-Westfalia, for the execution of the training programs.

YOUNG PEOPLE AND ATHLETICS IN THE GDR

Klaus Schonberger

Athletics in the GDR have continuously advanced since the country's access to the international sports arena. Year after year GDR athletes win first places and medals in the most important international championships. Around the world people speak of the 'secret' of GDR sport and especially of athletics.

The basis of these successes is a well-planned development of sports. This is supported in every respect by the state, which is very favourably disposed to the mass character of sport and, above all, to the promotion of children and youth sports. The XI Congress of the Socialist Unity Party of Germany, held recently, once again stressed the desire to develop sports as a part of the daily life of an increasing number of people and especially of young people. In Directives issued by this Party Congress, the development of sports was specified as Party program and, thus, as state program: *In promoting physical culture and sport, emphasis must be placed on both the mass character of such activities and on the need to increase performance levels . . . Consistent promotion of competitive sports and young athletes, the systematic development of sport-related sciences and medical research, and the lasting improvement of the facilities and equipment for training and competitions will prove increasingly effective in stimulating athletes to top performances and medal-winning participation in the Olympic Games, World and European Championships and other international meets. It is necessary here to make comprehensive use of the results of science and technology.*

A short extract of the Youth Law of the GDR (1974) shows that these are not new demands and statements, but that they have been prescribed in the law of the Republic for many years. Article 34 of the Youth Law reads: *Physical culture and sport belong to the life of youth in the socialist society. Regular participation in sports is a need and a task of all young people to develop their personality. The socialist state guarantees physical culture and sport in all fields of life and promotes the activities of the German Sports and Gymnastics Union as the initiator and organiser of sports.*

The German Athletics Association (DVfL) of the GDR as one of the biggest GDR sports associations, harmoniously integrates itself into this development process.

According to the membership figures, the DVfL of the GDR is placed fourth in the country. At present, there are 189,479 members in the athletics association. It is an important fact that 80.8 per cent of the members of the DVfL of the GDR are children and young people. One can say with certainty, it is the association paying greatest attention to the development of athletics for children and young people. The following figures illustrate the structure of the DVfL of the GDR:

1,625	members under 6 years	=	0.9%
94,302	members of 6-14 years	=	52.8%
30,654	members of 14-16 years	=	17.1%
17,838	members of 16-18 years	=	10.1%
34,445	members over 18 years	=	19.2%

Additionally, there are 10,611 athletes active in two sport associations.

The interest taken in athletics as well as the successes of top-level athletes of our association in international sports events have considerably and continuously contributed to an increasing number of young members as is shown in the following figures:

Year	Children	Young people
1957	9,147	19,584
1970	61,490	29,492
1975	85,076	41,529
1980	92,759	45,028
1985	95,927	48,492

But a large number of participants is only one side of the medal. The association would remain unsuccessful without management structures, or people to set the whole complex of children and youth sports in motion. For this reason, the DVfL of the GDR is interested in a strict management system guaranteeing permanent all year round sports exercises, training and competitions.

The central management, the Presidium of the association, co-ordinates all questions and tasks with the 15 county athletics boards and the 260 district athletics boards. In approximately 2,800 athletics sections, which are the smallest units of the association's structure, countless voluntary helpers, instructors and officials put the programs of the association into practice.

The Athletics Association of the GDR takes pride in its members who enthusiastically devote their spare time to sports. Above all, they educate our children and young people to become fighters and engaged young personalities who, in addition to sports, stand the test in daily life too. In interviews, most of our successful athletes mention as the cradle of their success their instructor and their sports section where they made their first steps in athletics. The 16,638 instructors of the association have created through their dedicated efforts the basis of the association's cadres and performance pyramid and have laid down the foundation-stone of many successes. It should be noted here that the ratio of instructors to athletes is 1 to 10. The fact that most instructors are awarded with honours of the association or with the title 'Meritorious Instructor of the DTSB of the GDR' shows that their work is highly appreciated. Their activities are respected and recognised in their working collectives and in local press media.

Understanding the popular basis of our association as well as its structure, without which any development would be impossible, the question remains how the talents are selected from the circle of the 80.8 per cent of members? How are they promoted and coached to become top-level athletes?

It is not possible to answer these questions comprehensively. For this purpose a more differentiated and detailed analysis and explanation would be required. Essentially, however, it starts with a quite simple but systematic and continuously practised system of screening and selection of talented children. In our country children start school at the age of 6 or 7 years. It is almost unnecessary to mention that the sports lessons are conducted with great attention from the very first school day. On the basis of proved teaching programs much importance is attached to the training in the various track and field disciplines. At the same time the children begin to take part in sport outside of their school lessons in the school sports clubs or sections of the GDR sports organisation DTSB, in which qualified sports teachers and instructors work with the young people. It is only logical that the co-operation between the sports teachers and the various sections of different sports clubs guarantees the successful screening of talents. They, above all, have the opportunity to find new talents among the children as well as to test their prospective aptitude for a sport. A carefully established and organised competition system aimed at these age-groups enables the instructors to find their young talents who meet the demands of the respective sport.

In this connection, the Spartakiad Games seem to be a magic word. Beginning with manifold school competitions in track and field, a pre-selection for future competitions is made. In regional competitions (eg several schools of a GDR district) an ongoing selection of athletes takes place and the winners of these competitions qualify for participation in District Children and Youth Spartakiad Games held at the end of each school year in early June. These competitions have become more and more the source of talents for athletics. From these competitions the talented children qualify for the next higher form of Spartakiad competitions — the County Spartakiad Games. In these meetings of the best young athletes of approximately 10-20 districts, participants have to show a very high ability level and the 'mesh of the sieve' becomes more narrow. Finally, the central competitions of the GDR Spartakiad Games take place in Berlin or Leipzig every two years. There, usually, nearly 2,000 athletes in the age-group 13, 14, 15 and 16/17 years compete in track and field for medals and points on behalf of their counties, districts, sports clubs and sections. One need not underline that following the above mentioned qualification system, this competition is the biggest objective of every young athlete. There are only a few top-level athletes in the GDR who did not follow the Spartakiad path. Heike Drechsler, Ulf Timmermann, Marlies Gohr, Marita Koch etc. — can all be found in the official protocols of these competitions, not always as winners but at least as participants. It is only too correct if we use in our association the slogan 'Spartakiad Games the jumping-off place to Olympics'!

Analogous to the Spartakiad system there is a championship system of the association starting with district championships, continuing through the county championships followed by the annually held GDR championships of several age-groups starting with the age-group 13 years at national level.

In top-level junior sports the systematic training starts with a general basic training. The most talented children from school sports clubs and sports groups of sections of the DTSB of the GDR continue to be coached at training centres of which, as a rule, one or more exist in each district of the Republic. This, mainly, takes place at the age of 10-12/13 years. Under the guidance of experienced instructors the systematic sports oriented training begins at this stage with the aim of realising talents. On the basis of scientific and pedagogical methods and principles, a manifold form of training generally prepares future high level performers and enables the determination of aptitude and selection of talented athletes. It also contributes to the education and training of all-round developed personalities. Under the conditions of daily life and the obligations to be fulfilled at home and at school, this first stage of training is carried out in the towns and communities of the country.

In the course of this phase of the child's sporting development, keeping in mind the specific features of the age and of the athlete's biological maturity, first examination, tests and competitions, especially in multi-discipline events, take place with the aim of determining the 'coachability' of the athlete, their capability, their readiness and their ability to take stress. Normally, the child in the age-group of 10-12 years will first compete in nearly 50-60 multidiscipline events. This underlines the fact that the principle of manifoldness is primary. In this connection, of course, the especially favourable age of learning is taken into consideration and, in addition to speed in general, certain basic sports motor abilities and motor coordination will be efficiently trained and developed. It is a matter of fact that real talents develop under equal conditions and in general training. The aim of this stage is to restrict the broad basis by finding out talents meeting the requirements of track and field disciplines, ie of the 42 Olympic disciplines, in the best possible way.

Having finished this first stage, the most talented boys and girls have the opportunity to improve their sports capabilities at a children and youth sports school or at a county sports club under the guidance of qualified coaches, instructors and teachers. But the path to the winner's platform in international sports events such as Olympic Games, World and European Championships is still very long. Now, training in groups of special disciplines. subject to a completely new rhythm of life and under other strains of life and training, only those who have really gained all qualities to reach highest performances will succeed. In the case of top level performance, of course, the assessments of the physical aptitude of the athlete play an important role, but more and more the athlete's entire personality is required. Attitudes, motivations, the ability of mobilisation, will, fighting spirit, and mental alertness are components which, as a result of the unity of education and training, play an important role in the development of a top-level athlete. Numerous competitions, tests, performance diagnoses and examinations increase for coaches in the sports clubs the value of an assessment of the sporting aptitude. At the age of 14 or 15 years (but there are, of course, cases of a later determination) it is already quite certain what discipline is the most suitable for the athlete.

In most cases the 15-year-old athletes have already achieved good performances in their future special discipline. The talent that begins to show very early in some athletes means participation in junior highlight events such as World and European Junior Championships as well as friendship tournaments of socialist countries is possible. We have had several examples recently in our association such as Ilke Wyludda, Ines Wittich, Kathrin Krabbe, Heike Tillack and Karsten Wichert.

This further path of specialisation, training and development of high sports performances is not followed by all athletes who have been delegated to sports schools. The athletes retired from active sport, who due to their individual upper limits are not able to meet the requirements of competitive sports, have all opportunities to continue their school and vocational training in the society. But the athletes who have cleared this hurdle as well now tackle the highest objectives of competitive sports under the guidance of well-proved collectives of coaches, physicians, scientists and sports managers. After highlights in junior events, successes in Olympic Games become their objectives. To this end they work systematically together with the management of the association and with the sports clubs.

Through a systematic process of screening and selection and a comprehensive promotion of competitive sports by the party and state leadership as well as by the incorporation of the knowledge of several sciences and, not least thanks to the dedicated activities of innumerable diligent volunteers, the GDR athletes have gained a good reputation for success all over the world and they want to keep it.

Klaus Schonberger is the Deputy Secretary General of the German Athletics Association of the GDR. This article first appeared in **New Studies in Athletics** *(1987) 1:9-14. It is reproduced with permission from the IAAF.*

APPENDIX ONE

CHILDREN AND LONG DISTANCE RUNNING
POLICY STATEMENT OF THE AUSTRALIAN SPORTS MEDICINE
FEDERATION CHILDREN IN SPORT COMMITTEE

Dave Roberts, Allan Norton, Alex Sinclair, Peter Larkins

Introduction

In the absence of definitive scientific evidence relating to the detrimental effects on children training for, and competing in, distance running events, and the wide range of maturity levels for any given age, it seems prudent to recommend conservative guidelines based upon potential, but currently unverified risk factors.

The following guidelines, therefore, should be viewed in that context. They represent a compromise between current practice, and what might be considered as ideal, and may be modified in the light of future research findings.

Recommended maximum competitive distances:

Age	Distance
Under 12 years	5km
15 years	10km
15-16 years	Half Marathon
16-18 years	30km
18+	Marathon

Recommended weekly maximum training distances: 3x competition distance.

Children known to be physically immature for their age should be limited to the maximum recommended distance for the age group below their own.

Further considerations and rationale

Notwithstanding the recommendations, ASMF supports the following statements endorsed by the American Academy of Paediatrics in 1982 which reads: *long-*

distance competitive running events primarily designed for adults are not recommended for children prior to physical maturation. Under no circumstances should a full marathon be attempted by immature youths (less than Tanner stage 5, sexual maturity rating). After pubertal development is complete, guidelines for adult distance running are appropriate.

The considerable benefits which accrue from regular aerobic activity must be weighed against the possible harmful effects of intensive training and competition on children. It should be understood that children do not need to run long distances to achieve an aerobic training effect.

Effects on the musculo-skeletal system

Particularly during periods of rapid growth, children are most vulnerable to musculo-skeletal injuries and disorders. Repetitive stress and resulting overuse syndrome may in the long term lead to musculo-skeletal dysfunction.

The effect of minor deviations which would normally cause few problems are magnified when running long distances, especially on hard surfaces.

It is recommended, therefore, that:

1. All children should have a musculo-skeletal assessment before embarking upon a training/competition program of long distance running.
2. That regular long periods of running or hard surfaces be avoided.

Physiological considerations

Apart from low economy of locomotion, there do not seem to be any underlying physiological factors which would preclude children from running long distances.

Children, however, are different from adults and when compared with adults are disadvantaged by a faster stride rate and poor tolerance to heat stress. It is recommended therefore, that:

1. Children should not be encouraged to participate in competitions designed for adults.
2. Weather conditions should be cool.
3. Children should be taught about ingestion of fluids before and during a race/training session.
4. Appropriate clothing should be worn.

Sociological considerations

There is a danger that the time required for training/competition in distance running may preclude a child from enjoying a wide range of social experiences.

Study, mixing with other children, developing other skills, etc., are important in normal growth and development. The Committee believes that the time devoted to running long distances should be kept in perspective.

APPENDIX TWO

CHILDREN AND ADOLESCENTS IN SPORT
A POLICY STATEMENT ISSUED BY THE AUSTRALIAN NATIONAL HEALTH AND MEDICAL RESEARCH COUNCIL

From an early age children are engaged in a variety of physical activities ranging from play to elite sport. Play is self-determined, individualistic and has no rules. It is spontaneous and self-pacing, there is continuous feedback and minimal evaluation. It allows for individual variation and can start and finish at any time. Games apply some formal rules to play activity and sport is highly organised. Generally, the rules in sport are in the hands of people other than players. There is considerable literature on the physical, psychological and social aspects of children in sport. Knowledge regarding criteria for safe participation, overuse injuries, motivation to ensure continued involvement and the long-term outcome of participating in sport is incomplete. However, the major deficiency appears to be lack of dissemination of important information to those involved — parents, teachers, coaches, physicians, and the children themselves.

The importance of play in normal development is generally acknowledged. Play enables a child to improve motor skills, assist socialisation, achieve success and subsequent praise, improve fitness, increase self-esteem and have fun. The importance of exercise for good health appears valid. Regular exercise is assoc-iated with better control of obesity. However, there is a need for further studies regarding the value of exercise for conditions such as coronary artery disease. There does seem to be an association between activity and reduced risk of coronary artery disease, but no consistent change in serum lipids. In spite of potential benefits of exercise, there is a continued decrease in time spent in exercise from 2.8 hours per week in adolescence to 20 minutes per week in the 5th decade of life. This suggests a lack of positive experiences and inadequate promotion of active lifestyle.

In the pre-adolescent and adolescent, the growth plates are open and growing rapidly. There is some information regarding susceptibility to particular injuries and different stages of growth but further information is required to determine whether sport or games are associated with a higher or lower risk of injury than free play.

There are considerable negative components to organised sporting activities. There are training demands such as costs, discomfort and time commitment. There may be considerable restriction of social life. There is the potential for anxiety associated with defeat and failure to live up to adult expectations.

It is important to establish the ages at which children are able to cope with physical and emotional stresses without being disadvantaged.

Physiology

Performance is determined by genetic, nutritional, climatic, health, sociological, psychological and training factors. The hereditary component contributes to build maximum oxygen uptake, neuro-muscular co-ordination and control of ventila-tion. This biological basis is modified by a complex interaction with psychological and socio-cultural characteristics which ultimately determine performance.

There is scarcity of information which enables us to understand the effects of training on musculoskeletal, respiratory and cardiovascular systems in children. There are a number of studies of short term effects of muscle training but overall evaluation is limited. Some suggest that children have the same increased aerobic fitness with training as adults, while others suggest that training has little effect in the pre-adolescent child. Most child participants certainly have a minimum of sustained physiological stress so that fitness benefits are minimal. There has been some suggestion that endurance sports such as swimming and distance running may increase growth. However, others have shown no significant effect.

Apart from controversy regarding the effects of training and sport on improving fitness and performance, there is also considerable lack of data regarding the potential for injury. It is uncertain whether increased mobility is associated with an increased or decreased incidence of sprains and dislocations. On the other hand, it has been shown that certain dental profiles are more prone to damage during sporting activities.

Although exercise training does not appear to harm physical growth in the long term, there is considerable discussion regarding the potential for injury in various sports at different ages. There is a wide individual variation in body builds, fitness and age of maturity. This appears to be particularly marked in boys where early maturers tend to get into organised sport. Further understanding is needed regarding the age at which children should participate in particular sports, the intensity to which their involvement should be developed and criteria for competition between different individuals. Apart from different ages of maturation leading to different participation in various sports, there is some evidence that sporting involvement may influence pubertal development. Boys playing football tend to be early maturers as do girls in swimming squads. However, girls in athletics, gymnastics and ballet often have delayed maturation, including menarche.

Age limits

There are wide individual variations in physical, psychological and social maturation. With advancing maturity there is an increase in body size, greater aerobic capacity, increased ability to store glycogen, increased strength, speed and power. There is maturation of motor skills which vary between sexes. Boys can often throw, catch or kick a ball by seven years of age whereas girls may not be competent at this activity until eight or nine years of age. At nine to ten years of age there is maximum skill development and improved co-ordination in both sexes although boys tend to be more competitive. Peak endurance occurs in girls between nine and thirteen years and in boys a little later. There is no difference in the effects on fitness of intensive activity between preadolescent boys and girls. There are no long term side-effects on menstruation, child-bearing or body structure. Excessive weight training does not appear to be of much value in pre-pubertal children. It does appear that some sporting activities should be related to maturation age rather than strict chronological age.

Children under eight years of age tend to play individually or in small groups such as family groups. They participate in various forms of free play, they change friendships and are critical of the opposite sex. Between nine and twelve years there is more co-operation and fun derived from games and sport. Awareness of self and others is improving and they begin to accept responsibility. Attention span increases. From thirteen years onwards they tend to master skills, understand rules, apply strategies and tactics, and are able to play with friends. It appears that this psycho-social development is important in planning participation in sport and that competition must be gradually introduced at the appropriate age.

Training

Activity stimulates bone growth, muscle protein, oxidative enzyme activity and possible DNA content of muscle. There is an increase in lean body weight mass and reduction in fat. However, short-term effects are not permanent and activity must be maintained. Performances in different sports have varying optimal levels of flexibility and strength for optimal performance and further information is needed regarding the kind of training and time commitment to obtain those optimal levels of strength and flexibility. Safety procedures to avoid injury need to be identified.

Drug misuse

Drugs are used in children's sport. It is mostly a problem in adolescence but there is the potential for increasing use in young children with increasing competition in this age group. Urine tests, for drugs are impractical and inappropriate in most children's sport. Therefore, it is essential that those involved must be educated regarding the ineffectiveness, illegality and risks involved with drug use.

Stimulants such as amphetamines and methyl phenidate have been used for many years although they seem to be less of a problem nowadays in sport. There is conflicting information regarding their effect. They possibly enable the participant to ignore pain, obscure fatigue and become more aggressive. It is doubtful whether they actually improve performance. High doses certainly cause severe psychological disturbances.

There is also conflicting scientific information about whether anabolic steroids truly increase performance. They certainly increase muscle bulk but there is some evidence that it is predominantly due to increased water content. They are potentially toxic and may produce oligospermia, testicular atrophy, gynaecomastia, raised serum cholesterol liver carcinoma, acne and early closure of epiphyses.

Nutritional aids are widely used in sport. There is no evidence of any increased benefit of high vitamin intake for sporting performance. Water is the only drink known to be of value in sport. The various preparations with sugar, known as '-ades' delay gastric emptying and water absorption. Similarly, salt tablets are potentially dangerous as they may also inhibit the absorption of water.

Narcotics, local anaesthetics and anti-inflammatory agents are potentially dangerous as they allow greater injury by reducing pain and allowing the participant to continue stress to the involved joint. Fortunately these are not widely used in children.

Nutrition

Informed nutritional counselling is essential. Most children in physical training do not ordinarily need an increase in any specific nutrient such as proteins, vitamins or minerals. They need water and energy rather than special electrolyte mixtures or high protein packs. There is no evidence that any nutrient will enhance athletic performance if taken in increased amounts. It is important that there is regular intake of water and energy and that inappropriate intake in relation to sport does not occur. Markedly restrictive diets to achieve desired weight and fatness should be avoided. Girls with poor diet, especially when associated with poor social circumstances, are at risk of iron deficiency.

Psychological impact

There is increasing conflict between the need for the fun of free play and the pressure to participate in organised sport. The demands of sport may reduce the time for play. There have been few studies on the psychological impact of various degrees of organised sport and most of these have been short term. Vigorous sport for the pre-adolescent may enhance self-confidence, enable the child to learn to cope with stress, assist with social adjustment and help release aggression. However, evidence for these benefits is not clearly proven and if the child is not emotionally mature enough to handle the stress of organised sport he may get excited and anxious. There is conflicting evidence on the relationship between physical activity, academic achievement and socialisation. Some show a positive association and others none at all. Does sport improve or decrease attitudes of 'fair play'? Does competition increase or decrease co-operation? Does sport release or promote aggression? Aggression is learned, even in sport. Does sport help self-esteem?

The stress does seem to be related to the child's basic competitive and anxiety state, levels of self-esteem and expectations of parent and coach. The tools for studying anxiety in children are limited. It is not clear whether stress in sport is more severe than other stresses faced by children, although for most children it does not appear to be excessive.

Self-esteem increases if the coach provides positive feedback. There is evidence that the effect of extrinsic rewards can be positive or negative. Extrinsic rewards may enhance, depress or have no effect on intrinsic motivation. It appears to be wise to avoid any substantial monetary contribution in extrinsic reward as the benefit is limited and potential disadvantages great. Children should appreciate playing for its own sake so that they will continue beyond adolescence. Many factors are involved in the enjoyment of sport including peer relationships, coaching behaviour and physical ability. The structure of sport and quality of adult leadership are important and the examples set by professionals or sports heroes may be significant.

There has been considerable interest in the reason for dropping out of sport. Identified factors such as over-emphasis on winning, adult pressure, unequal opportunity to play in games, inadequate fun in games, training especially when young, and insufficient physical activity. Many paediatricians see children with psychogenic abdominal pain due to parental pressure. These important problems should be identified so that an optimal environment can be provided for children to participate in sport and develop the interest as a life-long activity.

Positive aspects of children's sport

It is, of course, desirable to prevent unnecessary injury or emotional disturbance of children, including that arising out of participation in sport. However, there are positive aspects of sport for most children; some of these positive aspects may be jeopardised by too rigorous an insistence on protection and regulation.

Risk taking
A certain amount of risk appears to be a normal and desired aspect of human behaviour. The excessive avoidance of risk, in contrast, is associated with distorted psychological development. Practice in taking risks and in making a personal decision about how much risk to take can be obtained on the sports field probably more safely than in unstructured activity in the creek or on the streets. This normal developmental process is subject to adult interference either to increase or to decrease the risk in comparison with the children's judgement.

Involvement with peers
For many children, sport provides a satisfactory way of establishing peer

relationships, particularly for children whose physical skills are reasonably good but who lack social skills.

Satisfaction in Achievement
Similarly, sport can be a vital source of narcissistic gratification for children with limitations in other abilities. It may be important for a child to be able to choose from a range of sports: for example, rugby football (whatever its faults) is one of the few team games in which a large, slow child can be a genuinely valued team member.

Physical Well-being
Physical fitness is important during childhood and also to promote a lifestyle for future years.

Personal Role Definition
Children's play progresses naturally from less structured to more structured activity, reflecting its function as a preparation for adult life. From the age of about eight years children enter a stage of increased autonomy, of personal responsibility for behaviour. Sport, with defined and agreed rules, provides a setting in which this autonomy can be tested in a relatively safe way.

Parents

The family is important in promoting and encouraging younger children's activities whereas coaches, teachers and peers become more important with older children. Parental encouragement can be beneficial when it promotes positive values, but it can be dysfunctional when winning is considered to be more important than the fun; expectations of the adults lead to a sense of failure; and parental involvement deprives the child of the opportunity of self-discipline and responsibility.

Clear guidelines are required for parental involvement in children's sport. Those that should be considered are:
— supportive approach — realistic goals, hiding disappointment, patience, appreciation, promoting obligation to the team and ensuring adequate preparation
— ensuring parents stay on the sidelines and avoid yelling instructions and derogatory remarks to players
— avoid interfering with the coach
— parents should be provided with information which will help them decide whether their child should participate. Factors to consider are:
  - time demands for parents
  - costs involved
  - safety
  - opportunity for the child to get a chance to participate
  - availability of coaching
  - evidence that the child will be happy in the activity.

The role of non-parent adults

Teachers
Clear guidelines are required for teachers to assist in organising sporting activities for their students. Criteria that they will need to consider are:
— aims
— personnel

- equipment — including variations required
- programs to allow participation, variety, appropriate time concentration span of the age of students, and the ability to learn skills
- attitudes to instill in the students
- safety
- communication with parents and other groups

Coaches

Coaches do need assistance to establish leadership skills as well as expertise in developing techniques. Most coaches have no formal training and many are parents. There is often a difference in what people think they are doing as a coach and their actual behaviour. Some willing volunteers get their vicarious thrills through the children.

Coaches must provide feedback and this should be positive reinforcement. They should de-emphasise winning and losing and promote fun. They should understand the physiology and psychology of training and be able to organise appropriate training sessions. They should have expertise in the care of injuries. They should be able to promote and encourage a healthy attitude to scholastic achievement and arts as well as sport. They must recognise individual differences between children. They should not interfere with family life by making unrealistic demands on their charges. They are an important role model for many children and should accept responsibility for their participation.

The Physicians

Physicians are frequently involved in pre-sport examination and in giving advice regarding intensity of involvement and management of injuries. It is not clear which physician should examine a child before participating in sport. In most cases, the child's own physician is the most appropriate person but there is some argument that a specialist with a particular interest in sports physiology and psychology may have a role. The physician with an interest will play an important part in providing advice and back-up for sporting bodies.

Physicians must become involved in a number of areas. They

- will be required to examine most children for sport participation. Information regarding features to look for should be widely disseminated.
- must be able to be an advocate for preventative medicine and have some knowledge of rules regarding particular sports and rules for protective equipment. They must be aware of those patients at risk, such as those with recurrent concussion, a single 'paired' organ eg one eye, kidney, and some forms of cardiac disease;
- should establish a program for the management of injuries frequently seen in various sports and also understand the requirements for rehabilitation;
- may need to educate players, parents and coaches in exercise physiology, prevention of injury and management of trauma;
- should be aware of the special needs of adolescents in areas such as obesity, drugs, pregnancy and sexually transmitted diseases which may be only brought to their attention through sporting activities;
- must keep careful records of involvement and patient management;
- should know the rules of the games and be able to appreciate the requirements of physical status and maturity rating for participation;
- should understand the current 'state of the art' regarding nutrition and drugs in sport. (Stackpole **Paediatric Annuals, 1984; 13:**592).

Medical issues
Sudden Death in Sport
There is always the risk of sudden death for children playing sport. However, it could not be justified to restrict exercise in general because of this risk. The risk can certainly be minimised by ensuring that equipment is approved, coaches are certified, appropriate rules for various ages are instituted, officials are supervising activities, training is appropriate and that there is a check examination before participation.

Factors in the child which may lead to sudden death include unrecognised cardiac abnormalities such as idiopathic sub-aortic stenosis, myocarditis or cardiomyopathy, anomalous left coronary artery, predisposition to arrhythmia in association with mitral valve prolapse or heart blocks. Children with systemic hypertension, pulmonary hypertension and conditions such as Marfan's are usually identified and certainly have an increased risk with some sporting activities.

Risks with particular sports vary. For example, collision risks are high in football, hockey and boxing; trauma due to high velocity objects occur in cricket and baseball; trauma associated with vehicles involved occur in cycling, motor driving and go-karts.

The environment may also predispose the child to serious illness or injury. High temperatures may produce heat stroke and dehydration. Children perspire less than adults and are possibly less tolerant to heat. Rules are necessary for acclimatisation to exercise in heat. Cold may induce ventricular fibrillation in extreme situations. Mountain climbing, hang-gliding, play grounds and pools may be associated with specific risks. Pools are present in 10 per cent of homes and are accessible at home or in a neighbour's backyard for 20 per cent of Australian children. Adventure play grounds are generally not associated with any increase in risk of death (Nixon, et al **British Medical Journal, 1981; 283:**410) but unsafe equipment may lead to severe trauma. Hard playground surfaces are a significant source of injury and should be replaced by materials which have high impact absorption characteristics.

Injuries
There are insufficient satisfactory studies of the problems related to injuries in children playing sport; such reports as exist are often short term, subjective and selective. Further information is needed regarding predisposition, prevalence, prevention and appropriate management of sporting injuries in children.

During childhood there are ongoing changes of the growth cartilage and articular surfaces and both of these are often affected by a variety of stresses. However, it is still unclear whether growing bones and joints are more susceptible to major trauma or recurrent micro-trauma than mature bones, and joints. Children certainly develop 'a little league elbow as do adults develop tennis elbow'. There may well be different mechanisms involved as well as differences in pre-disposition.

There is some evidence that there is a lower rate of injury in pre-adolescent sport compared with adolescent sport and that injuries that do occur are usually minor. Solomon, et al (**American Journal of Sports Medicine, 1980; 8:**325) found that children playing youth soccer under 10 years of age had an injury rate of 1:1,000 while those over 10 years of age had an injury rate of 7.7:100.

Guidelines are needed for physician involvement in the management of injuries with sport. Information regarding initial assessment and triage would be valuable to most physicians. Sports which require the presence of the physician should be known: this should be rarely necessary for junior sports. Physicians should be able to provide training for coaches in the management of injuries.

Emergencies
- *Head injuries:* the importance of an airway, assessment of conscious state and localising signs need to be pointed out.
- Neck injuries are rare with children but occasionally occur in gymnastics and with contact football.
- Respiratory trauma is usually only a problem when the airway is traumatised or a lung is ruptured.
- Cardiac emergencies are rare
- Abdominal injuries require careful observation and referral if the patient is in severe pain or is shocked.
- Musculoskeletal problems are common. Information is required regarding first aid, manipulation, splints, blood loss and compartment syndromes.
- Lacerations are common and often referred.
- Cold injury and heat exhaustion.
- Eye injuries.
- Lower limb injuries increase after age 15. Sprains and contusions are the most common. They are seen most frequently with cycling, basketball, football, cricket or baseball, skiing and injuries with playground equipment. The patello-femoral pain syndrome is seen in young athletes and avulsion injuries are occasionally identified.
- Oro-facial injuries are perhaps one of the most common of all sporting injuries. Information is required regarding first aid, manipulation and splints.

Overuse injuries
Overuse injuries are not well understood by primary care physicians. They usually occur when a child changes to a new sport or is involved in an intensive training program. They produce pain and stiffness and may be bilateral. To excel in sport today, young athletes often train for 3-6 hours per day and train longer, harder and at an earlier age. Overuse injuries are probably related to microtrauma, chondromalacia, fasciitis, shin splints or stress fractures. Further information is needed regarding these injuries and guidelines regarding the extent of participation following injury is required.

Injuries in specific sports
Both the frequency and type of injuries vary in different sports. A few examples make the point: Dicker, et al (**Australian Physician, 1986; 15:**455) reported one injury per 21 man risk hours in professional Australian Rules football. Davidson, et al (**Medical Journal of Australia 1978; 1:**247) reported one injury per 3.6 man risk hours in senior rugby and one per 400 man risk hours in schoolboy rugby. These were mainly fractures in the 16-18 year age group related to position on the field.

- Competitive swimming has been reported to produce anxiety rather than stimulation in large proportion of children.
- Fast bowling has been associated with stress fractures of the vertebrae (Elliott and Forster, **Journal of Human Movement Studies 1984 10:**83).
- Horse riding is associated with an increased risk of head injury which can be reduced by the wearing of head gear and adequate supervision (Nixon, et al **Safety in Childhood,** CAPFA).
- Weight lifting produces an increase in blood pressure and bone damage.
- Long distance running is associated with increased joint injuries.

- Gymnasts have more musculoskeletal injuries than controls (Garrick, Requa, **Journal of the American Medical Association, 1978; 239:** 2245).
- Forty-eight percent of pedal cycling injuries are head injuries and 80 percent of deaths are due to head injuries. An accident rate of 44:100,000 population have been reported (M. Lugg W.A. Health Department). Competitive cycling may be associated with an increased risk in children.
- Eye injuries account for approximately one per cent of all injuries in most sports, especially ball games such as squash.
- There are inadequate data regarding the prevalence of injuries associated with the use of trampolines.

Girls in sport

Some have claimed that girls are at increased risk of certain injuries. Apart from patello-femoral pain syndrome and some stress fracture, there does not appear to be any significant injury increase in girls. The menstrual cycle does not appear to affect performance or disposition to injury. There is continued discussion as to whether girls' and boys' competitions should be separate. Performance levels at present are different but this may not always be an issue since many of the differences are more social than physical. There is very little difference between pre-adolescent boys and girls.

Oligo or Amenorrhoea
Pre-pubertal girls involved in heavy endurance training do have delayed menarche in some cases. This is particularly marked in ballet dancers and gymnasts. The cause is uncertain. Some argue that the delayed menarche pre-selects those who will undertake those particular activities. However, others claim that nutritional factors, stress factors or possibly hormonal factors may play a role. There is certainly a hormonal response to exercise although the details vary from one study to another. There is some evidence of hypothyroidisms, hypopro-lactinaemia and possibly hypothalamic changes. This has raised the hypothalamic involvement with exercise and anorexia nervosa (Vegersky, et al **New England Journal of Medicine; 1977; 297:**1141). Post-pubertal girls do have an increased incidence of oligo or amenorrhoea associated with endurance sports. Twenty to fifty per cent of post-pubertal adolescents have been reported to have these menstrual disturbances compared with 5-15 percent of controls (Baker **Fertility and Sterility, 1981; 36:**691). There is argument as to whether these should be investigated when they occur. It is certainly risky to assume delay is always due to exercise. If delay occurs beyond 16 years then a careful history and examination is essential and one should consider measurement of gonadotrophin, prolactin, thyroid function, skull x-ray, bone age and karyotype. It is argued that hormone replacement should be considered at this stage. It is certainly unnecessary under 16 years of age, may be optional between 16-18 years of age and is recommended over 18 years of age. Failure to replace hormones may be associated with psychological problems and hypoestrogenic state producing osteopenia (Ayres, et al **Fertility and Sterility, 1984; 41:**224).

Oro-facial injuries account for between 10-20 per cent of all injuries to children participating in sports. There are inadequate data regarding the incidence of oro-facial injuries associated with leisure activities (eg. skate boarding bicycles) but these are thought to be of similarly high incidence.

Recommendations

The principles for participation in sport should be:

— fun and enjoyment
— socialisation
— developmental learning
— success
— democracy
— encouragement
— recognition and acceptance of individual differences.

The aim of sport is among other things to help a child become fit and competent. Competition and the outcome should not be the primary expectation. Children must be protected from the human experiments of athletic training in organised sport. Some argue that a consent form should be required to participate.

Details are required regarding medical evaluation before participating in sport. Physicians require information which will help decide whether a child is fit to play. Factors that should be considered include personal history, routine physical examination plus consideration of sex, age, height and weight percentiles, body habitus, joint function, co-ordination, maturity rating and fitness. The type of sport must be appropriate for the child's maturity age, not necessarily chronological age. Children should be examined at least once, although a follow-up examination may be warranted for those involved in intensive organised sports. Children who should be excluded from any sport include those with cardiac abnormalities such as idiopathic hypertrophic sub-aortic stenosis, aortic stenosis, primary pulmonary hypertension, anomalous left coronary artery and Marfan's syndrome. These are often diagnosed on the history rather than the murmur.

Children who should be excluded from specific sports include those with hypertension. Children have an exaggerated blood pressure rise with exercise compared to adults. It is uncertain whether a more markedly exaggerated blood pressure rise may be indicative of future hypertension or not. Systolic and diastolic pressure both rise in weight lifting while systolic pressure alone tends to rise with running and cycling. On the other hand, regular endurance dynamic exercise may reduce blood pressure. These factors need to be considered in relation to the blood pressure and participation in sport (Fidler, et al **Pediatrics, 1979; 64:**579).   Those children who should be protected from contact sports include those with single 'paired' organs (eyes, kidneys, testes), those with abdominal organomegaly (liver and spleen, especially seen in glandular fever), multiple concussion episodes.

— Rules should be established to
     - avoid overuse injuries
     - avoid head injury by the use of helmet
     - avoid dental injuries by the use of mouth guard
     - teach children to practise break falls
     - ensure equipment is safe
     - that the rules of play should be adequate
     - that the proper warm-up exercises are carried out.
— First aid kits should be available and rules for managing common injuries established and well understood.
— Plans for action when a player is actually or apparently injured should be established. Criteria for removal from play should be determined. A transport and referral system should be planned and available.
— Sports should be classified as suitable for different ages and degrees of fitness:
     - contact — football, hockey, lacrosse, rugby, wrestling
     - limited contact — basketball, soccer, volleyball

- non-contact — running, fencing, gymnastics, skiing, swimming, tennis
- moderately strenuous — badminton, netball, golf, tabletennis
- non-strenuous — archery, bowling, shooting.

— Sports training should be considered within maturation levels. Expectations must be realistic.
— Lines of authority should be established. Supervision should be ensured. Officials should be given the power to deal with infringements.
— Equipment must be evaluated. Playground equipment must be designed with optimal safety in mind. Optimal consideration for trampoline use must be considered.
— Rules for training programs and for particular sports must be established. Modifications must be made to suit the needs and capacity of children. Junior versions of adult games can be encouraged (eg. Kanga Cricket, Junior Hockey, T-Ball). Rugby can be made safer by reducing the number of players, skill requirements with modified scrums, shorter time per half and smaller size of field.
Information regarding specific sports is available from the National Health and Medical Research Council, Departments of Youth, Sport and Recreation and Australian Institute of Sport.
— Parent education programs must be undertaken to ensure understanding that a positive environment must be established, preventive programs formulated and sporting injuries appropriately dealt with.
— Records must be kept.
— Consideration regarding the role of material rewards (ie. trophies) must be carefully given. These have only limited value in sport.
— Opportunities for participation are vital. Details of selection processes must be determined.
— Children must be involved in early planning and evaluation.
— Early specialisation should be discouraged.
— Specific rules must be developed for high risk sports, eg. scuba diving should probably be limited to older adolescents and excluded for children with spontaneous pneumothorax, cardiovascular disease and epilepsy. Asthma, middle ear disease and diabetes may be particular problems.
— Rules regarding the use of nutritional supplements and drugs should be considered. There is need for further research.
— Ethics Committees for sporting bodies may need to be set up. Legislation may be required for some changes.
— National surveillance of various injuries in different sports should be supported.
— Physician involvement should be clearly defined with regard to pre-sport check, presence at specific sporting activities and a source of information to educate others involved.
— There is a need to find out what sport does and does not do. Information regarding exercise threshold for injury in young children is needed. Long term effects of elite sport activities need to be determined. Understanding of overuse injuries is vital. Follow-up studies of those with exaggerated blood pressure response to exercise is required. Long term prospective studies are necessary to find out why children drop out of sport as this puts many off a beneficial life-style.

Looking to the future, it is absolutely essential to encourage young girls to participate and to ensure they continue to participate. Baseball, hockey, and soccer illustrated here all have such modified versions for younger players and beginners. The AUSSIE SPORTS Program of the Australian Sports Commission is particularly important for junior players.

Right: T Ball.
Photo: Australian Information Service.

Left: Junior Hockey.
Photo: Australian Institute of Sport.

Right: Soccer.
Photo: Katrina Bridgeford. An entrant in the
1988 ACHPER/Bicentennial Authority
Photographic Competition.

SECTION SEVEN
PROMOTING WOMEN'S SPORT

AN INTRODUCTION

Ken Dyer

This book is concerned primarily with the benefits that sport can give to women. In particular it is concerned with how women's participation in sport can be increased in the years ahead and how their performances in all sports can better match their potential. These are matters of making sports available and attractive to girls and women at all stages of their lives and of understanding those aspects of their biology which might require special training or coaching regimes.

Part of the means of achieving a general acceptability of all forms of sporting endeavour among women and making them attractive is to show, by media exposure, that the sports are popular, fun, skillful and accessible to women. For some women at the top of their sports there is fame and fortune to be won and they can become heroes and role models to younger generations still at school.

Sport in the 1980s is dominated by money and the media. This domination is of a different sort at the levels of elite and international sport on the one hand, and at club level and recreational sport on the other. At elite levels in those sports which command media attention and therefore large sponsorship deals, players are placed under increasing pressure to perform and their role is changing from one of 'sportperson' to 'entertainer'. This trend may be much less pronounced and less widespread in women's sports than men's, but it is important nonetheless. It is reported, for example, that when distance runners Zola Budd and Mary Decker were rematched in London in 1985 after their dramatic encounter in the Los Angeles Olympics 3000m in which Decker fell and was injured and Budd partly as a consequence finished only seventh, they were paid $90,000 and $54,000 respectively — for less than 10 minutes TV exposure!

This sort of commercialisation is of course a very mixed blessing — but there is a very strong argument which says that if men sports stars can earn thousands or even millions of dollars for a year's work, then why can't women. The usual response from sponsors is that sportswomen aren't so popular and therefore do not command media attention as do men. But, as has often been pointed out, it is the media themselves, particularly television in this day and age, who largely create the popularity of sports and build up the participants to superstars.

In terms of number of participants and spectators, women's netball, hockey, swimming, basketball, golf, gymnastics and tennis, to name but a few sports, are as popular and as televisual as the best of men's sports. And yet as Helen Menzies shows in her paper in this section, the attention given to women's sports by all sections of the media is quite appalling and has changed very little in the last 8 years or so.

219

The reasons usually given for this lack of media attention are usually quite wrong and often absurd as well. The question is how to change the situation. The government enquiry into Women, Sport and the Media of 1985 recommended among other things the establishment of a special Women's Sport Promotion Unit. After some delay the Unit was in fact established and the conference, which this volume records, saw the official launch of the Unit. A statement of the aims, objectives and mode of operation of that Unit is therefore a most important part of this book. It is presented as an appendix to the article contributed to this section by Margaret Pewtress, the Chairperson of the Unit.

Most sports men and women don't aspire to be elite performers. They want the benefits of health, fitness, fun and companionship which club and recreational sport brings. But money is still required at this level for equipment, ground maintenance, travel and a myriad of other things. And for a sport to prosper and grow it needs both more money and sufficient publicity to attract new players and where appropriate, spectator support. The final paper in this section provides an insider's view — from both sides of the fence as it happens — of some of the problems of sponsorship, funding and money raising. This is important because, as in so many other things, it is not an area in which women traditionally have much experience. Like the skills of sport themselves it is an area which requires careful training, continual practice and full recognition of its importance. Like the acquisition of sports skills by women, it is an area which is changing, but only as a result of continued pressure for change by women on behalf of women.

WOMEN'S SPORT: TREATMENT BY THE MEDIA

Helen Menzies

The background

One of the most succinct statements of the importance of this topic was made in a report entitled **Women Sport and the Media** which presented the conclusions of a National Working Group on women in sport which reported to the Commonwealth Government in 1985. Because of its importance I quote the introductory paragraphs at some length.

> The media and sport provide two powerful socialising influences in Australian society. They provide evidence of, and an opportunity to emulate, role models on which people, especially young people, base their attitudes and behaviour. The confluence of those two elements — that is, when sport is presented in the media — creates a highly potent socialising influence. We believe that the subconscious 'message' from the way in which women in sport are presented is that their activity is not intrinsically as worthy or important as men's sport.

> It is the basis for attitudes which are evident and well-documented within the media and in other key influencing bodies relating to sport which devalue the sporting experience when it involves women.

> We believe that, as much as the media, especially television, reflect the community within which they operate, they also inevitably shape and direct attitudes, behaviour and priorities. What is seen on television, heard on radio or read in the newspapers, sanctions what is acceptable or expected. What does not appear in those forums can end up being trivialised, ignored or rendered unable to compete with other 'normal' activities when it comes to establishing and sustaining a priority either for resources or general attention and concern.

We believe that, in general, women's sport in Australia, and the involvement and participation of women and girls of all ages and at all levels in the community in either elite or recreational sport, has suffered the consequences of a long tradition of prejudice and lack of concern. That situation has been both reflected and to a large extent caused by the inadequate coverage of women's sport in the media.

In a country like Australia, where sport **is** so important, and where the media **do** decide attitudes, the value of women's sport winning a place in the media can't be over emphasised.

[Abby Hoffman makes a similar point in her paper on the Canadian experience reported in this book. Her anecdotal and impressionistic account of some of the coverage of Women in Sport in Canada and internationally, complements this paper in a valuable way. She emphasises the equally important aspect of the nature and quality of the coverage of women's sport *Ed.].*

I am assuming that we all share this basic analysis. Getting women's sport into the media is war: war is hell, but given a good battle plan we can trot off triumphantly into the sunset at the end of the last reel. I will give you an example of the sort of things I mean by strategies and battle plans. It refers to the conference which this book reports.

Once it had been decided to hold a Women's Sport Conference, this could be thought about in two ways:

1. By considering what should happen at the conference;

2. By considering how the conference itself could be used as a strategy.

For one thing, having a conference in one's own city is a help. It focuses attention, raises issues, jogs consciences. There was, for example, an excellent response from the Adelaide media to this conference both in terms of the pictures made available for display at the conference, and the coverage of the conference and the issues with which it is concerned in newspapers and on the electronic media.

Sometimes, too, individual sessions can be planned to serve wider purposes. For example, for this particular conference I wrote to 25 capital city newspapers and 45 capital city radio and television stations around Australia asking them what their policy on the coverage of women's sport was, what priority they gave it, who were their women's sports journalists and/or who actually covered women's sports. One outcome of such an exercise is that you get some interesting information. An added outcome is that the exercise itself serves to congratulate people who are doing things well, to prod those who aren't, and hopefully make everyone think about the issues.

Some of the pictures sent by the papers to which I wrote for the conference are reproduced in the pages of this book. Almost as interesting were the responses from the papers who didn't send pictures. For instance journalists from both **The Australian** and **The West Australian** phoned to say how horrified they were to find how few photographs their papers had of sportswomen in action, and **The West Australian** actually commissioned someone to go out and take some. So initiatives such as this can have important immediate consequences. But it is to a longer term strategy which I now turn.

The surveys

One of the important ideas behind the particular information-gathering exercise I have just described was to allow comparison with statistics gained in surveys taken in earlier years. The first of these dates from 1980 and arose as the result of an earlier conference.

In February 1980 a State conference on women in sport was organised by the then South Australian Women's Adviser to the Premier, Rosemary Wighton. Afterwards, Rosemary convened a group of six women to look at recommendations from the conference, and that group decided to take up the issue of media coverage.

We set as our long term goal the getting of increased and better media coverage for women in sport. The first of our short term steps to that goal was to determine precisely the amount of coverage actually given to women's sport. So our group did a content analysis of Australian capital cities' daily newspapers and TV channels during one week during May 1980. Those results were then circulated widely, sent out under the heading of the Women's Advisory Unit of the Premier's Department, hoping that this would give it sufficient status to ensure it more than a second glance. The survey got extremely good coverage on radio, TV, and in the press, both in South Australia and right round Australia.

The results of the survey were extremely revealing:

— In that week, women's sport averaged two per cent of all available sports space in all capital city newspapers.

— On average, four times as many men's as women's sports were featured in the results sections of the newspapers.

— On average, there were 12 times as many graphics devoted to men's as to women's sports.

— Eighty per cent of sports space was given to racing and various football codes and of that 80 per cent, more than half went to racing.

In order to gauge whether or not that situation had improved in four years, the National Working Group on Women in Sport undertook a similar survey for the corresponding week in May 1984. The results of that survey were equally revealing, and, considering the time that had elapsed, disappointing:

— In 1984, the space in the sports section of papers devoted to women's sport was 1.3 per cent.

— Five times as many men's as women's sports were covered in results sections.

— Space given to football decreased by 11 per cent, due mainly to Olympic Games lead-up stories.

Table 19: The treatment of women's sport in Australia by the capital city newspapers

		1980	1984	1988
Percentage of total sports	Men	96.2	95.9	95.8
report space given to	Women	2.0	1.3	2.5
Women's sport	Shared	1.8	2.8	1.7
The number of sports	Men	18	15	16
reported	Women	6	7	5
	Shared	3	3	3
Percentage of total sports	Men	96.2	95.9	95.8
report space given to men's	Women	2.0	1.3	2.5
and women's sport	Shared	1.8	2.8	1.7
Number and percentage	Men	50 (90%)	49 (93.1%)	57 (87.3%)
	Women	4 (7%)	3 (3.5%)	5 (7.5%)
	Shared	2 (3%)	1 (3.4%)	3 (5.2%)

A precise replication of the 1980 and 1984 surveys, carried out in the corresponding week of the year and allowing direct comparison was carried out in May 1988 by Dr. Sandy Gordon's group in Perth as reported in his paper in this volume. Briefly the results of his group are as follows:

In 1988 the percentage of that area of the paper given over to sports reports allocated to women's sport had increased slightly to an average of 2.5 per cent. But there were 16 men's sports reported and only 5 women's. Of the space devoted to sports results, 8 per cent was for women's sports; and of all the sport graphics (photographs, diagrams etc) only 7.5 per cent were for women's sports. A summary of the principal findings of these three surveys is given in Table 19. Virtually nothing has changed in these eight years despite all the attention given to women's sports by educators and politicians, all the equal opportunity legislation and all the expansion of women's programs in the Olympics and the like. Clearly much remains to be done.

Further interesting comparison is between the number of sports journalists in the years 1980 and 1984 and to set these figures against the numbers for 1988: that came in response to the letters I sent out to the 25 capital city newspapers.

The 1980 survey found that three newspapers had one women's sports journalist each. In 1984 the figures were 15 women's sports journalists in 10 newspapers, and two women radio sports journalists. In 1988, the situation had clearly continued to improve. There were seventeen women's sports journalists named from thirteen newspapers, eight women's sports journalists in 12 radio stations, and 10 women's sports journalists in 17 television stations. This is particularly encouraging, given that there was not a 100 per cent response to my enquiries.

To further update the information about media coverage for 1988, I analysed the coverage of women's sport given by the morning papers throughout Australia for the week February 15th to 20th. The numbers of articles carried by the papers and the number of photographs carried by the papers is set out in Table 20.

The paper which had the most number of large articles on women's sport was the **West Australian**, while both the **Advertiser** and the **Canberra Times** had the most number of medium sized articles and the **Daily Telegraph** had the most number of small ones. In overall total the **Advertiser** and the **Canberra Times** tied on 16 articles each. Considering photographs, the **Mercury** in Hobart had five excellent action photographs and the **West Australian** had the largest number of non-

Table 20: Articles on women's sport carried in capital city morning papers, February 15-20, 1988

Newspaper	Articles				Photographs	
	Large	Medium	Small	Total	Action	Non-action
West Australian	5	6	2	15	3	8
Advertiser	3	13		16	3	
Canberra Times	2	13	1	16	4	
Mercury	4	5	1	10	5	2
Daily Telegraph	2	2	4	8	1	2
Courier Mail	4	1		5	2	1
Sydney Morning Herald	1	1		2	1	
Age	1		1	1		
Australian		1		1		1
Herald	2			2		1

Table 21: Number of women's sports given coverage by capital city morning papers, February 15-20, 1988

1980	Golf, hockey, athletics, racing, netball (5)
1984	Basketball, golf, tennis, swimming, netball, gymnastics, hockey, squash, underwater hockey (9)
1988	Hockey, softball, rowing, squash, cricket, athletics, equestrian, lifesaving, veteran aths, basketball, cycling, abseiling, diving, skiing triathlon, bowls, golf, skating, touch football, horse training, swimming, gymnastics, motor racing, disabled athletics, powerboat racing, tennis, water skiing (27)

action, but it is depressing that the three papers which claim to be the most prestigious morning papers in Australia had but one each.

Let us now look at Table 21 which sets out the number of women's sports given coverage in capital city morning papers. This simple listing of the number of women's sports covered shows a definite improvement over the last few years. So the picture is not totally gloomy.

I will now turn to the responses to the letters which I sent to newspapers, television and radio stations. These are summarised in Tables 22, 23 and 24.

First Table 22, the newspapers. Notice first, the response from the **Perth Sunday Times** that says *No women's sports journalist except some casuals, who represent the minor sports, like softball*. The perception of women's sports as minor is one of the major barriers we still have to overcome. [Recall in this context the rhetorical questions which Abby Hoffman asked about Olympic representation in her first paper in this volume. Why, she asked, did men's baseball get a place in the 1988 Seoul Olympics but women's softball did not. The perception of women's sports as minor will not be easily overcome *Ed.*].

The response from the **Sun** and the **Sunday Sun** in Brisbane to the question concerning their policy on the coverage of women's sport is an interesting one. The editor there said that he wanted to increase the coverage of women's sport but lacked the women journalists to do it. This is an issue that comes up very often and it is encouraging to note the figures coming out of the BA Sports Studies course at Canberra CAE. Currently of the 21 students majoring in journalism, 11 are women and of the first set of graduates, 10 of the 12 were women. Given a continuation of results like that, this aspect of coverage of women's sports could be revolutionised in very short time.

The final point worth highlighting from Table 22 is the list of newspapers that did not respond. All of the Sydney papers are conspicuous by their absence, as is the national daily **The Australian**. This depressing observation confirms what was found in both 1980 and 1984, and it seems clear that particular strategies are needed in these very important areas.In Table 23, there is a very interesting quote from Radio 3DB in Melbourne: *If the sport is big enough, in terms of listener involvement, I'll cover it. Minor women's sports, like netball and so forth, would only deserve a line or two against big sports like Australian Rules*.

This perception of reality has clearly not yet been shaken by knowledge of the fact that netball has more participants Australia wide than Australian Rules.

Also in Table 22 are responses from the two radio stations in Adelaide which cover sport. Both of them, you will see, are very positive in their attitude towards women's sport. If we were being cynical we could probably say 'Oh, yes! But all

	...on ...res*	Women sport journalists?	Policy on coverage of women's sport
		One	No distinction between men's and women's in journalists of allocation of space. 'We have increasingly recognised the importance of women's sport.'
West Australian Western Mail (Perth)	Yes	One (currently freelance) Covered LA Olympics	No difference between men's and women's sport.
Sunday Times (Perth)	No	'No women sports journalists except some casuals, who represent the minor sports, like softball.'	
Age (Melbourne)	Yes	One freelance Three who cover some women's sport	
Canberra Times	Yes	All cadets trained in sport — one as assistant sports editor, though few women go on with it	
Sun (Melbourne)	Yes	One covering both women's and men's Two others covering particular sports Others as needed	'Strong emphasis on women's sport' Priority: public interest
Courier Mail Sunday Mail (Brisbane)	No	One	'Coverage of women's sport is now better than it used to be'
Sun Sunday Sun (Brisbane)	Yes	Two part time Publicity Officers from sports get contributors' rates	Want to increase coverage but lack the women journalists to do it
News (Adelaide)	Yes	Two	Two fulltime women sports journalists since 1982
Sunday Mail (Adelaide)	Yes	Three (two in restricted areas)	The best stories of the day Matter of priorities, space, traditions, commitments. 'Can't judge newsworthiness by a number of participants.'

No response
Sunday Observer (Melbourne)
Sun Herald (Sydney)
Sunday Telegraph (Sydney)
Sydney Morning Herald (Sydney)
Daily News (Perth)
Mercury (Hobart)
Sunday Press (Melbourne)
Australian (National)
Times on Sunday (National)
Daily Mirror (Sydney)
Daily Telegraph (Sydney)
The Sun (Sydney)

* Pictures of sports women sent

225

Table 23: The response of capital city radio stations

Name	Women sport journalists	Policy on coverage of women's sport
ABC radio/TV (Adelaide)	None	'The ABC gives fairly extensive coverage of women's sport and its policy is to maintain such coverage.' Reports, summaries, results, guests
ABC radio/TV (Perth)	5 with areas of specific coverage	Same as for men. Factors: public interest; resources; schedules All major and other relatively important women's sports covered
ABC (2CN) (Canberra)	None	
ABC (Sydney)	One sports trainee on a 2-year contract	Regularly cover all major women's sport events. Claims to be only station to have regular reports from World Netball, Federation Cup, women's cricket tour of UK
3DB (Melbourne)	None	'If the sport is big enough, in terms of listener involvement, I'll cover it. Minor women's sports, like netball and so forth, would only deserve a line or two up against big sports like Australian Rules.
4BC (Brisbane)	None '. . . and from that you should read bias neither pro nor con; to my knowledge we've never had an applicant	No different from men's Decisions based on 'the likely responses from an audience'
ABC: 4QR (Brisbane)	None. One from the non-sport staff does some tennis. Casual interviewer/ producer for Saturday morning Sports Extra	
5DN (Adelaide)	None, but Ken Cunningham's top drive time show gives 'comprehensive coverage'. Examples: regular segments on netball, softball, basketball, hockey, eventing, cycling. In the last 6 months, interviews with 31 other women. During cricket tour to England, 15 overseas phone interviews	
5AA (Adelaide)	None. But: 'Women's sport has always been a high priority on our Station and has always been covered on the merit of the participants as athletes in their own right, never in a condescending manner. The importance of women's sport will always ensure that it remains an integral part of our programming.'	
ABC (Hobart)	One program officer who has regular sports news shifts and provides occasional reports.	Coverage of sport, leisure and recreation activities in which women are well-represented
7HT (Hobart)	'Firstly we have no women sports journalists on our staff	'Secondly the coverage of all sport is the responsibility of our Sports Editor, and finally priority is given according to news value.'
ABC radio/TV (National)	One. Only woman sports reporter regularly involved in national broadcasts on the ABC. Covers individual sports, regular sports news shifts; very successful 'Inside the Back Page' series of Bicentennial segments for Sports Arena.	

Table 24: The response of capital city television channels

Name	Women sport journalists	Policy on coverage of women's sport
Channel 7 (Canberra)	One	If we hear about it we cover it — the ball is in the court of the sports. Head of Sport has attended seminars to advise women's sport groups.
Channel 7 (Sydney)	One (for past four years). At first mainly women's sports, now general.	No particular policy: up to the producers and journalists
Channel 9 (Sydney)	None	Wide World of Sport includes women. Winter Olympics coverage: no discrimination.
Channel 2 (Melbourne)	None: not on policy. Get female applicants, but against them is lack of journalistic experience. Bring in specialists for particular events.	Do limited coverage of major events, all 'packaged' for magazine programs like Sports Arena. Packages on 11 women's sports last year.
Channel 7 (Melbourne)	One (Football)	
Channel 10 (Adelaide	None	Policy is that we cover the best that's on that day.
Channel 9 (Adelaide)	One with the News department.	Telecast local women's netball final. Also: tennis final, and segments in sports roundup show, the news, C'Mon Kids, and many other programs.
Channel 9 (Perth)	None	Does not discriminate
Channel 9 (Launceston)	None	Same as for men: 'The number of competitors taking part and the state of the event.' Northern netball roster given regular slot on World of Sport.
Channel 9 (Hobart)	Girl's report of sport in two children's programs. Women presenters from many sports do segments on World of Sport.	
ABC (Brisbane)	One, Sports producer	Liaise with Publicity Officers of women's sports, especially at national and state level. Coverage of local competition.
Channel 7 (Brisbane)	Used to employ one but she went to Melbourne to live.	
Channel 9 (Brisbane)	None, but 'this is a choice on the part of journalists, not discrimination.	'The major sporting events are more likely to be played by men. We believe that the majority of 'our viewers want to watch sports which depict the highest level of skill.' 'It is the viewers who tell us what they want to watch and we respond.'

227

Table 24: The response of capital city television channels (cont'd)

Name	Women sport journalists	Policy on coverage of women's sport
Channel 0 (Brisbane)	One (Is part of 10 Network team for Olympics in Seoul)	As with everything, on the basis of 'news value and the degree of interest to our audience.'
Channel 10 (Melbourne)	One, general sport	
Channel 7 (Perth)	One plus one sports producer	Cover both men's and women's.
No Response ABC (ACT) ABC (Sydney) SBS (Sydney)	Channel 10 (Sydney) Channel 9 (Melbourne) ABC (Hobart)	

they have done is learn the correct words to say'. And that may perhaps be true at least in part. But on the other hand you can see from the information they give that they in fact do cover women's sport and probably better than any other radio station in the country. That is not an accident or a result of good luck. I would argue that it is a result of the sort of strategy described in this paper which began in Adelaide eight years ago.

It is interesting to note the number of replies from the ABC shown in Table 23. There is clearly a sense of obligation and a sense of responsibility about the coverage of women's sport in the national network. This is worth pursuing.

The ABC in Melbourne gave some interesting information. It says the station does limited coverage of major events and items now are 'packaged' for major programs like Sports Arena. There were packages on 11 women's sports last year. I think it is worth keeping in mind the idea of packaging rather than trying to sell the whole of a sporting event to a media outlet.

The comments from Brisbane, Channel 9 are depressing: *The major sporting events are more likely to be played by men. We believe that the majority of our viewers want to watch sports which depict the highest level of skill. It is the viewers who tell us what they want to watch and we respond.*

I think this is a very good summary of two of the prevailing myths which media use to justify their continued lack of coverage of women's sport viz: that women's sports are unskilful, and that media respond to expressions of interest. I say that the media **create** that interest.

Table 23 shows once again a low number of responses from the two biggest cities, Sydney and Melbourne. It also shows, as did Table 22, that Adelaide does very well in all aspects of media coverage of women's sports compared to other cities. This owes a lot to the efforts of the last eight years. Efforts in this area can be rewarded.

The issues raised

One of the responses to the original 1980 survey was from sporting editors who said that one of their main problems was that there were not any women's journalists. At this time I was studying sports journalism and had done some work experience at **The News** in Adelaide. So when at the end of the year in the 'Silly

Season' **The News** was looking to fill in some space, the sporting editor remembered me, and remembered the survey and the lack of coverage of women's sport, and offered me the chance to write a women in sport column once a week. As soon as I began doing that, the women's network in Adelaide flooded **The News** with calls and letters saying how they had never bought **The News** before but they would do so now because it was finally covering women's sport. Instead of writing an article a week I wrote an article a day and the calls and letters kept flooding in. Eventually, the editor said *Look, we'll give you a full time job if you'll just stop your friends from ringing up.* Once one of the Adelaide papers had a women's sports journalist the other one got one. Then the first paper got a second, and so the second got a second and really it has gone on consistently from there.

Those strategies of analysis and action can be used anywhere to overcome the barriers to coverage to women's sports in the media. What are those barriers to coverage? They can be illustrated by listing four paradoxical dilemmas:

First dilemma:

— There is comparatively little coverage of women's sport by the media.
— The media say they cover what people are interested in.
— People are interested in what they know about.
— People don't know about women's sport because it is not covered in the media.

The second dilemma:

— There is a need for more women's sports journalists.
— Women are not appointed as sports journalists because they haven't had the experience.
— They can't gain the experience because they don't get the jobs.

The third dilemma:

— Media gives coverage to events that attract sponsorship.
— Events attract sponsorship if they have media coverage.

The fourth dilemma:

— The media say that women's sports do not provide them with information.
— Women's sports say they try and try to get coverage and in the end give up in frustration.
— The media say they are hungry for stories.
— Women's sports say they have plenty of stories.

Some ideas for overcoming those barriers emerge from the media replies that were sent in response to my original letter of enquiry.

Perhaps the first point is that any sport should consider whether it really wants media coverage. Because the fact is there will be a cost. One of the things the sport will lose is privacy and the capacity to wash its own dirty linen in private. One of the things the sport will gain will be stars, and that has some problems as well.

Assuming, though, that you have decided you do want media coverage, these are some things to remember:

— Don't treat the media as a public relations firm for you. Don't assume you will only get coverage of good news.
— Look for what is marketable in your sport.

— Appoint a public relations officer with 'news sense' or with a willingness to learn.
— Promote characters and personalities; people want to read about people.
— Establish a line of communication with a journalist on a personal basis.
— Be regular in keeping in touch.
— Know what the deadlines are, and meet them.
— Push to have specialist women commentators brought in for particular events.
— With television, make your aim be to have packaged highlights in major magazine shows, rather than the complete event at graveyard times.
— And the most important thing of all, thank people when they have given you coverage.

[This list should be compared with the points made by Julia Morant in her paper on marketing and sponsorship of women's sport later in this section. Between them these two presentations by thoughtful and active professionals and the information booklet reproduced as an Appendix to Julia Mourant's paper, cover most of what is important and illuminating in this field *Ed.*].

Some other quotations from replies to my original letter are also illuminating and informative.

— *Last year we ran a five part series on why women's sport doesn't get the coverage it deserves. We asked for suggestions from sportswomen. We got three letters.* (Brisbane sports editor)
— *The ABC has a charter obligation to cover widely, and David Hill is pushing for 'relevance' in the market place.* (Melbourne sports editor)
— *The situation has never been worse in Melbourne in relation to women's sports* (Sports journalist)
— *The coverage of women's sport has dramatically improved* (Brisbane sports journalist)
— *The* **West Australian** could not find good enough pictures in its library to send to this Conference, so now it has commissioned a photographer.
— **The Australian**'s pictorial desk was 'appalled' at its own lack of pictures.
— *We should get off our backsides too.* (Adelaide sports editor)
— *My job has been frustrating. I do believe once women are in the position to be sports editors or the young males of today grow up under anti-discrimination principles, then we won't have the battle.* (Brisbane sports journalist)
— *I'm a man in the job. A woman in the job would do something different, I'd have to concede that.* (Adelaide sports editor)

Finally, having looked at the barriers and what is needed to overcome them, we now move on to look at the strategy for doing that.

There are two parts to this, firstly the process and secondly the player.

Part A — The process
— Get the statistics that prove your point.
— Get support from other women; and from people in status positions.
— Define your shared goal.

— Detail the steps needed to reach that goal.

— Take them!

Part B — The player (you)

Be:

— Confident

— Calm

— Rational

— Calm

— Determined

— Calm

— Persistent

— Calm

— Professional

— Calm

— Expert

— Calm

— As angry as you need to be

But

— Calm

Finally, a quote for you to summarise the lessons which might be learnt from this particular paper — indeed all the papers printed in this volume. It comes from American ice hockey player Reggie Leach, who said:

success is not a matter of spontaneous combustion, you have to set yourself on fire

THE WOMEN'S SPORT PROMOTION UNIT

Margaret Pewtress

The Women's Sport Promotion Unit (WSPU) was established late in 1987. It was formed at the same time as the Minister for Sport announced the **National Policy and Plan for Women in Sport**. The WSPU is a committee of the Australian Sports Commission (ASC), the statutory authority which advises the Minister in relation to the promotion and development of sport in Australia.

How did the WSPU evolve? It represents the efforts of many Australians, who for many years have worked hard to ensure a better deal for women and girls who play sport. The problems facing women who participate in sport were precisely documented in **Women, Sport and the Media**, a report to the Federal Government, from the Working Group on Women in Sport, published in 1985. The principal recommendations of that report are reported here as Appendix One. The ASC was asked by the Minister to analyse the recommendations of the report and to advise the government on further action.

This brief presentation will indicate some of the points which emerged during this debate, as I believe they are important to the successful promotion of women's sport.

Firstly the point was raised that women's sports were no different from minor sports; these also suffered disadvantage, in terms of promotion, funding and media coverage. It appeared obvious that if the debate was going to focus on a major versus minor sports issue this would cloud the fact that women's sports faced other inequalities besides the 'minor sports' tag. It was relatively easy to prove, in terms of registered members and international achievements, that many of the women's sports deserved to be seen as major sports. The point was then raised that perhaps this was a women's issue or a social issue and not an issue that should concern a National Sports Commission.

It was pointed out that one of the main objectives of the ASC is to increase the level of participation in sport by all Australians. Statistics show that less women than men participate in sporting activities and the drop-out rate of teenage girls from sport exceeds that of boys. It was clear that if the ASC was going to achieve one of its main objectives, that is to encourage more Australians to participate in sport, women and girls needed to be targeted.

Next we came to money. The main recommendation of the Working Group on Women in Sport was *That a Women's Sport Promotion Unit be established, under the auspices of the Australian Sports Commission*. At this stage the sports budget was fully committed and it was argued that if the Government wanted the WSPU to be established, extra funding was required. In summary, the issue of women's sport stayed on the agenda, but a WSPU was not established. Instead the Task Force for Women's Sport was formed and it was given the task of preparing a National Policy and Plan for Women in Sport. The Task Force comprised three commissioners: myself, Vicki Cardwell, and Jim Yates, plus co-opted member Wendy Ey. We finally developed a draft policy and then distributed it widely for comment from those who had been closely involved with women's sport. The Task Force presented the final draft of the National Policy and Plan for Women in Sport to the ASC in November 1987. It was quickly formally adopted and the Minister announced that the WSPU would be established with an initial budget of $50,000 — the budget is modest but it is a start.

So now we have a policy and a WSPU — what is it going to do?

There are 14 policy statements listed in the National Policy: targets are pin-pointed for each statement and the strategies to achieve these targets are set out. These policy statements and their associated targets are included here as Appendix Two. In this presentation I will simply mention briefly some of the activities that the WSPU has already put into action.

1) The Unit will function as a clearing house for information on women's sport. Many of the groups I have spoken to have emphasised that an information network should be our first priority, particularly with regard to what funding is available at state and national level.

2) The Unit will attempt to document the services that are available at state and federal level. To maximise funds already available, we consider it is essential to establish a States-Federal network, thus allowing all women involved in professional development in the sports arena to share ideas.

3) The lack of media coverage for women's sport is seen as a major problem.

Without appropriate role-models it will continue to be difficult to increase female participation and interest in women's sport. We must ensure, however, that it is not just flavour of the month coverage — the real point is to ensure that women playing sport is accepted as the norm and an integral part of Australia's mainstream sports culture. The Unit will pursue all available strategies to gain increased media coverage for women's sport. In this area I find it difficult to remain positive. I have been advised by wise people not to bucket the media, so I will merely say this — I hope that those who decide what to report in sport will take an objective look at what they are reporting — does it represent all the Australians who play sport? Currently women's sport gets less than 2 per cent of the coverage and this is not equitable.

In conclusion, I believe that if the WSPU is to achieve its objectives it is essential that women become more involved in the administration of sport, and this is why conferences such as this are so vital if women are to develop professional sports administration skills. Finally, we believe that all the problems facing women in sport have been clearly documented and now is the time to set about solving them.

APPENDIX ONE

The Recommendations from the report to the Federal Government on Women in Sport 1985

Recommendations regarding the Women's Sport Promotions Unit

1. That a Women's Sport Promotion Unit be established, under the auspices of the Australian Sports Commission, but reporting directly to the Federal Government, to fulfil the following functions:

   — to provide advice to the Government on all aspects of women in sport in Australia

   — to liaise with government departments and authorities

   — to faciliate, promote, monitor and report on the coverage of women's sport in all media

   — to monitor and report on the allocation of government funding to women's sport

   — to work with women's sporting associations to assist in developing skills in media liaison and sponsorship negotiations; to undertake research into the reasons behind media and public relations company decisions on advertising and sponsorship

   — to examine particularly the problems facing women's administration in associations and to offer direct assistance, for example, in conducting seminars and helping to develop and promote training courses

   — to facilitate and promote improvement in general public relations and media liaison skills

   — to act as a tribunal to investigate and act upon complaints and problems brought to its attention

It is envisaged that the Unit would be established for an initial period of three years and would comprise no more than five people; membership should include media and public relations expertise and should also include representation from the Office of the Status of Women. The Unit would be serviced by a small secretariat within the Australian Sports Commission. It would be funded as part of the overall ASC budget.

The Government should appoint the chairperson and the other members. The chairperson and at least a majority of members should be women. It would present an annual report that would evaluate its own performance and outline achievements, problems and goals covering all the specific areas nominated, including action taken or in hand to address and implement the specific recommendations of this report.

The Unit would actively encourage the establishment of, and full co-operation with, similar units in each State and Territory.

2. That the Federal Government, as part of a wider survey of sport in general, undertake a major survey to define the scope and nature of women's sport in Australia today and use the results of that survey as a 'baseline' to monitor changes and trends in the future; and that the future census collections provide information on general trends on participation and fitness.

3. That research be undertaken, and the results widely published, to determine the relationship between women and information and publicity about sport in the media and the reasons why girls drop out of sport in secondary school years.

4. That the Women's Sport Promotion Unit be responsible for evaluating the provision of assistance through State and Territory education departments, and through the Commonwealth Schools Commission, to sport in all primary and secondary schools; the results of the monitoring to be published regularly to evaluate the development of more equitable funding.

5. That, where government funding is involved, facilities for women's sport be assessed and upgraded where they are currently below standard.

6. That, where government funding is involved, facilities be provided or adapted to cater for major women's sporting events; or, where facilities already exist towards which government funds have contributed, access to those facilities be monitored and reported on the ensure equitable access.

7. That all major sports centres and facilities be provided with adequate child care facilities.

8. That government assistance to sports associations be equitable, bearing in mind the need to be flexible to respond to changing and different priorities and demands.

9. That government assistance to sports associations should not be dependent upon the amalgamation of women's and men's sporting associations.

10. That the Australian Sports Commission be required to amend application procedures for the Sports Development Program and other assistance programs to ensure associations are required, as a condition of receiving Federal Government assistance, to report on the division of resources between women and men and action undertaken to provide equality of opportunity for women and girls in their sport.

11. That the Women's Sport Promotion Unit be responsible for collecting and disseminating widely information about government sports assistance programs and policies and other opportunities for assistance available to women in sport.

12. That the Women's Sport Promotion Unit develop resource materials and circulate them widely advising women in sporting associations on how to work with and liaise with government departments and authorities.

13. That federal government funding to disabled sports groups be increased to allow greater attention to the needs of disabled sportswomen.

14. That the Federal Government implement a major public awareness campaign including resource materials such as posters and calendars to promote the achievements of women in sport in Australia and to encourage women throughout the community to become involved in some form of sport at whatever level.

15. That the Women's Sport Promotion Unit provide regular briefings to the media on events and changes in all aspects of Australian sport affecting women and girls in sport.

16. That mixed participation in sport and physical education at primary school be encouraged.

17. That the Women's Sport Promotion Unit collect standardised high quality information about government funding at all levels to sport, including details of the break-up of funds between women and men.

18. That greater attention in teacher training courses be given to the needs of, and attitudes towards, women in sport; and that the Women's Sports Promotion Unit liaise with education authorities to ensure specialist courses in teacher colleges concentrate on women and girls.

19. That the Women's Sport Promotion Unit liaise with teacher training colleges to encourage all teachers to undertake at least Level 1 accreditation under the National Coaching Accreditation Scheme in at least one sport.

20. That the Women's Sport Promotion Unit liaise with education authorities to encourage and monitor the appointment of specialist physical education teachers in all primary schools.

21. That the Australian Coaching Council be asked to review all training courses and materials to ensure they reflect the needs of women in sport.

22. That the Women's Sport Promotion Unit obtain information on the division of government and private funding for sport in schools between girls' and boys' sport.

23. That modified rules sports be introduced to all primary school students as an integral element in an overall physical education program that emphasises participation, co-operation, recreation and the learning of a wide range of fitness and movement skills, and not exclusively competition.

24. That the Women's Sport Promotion Unit liaise with curriculum development authorities to develop a women in sport unit for all school curricula and the promotion of resource materials to assist schools to expose children to a wide range of information about sporting opportunities.

25. That the Women's Sport Promotion Unit seek information from local governments on the distribution of local government resources to women's and men's sports in areas such as facilities, equipment, assistance with travel to competition and so on.

26. That the Women's Sport Promotion Unit seek from the Office of the Status of Women and the Human Rights Commission information on the impact of the Sex Discrimination Act on all aspects of activity that affect women, with particular reference to its capacity to assist in breaking down the barriers for women and girls in sport, and other areas of related research.

27. That the Women's Sport Promotion Unit, in consultation with the Office of the

Status of Women, monitor and report on the impact on women and girls in sport of wider, community attitudes towards women and, where possible, recommend action to be taken to address and overcome remaining problems and difficulties.

28. That the Women's Sport Promotion Unit liaise with the Occupational Health and Safety Commission when sport and fitness programs in industries form part of health promotion programs, and assist in developing further such programs in particular for women in the workforce.

Recommendations regarding the media

1. That the Women's Sport Promotion Unit liaise with media organisations to seek:

   (i) more equitable coverage of women's sport in news and general information programs in all media outlets, especially the ABC and SBS and the provision of a comprehensive sports news and results service;

   (ii) the employment of more women sports journalists and broadcasters;

   (iii) the assignment of women sports journalists and broadcasters to general sports and more journalists to cover all aspects of women's sport;

   (iv) sponsorship to provide annual scholarships to train cadet women sports journalists and broadcasters;

   (v) the development of training opportunities for women sports journalists, including in-service courses.

2. That the Women's Sport Promotion Unit report at least annually on progress made towards each of the objectives outlined in recommendation (1) above.

3. That the performance of media outlets in covering women's sport be monitored and reported on by the Women's Sport Promotion Unit.

4. That a women in sport 'encyclopaedia' be produced providing information about the history and achievements of Australian women in sport, and that the publication be regularly updated and made available to the media.

5. That an annual diary of major events and competitions in women's sport be produced and made available to the media, and that a handbook be prepared outlining the programs available to publicise women's sport-type of program, producers, deadlines, etc. — and made available to women in sporting associations.

6. That the Australian Broadcasting Tribunal, in the context of evaluating the performance of individual commercial and public broadcasting and tele-vision stations, concentrate on the coverage of women's sport under both the Australian content and the 'adequate and comprehensive' provisions, and that, if no significant changes in coverage have become clear in two years, the Women's Sport Promotion Unit recommend to the Federal Government amendments to licence conditions to require more equal coverage of women's sport in line with the spirit of the sex discrimination legislation.

7. That the Special Broadcasting Service investigate the possibility of using its existing community information and current affairs programs to provide information to ethnic women and girls about the opportunities for involve-ment in sport and fitness activities.

8. That the Federal Government offer a significant annual prize for the best

coverage of a women's sporting event by a journalist or broadcaster and to the best media organisation for overall coverage of women in sport.

9. That the Women's Sport Promotion Unit liaise with the Australian Journalists' Association to examine the possibility of developing an agreed set of principles and values to guide the coverage of and reporting on women in sport.

10. That the charter of the ABC be amended to include 'sport' so that it will be required to 'encourage and promote all sports in Australia, including women's sports'.

Recommendations regarding sport associations

1. That the status and role of publicity and media relations officers be upgraded where that position is not already filled by someone in a senior management position.

2. That all associations be advised of and encouraged to use the services of AAP and Telecom's Sportsfone to publicise results and events.

3. That, where an organisation or association receives funding from the Federal Government, it be required, as a condition of receiving that assistance, to report annually on the distribution of resources, access to facilities and provision of equipment; the report should include details of the levels of funding provided in these areas to women's and men's sport and, where that funding is unequal, should provide an explanation. Long-term development plans should indicate specific action to be undertaken to resond to the need of women within the sport.

4. That the Australian Institute of Sport and other organisations responsible for specialist coaching and sports science services and programs be required to report on activities and funding to provide assistance to women athletes and teams, and that women be equitably represented on coaching and sports medicine staff.

5. That, in consultation with the Women's Sport Promotion Unit and the Sports Aid Foundation, associations develop long term plans to generate and sustain sponsorship for their sport.

6. That all associations which receive funding from the Federal Government be required to ensure that at least one athlete (from the men's and women's element in their sport for mixed sports) be appointed to their board of management or top decision-making body.

7. That all associations provide a forward calendar of events to all their members, especially women, to assist them in planning to take account of other commitments and priorities.

8. That associations develop training opportunities to encourage women to become involved in administration to the most senior levels.

9. That women be encouraged to become referees, umpires, etc., in all sports, including men's sports, and that courses designed to achieve this objective be well publicised and held at times that enable women to participate.

10. That selection criteria for the appointment of coaches, managers, team officials, sports science personnel accompanying national and State teams where government funding is involved be made public.

11. That all 'umbrella' organisations in sport — for example the Australian

Olympic Federation, the Australian Commonwealth Games Association, the Confederation of Australian Sport and the Australian Sports Commission — be required to publish details of procedures to select members, the method of appointment, and operational information.

Recommendations regarding groups with special needs

1. That the Women's Sport Promotion Unit give consideration to the needs of special groups within the community.
2. That the Australian Institute of Sport and State institutes increase the provision of their services and skills to both disabled and rural women in sports teams and individual players.
3. That the Aboriginal Sports Federation be asked to undertake a study of the sports need of Aboriginal women in Australia, with a view to recommending specific programs and services to be developed to meet them.
4. That the Australian Sports Commission be asked to look specifically at the needs of elderly women in the development of its overall action plan for sport for the elderly; and to provide information on sporting opportunities for elderly people to appropriate organisations and groups.
5. That sports associations receiving government funding be asked to report to the Women's Sport Promotion Unit on programs and services provided to encourage women in urban areas to participate, and on access to facilities for all special groups.
6. That programs be developed by community welfare and other relevant departments to provide sporting opportunities to women in prisons and other institutions.

APPENDIX TWO
The Australian Sports Commission Policy on Women in Sport 1987

Policy Statement 1 — Promotion

It is an ASC objective to improve the promotion of women in sport.

The ASC will seek to encourage similar promotion of women in sport by other governments, the media and sporting organisations.

1.1 Targets
To increase:

— awareness and focus on the achievements of women in sport

— the quality and quantity of media coverage

— sportswomen role models in the media

— opportunities for sponsorship

— awareness of women's participation in sports.

1.2 Strategies
It is an ASC objective to:

— undertake a public awareness campaign on the values and benefits of 'sport for all' reflecting accurate and realistic role models for both women and men, (eg a 60-second community awareness message depicting women participating as part of a wider campaign)

— develop and distribute material that raises awareness and promotes equity and women's participation in sport

— negotiate with relevant media organisations to develop a TV/magazine/newspaper series on women's achievements in sports

— develop a logo for the Women's Sport Promotion Unit (WSPU) which could be used for promotional purposes

— target specific audiences and groups, both within and outside the sport system, for promotion materials, and develop and distribute materials appropriately

— prepare an educational program for women athletes and administrators on media relations and sponsorship negotiations

— produce a video portraying successful female sportswomen participating in their sport; this video would be widely promoted in schools

— prepare a series of publications on women in sport, eg booklets on issues of women in sport:
  - training techniques for women
  - elite sportswomen
  - media relations
  - sponsorship negotiations

— support other organisations promoting women in sport. Wherever possible co-ordinate with other bodies and set up support networks on issues relating to women in sport

— support or endorse organisations, programs and products which encourage women in sport.

Policy Statement 2 — Leadership Development

It is an ASC objective to support and encourage increased involvement by women at all levels of sport administration and development in Australia.

2.1 Targets

To increase opportunities for women to gain:

— sports development skills

— positions in decision making areas.

2.2 Strategies

It is an ASC objective to:

— initiate follow up seminars to the 'Playing the Game' Workshops

— ensure that all ASC seminars take into account the needs of women in sport

— assist women to gain skills in media liaison and sponsorship negotiation, eg workshops, publications

— actively encourage women to apply for positions as coaches, administrators, referees/umpires and officials

— prepare and distribute publications that will assist women on media liaison and sponsorship negotiations

- encourage National Sporting Organisations (NSOs) to include women admistrators in any mixed team
- ensure that any Sports Talent Encouragement Plan (STEP) Coaching Program includes women coaches
- advocate that women be fully represented on decision making bodies in sport
- compile a directory of women in management positions in sport and monitor the trends.

Policy Statement 3 — Participation Development

It is an ASC objective to increase the quality and quantity of opportunities for all women to participate in sport as athletes, coaches, administrators or officials. This includes those individuals whose disadvantage is compounded by their 'group' membership, eg women with low socio-economic status, older women, women of non-English speaking backgrounds, Aboriginal and Torres Strait Islanders, women geographically isolated, institutionalised women, or women with disabilities.

3.1 Targets
- to raise awareness and educate the community that women do and can participate in sport
- to increase opportunities for participation in sport.

3.2 Strategies
It is an ASC objective to:
- *develop a community awareness message (60 second or a series of advertisements) to focus on a range of women participating in sport and encouraging other women to participate*
- *liaise with officers managing the Girls and Physical Activity Project to assess appropriate special measures which could be undertaken by the ASC to introduce girls to a wider range of sports*
- *liaise with relevant agencies (eg schools, national sporting organisations, government bodies) to encourage special measures to be developed to assist women and girls to participate in sport*
- *develop a database on sport participation rates and include indicators that trace the involvement of women and girls give priority funding to projects that aim at increasing participation by women in their sport.*

Policy Statement 4 — Elite Level Participation

It is an ASC objective to encourage sports organisers to ensure that women enjoy fair and equitable opportunities, support, incentives and rewards in international and national levels of sport.

4.1 Targets
- to ensure that elite female participants have appropriate access to services such as coaching, funding, travel, facilities and to the rewards of participation at the elite level.

4.2 Strategies
It is an ASC objective to:
- ensure that all its programs and policies are based on equitable criteria

- encourage other organisations (eg NSOs, governments) to operate their sports programs on any equity basis
- collect and analyse data on opportunities and support for females in sport at the national and international level
- review support and assistance given to bodies if they are found to be inequitable.

Policy Statement 5 — Junior Sport

It is an ASC objective to encourage junior sport and in particular mixed participation and modified sports at primary school level and club level.

5.1 Targets
- to increase opportunities for mixed and modified sports at primary school level and club level.

5.2 Strategies
It is an ASC objective to:

- encourage those organisations responsible, to support mixed participation in sport at primary school
- encourage the adoption of AUSSIE SPORTS in all primary schools
- collect and collate material on why children (particularly girls) drop out of sport
- initiate a program targetting high school aged girls (through schools and community clubs) to become involved in and remain in sport
- liaise with the Girls and Physical Activity Project to examine what has already been done and how the ASC can assist the promotion of girl's sport
- liaise with State and Federal Departments of Education concerning projects to develop self-esteem of girls through sport
- ensure that NSOs consider equity matters in their junior development programs
- reflect the above issues in its own programs particularly AUSSIE SPORTS and the Applied Sports Research Program.

Policy Statement 6 — Education

It is an ASC objective to encourage the appointment of specialist physical education teachers in all schools. The ASC supports greater attention in teacher training courses to the needs, realities and perceptions of women and girls in sport.

6.1 Targets
To encourage:

- the employment of more specialist physical education teachers in all schools
- greater attention to women in sport in teacher training courses.

6.2 Strategies
It is an ASC objective to:

- encourage departments of education to appoint physical education teachers to all primary schools

— encourage tertiary institutions to provide greater attention to women in sport issues in teacher training courses

— investigate the proportion of female sports educators

— promote AUSSIE SPORTS resources and in particular those resources that address issues facing women in sport.

Policy Statement 7 — Media Coverage

It is an ASC objective to encourage the media to ensure that the amount, style and presentation of coverage given to women in sport is fair and unbiased.

7.1 Targets

— to increase the quality and quantity of media coverage

— to encourage media representatives to more effectively cover women in sport

— to encourage the employment of more women journalists.

7.2 Strategies
It is an ASC objective to:

— lobby the media to increase the quality and quantity of media coverage of women in sport, including encouragement of more journalists (especially women) to be trained to cover women in sport, eg encourage the media to learn the rules or codes of women's sport so that they can present women's sport more accurately and positively

— monitor the media continually, congratulating them on good quality coverage of women in sport and registering disappointment of poor quality reporting

— encourage NSOs to assist by preparing a list of their supportive media contacts. These contacts can be approached to be involved in writing/reporting on women in sport

— encourage NSOs to write to the Australian media

— challenging sports editors, producers and journalists to allocate more space and time to women's sport

— assist NSOs to develop skills in media liaison skills, keep NSOs informed on publications available on media liaison

— encourage the public to register any disapproval of media coverage with the Australian Broadcasting Tribunal.

Policy Statement 8 — Sponsorship

It is an ASC objective to actively encourage the sponsorship of women in sport, and assist sports administrators to develop skills in public relations, promotion and sponsorship negotiations.

8.1 Targets
To increase:

— the sponsorship given to women in sport

— the marketing skills of representatives working with women in sport.

8.2 Strategies
It is an ASC objective to:

- maintain a register of elite female athletes and inform potential sponsors of sportswomen able to help them promote their product
- raise women's awareness of the costs and benefits of promotion and sponsorship activities
- conduct workshops and produce publications on gaining sponsorship and promoting women in sport
- establish a library of action photos and resources, featuring women in sport.

Policy Statement 9 — Funding

It is an ASC objective to ensure that its funds are equitably allocated between females and males, and encourage other funding bodies to adopt and maintain equitable funding criteria.

9.1 Targets
- to ensure that funds are allocated according to equitable and objective criteria
- to require funded bodies to demonstrate commitment to equity.

9.2 Strategies
It is an ASC objective to:

- base its funding on objective criteria
- require funded bodies to account for the use of funds allocated for women's programs
- liaise with NSOs and Departments of Sport to analyse their allocation of funds to sports and between males and females
- publicise funding trends and decisions by governments, and national sporting bodies.

Policy Statement 10 — Sports Facilities

It is an ASC objective to work with governments and other relevant organisations — Commonwealth, State and local — to develop, upgrade and maximise use of facilities consistent with a sporting environment that provides equal opportunities for men and women.

10.1 Targets
- to ensure equitable access by women's sporting groups to all sports facilities.

10.2 Strategies
It is an ASC objective to:

- Encourage agencies to fully account for the needs of all women in relation to sports facilities, particularly in terms of:
  - planning of facilities
  - access to facilities
  - upgrading of facilities
  - support for facilities for child minding (especially in all new buildings)
  - maximising use of facilities by appropriate design, and where necessary the modification of design
- access data on the quantity and quality of sports facilities in this country

— fully consider women in its funding decisions
— assist women's NSOs to negotiate with local governments for an equitable share of and assess to local facilities.

Policy Statement 11 — Amalgamation

It is an ASC objective to support and assist the process of amalgamation of sporting organisations, where there is mutual agreement between the women's and men's organisations and where there are necessary safeguards in place to ensure that women will be adequately represented.

11.1 Targets
— to encourage the efficient administration of sporting organisations
— to assist with amalgamation where there is mutual agreement between parties
— to ensure full protection of the rights and opportunities of women to participate at all levels of sport in the future management of the new body.

11.2 Strategies
It is an ASC objective to:
— where there is mutual agreement, assist the amalgamation of men's and women's national sporting organisations
— provide and review guideline for amalgamation to NSOs to ensure women are represented in the decision making processes of their sport
— monitor and report on progress in sports where amalgamation has taken place.

Policy Statement 12 — Research

It is an ASC objective to encourage, undertake and commission research on women in sport and encourage such research to be widely analysed and distributed.

12.1 Targets
— to collect and collate research already undertaken in areas affecting women in sport
— to commission new research in areas of need to distribute research findings and encourage practical applications.

12.2 Strategies
It is an ASC objective to:
— collate and distribute details of research already completed on women in sport issues
— undertake or commission research and analysis into the problems and issues affecting female sports participation, and encourage the undertaking of such research by other agencies, eg educational institutions
— request the National Sports Research Co-ordinator to collect and collate material on women in sport and to undertake a series of 'State of the Art' reviews or 'Fact Sheets' on issues
— undertake or commission research such as:
  - why girls drop out of sport
  - women's fitness and participation in sport

- media coverage of women in sport
- factors influencing attitudes towards women in sport
- women's performance in sport
- implications of the Sex Discrimination Act.

Policy Statement 13 — Liaison and Information Exchange

It is an ASC objective to be an agent for the collection and dissemination of information about women in sport and, where possible, co-ordinate such activities with our agencies.

13.1 Targets
- to increase the 'bank' of information about women's participation in sport
- to collect and distribute information about women in sport
- to increase awareness and knowledge about women in sport.

13.2 Strategies
It is an ASC objective to:
- request bibliographies on women and sport form major libraries
- establish a photo library on women in sport
- develop a directory of agencies/persons with expertise in the area of women in sport
- continue to publish a diary of events, with women's events identified
- consider the publication of a sports encyclopaedia and other publications to publicise data and information collected.

Policy Statement 14 — Program Development and Evaluation

It is an ASC objective to ensure that the needs of women and girls are identified and taken into account in the development, implementation and review of all ASC programs and encourage all levels of government and sporting bodies to take a similar approach towards sports policy and program development.

The ASC will design and implement mechanisms to monitor and evaluate progress towards achieving equity for women in sport.

14.1 Targets
- to ensure that women's needs are fully taken into account in all ASC policies and programs
- to ensure that all programs and policies are monitored and evaluated, and that the implication for women in sport are noted.

14.2 Strategies
It is an ASC objective to:
- assess and revise all policies and programs over the next three years to ensure that women's needs and other equity considerations are being taken into consideration
- recommend that State/Territory Governments (where it has not occurred) establish a women's sport committee or appoint an advisor to assist the Minister for Sport and Recreation to make decisions which affect women involved in sport
- inform the Sport and Recreation Ministers Council of the Women in

Sport policy and encourage state/territory departments to support its implementation

— encourage all levels of government and sporting umbrella groups to take into account women's needs, and commend such action when it occurs

— review requirements for NSO development plans to ensure the needs of women are taken into account. Encourage NSOs to recognise the needs of women in their policies and programs

— encourage NSOs to review and report on the number and quality of events/carnivals in which women can participate — either as separate events or part of existing events

— review progress on all priorities and actions outlined in this policy

— develop and review related evaluation procedures regularly to assess their adequacy and relevance.

MARKETING AND SPONSORSHIP OF WOMEN'S SPORT

Julia Mourant

This paper is written by someone who is a media executive, a sponsor of sport and a member of sporting organisations. As a sponsor of sport, I will begin by presenting the sponsor's point of view. Most sponsorships are negotiated with private enterprise companies because any money that sports organisations get from a government source is usually in the form of either a grant or a loan. When they receive money from a private sponsor it is almost always a gift. A sponsor first of all has to earn that money that they are giving away. This means that in the case of a company such as Coca-Cola, their employees on the factory floor are making a product and that it is being distributed by other employees; it means that their sales teams are out there selling and they are putting stock and product into shops which then generates cash flow. Coca-Cola employ in South Australia several hundred people and keep a fleet of over a hundred vehicles on the road simply to move their products. In addition to all the direct costs associated with these activities, they have to make enough to pay workers' compensation insurance and payroll and other taxes. They must put money aside for future development and growth. The list just goes on and on.

All of the employees of a company like Coca-Cola are working for the same goal, which is to make a profit so that the company can keep on going. Once the shareholders have been paid out of any profit which is made after all these activities have been taken care of, then any money that is left over can be available for sponsorship purposes. All sporting bodies know that Coca-Cola and other companies have got some money available for sponsorship; the fight is therefore on to get that money. It is not a foregone conclusion that any organisation will get money if they apply to any company for a sponsorship. Even if they go and ask for it really nicely. As a sponsor, I am really tired of hearing the phrase *It's not fair that X got dollars and we didn't*. Fairness really has nothing to do with it.

Sponsors' dollars will only be distributed to those sports that maximise the sale of a company's product. The organisation is into sport and the company — any private enterprise business — is into promoting and selling their product. The company's dollars have been earned. The sports organisation is looking for a handout. But, when they take that handout, what are they going to give back? A pleasant smile is not enough and it never has been.

As a sponsor, I can tell you that it is not enough. As an employee of the television station Channel Nine in Adelaide, I get to give away their money and their commodity which is air time. In my capacity as the Publicity and Promotions manager for Channel Nine, I deal with all those sponsorships and Channel Nine has curbed its spending dramatically in this area. My company has given money and air time to a lot of sports and in return, in several instances, we have been excluded from the publicity and the advertising of these organisations. Our resources often were not used: for example the sports organisation may have had a special event happening but did not ring our newsroom about it. It would have been easy to pick the phone up and dial the same number that they use to ring me and ask me for the dollars to sponsor their event! They could have said 'We've got this event happening and we would really like you to come out and have a look at it.' But often we didn't get even that; nobody rang the newsroom to say that these things were happening!

Any publicity that was generated for those sports was usually generated by my department. I look after my company's dollars and I often say, 'Hey, that might be a good story'; but then when I get out there it is often like extracting teeth. 'Can I get two people to photograph with X?' 'Oh. Oh, can .... Oh no. Well, you have to ring ...' And then you start the merry-go-round. There are sub-committees of committees of splinter groups of all sorts of things. And you go round and round in circles trying to organise a few photographs and obtain some simple facts and figures. In the end, it is easier to say, 'Oh I give up'. It is much easier, right?

So what happens to that sponsor in the end when having given them money for 12 months; they do not give even a summary saying what happened to their sponsorship dollars. What should a sponsor think or do when, as is often the case, there is no contact to say, 'Look we've had these fabulous successes', or 'We've had this real bummer of a year, but next year is going to be even better so just hang in with us'; 'All these athletes of ours did tremendously well and thanks to you giving us your dollars and lending us your name. We were able to get a better junior program up and running and gain some more minor sponsors which gave us some more cash flow'; 'Thanks very much because you gave our sport a higher profile'.

Often when I get back to bodies such as these and say, 'Look, you know we gave you money; we helped you out; we gave you air time which is a very expensive commodity. Why didn't you get back to us?', I get answers such as 'Oh, we didn't think it was our responsibility', or 'We didn't have anybody to do it'. (Quite what **it** was I don't know, because everybody uses the telephone day in day out). 'We're sports people not advertising agencies. We didn't think you'd be interested'. That last statement is a real killer, because if the sponsor is not interested in the first place, they would not give you a cent. They have already indicated their interest by virtue of the money, time, product, resources etc, that they have provided.

If you do not really disbelieve all that I have said so far, put me to the test; go to your sponsors and ask them what they are getting from you. I would suggest, though, that most women's sports are being sponsored by companies in which the senior people are actually friends or they have family or business ties with people in the sports organisatons. I suggest that not enough work is being done to break into the corporate market. It is really no different from men's sports and children's sports, but both of those sporting areas are actually gaining big corporate dollars on a national and state level.

Having gone through all that I have just described as a sponsor, I have often also been disappointed that our Managing Director and the General Manager were only invited to one event. And that was the day they handed over the cheque. At no time in my nine years employment with Channel Nine has any of the sporting bodies we have supported ever got back to us and said, 'Listen, you've got 280 people working there; what say we offer you a $2 discount for all your staff and you get them to roll up, because you know they look like a great bunch of people'. But we have never ever got that. There have been no initiatives back the other way; we have handed over our airtime and the dollars, then we have been ignored until the same time next year. The same letter, just the dates whited out and typed over again, arrives to say, 'Thanks very much. We'd like the same again; we'd like 15% more this year because of inflation!'

Not only do some sponsors like myself hand over the money, but then we go out and have our own advertising signs done. And then we trot down to wherever the event is and we put them up ourselves. And then we maintain them. Why should we do that? Surely that is not really the sponsor's responsibility. Well, it is our product — we are the ones out there in the market place. I would hate to see a Channel Nine sign that looked tatty; that had not been secured to a wall properly and had fallen down; I would hate to see a Channel Nine sign that had been battered around by the elements and did not look good. I do not want my sign to be on the third door round the back, or just propped up against the wall somewhere. I want it to be in the best place, so I get the signs made. I usually go down and put them up; and then we maintain them. So the sponsors are not only handing over money, but they then have got to look after their own image. A lot of sponsors get really cheesed off because they have not only given money but end up looking after their own interests as well. A considerable further worry and expense.

So, before a lot of sporting bodies ever go out and pitch for international events, I would like to offer a word of advice: there are professional organisations that not only will help you if you go to them and say, 'Hey, there's half a chance that we could get the All Australian Women's Marble Championship in the middle of Wayville Showgrounds in 1990, what would be the chances?' They will help you do your proposal and help you get the sponsorships. Yes, they would take a fee for that, but they would not only help you put the package together, but help you run it as well. You need such organisations because really, you are asking to be shown to the world as professionals. Too often in this aspect sporting organisations are all amateurs. They all work at something else. I am a professional publicity person — Promotions and Marketing — I find it very easy. But most sportwomen find it very difficult to do what I do for a living. Let me tell you I cannot run 400 metres either.

As a sponsor, I now put all my energy and money into training camps and schools for young sports players. We are currently involved in cricket, tennis, soccer, water sports, baseball and softball and I would like to take this opportunity right here and now to say that the baseball and softball coaching clinics are some of the best that I have ever observed. I just love them.

I go down there and the kids laugh and they have the best fun and they are learning some of the best skills that I have ever seen and it is all due to the organisation and the skills of the head person. I put our resources now into such areas, knowing that there will be changes in the future, hopefully coming from conferences like this. I concentrate on areas where I can see that there are things that can be done to change the present situation. I want to ensure that young people going to those camps are trained properly to gain the benefit of what is learnt from conferences like this.

As a media executive I did not get to where I am now by waiting for somebody else to do a job. I have got on and done it myself. So, to help sporting bodies with little or no media skills, I spent a great deal of my time putting a publicity manual together. I then offered it around at no cost to sporting bodies, with the additional offer of me conducting media workshops for their clubs or bodies so that I could share my skill and help sports get ahead. It was a genuine offer and I gave up my personal time and energy and my skills to help sports people gain publicity. I circulated about 200 copies, but I know of only one person who used the manual and that is a woman involved in this conference. Consider this from the opposite perspective. If I went to a sports coach or indeed almost any sports person, they would, no doubt, give me some coaching along the following lines: 'Julia, this is how you run properly; this is how you get to do 400 metres. Here's a little advice on training; do that for X amount of time and this for X amount of time and in the end you will run 400 metres — it might take you an hour, but you'll get there'.

I am a professional publicity person. I am not going to do your job for you, but I am only too willing to give you a little bit of 'coaching'. The objective is to be able to run publicity and it is only going to be 100 metres. I will give you a few training sessions and you'll get there — it might take you an hour but you will get there. I repeat that only one person took me up on my offer in South Australia. So what I am saying is, 'It's easy to say boo, hiss, sponsors don't do this and it's not fair and the media don't do that', but at the same time the media in one instance offered to make available some of its skills. The answer, essentially, was 'Thanks, but no thanks'.

Let me finish this section by recalling one small but typical incident. A few days before this conference started, a journalist from Channel Nine's newsroom, rang the organisers of the conference to enquire about doing some footage on one of the overseas athletes. They were told that the athlete concerned had just finished on the track. Our response to that was, 'Why wasn't there some contact with the newsroom to say that there was an international athlete running, leaping, bounding here in Adelaide and that if you want some great footage, grab a camera and get on down because we'll be only too happy to show you where it is?' So it was a great story that this conference missed. A story like that would have helped your conference sponsor immensely. [As an Appendix to this paper, I have included the **Handbook on Handling the Media** which was prepared specifically for activities during Women's Week, in Adelaide, March 1988, of which this conference was one. The lessons it contains are quite general though — only the names would be different for other times and other places *Ed.*].

I would like to conclude with some comments as a member of a sporting organisation — my final involvement in sport. I absolutely love soccer — I watch women's soccer, but I am actively involved in the Adelaide City Soccer Club. My role in the club is to earn sponsorship dollars. We, the Committee (there are four of us) would sell anything that will earn us money. We have sold all the players. Their wives and girlfriends are not very happy, but we have sold them anyhow. The program and the tickets look after all the sponsorship and we organise one major fund raiser event every year. It is very hard work, because a team in the National Soccer League, I am sure you will realise, requires a lot of money to keep them on the road. But we have a target; we start very early; and we actually plan ahead. Last October, for example, we were already selling our sponsors on the kick-off date of

January. We do clever things for those companies that say: 'Yes, we'll be a sponsor, but it's a bit much to give you $500 straight up'. We say, 'Fabulous, we'll invoice you quarterly, smilingly'. And so we invoice quarterly. Some companies say, 'Yes, we'd like to be a player's sponsor, but things are a little bit tight'. We invoice them monthly. So it is not a matter of having a huge cheque; doing is by working out in the long run how much money is incoming. We work it out on a monthly basis and that gives us a cash flow, so that we are budgeting our club.

And I might say that we have yet to be disappointed so far as any one by one payment from a sponsor is concerned. So sponsorship is not just one big fat cheque once a year. You can say to a sponsor, 'Look, we've got a telephone and a car to run us around to get us all the things that we need, would you pick up the tab for our telephone bill and we can advertise your sponsorship on our car. These are the phone bills for last year. This year we can expect a slight increase — would you mind doing that?' This gives this sponsor a purpose. Sponsors just do not like handing over a big sum of money and not knowing what happens. You can always justify in retrospect on paper what you spent the money on. But too often at the end of the year it is not easy for sports organisations to know what they really did spend the money on.

So, learn to use your sponsorship and use it to your advantage. When you are successful with an approach to a sponsor, do creative things with their money. Most of those sponsorship dollars come from companies where people on the factory floor had to earn the money first of all before they gave it away.

APPENDIX
WOMEN'S SPORT AND RECREATION IN THE MEDIA

An Information Booklet prepared by the
South Australian Department of Recreation and Sport

What this booklet is about

The purpose of this booklet is to improve the relationship between people in the media and women and so to take a step closer to better coverage of women's sport and recreation.

Advice given in this booklet is by no means intended to be prescriptive. It is intended to promote a better understanding and broader knowledge for all those directly concerned with communication between the media and women's sport and recreation.

It is generally agreed that the participation of women in sport and recreation depends a great deal on the images and models portrayed of women in sport in the media. As indicated by the Women, Sport and Media Report, compiled by Senator Rosemary Crowley's Working Party, plus the participants in the recently convened Women in Action Conference, Adelaide, there is much room for improvement in media portrayal of women's sport in SA.

The media has the power to shape the attitudes of people of all ages to physical activity — it therefore does not just reflect sport and recreation that people want to hear, see or read about.

So as to develop more positive images of women's activities it is important to inform the media as to the ways in which women want to be portrayed, just as it is important to inform women as to how they can encourage better images through more organised contacts with the media.

Towards the above aims, this booklet provides practical advice as to how women can deal with the media, who to contact and when, and what forms of contact may be effective. The media is advised about how to portray women and who to contact and when.

The information in their booklet has been compiled in response to receiving information from both women in sport and the community, and employees in the media. Therefore, it is **first hand** advice about what both parties are requiring to improve the sports woman's image.

Feedback from sportswomen and women in the community

In recent years there has been considerable public comment from the women in our community about their concern for the poor portrayal of women's sport. It is well accepted that a portrayal of good role models in sport serves to encourage people to maintain an involvement in a sport. There is clear research and evidence that indicates that women are generally poorly portrayed in the media either by inappropriate reporting or no reporting at all. Women's general dissatisfaction with this poor portrayal has been evident through their lodging of public complaints, decline in purchasing of newspapers and participation as an audience to TV and radio.

To confirm that women in our SA community are still concerned about their inappropriate portrayal through the media, a series of consultative processes with various members of the community was conducted. These were in the form of:

— personal interviews with elite sportswomen
— public opinion survey conducted in the Mall
— attendance at public meetings organised by women
— attendance at sportswomen's meetings

The overwhelming response to the question of whether the women were happy with the current portrayal of sportswomen was **no**. Another major concern for the media to note was that the women also acknowledged they now no longer purchase or view the particular medium that portrays sportswomen inappropriately.

Obviously, the ultimate aim of improving the media image of women in sport is to encourage more women to take part in such activities. But, as indicated, the standard of the present portrayal is not acceptable to many of the media's audience.

It is recognised that it is not always the 'fault' of the media that there is inadequate coverage of sportswomen. This booklet also includes information for women on ways they can improve their communication with the media. However, it was evident that women in the community are very unhappy about their present image. They have provided some guidelines on how they would like to see themselves portrayed. These guidelines are provided for your benefit.

Also included is a current listing of contacts for women's sporting groups. These should assist in gaining up-to-date information related to the women's sport or recreation.

Advice on how women want to be portrayed in the media

— Females represent approximately 51 per cent of the population but have less participants than males in active recreation in South Australia. The media has a role to play, along with other social institutions in helping to promote women's activities in such ways that encourage more females to be active.
— The more often positive models of women being active are portrayed in the media, the more likely it is that the young will follow suit.
— The implication is for the need to have increased air time or column space devoted to women's activities.
— Promotion of 'non-traditional' women's activities will encourage women to take part in a broader range of activities in their own recreation time.
— The public wants to have the opportunity to know about the widest range of sport that is available.
— Women want more action photographs and film so that it reflects the vigorous activities they are involved in.
— Women want like language choice in the media to reflect more an equal status of men and women. Hence the need to avoid terms such as 'girls' or 'pretty' when male equivalents of these terms are not used in covering men's sports. Language in general should complement any coverage of the sensation or controversial.
— Avoid trivialising women in sport by focussing on just one aspect of the sport or an aspect of the women involved that is irrelevant to the sport being played, eg a controversy in the administration; or the private life of a participant.
— Consider placing articles or items in a newspaper or program in more prominent positions or at more prominent times.
— Women in high and low participant sports want to read more about what they are involved in.
— When editing press releases check back with the correspondent — the courtesy and concern will be appreciated.
— If the activity is played by men and women separately, devote equal space and time to separate articles on each.
— Appoint more female and male journalists who have a specific task of covering women's sport and recreation.
— Always portray women's sport on its own merits and not in direct comparison with men's sport. Consider women's sport as different, not as superior or inferior.
— Persistent, consistent and professional contacts by women with the media, now and in the future, should be rewarded. Have the topic discussed at policy level with a view to making a commitment over a substantial period of time to cover women's actiities more.

Using the contact list

The format is self-explanatory and provides opportunities to make contact with associations and groups from the most prominent, traditional and competitive through to the least traditional and non-competitive.

While women are urged to be persistent with the media, this listing makes it more possible for the media to also 'make the first move'.

Feedback from the media

As indicated in the 'Wise Words to the Media' Section, many woman are unhappy about the present image of sportswomen in the media.

To gain information related to the media's response to such complaints, contact was made with media personalities, sports editors and reference to the **Women Sport and The Media** report was carried out. In general the media accepts responsibility for this poor coverage due to many factors, including poor market research, basic individual prejudices and restraining policy.

Given these constraints the media emphasised the importance of receiving good clear and precise information from the women's sports. On most counts the media suggested the information it received was inadequate. So as to assist women in sports to improve their image, this booklet includes informtion received from media personalities related to how to achieve good communication. The guidelines, in the whole, are an adaptation of Helen Menzies' 'Making it into the Media' with added information received from local media personalities. They are designed to **help you** to improve your coverage in the media. It includes a listing of media contacts and alternative methods of promoting your sport.

Advice on what information the media want to receive

In general, the establishment of a Publicity Officer was strongly supported by media employees.

The following guidelines on the duties of the officer will assist both your organisation and the media's ability to promote your sport.

The Role of the Publicity Officer

Every sport and recreation organisation needs a publicity officer. The person should have high status in the organisation, know the sport well and be prepared to be **persistent** and **consistent**. The person should be an independent worker who will report back to the group and who is available to be contacted at all times.

Duties (not in order of priority)
- Persuade others in the organisation of the need for media coverage.
- Arrange access for the media to participants, coaches, administrators.
- Have all information readily available: key dates, key people and how to contact them, records and record holders, team selections, history.
- Keep up with interstate and overseas news in the sport.
- Arrange interviews with visiting stars.
- Keep a cuttings file, not only of her own sport, but of similar sports to analyse how they made it into the media. Learn about the styles used.
- Contact suburban press with local or junior stories and results. Send also black and white photographs.
- Keep in touch with media contacts, once they are made. Maintain friendly relations and see key people in the media in person if possible, including the comperes of sports shows.
- Send media contacts newsletters of the organisations.

— Think of feature stories, and 'sell' the ideas for those to the media. Consider magazine, current affair or 'features' programs and columns as alternative avenues for these.
— Tell the media if you are giving the same story to rival media. Don't necessarily give stories to all media — be selective.
— If you want coverage, you must accept that all aspects of your organisation may be reported — the sensational and controversial along with the 'good' bits that you want.
— Phone and write letters of thanks for good coverage — not just to journalists, but to bosses, eg the sports editor.
— Be constructive and quick in making complaints of unfair or inaccurate coverage. Be sure of the facts and first phone the journalist to see what went wrong. Make your views known in a calm and rational manner.
— Issue press releases well ahead of time. All media outlets like them and prefer varying periods of notice.

The Publicity Officer Contacts the Media
— Phone sports journalists of newspapers, TV and radio stations or their editors, program directors or producers.
— Say: who you are; who you represent; your aim in making contact; ask for an appointment.
— Visit the media person and find out how you can gain the best coverage and what kind of stories are required. Observation of written and visual styles will assist this learning.
— Make yourself aware of deadlines.
— Ask whether a particular reporter could be assigned to deal with your sport or activity.
— Find out how you can arrange for photographs to cover your sport and the sort of photographs wanted.
— Keep contacts with journalists etc to the point and don't hold them up.

When There is a Story About an Event or Person in Your Sport, Issue a Press Release
— **Remember**: news is about people, individuals not just teams; it is about novelty, drama; the sensational. 'Angles' to stories can be manufactured.
— Press releases, if modelled on the style of sentences and paragraphs of the media, will save journalists time and increase your chances of publicity.
— Work out: **what** you want to tell people about, **whom** you want to tell, and **what** is newsworthy that you could tie your message to.
— Check ahead that your event does not clash with other major events.
— Use headed note paper, a typewriter and include the date.
— Choose a short simple headline and have a snappy opening sentence which captures the main plot in an eye-catching way.
— Lead sentence should cover what is happening, who, when and where.
— Keep sentences short and simple and concentrate on facts and key points in order of importance.

— Include direct quotes, if they are colourful or controversial or you want to get over an opinion rather than a fact.
— Use language that everyone not involved in the sport or activity will understand.
— Keep the overall release short.
— Follow sending of the release with phone calls to check that it has arrived and to see if it will be followed up. (eg send release 6 weeks in advance; send more details one to two weeks in advance; phone two days before the event.
— Use double spacing and type on one side of the paper only.
— Use wide margins (about 4cm) on both sides of the paper — for the sub-editor, and use A4 paper.
— Never split a sentence over two pages.
— After page one, number each page at the top and put 'more' at the bottom if there are more pages.
— After the final sentence of the release, put 'ends'.
— Use staples rather than pins or paper clips, and do not underline anything (underlining has a particular meaning for sub-editors and printers).
— Send release to media office by TELEX — facilities are at the GPO 24 hours a day.
— Send the press release to Australian Associated Press (AAP) to save time and get multiple coverage. AAP sends teleprinter stories out 24 hours a day to hundreds of outlets.
— **Always** put the name and telephone number (work and home) of at least two contact people including publicity officer, coaches and sportswomen.

Hints on Developing Good Communication Skills
— Believe in yourself; that you have a story to tell; and **persevere** in your efforts.
— If you are phoning in news, spell difficult words and names. If it is to be read out put the phonetic pronunciation of names in brackets, labelled 'pronounce . . . .'.
— **Always** be consistent and regular in contacting chosen sections of the media.
— Call a press conference for **really** big news or a VIP. Announce it by a press release for no later than 11.30am, give journalists a sheet of background information and have phones available. Arrange separate interview times for paper, radio, TV.
— If an interview with you has been set up, phone the day before and ask the interviewer how long it will be and what the questions will be about.
— If phoned for an immediate interview or answer and you want time to think about it, say you will phone back in a few minutes.
— Choose knowledgeable representatives for interview — appearance is important on TV and voice on radio.
— Have a knowledge of the facts before being interviewed — and take a list of the main points with you.
— Speak slow and low in interviews. Nervousness makes people speak higher and quicker.

- Look at the interviewer if on TV, not the camera.
- Practise interviews on video, cassette recorders or by role playing.
- Don't get angry with an interviewer, eg don't say, 'I don't think that's a fair question/comment', **but say** 'anyway the important thing I want to emphasise is . . .'
- Ask to start an interview again if you don't like what has happened to that point.
- If a question seems designed to trivialise you or your sport, you can say you are not going to answer that question, and why.
- Ask to have a story read back to you before it is used and simply point out errors of fact or emphasis.
- Encourage the photographer, camera operator to capture your sport seriously, portraying action.
- Write down the main points you wish to make before phoning a member of the media.
- Always leave a clear message asking for a person to call you back, leaving details about your enquiry.
- Always make use of any phone answering machine. It saves time and is often the only way to contact a person.
- If you are hard to 'catch', why not have an answering machine? It gives the media a better chance of contacting you.

Many of the most popular of women's sports rely on grace, skill, precision and artistic interpretation. Why have these been so persistently under-valued in sport?

Right: State representative Jenny Wilson diving at the SA Aquatic Centre.
Photo: Doug Nicholas. Thanks to the Girls and Physical Activity Project.

Left: Bowls — not just a game for senior citizens.
Photo: TAS Photographics. Thanks to the Australian Institute of Sport.

Left: The 1988 Australian Trampoline Championships.
Reproduced with permission of the Bicentennial Authority.

Right: Ann Maree Kerr, 1984 Australian Champion and Olympic representative at rhythmic gymnastics.
Photo: Warwick Forbes.

SECTION EIGHT
SUCCESS STORIES

AN INTRODUCTION
Ken Dyer

One of the threads which runs through many of the preceding pages is the great significance of successful sportswomen as pioneers, role models and heroes for the next generation. Women in sport, as in most of other areas of human activity and endeavour, owe a great deal to the determination, the persistence, the hard work and the successes of those who have gone before. One of the most important features of the Conference that this book reports, therefore, was the presence of some of the all time greats of women's athletics. These athletes, among other things, provided to conference delegates their personal stories — how they trained, how they overcame adversity, how they organised their lives and what their thoughts are on competition of yesterday, today and tomorrow.

This section collects together the talks which these athletes gave and the answers which they gave to a short panel discussion session held towards the end of one of the days of the conference. These are important personal statements and opinions. They varied in the manner and length they were given to the conference and hence they vary in length as presented here. That is not the important point. What is important is that these athletes did achieve great things — sometimes against great odds. They were in Adelaide to tell us how and why they achieved what they did achieve and to inspire the next generation to go even faster, higher or further.

Doris Brown-Heritage

Doris Brown-Heritage is one of the pioneers of women's long distance running. In 1954 she broke the US 440 yards and 880 yards records, just about the longest distances women could run at that time. Between 1967 and 1971 Doris was the US and World Women's Cross Country Champion, the only person ever to have won the latter title five times in a row. In 1968 and 1972 she was in the US Olympic team for the 800m and 1500m finishing fifth in the 1968 800m. By 1976 she was running marathons fast enough to break the Canadian record and in 1983 held the Masters mile record.

Doris is currently an academic, a distance coach in the US and is a member of the IAAF Cross Country and Road Race Committtee. Her paper in this section is a valuable personal story of the problems faced and overcome by pioneer women distance runners.

Gaylene Clews

Gaylene Clews, as well as being the Australian Cross Country Champion 1976/78 and a member of the Australian Cross Country Team 1976/81, has taken up that most demanding of activities, the triathlon. She was the world ranked female 'sprint' triathlete in 1985.

She is also an author, having written **de Castella on Running** with Robert de Castella, and has contributed various papers on aspects of women, sport and equality in recent years. Her paper in this section is concerned very much with issues of personal development for sportswomen.

Majorie Jackson

Marjorie Jackson is one of the legends of Australian and World Athletics. Her story essentially begins on a day in February 1949 in Sydney. There was that day a huge crowd at the Sydney sports ground — they were there to watch one of the greatest ever women world track stars Fanny Blankers-Koen who was to race against some local people. The 100 yards was considered by the experts to be merely an exhibition run by the Dutch woman, but instead she found herself beaten by a skinny young 17-year-old from Lithgow who was wearing a pair of shoes that were far too big for her and were stuffed in the toe with paper. No-one took that result seriously — the win was obviously a fluke. A few days later there was another race over 100 metres. Lithgow Flash Marjorie Jackson again went to the front and she stayed there. Over the next five years Marjorie sealed her reputation as the fastest woman in the world by setting new world records for the 100 yards, 100 metres, 220 yards and 220 metres. She also collected seven gold medals, five at the Commonwealth Games and two at the 1952 Helsinki Olympics in the 100m and 200m. In 1977 after the death of her husband, the Olympic Cyclist Peter Nelson, she formed the Peter Nelson Leukemia Research Fund and just before the Conference received a Community Service Award from the Unley Rotary Club for helping raise more than one million dollars in research money.

Mary Peters

Mary Peters is one of the most outstanding of all the women athletes who were present at the conference and are represented in this book.

She represented Northern Ireland at every Commonwealth Games between 1958 and her retirement in 1974. Among her achievements were second in the shot in 1966, first in the shot and Pentathlon in 1970 and first in the Pentathlon in 1974. In the Olympics Pentathlon she was fourth in 1964, ninth in 1968, and first in 1972 with a new world record — truly an amazing record.

Since her retirement from active athletics she has been a tireless worker for youth and sport in her native Northern Ireland and in the rest of the UK. She was team manager for the British Women's Athletics team 1979-84 and currently runs a Fitness Centre in Northern Ireland. The keynote address which she gave to open the Conference is presented in this section.

Ruth Fuchs

Ruth Fuchs is a Sports Scientist from the German Democratic Republic. Before that she was for eight years or so, the World's greatest woman javelin thrower. She began her domination of the women's javelin with a world record throw of 65.06 metres. She won the 1972 Olympic title in 63.88 metres, an Olympic record. By 1976 Ruth Fuchs had increased her world record to 69.12 metres and in winning the Olympic title set another Olympic record of 65.94 metres. She continued to be the Queen of Javelin until 1980, setting yet another world record of 69.96 metres. She finished eighth in the 1980 Olympics. Between 1970-80 Ruth took part in 129 competitions, winning 113 of them including 30 straight from 1972 to 1974, a unique record. She gave three papers to the conference which appear in other sections.

Irena Szewinska

Irena from Poland is known as the amazing Irena Szewinska; she ranks, along with Shirley Strickland, as one of the most successful female track and field athletes in Olympic history. She has won the total of seven medals, three gold, two silver and two bronze. In 1964 she won gold in the 4 x 100 metres relay, silver in the 200 metres with a time of 23.1 and silver in the long jump with a distance of 6.60 metres. In 1968 she won gold in the 200 metres in 22.5 seconds — that a world record — and bronze in the 100 metres in 11.1 seconds. In 1972 she won bronze in the 200 metres and in 1976, gold in the 400 metres with a time of 49.29, another world record. She was the first women to break 50 seconds in the 400 metres in her second race over that distance. Between 1974 and 1978 Irena won 34 straight 400 metre finals. As well as participating in the panel discussion, a training schedule of Irena's, which she described at the conference, is presented in this book as an Appendix to the paper given by Terry Dwyer on Training for Women, in Section Five.

THE JOY OF BEING A SUCCESSFUL SPORTSWOMAN

Mary Peters

The participants in the conference of which this book is a permanent record are a very select group of people. They are concerned about women, about women participating in sport and the opportunities which such participation provides. In the UK at the moment, the theme is 'What's Your Sport?' I believe we must ask this question over the whole world of both men and women.

My sport was athletics. I was born in Liverpool, England during the war. I had a brother three years older than I, so we became very competitive. At the age of eleven we moved to Northern Ireland. Beside our house was a piece of waste ground. I got a spade and dug a long jump pit in the dirt. My mother was not very happy when I came in with dirt on my shoes but I was very happy when I jumped an inch or two further. Later the family moved to Portadown and the headmaster of the school I attended there was a very exceptional man. He tried to get every pupil in his school to take an interest in sport. I was not very good at anything and one day, when attempting to play cricket, the headmaster suggested that I go and meet the athletics coach. I thus met a man who was very keen to see people progress in sport. My father was also very ambitious for me. He bought me a very unusual present for my 16th birthday — a load of sand! I would have preferred a pretty dress, but the sand was deposited on the driveway and I had to carry it to the back to make a high jump pit. Worse was to come. On my 17th birthday I got a load of cement. That was to create Northern Ireland's first shot put circle. Before that we had put the shot on grass using spiked shoes.

At that time the National Athletic coach in Northern Ireland was Franz Stampfl. I never met him then, although I did meet him later in Tokyo, but he did have a great influence on the development of women's athletics in Northern Ireland — much as later he had a great influence on women's athletics in Australia.

My first Commonwealth Games was at Cardiff in 1958. I was 8th out of 9 in the high jump; I was 9th out of 10 in the shot put. I was also in the 4 x 110 yards relay. There were four girls from Northern Ireland competing in the athletics. One was Thelma Hopkins the high jumper who later won a silver medal at Melbourne, one a javelin thrower, one a sprinter and me an all-rounder. We were entered in the relay. As I, the third runner, passed the baton to the fourth runner, the Aussies were breaking the world record at the other end of the track. but it was an experience and I liked it.

I decided I would continue training. My only brother John migrated to Sydney in 1961 and I gained my first international vest that year. I had trained as a teacher of home economics and was teaching this subject when I first took part in an international match at the old White City stadium in London. I knew that my event was televised. I returned to school on Monday morning and walked in with my shoulders back and my chest out, hoping that some of the pupils would have seen me. They had. One little girl said to me *Miss, I saw you on the television on Saturday.* I said *Did you?* She said *Yes, and my brother said to tell you that you were a dead loss.* Well I was, because I was fourth out of four — but I enjoyed it. And I decided that if I trained a bit harder I could perhaps get to Perth in 1962, compete there and then cross Australia to see my brother. Well I did make the team and finished 4th in the shot put.The next Games to come along were the 1964 Olympics and the Pentathlon was on the program for the first time ever. So I trained hard and made the team. I shared a room with Mary Rand and Ann Packer. Mary won a gold, a silver and a bronze medal. Ann, but for Betty Cuthbert, would have won two gold medals, but she won a gold and a silver. I was fourth in the Pentathlon. Mary and Ann hammered nails into the walls of their room so that they would have somewhere to hang their medals when they came back from the track. I did not. But I still enjoyed it all. I enjoyed seeing them get their medals, telegrams and flowers. So I decided to carry on training.

There was still no Pentathlon in the Commonwealth Games program and I was not really a big enough girl for a shot putter, so my coach decided it would be a good idea if I gained about 10 or 12 kilograms in weight, which would help me win the gold medal in the shot put.

But I hated putting on all that weight. I wore my coaches wife's maternity dresses because my shoulders were so big. I had a new experience at these Commonwealth Games. For the first time we women competitors had to undergo sex tests to prove that we were women. I now have a certificate on my bedroom wall to prove that I am really a woman! As the years went by these tests changed their nature and their name. By Los Angeles in 1984 they were called 'gender clarification tests'.

I finished 2nd in Jamaica despite all my efforts at putting on weight. My coach was bitterly disappointed in me. He said I was a failure and if I took the attitude I did in being pleased at finishing second, I might as well retire. But I liked athletics. I enjoyed the travel. I enjoyed the friendships. I even enjoyed the hard work of training in the cold and the rain. So I decided to continue and aim for the next Olympic Games in Mexico 1968.

My most vivid memory of these Games was Vera Nikolic who competed in the 800m. She had broken the world record that year and was favourite to win. In the final of the race she ran off the track distressed; the reason was that the Yugoslav government had printed a stamp featuring her which they intended to issue when she won her gold medal and the pressure was too great.

I remembered that well but still wanted to succeed. However I was injured in Mexico and finished 8th. Time was passing. I was getting old! I decided that the next Commonwealth Games was make or break. I had to win a gold medal then or never. I was lucky. They included the Pentathlon in the 1970 Commonwealth Games in Edinburgh and I managed to win that and the shot put. Success tasted sweet. I was 31 years old. Not many athletes of that age carried on, but I felt that I could still do well in Munich.

So I had a year's rest, gathered my thoughts, changed my high jump style to the Fosbury Flop, which at 33 was quite a feat. But it worked; because the first time I tried it I jumped higher than I had ever jumped before. I won a travel scholarship so that I could go to the USA to train in the good weather, away from the troubles of Northern Ireland and on a synthetic track. I spent 6 weeks training hard.

When I got to Munich, the omens seemed to be with me. The manager of the British team was Arthur Gold (A Gold!) and he presented me with my number 111! In the Pentathlon I had to compete against Heidi Rosendahl the local favourite and Burglinde Pollak the East German winner of so many titles. But I knew that if everything went right for me I could win.

The first event was the hurdles and I ran a personal best of 13.29. Then in the shot I did a pentathlon personal best of 16.20. We had to wait for several hours before the high jump. I jumped and jumped and suddenly I realised that there was no one left in the competition. For the first time in my life I was centre stage. I was being watched high jumping. The only other competitor in the stadium was Wolfgang Nordwig pole vaulting at the other end. He vaulted and the crowd roared; I jumped and they roared — for me! And it was lovely; and I jumped higher then I have ever jumped before — 1.82m. I then had to get back to the village and try and sleep that night knowing that my two weakest events were to come and that they were Heide Rosendahl's strongest. I was in the lead. I did enough in the long jump — 5.98m a very mediocre jump and I was told that I had to run the 200m faster than I had ever run before to stand a chance of the gold. I ran scared I assure you; but I did it managing 24.08 and I won the pentathlon by the barest margin of 10 points. I was the happiest girl in the world.

That evening we had a celebration party. The Belfast evening paper, the **Belfast Telegraph** telephoned me to say that they wanted to establish a trust fund to commemorate my win. How would I like the money spent. I had no hesitation in saying that I wanted it spent on a decent track so that the young people in Belfast could train on a better one than I had had to use which was full of pot holes.

So when I returned from Munich we started the Mary Peters Track Fund. I was invited to give speeches and TV and Radio interviews. At every appearance I collected money for the track. And over the years we collected £100,000, enough to pay for the Mary Peters track, where we now hold many international meetings.

I still hadn't finished with athletics. Partly because my family lived on this side of the world, I decided to make the Commonwealth Games in Christchurch my swansong. At the age of 35 I won the final gold medal of my athletics career. And there I decided to write my book **Mary P**; I did some parachute jumping and went to the Prague European Games as a commentator.

In 1977 I opened a health club in a town just 12km from Belfast to encourage people to take an interest in their health and fitness. One of my first members, a lady named Sadie Smith came to us weighing about 125kg. During the first year she lost nearly 50 of the kilograms — not, she said, because of her health but because if she died she was worried that they would not be able to get the coffin downstairs! But we have all sorts out in our club. My most senior member, for example, is an 84-year-old retired doctor who comes because she has stiff joints. We have a heart transplant and we have people rehabilitating after major surgery or after sports injuries. We also have international athletes preparing for Olympic or Commonwealth Games.

In 1980 I was invited to become manager of the Great Britain women's athletics team. I didn't realise the hard work that was involved. We worked from 5am until midnight very often. But the joy of sharing the success or of commiserating with the failures of the athletes was very interesting. I did the same job in Los Angeles and remember particularly the joy of Tessa Sanderson, the first coloured athlete to win a medal for Britain and Seb Coe's second triumph in the 1500m. First is first and second is nowhere was his philosophy. I retired then from management, believing I had done my part and someone else should take over. I am now President of the Northern Ireland Women's Athletic Association and Patron of the Northern Ireland Men's Athletic Association, so I am still very involved. I am a member of the Sports Council for Northern Ireland. I am a foundation member of the Ulster Games and am a member of the Ulster Sports and Recreation Trust which gives grants to our budding sports stars. I have learnt to survive and I have taken up bowls.

By the year 2000 I will be collecting my pension. The sports stars of 2000 are still at school — so their success is in our hands. Will we have even more improved track surfaces? Will sponsorship money still be available? Will politics still dominate sport? Will all international stars still have to be full time sportsmen and women. Will media pressure still exist and will the media be interested in women's sport? Will we see an end to drug taking? How much more advanced will training shoes and running shoes become? But most important of all will women still enjoy sport?

Sport was good to me because of the enjoyment, the friendship, the travel, good health and fitness, and the confidence which it helped to build in me as a result of my achievement. The outcomes of my success have been: pride in representing my country, the pleasure in helping charities, and still travelling all these years on.

WOMEN'S DISTANCE RUNNING: PAST, PRESENT AND FUTURE— A PARTICIPANTS VIEW

Doris Heritage

Running: early beginnings

Legend has it that Pheidippides ran home to Athens from the battlefield of Marathon to report victory by the Greeks over the Persians. Having delivered the news he fell dead of exhaustion. Distance running was not a part of the Ancient Greek Olympics and women were not even allowed to watch any event in the Olympics for much of their history until the city of Sparta, unlike Athens, eventually encouraged its women to train and compete equally with men. Prior to their admittance, Greek women had age division competition in a quadrennial festival of one event — a 500 foot run.

Equally as fascinating as the myths of Pheidippides and the sketchy tales of ancient Greek Olympic festival ideals of wholeness, beauty and laurel wreaths, are the stories of Mr. Robert Dovers' Olympic Games upon the Cotswold Hills. This quadrennial English revival of the Games began in 1603 and lasted until 1852 with a break only for the English Civil War. There were Greek struggles to reinstate some make-shift Games in Athens from 1859-1888 and various other Olympic-type festivals in England, Scotland and Canada.

The modern Olympics began in Athens in 1896 to honour the classical Greek festival; a marathon of near 40k was contested on Pheidippides' course, from Marathon Bridge to Athens. In today's Olympics there is always at least one country which is unhappy about something. At the first of the modern Olympics it was the Americans; they arrived only 10 minutes instead of two weeks before the first event, no one having told them that the Greek Calendar was being used. They still won a lot of medals, however, and the Greeks had none when it was time to close the Games with the marathon.

Twenty-five Official competitors and one unofficial runner named Melpomene started the race. She must have been the first runner to have her entry refused because of her sex. She sneaked into the race (like my friends and I of more recent historical times!). She did finish and her unofficial time was about 4:30. Perhaps like early American marathon women runners she had to note the number of the guy who finished in front of her and look up his time and place in the newspaper results. [The total number of official competitors is uncertain and many doubt that Melpomene actually competed, but the story is widely believed and her time is often quoted *Ed.*].

Back to the race — the French leader was hit by his coach's bicycle at 30k. The Australian 800 and 1500 metre champion Edwin Flack then led until about 33k, where a little Greek shepherd, water or mail boy named Spiridon Louis claimed the lead and went on to win the race in 2:58:50! Being an honest, married man, he turned down the wealthy merchant's daughter and all of the rest of the under-the-table substantial offerings to retain his Amateur standing — so they say; except for a horse and cart. History does repeat itself!

Spiridon's preparation no doubt was part of the reason his face was twisted in pain during the race. He undertook no real training but did run two marathons for practice on the Olympic course! He had no food, only prayer the previous day, and ate a whole chicken just before the race! In fact there were only 9 official finishers including eight Greeks! It is rumoured that the organising Committee went out to search for participants among the sailors on the ships in the harbour of Piraeus rather than accept the entry of any women.The next Olympic Marathon in Paris had a course change at the starting line and a suspicious French bakery delivery courier who knew the new route and the short cuts won. His name was Michel 'Rosey' Theato and his time was 2:59:45.

The current standard distance of 26.2 miles (42,195m) was first run at the London Olympics of 1908 in order, it is said, that the start could be at the Royal Palace of Windsor and the finish in front of the Royal Box half-way round the White City track at Chiswick in London. Again there was controversy with the Italian runner Dorandro Pietri collapsing several times before the finish, eventually being helped over the line and hence disqualified.

But still there were no women runners in the marathon (or any other track event) in the Olympics. Not until 1918 did Marie Louise Ledro, a French woman, run the first 42.2k marathon and not until 1928 did women get onto the Olympic track.

The real action for distance running in these early years was the flame of professionalism between about 1700 and 1930. England and the US in particular saw distance races motivated by lots of money. A distance race, which could be anything between 4 miles or 24 days, might bring $10,000 in prize money — twice the annual salary of 1850 in America. English sponsors were public houses, while in the US horse tracks on the horses' days off provided the purses. US spectators liked to see their Indian and Black minorities beat English athletes. In 1863, an American Indian Hagasadari or Louis Bennet, but universally known as Deerfoot, was earning lots of money in England winning races between four miles and an hour. His success was attributed to tactics — Deerfoot was the first to employ surging. In 1884, $4,000 was paid for 623 miles in six days and nights of running — that is a lot of money and a lot of corners. The contest was held in Madison Square Garden, New York, an indoor facility!

Womens' opportunities were less frequent but they did exist. Amy Howard offered challengers a 20-mile handicap for a six-day go-as-you-please race in San Francisco in 1881. The prize was $1,200 for 320 miles or more.

The amateur tradition can be traced back to running events organised by the private schools and colleges in England from 1830 onwards called 'Hare and Hound's' or 'the paper chase'. A paper dropping group ran first, pursued by a second group. As these school runners grew up and felt silly chasing paper, formal cross country races were established, helped by farmers who did not like paper and runners going everywhere.

Through the early years of this century, women were swimming and playing tennis in the Olympics, but their applications to take part in track and field were refused several times. Several international track and field competitions, including four Women's World Games were sponsored by a Women's International Federation which had been formed in 1921. The IAAF finally allowed five events in the 1928 Games, with 800m being the longest track event. The result of that race set women's distance running back 40 years at least!

What was known as 'drama' in men's races was labelled 'frightful' in this women's race. Several women collapsed at the finish, as had often been the case in men's races. Three of the women broke the world record and six finished capably. Officials from several countries, including the US, jumped on the IAAF to cancel this 'frightful episode' from future Olympic Games. This they did until 1960. Prevailing attitudes of the time were: *Women are not physically fit for the excitement and strain that competition affords* and *Let women play for enjoyment, not specialise to win*. These officials obviously had not read the Bible which speaks of running so as to win your race (and says something about preparation too, and that's all in the New Testament, not the Old!).

Running: the present

During the 1950s and the 1960s, doctors supportive of women's running were accused of professional irresponsibility for encouraging women to use their inherent endurance and stamina. US women athletes jumped into men's cross country, marathon, even track races. It was either that or race only 200 metres or run by one's self. World records did not count if the track had no curb or only two athletes ran in the race. In the US the only facilities were scholastic facilities, and most of these had rules about not allowing girls on tracks. And where did a girl get money to travel to a national meet? Or buy running shoes to fit? Or get a coach?

Even times far in excess of world records made no impression on those holding the purse strings. It was a bit lonely training all year for maybe two races. All in all there was virtually no encouragement for women distance runners.

By 1967, when men had run a world championship cross country race for 100 years, women finally had that opportunity. This became the distance event for women internationally. Initially it was only 1¼ miles but was gradually lengthened, and in April 1988 had reached 6 kilometres.

Let me inject a personal note to try and get across what this revolution has meant for women.

Never having travelled before, that first cross country championship in Barry, Wales was a memorable experience personally. My coach and I managed to borrow enough money for the plane tickets. The US did not send a team but I thought if I did well enough we might get a team the next year. (I did and we didn't, but we all begged and borrowed and got enough money in 1968 for the second one anyway.)

Besides the thrill of victory over the English at home, visiting with Maria Hartman and hearing stories from others of the original women Olympians (not Melpomene!) and travelling in Europe for a few days with no money was quite exciting for us. The Hotel Fly-In across from the Amsterdam Train station was it! And with no money for the toilettes, we could have been stranded in the train station if we were not so fast!

My memories of the first International Championship are beyond description. The thousands of spectators lining those Welsh football fields and cow pastures, half of them all the way from Belgium to support Roelants in his perennial victory in the cold, windy, cross country weather with lots of mud and drama. That first post race celebration, in which runners from all over the world clapped and stomped wildly and stood for the first women's race results. These gave us the greatest reward possible — to be honoured by our male peers, coaches, and each other.

For women, distance running need no longer be only the political statement it recently was. Now the world class foot racing headlines read: Moe vs Marot, Waitz vs Tinari along with Barreto vs Solly, and Martin vs Audain. The marathon times for women's races now appear in the newspapers with athletes from many countries being represented: 'Martin runs 2:23 in Japan' says a recent headline. It is not so long ago that such a time would have made a headline as a world men's record. It is faster than ever Zatopek ran a marathon. [Not quite, but still fantastic Ed.]

The 1987 money winners in road racing start with Rosa Mota and Liz Lynch McColgan followed by Ibrahim Hussain. Not only have much higher earnings gone to women of late but their running opportunities are much improved.

In 1975, Dr. K.F. Dyer of the University of Adelaide confirmed for women what they knew already: *Factors such as differing degrees of social encouragement and differing levels of expectation are important factors in female athletic performance. Absolute differences in ability between men and women are less than supposed and biological differences less important in causing them.* He used 800m as a comparison (no other choice then!). I want to add a few words about the marathon.

800m	1934	1954	1974	1988
	1:49 M	1:48.6 M	1:44.6 M	1:43 M
	2:17 F	2:12.6 F	2:02 F	1:54 F
Marathon	1896	1953	1969	1988
	2:58:50 M	2:18:40.2 M	2:08:33.6 M	2:07:12 M
	4:30 F		3:07:26 F	2:21:06 F

In 1969, the woman who ran the first sub 3:10 marathon was a mother of two, Anni

Pedeerdkamp, a Van Aaken athlete. Then in 1971, women ran under 3 hours (2:55:22 by Beth Bonner, and 2:49:40 by Cheryl Bridges at Culver City).

In the US in 1972, women were allowed to compete in the same events as men, but separate starts were required with the women 10 minutes ahead. The women simply sat and waited after their gun was fired until the men started. They then had the ten minutes added to their finishing times. In 1973, Germany had a national marathon championship for women followed by the US in 1974. In 1975, 2:39:11 by Miki Gorman, at 41, brought the time from over 3 hours to under 2:40 in ten years! 1984 was a great milestone for women with the Olympic Marathon, and the record coming so near to 2:20. Now a 10k has finally appeared in the 1988 Olympics. (But when do we get the 5k?).

And there are other promising additions: next year junior women will have a championship cross country event (even if it is only 4k) to go with their distance events in the Junior World Track Championship. Men now want a 15k road championship alongside what is now an annual women's event at this distance.

'Glory lies not only in accomplishment but in a bright future!'

Training: the recent past

During the 1920s it was customary for serious runners to train by giving themselves time trials several times each week, along with calisthenics. That was about it. The Scandinavians had previously contributed forest runs of several hours including pace change and hills. The fabulous Czech runner Zatopek in the 1940s intensified and formalised Swedish fartlek (taking the fun out of it in so doing) inserting full speed 200s and going over two hours in each training session. He also did 50 x 400m and other high volume repetitions of slow intervals. 'He went at it like a madman' according to his own accounts and won all the Olympic medals, becoming the centre of sport cult of his day. He lifted his wife, Dana, for weight work, which was about it for any mention of women and distance training then.

Until Zatopek's time, athletes were the principal instigators of new training ideas. Then various schools of training began to emerge, with the balance of creativity shifting toward coaching. Russian coaches were deeply influenced by Zatopek and based their training on lots of precise intervals (Kuts won two gold medals in the 1956 Olympics and his style was 25 x 440 at 63-67, jogging 100m between each in 30 seconds). Percy Cerutty of Australia included sandhills, and special natural diets along with a mileage base and **no women**! In fact, at the 1968 Olympics in Mexico City, this leader of our sport who had coached some of the greatest middle distance and distance runners of all time was so abusive to those of us riding the same bus to our 800 metre Olympic race, that he was nearly thrown off the bus by some male sprinters.

In the 1950s and 1960s, coaches from all over the world, like Lydiard of New Zealand and Mulsk of Poland, were placing endurance training in the forests and on roads at the centre of training philosophies. Dr. Ernst Van Aaken of West Germany was one of these. He gave special attention to women, believing their endurance capabilities suited them for running. A few medical men of the 1960s began to speak out for women as well, defying the rumors about child bearing problems, muscle bound results and the like. So we were able to sneak into more marathons and finally have cross country races.

After the mile high Mexico Olympics in 1968, doctors and scientists became more active in the science of running. They were desirous of confirming what coaches were directing. Bill Bowerman's hard-easy rhythm system, with date pace-goal pace training added to the Gerschler-Reindells-Stampfl German intervals in conjunction with a Lydiard mileage base, gave doctors, nutritionists, bio-mechanists, physiologists and psychologists a plethora of data for examination. By 1968 Bowerman's **Jogging** and Cooper's **Aerobics** books had appeared and mass participation of both men and women in road running and especially marathons developed thereafter throughout the world. While world and Olympic records were improving for men, women's training was following a similar pattern to theirs. But first women had to progress politically. Like our male counterparts, we were riding bicycle ergometers, having muscle biopsies and blowing underwater weight bubbles. But we were also diluting our training through having to focus on sports governing bodies, legal assistance, fund raising and the media.

The best of our runners were only able to compete at 5k internationally in cross country. In 1960, 800m had been reinstated in the Olympic Games with 400m coming in 1968 and 1500m in 1972. But literally nothing was available for long distance runners. On the bright side, Greta Waitz, Lisa Martin, and others young enough to survive to the present, did have a good speed base! Athletes like Ingrid Kristiansen, Bente Moe and Lisa Weidenbach did bring some great cross training and endurance background as skiers and swimmers.

Training: the present

If statistics, doctors and lawyers were the means to 'gaining inches so women could go miles' in the recent past, exercise physiologists, biomechanists, and psychologists are helping to take some of the guess work out of 'train-as-you-feel' and providing guidelines between 'no pain, no gain' and junk mileage. Science is helping us deal with the information explosion. Specificity along with moderation, variety, and periodisation of long-term training plans are especially helpful to elite female athletes, for **more** is no longer the key to increased success. **Smarter** is better now.

Leaders in exercise science from around the world, like Francisco Conconi, Jack Daniels and Dario Herrera define three major parameters affected by training that will improve running performance.

1. Maximum oxygen uptake ($\dot{V}O_2$max) is the greatest amount of O_2 the muscles can utilise while exercising intensely. It is sport or muscle specific and requires specificity of training — run to be a better runner and run a specific pace; for a distance runner it is about the speed you can go for 11 minutes or about 2 miles.

2. Anaerobic threshold, the limit above which anaerobic processes take over and oxygen debt builds up, can be extended by some running at about 85% of $\dot{V}O_2$max.

3. Running economy is the third area, requiring some training at 70% of $\dot{V}O_2$max. This is the cross training area, to some extent.

To these, pace, speed and rest categories of training are carefully calibrated into a periodisation format along with detailed scheduling of competitive options. Women have particularly benefited from this scientific input. Previously they tended to train like men, or like some outstanding woman champion. Now we know that each of us must progress individually for best returns on our effort.

Science has constantly been updating information of importance to the modern distance runner. Alternative/supplemental training in swim pools, on bicycle ergometers, and now on treadmills that go 380 metres/min with adjustable incline are the state of the art today. Monthly blood chemistry evaluations assist with diet monitoring and precautions against overtraining, as do charting for symptoms such as a rise in morning pulse or temperature, signs of constant thirst, weight loss, or inability to recover from previous workouts.

Research shows that a well hydrated, low fat, complex carbohydrated diet, significantly enhances muscle glycogen concentration and energy availability. (Low resistance clothing and light shoes help conserve these energy stores!)

The importance of sound nutrition cannot be overestimated. Many athletes see food as a fattening enemy rather than an energising fuel. About 2000/cal daily are necessary for optimising adequate supplies of nutrients, including such elements as iron for prevention of anaemia and vitamin C for iron absorption. Calcium is of particular concern because of its relationship to bone density and osteoporosis and in conjunction with oestrogen levels and amenorrhea.

Great emphasis continues to be placed on the need for athletes to reach maximum strength, speed and endurance by reducing their body fat stores to low levels, and thus a tendency toward eating disorders exists, again in conjunction with amenorrhea. Athletes are willing to spend several hours daily working out, getting physical treatment, doing exercises to prevent injuries, and listening to motivational tapes. Yet they withold optimal fuel supplies. They forget that the body is the temple of the soul, an excellently constructed machine with an incredible ability to perform if it is supplied the appropriate fuel.

Medical science has developed means for boosting and blocking a variety of the body's enzymes or catalysts, particularly in relation to catastrophic illnesses or injury. Enhancement of athletic performance by ingestion of such substances as steroids, or other catalysts, is of grave concern to sport scientists for health reasons as well as to sport federations trying to ensure fair and safe competition.

The science of sport psychology is another avenue of present day excellence orientation. Melpomene and other pioneer athletes did not have available this science to them because it has only recently been fully developed. Champions are positive in approach to life and their sport. They believe in themselves and their God-given talent. Their focus and concentration is absolute. They employ positive visualisation, creative imagery and positive self-talk techniques. They analyse losses carefully to refine technique, improve strategy and boost performance levels and they do not see themselves as losers. They put defeat behind them quickly and look ahead to new challenges.

They always have goals. Sport psychology is all about self-esteem. The Bible says to respect your neighbour as yourself, sport psychology now provides worthy tools for strengthening self-esteem as it relates to athletic excellence on an individual basis.

Today's elite distance runner is tough-minded, self-defined, independent, more outgoing, confident, focused, less likely to be running to escape than to accomplish — running to win rather than running not to lose! She is increasingly beleaguered by demands on her time by marathons and long races that bring about considerable wear and tear on her body. So she is turning more and more to shorter races, to attack her greatest weaknesses — lack of speed and overuse and its injuries. She is replacing quantity with quality — the track once or more a week, the weight room regularly, the pool and bike **before** they are the only options. Economy and intensity are the trends of the future. She regards running as a positive influence on her life and plans to run until death (that's different than running to death!). Yet she is still ambivalent about the pressure of competition.

No longer does she identify sex discrimination as her most pressing problem unless she is a 5k specialist. Balancing running, family and career is now the number one focus. She does manage to keep a balance, but running is seldom the aspect she neglects any more if one area has to suffer.

In the US, research studies show that among marathon runners, most of those who commenced running later in life after the 1972 Title IX Federal Law, did it to lose weight, get fit, or to find a new activity ... *It changed my life; I excelled; I loved the demands, challenge, rewards, rapid results, competition.*

The younger runners, the first generation of females to come through scholastic and collegiate cross country and track programs, could finally express Olympic ambitions — the 1984 marathon and now the 10k. There will always be room for a Priscilla Welch, Lisa Weidenback, or Bente Moe from a swimming background, but the younger athletes with a strength-speed track background who also possess endurance will be discovered earlier, as, in general, they are among men, and among women of some other countries.

A positive attitude in general seems to be the greatest influence of running upon athlete's lives, as a means for self-expression — an art form!

Running and training: the future

As an information explosion characterises the present status of running, what will the future hold — besides a 10k in the 1988 Olympics and a junior women's cross country championship? What would be on your wish list for the future? Five ounce shoes are here already. Looking good in a hooded racing body suit might take some dramatic goal orientation and visualisation for some of us, as will a $15,000 treadmill. Confronting a needle for monthly blood testing might also be challenging to some. Balance is the fine art of resting and training — of knowing more isn't better but smarter is better, knowing **self** well enough to individualise with confidence about training and racing — protecting one's own talent through prevention, learning first how to **train to train** and how to **train to compete** — to race well, then finally learning how to progressively train — to leave the comfort zone of what has worked before for the challenge of going beyond — leaving the good for the better — to accomplish what has not yet been done! Leaving the good for the better. Balance means never having to say: 'I can't understnd what's wrong with these matches; they burned fine yesterday!'

Famous New Zealand miler John Walker, the man who has run more four-minute miles than any other, said recently that like the US *New Zealand is not producing the great runners it once did — greed, laziness, unwillingness to sacrifice, fondness for sitting in front of the video, partiality toward the automobile, all destroy incentive. Who wants to go out on the hill in the rain and wind and run 20 miles when he could be home with a sweet and a warm fire? Maybe today's runners want to win an Olympic medal in a lottery.'*

John is not merely talking underachievement here. It is discipline that is symbolised. The small details that make the big differences — overtraining a few miles, one too many races, one more moneyed race, or missing a few stretches for several days. **When you care enough to pay a great price in daily detail, you do not give away the outcome nearly so easily.**

The present information glut makes the future a time for small details. Organisations may squabble about pacing. Athletes will digitise training responses. Details. Details! Is all this really fun any more?

Ingrid Kristiansen is a lady who demonstrates the future now. She has transported whole stadiums of spectators past limits they could only know vicariously through her vision. Such was her 1986 European Championship 10k. And again, her 1987

World Championship, only this time she demonstrated new courage, perhaps learned from another courageous champion, Joan Benoit, in the 1984 Olympic Marathon. Both went where they had never gone before without the confidence of invincible health — new champions!

Priscilla Welch is also the future. At 43 she is one of the world's best marathoners. She is quoted in the news as leaving the cars and money to her husband and taking her pleasure in enjoying her races. She prepares specifically, has faith in her careful preparation, and concentrates during her training and races.

She believes the men around her in the New York Marathon may have had more fun during the race while she concentrated, but she had the greater pleasure in her results. She expects to improve, pays the price, applies the scientific information, but also balances her extremely tough training and family involvement, the information explosion, the finite details necessary to be excellent, her lack of athletic background in years and her masters status. Her eyes are on the prize. It's **doing** not **getting**. She loves **people** and uses **things** — not the other way around. These characteristics will never be outdated. They are the future as well as the past. Science is now. How we use it is the future — focused, balanced, flexible, moderated yet specific and with fresh courage.

My future has another fantasy. Nineteen-year-old Kenyan runner Mary Kipruto's story is an illustration. Perhaps her training is not so scientific, her clothing not the latest fashion, her races not substantiated by electronic timing. She has even brought a return to the days of sneaking into mens' races, this time in Italy and in a false beard! By age 19 Mary Kipruto had apparently exceeded several distance records — 29:29 for a 10k, 25k in 1:22:06, a training mile in 4:17.2, a marathon in 2:19.

But times are not the issue here. As a young African mother and a farm wife her lifestyle does not lend itself to prioritising her running assets. And hers is not an isolated case. My own experience trekking in the mountains of Nepal, substantiates how subsistence level lifestyle may provide equality in the size of the loads men and women carry and how children cover 20 miles or more a day at high altitude going to school and carrying firewood. But it's not good pace work. Running for sport, freedom, or excellence can never be a priority, or even a thought, when starvation is constantly at the door.

Back to Africa: Mary's plans do not include a new country or career. The problems were insurmountable. And other problems are too great to be overlooked as well. How will we assure such athletes that their dreams and efforts can be realised?

All runners need the opportunity to train and compete for our sport to have true champions. Each human being has unlimited potential and should go where her dreams and expectations are allowed to take her. Along with seeking to balance the art and science of training with the love of running, the people and places, the challenge and freedom running affords aesthetically, the runner of the future will be doing her part to assure such opportunities for all the future runners of this Earth. Only then, will she be able to honour the competition with her most rewarding effort.

WOMEN, ATHLETICS AND SELF-ESTEEM: THE ATHLETES VIEW

Gaylene Clews

Introduction

From the time I was a small child I knew my ability in sports singled me out as special. Throughout my childhood sports developed in me a sense of self-worth, confidence and a willingness to try. Team sports encouraged good social skills and an aptitude towards work that was expressed scholastically as well as physically.

My participation in sports enabled me to enjoy good physical co-ordination and strength with a sense of direction and purpose. Everyone knows about those qualities and the positive aspects of sports, but what is less spoken about are the underlying conditions through which women play sports. Conditions that are present during our childhood and continue through our adult lives.

Sport is a mass of contradictions for the female athlete. To win we must be dedicated, aggressive and strong, displaying qualities respected in men, but to be permitted to play we must remain gentle, supporting (like women are 'supposed to be!').

To distance running women bring their femininity and enthusiasm but to be successful we are encouraged to be androgenous. Obtaining light and sinewy bodies often suppresses normal female hormonal functioning. This can lead to long-term medical problems, all in the pursuit of performances closer to those of men [see, for example, the papers by Dick Telford and Peter Brukner in this volume which discuss some of the physiological and more medical issues *Ed*.].

As women, more so than men, we compete for others: coaches, families and friends. Success and living up to others expectations determines how we feel about ourselves and whether or not we live, happy, well balanced lives. In light of the recent controversies concerning steroid taking, anorexia and depression in women athletes, we must ask ourselves for whom are we competing and why?

Body image and female self-esteem

We all lead complex lives like an intricate web in which we are the centre. The strands of the web represent life's many facets: spiritual, family, social, physical and others. When our self-esteem is high and we are balanced individuals, the web remains intact if one or two of the strands are temporarily fractured. **But** if we concentrate everything good we feel about ourselves, into a single strand of the web, a single facet of our lives, our world is likely to crumble if that strand frays. This paper is an attempt to articulate some of the ebb and flow changes that affect female athletes, their self-esteem and consequently the quality of their lives.

As coaches, administrators, families and friends the most important assistance we can offer our women athletes is to help them develop positive self-images and balanced lifestyles. Both of which are conducive to better athletic performances and greater female participation in sports.

On both a social and personal level a female's participation in sports at times is confusing. For example, how does the young adolescent woman balance the desire to be athletic with her rapidly changing body? The trim taut figure that enabled her to run unencumbered with agility and speed is changing. Her breasts swell, and for a while they are tender and uncomfortable. During menstruation her stomach may cramp and her thighs feel heavy and lethargic. Where before she was finely built she now has a fuller figure leaving her feeling differently physically and emotionally.

She may resent the changes in her body, and see them as inhibiting. She knows that a more androgenous body type is desirable for optimal athletic performances; performances that make her feel special, that make her feel loved. Her rejection of these normal feminine changes may result in a traumatic and emotional time for her. In the worst case she may become another anorexia nervosa statistic or attempt to retain her pubescent body shape.

Or she may welcome these changes in her body and enjoy her flowering into womanhood, but reject anything that she sees as interfering with her being accepted as a young woman instead of a girl. She may shy away from sports if she feels that they detract from her femininity.

Anything too competitive, aggressive or physical may be seen as contradictory to to the soft, supporting and gentle qualities that she associates with being a woman. During this time she may slide out of the sports arena altogether and be more inclined to watch her boyfriend's football game, than to participate in anything athletic herself.

It is important for girls to understand the adolescent changes occurring in their bodies, so that they may make smooth transitions from young girls to young women with positive body images. Poor body image and low self-esteem in adult women can contribute to self-abuse in the form of taking anabolic steroids or developing anorexia. Both the drug user who uses steroids to increase body strength and the anorexic who uses self-induced starvation to maintain an abnormally lean body for supposed optimal athletic performance, are self-abusive. Both are striving for improved athletic results by rejecting their femaleness and endeavouring to streamline their bodies into androgenous shapes to closely resemble that of a man's.

Why do women risk osteoporosis, an inability to bear children and liver and/or other organ damage for the sake of an athletic performance? Is it just a reflection of their own low self-esteem, or is it a reflection of a wider social attitude that rewards the victor irrespective of the costs?

Distance runners equate thinness with high performance potential, high performance with love and therefore, thinness with love. This is totally understandable in a society where fat is rejected, but even more so when total per cent body fat can have a direct impact on livelihood.

Fatness is an embarrassment. It is seen to reflect a lack of willpower, and suggests a weakness of character. It leads to questions being asked about the fat person's dedication to her sport. These negative connotations are presented socially and internalised individually, resulting in many women being their own worst enemies when it comes to self-acceptance and self-love. Many of us have great difficulty in just simply loving ourselves, not in an arrogant or egotistical way, but in a self-appreciative way. We often restrict ourselves because we reinforce negative self-images, instead of inverting them into positive and constructive beliefs.

A simple example of this is the number of women who refuse to participate in sports because they are 'too fat' and think people will be critical of them. In fact, it is they, who are too critical. They could easily invert a negative perception and make it positive by thinking 'I feel good, here I am out here exercising, doing something constructive and positive about my health and my self image'. We should all accept that we are okay as we are and learn to respect ourselves for what we can do, not criticise ourselves for not doing what other people think we ought to do. In our society we know that everyone loves a winner. For most of us however, life is full of seconds, nearlys and almosts.

Personal development

When I was a child I took myself too seriously and thought that the world revolved around under-age swimming competitions. A small spastic girl in my first grade taught me what it was like to just belong. She was almost a perfect child, except for her limbs that buckled and jerked in braces underneath her thin fragile body. Unfortunately, almost was not good enough; she was ostracised in the playground and struggled for acceptance in a cruel way. I remember, however, her beaming smile when I invited her to play tag. Enthusiasm and happiness radiated from her because she had been given a chance to just belong.

She knew true appreciation for so many of the abilities that I took for granted. The gifts of motion, agility, strength and control . . . gifts that I always wanted to be better. Is it in striving to be better that we are supposed to learn and find ourselves? Or is it in the striving that we lose ourselves, never being satisfied with who we are, but always deceiving ourselves into believing that we will be someone better in the future? I suspect it is a little of both. We must be more accepting of ourselves just as we are if we want to maintain balance and harmony in our lives.

This by no means implies that we become complacent or stop striving for improvement. **But** we live in the present so we must be satisfied with the present. We can certainly look forward to the unfolding future but if we always live for the future we miss out on a lot of the rewards and pleasures of today.

As athletes, we may never be satisfied with what we have achieved if we are always seeking the next opportunity in an endless pursuit of transitory goals. 'If only I could run a sub three hour marathon, then I would be really happy.' 'If only I could win an Olympic gold medal then all of my dreams would come true.' When we start making material or prestigious gains largely responsible for our happiness we are likely to end up disappointed and disillusioned.

Happiness is not found in acquisitions, but in a philosophy and attitude towards life. Yet too many athletes continue to pursue results and performances in order to achieve fulfilment . . . to feel loved. When one goal is reached they must achieve another, and then another, to be content with who they are and how they feel about themselves. When they fall short in their sporting pursuits they are dissatisfied with their lives in general.

Just as the adolescent girl may be confused about her body image as she makes the transition from a girl to a woman, so an athlete can be frightened during a low period in her career, coping with injuries, or retirement. This is particularly true if everything good she feels about herself is too closely interwoven in her ability to perform athletically. To cope with these changes and fluctuations she must appreciate herself for the capable, competent human being that she is.

In my own career I have struggled with periods of low self-esteem when my sporting life was under change or stress. Most sportswomen would say the same.

Support for athletes

The role of an athlete's support group is to endeavour always to be positive in their approach towards the athletes and their sport while at the same time encouraging them to be all round individuals, in all aspects of their lives. There is a tremendous amount to be gained from good communication skills between support groups and athletes, with respect to body image and performance, self-confidence and performance. In offering our support, our greatest responsibility is to develop well-educated individuals capable of making independent decisions and not becoming totally dependent on the decision-making of those around her.

Coaches must be clear in their communications and attempt to enhance athletic performances through positive reinforcement. An athlete should never be made to feel responsible for the happiness of others, because others have reflected their own egos into the performances of the athlete. As simplistic as it sounds, this is not easily accomplished. A coach's reputation and his/her credibility is often dependent on the achievements of the athletes he/she coaches.

A coach who is too dominant will hinder an athlete's growth by not providing her with the opportunity to develop self-reliance, especially if she feels strongly indebted to the coach. A less aggressive trainer, on the other hand, can enhance athlete self-esteem by involving the athlete in decisions affecting training sessions, racing schedules and good competitive skills. This encourages the athlete to take responsibility for herself, her self-image and her athletic performances. If she feels certain relationships or beliefs are negative and detrimental to her performances she must know that she has the power to change them.

A family support system, where a parent or spouse may feel as if they have left skills of their own undeveloped, in order that the athlete be given the best of every opportunity to perform, may feel desperately let down and disappointed if the performances aren't forthcoming. Especially if they have become dependent on the athlete's achievements to feel satisfied and fulfilled in their own lives.

Administrators have been known to make difficult selection policies and to be unrealistic in their expectations of a team's performance, because their financial status — through sponsorship or government funding — may depend on the team's ability to perform internationally. Consequently, they too, are redirecting their own needs into the performances of the athlete.

It is a complex social structure in which we live. The mechanisms of that structure shape how we feel about ourselves in a very intimate way. As athletes we want to give back to those individuals and groups of individuals for the time, finance and energy they have invested in us. The best way we know how to say thank you is through our performances. We say thank you when we perform well. Unfortunately if we feel too great a responsibility to perform for others we may lose our sense of self.

Sometimes we hold onto negative beliefs as an easy way out of confronting a much greater challenge. For example, an athlete who is frequently injured may choose to believe that her injuries are just repeated bad luck. Or, she may reflect the responsibility for those injuries onto someone or something else. 'My training sessions aren't right,' 'there is something wrong with my shoes', 'the road surface is too hard', or any one of a multitude of other possible explanations. In reality she may have sub-consciously set herself playing the role of a great survivor in the face of adversity. She may be good at producing comeback performances, without the responsibility of having to stay at the top for any extended period of time, because predictably she'll fall victim to another injury.

We are not individuals whom the world acts upon, but actors in control. If we choose to belie responsibility for ourselves onto others we are just giving away our own personal power. If an athlete believes that she will never race well unless she obtains a certain body weight, it is not surprising then, that she has such a difficult time achieving her desired weight. Once achieved she must perform, or else a belief that she has clung so diligently to, that has shaped her self-esteem and affected her athletic performances, is threatened.

We as athletes must be willing to let go of beliefs that are negative and limiting. We must accept our own personal power and the control that we have over our lives. As we develop confidence and judgement, however, we must also recognise the limits of our own knowledge and retain an open-mindedness that allows us to accept advice. Advice and recommendations from the educated and experienced, the physiologists, nutritionists, coaches, and sports medicine personnel.

No individual has all of the answers. There are times when we have difficulty in seeing the fine line between a healthy development and an unhealthy one. Take the athlete who may be encouraged to weight train for increased muscular strength. She is readily rewarded with improved athletic performances and positive affirmations from others for enhancing her skill; she now firmly believes that stronger is better, she starts to look outside the weight room for every small gain and improvement that she can find.

Steroids present themselves as an attractive option and she incorporates them into her training schedule. Increased strength is now being developed at the expense of her long-term health, she has lost control of her reality and her judgement is wrong. Stronger is no longer better and that belief must be replaced.

Just as athletes and coaches don't hold all of the answers nor do members of sporting administrations. Administrators lack the knowledge to know always what is in the best interest of the athlete. They too must be prepared to be open-minded and listen to the advice of the educated and the experienced in their various fields of expertise. Repeatedly we see members of the administration scheduling athletic events to coincide with optimal television viewing times, with little consideration of the health and performances of the competing athletes.

Administrators must communicate with those they wish to aid, in an advisory rather than dominating capacity. They must be conscious of not reflecting their own goals into the peformances of their athletes. This can only be achieved through compromise, where there is no communication there can be no compromise!

Whether as children or as adults athletes develop a strong sense of self-worth, confidence and a willingness to try and achieve. Team sports encourage good social and administrative skills with an aptitude towards work that is often expressed scholastically as well as physically.

Participation in sports by women enables them to develop co-ordination and strength with a sense of direction and purpose. Sports help all of us to develop positive self-images that are reflected in all aspects of our lives.

I believe by understanding more about the social and personal relationships that surround us in the activities that we do, we will not only produce better athletes and well-rounded individuals, but better coaches, administrators and support systems. All of which are conducive to greater and more successful participation by women in sports. For we are no greater than our perceptions of ourselves.

COMMITMENT

Marjorie Jackson

My ambition always was just to represent my country at the Olympic Games. In my athletic days we just didn't have the facilities they have today. I used to train for the Olympics by the lights of a motor car on a makeshift cinder track in Lithgow. The Olympics held in Helsinki in 1952 were out of season for us and we had to train totally without competition. When I was selected for the Olympics, the people of Lithgow banded together and paid for a cinder track to be put down. We just didn't have cinder tracks in Australia, but knew we would have to run on them in Finland. But unfortunately the money ran out and there was no money left to put any lights up. Lithgow in the middle of the Australian Winter, June and July, is dark and foggy. I had to train after work in the dark. One person, who we thought was rich, owned a motor car and he used to park his car at the end of the track and shine his lights down the track. I used to more or less feel with my feet for the middle of the track and then set off. The car lights didn't do much more than light up the last ten metres of the track and looking back I am surprised I didn't break my legs. That's how I trained for the Olympics! My philosophy is that commitment should always be 100 per cent. I gave 100 per cent of my life for four years to represent my country at the Olympics. People must understand that nothing else is possible.

I don't believe a winner is just the person who comes first. I believe a winner is someone who improves on what they have already done. If you can live with who and what you are, that is the most important thing.

[Marjorie Jackson went on to win the 100m at Helsinki in a time of 11.65 and the 200m in a time of 23.89. She would almost certainly have won another medal in the 4 x 100m relay had the Australian Team not dropped the baton at the last changeover Ed.].

Irena Szewinska

I began my athletics career quite late — I was 15 years old when I began training. I began running at school in school competitions. I was fairly successful in these competitions even without training and people said I should begin training seriously.

My school was in contact with the club Polonia, and one of the officials from this club, a former Polish javelin record holder, formed a group of boys and girls to begin training. This was the start of a 20-year career on the track from 1961 to 1980.

My first Olympic Games was 1964 in Tokyo where I won three medals. This was a very short period of time — particularly as in these early years I trained only 3 or 4 times a week and the training was not specialist sprint training. In fact, the first Polish Junior record I broke was in the High Jump. Later I began the Long Jump, then the 200m and only at the end of my career did I take up the 400m.

Training is always a problem for a woman — particularly if she wants to have a family. I decided in 1969 that I would retire. I competed in many events 100m, 200m,

Relay and the Long Jump. At major international events such as the Olympics or European Championships, there were various qualifying rounds in each of these events, which is very exhausting. By the end of each season, I was very tired. This tiredness was both physical and psychological. At the beginning of each event I was always very nervous — if I wasn't nervous, my results weren't good. I liked big competition and my best results always came in big competitions. For example, in each of the events in which I won a gold medal, I broke the world record. So big competition helped me — but made me very tired.

So I decided to rest for one year in 1970 — and in that year my first son was born. When I began the second part of my career I felt as if I was just beginning again. And it was this, I think, which allowed me to carry on competing until 1980. Without this one year rest, it would not have been possible for me. In addition, women who compete after having a baby, feel much better and are much stronger, and it therefore certainly helps their athletic career.

During my sports career, I had a total of five coaches: three before I had my baby and two after — the last being my husband. I think it is a good idea for athletes to change coaches from time to time. Each coach has his or her own methods and ideas. Athletes can become too familiar and therefore bored with the exercises and routines favoured by one coach. They will respond very positively to changes — even though the fundamentals of sprint training or technique practice remain the same.

[Irena Szewinska has provided us with a copy of an example of the year-long training program she adopted. This has been included in Section 5 on Coaching and Training as an Appendix to the paper by Terry Dwyer *Ed.*].

SOME QUESTIONS AND ANSWERS

Irena Szewinska, Ruth Fuchs and Mary Peters then answered questions from delegates to the conference. An edited version of these questions now follows.

Q. Do athletes today start competing too young ?

Mary Peters I believe that athletes should enjoy their sport. If they are young and yet are not pushed by their parents and enjoy their sport then there are no problems. As they get older then they may want to do other things — go to the beach or to discos. But if they get rewards from their sport such as travel and friendship then these will overcome the other attractions. Age is no barrier if children enjoy what they are doing.

Irena Szewinska It depends of course on the sport. In a few sports like gymnastics and swimming children should start training early. In athletics it is less important to begin early. Young children can begin early but should only train lightly twice a week — more like play really. Training should never be hard in the early days —enjoyment is much more important.

Ruth Fuchs Early training should be mixed — some sprinting, jumping, throwing and distance running. This will provide a basis for later specialisation. But most of all it will let children have fun doing different things.

And that is the most important thing of all. Mary Peters is the best example of all.

Q.Is there any organisation in overseas countries equivalent to the Australian Little Athletics organisation which provides competition for children from age eight upwards ?

Mary Peters In the UK all junior athletics is done through the schools. When I attended a Little Athletics meeting, I was horrified at the attitude of the parents. They stood on the sidelines screaming at their children to win for the glory of the parents. I was glad that never happened to me. My father wanted me to win — but he never pressured me. Winning is important, so is competition — but it isn't everything. Fun is much more important.

Irena Szewinska In Poland, competition is organised between primary schools : these are the Spartakiada. The schools are in contact with the clubs and the best children may train with the clubs — but most of the activities are for enjoyment through the schools Spartakiada.

Ruth Fuchs Athletics in East Germany begins both in the Federation and in schools start at the age of eleven. Spartakiada start at the age of twelve and continue until the age of fifteen for girls and sixteen for boys when junior sports begins.

Q. Is there any problem for the adjustment of athletes when they have finished their competitive years because of the career years they have missed?

Irena Szewinska I used to miss quite a lot of my high school — two or three weeks at a time because of my attendance at international competitions. But I still finished high school and attended university, gaining a degree in economics. So I believe an athletics and academic career can be combined. I believe it is most important for sportspeople to have something outside sport — a family, a career and other interests. Somebody has to be last in competition; for those people it is important to realise that they have other opportunities.

Mary Peters When I competed, many of my fellow team members were school and college teachers. Now I believe it would be a very small number of team members who have careers of this sort.

Ruth Fuchs It is the intention in the GDR that all athletes should combine the careers of athlete, profession or university. But the non-sport career is simply taken more slowly. I finished my school career in the normal time — started my college career slowly and finished my first two years before concentrating entirely on my athletic career. I then went back to university for a further six years and completed my doctorate in psychology. I took nearly nine years for an academic program which normally takes about six. People need other challenges in life as well as sport.

REFERENCES

American Dietetic Association Reports (1987) Position of the American Dietetic Association: Nutrition for physical fitness and athletic performance for adults **Journal of the American Dietetic Association 87(7):**933.

Bales, J. (1986) Lessons from the GDR **Coaching Review** Sept/Oct pp.30-32.

Bandura, A. (1977) **Social learning theory** Englewood Cliffs, Prentice-Hall.

Bennett, R. et al (1987) Changing the rules of the game: Reflections toward a feminist analysis of sport. In **Women's Studies International Forum 10(4).**

Better Health Commission (1986) **Looking Forward to Better Health Vol. 3.** Canberra, AGPS.

Better Health Commission (1987) **Towards Better Nutrition for Australians** AGPS, Canberra.

Bierhoff-Alfermann, D. (1983) Women in track and field athletics: self image and social expectation. In **Women's Track and Field Athletics** IAAF/DLV, Darmstadt. FR Germany.

Birke L. and Vines G. (1987) A sporting chance: the anatomy of destiny **Women's Studies International Forum. 10(4):**337-348.

Birrell, S. and Richter J. (1987) Is a diamond forever? Feminist transformations of sport. In **Women's Studies International Forum 10:**4.

Bloom, B.S. (Ed) (1985) **Developing Talent in Young People** Ballantine, New York.

Blue, A. (1987) **Grace Under Pressure: The Emergence of Women in Sport** Sidgwick and Jackson, London.

Brook, N.D. (1985) Conditioning and the growing athlete **Athletics Coach 19n.4.Dec.** pp 31-35.

Brotherhood, J.R. (1984) Nutrition and sports performance **Sports Medicine 1:**350.

Brownmiller, S. (1976) **Against Our Will: Men, Women and Rape** Penguin Books, Harmondsworth.

Bryson, L. (1987) Sport and the maintenance of hegemonic masculinity. **Women's Studies International Forum 10(4):**349-360.

Bushby, R. and Jobling, I.(1985) Decades of sport and the shape of Australian womanhood. In **Fit to Play. Proceedings of the First Australian National Conference on Women, Sport and Physical Recreation** New South Wales Women's Advisory Council to the Premier.

Campbell, D.P. (1974) **If You Don't Know Where You're Going You'll Probably End Up Somewhere Else** Argus Communications, Allen, Texas.

Cann, C.E., Martin, M.C., Genant, H.K., and Jaffe, R.B. (1984) Decreased spinal mineral content in amenorrheic women **Journal of the American Medical Association 251(5):**626-629.

Carrigan, T., Connell, R.W. and Lee, J. (1985) Towards a new sociology of masculinity **Theory and Society 14(5):**551-604.

Clarke, A. and Haag, K. (1988) Unpublished data collected for Exercise Participation Among Working Women Report, SA Department of Recreation and Sport, Health Development Foundation.

Commonwealth Department of Health (1986) **Dietary Guidelines for Australians** AGPS, Canberra.

Connell, R.W. (1987) **Gender and Power** Allen and Unwin, Sydney.

Daly, J. (1982) **Ours Were the Hearts to Dare** Published by the author, Adelaide.

Daly, M. (1978) **Gyn/Ecology: The Metaethics of Radical Feminism** Beacon Press, Boston.

Deakin, V. (1987) Premature osteoporosis in the female athlete **Excel 3(4):**June, 16.

De Beauvoir, S. (1960) **The Second Sex** Four Square Books, London.

Dill, D.B., (1967) A longitudinal study of 16 champion runners **Journal of Sports Medicine 7:**14-27.

Dinnerstein, D. (1977) **The Mermaid and the Minotaur: Sexual Arrangements and Human Malaise** Harper and Row, New York.

Drinkwater, B.L. et al (1984) Bone mineral content of amenorrheic and eumenorrheic athletes **New England Journal of Medicine 311:**272-281.

Dworkin, A. (1981) **Pornography: Men Possessing Women** Women's Press, London.

Dyer, K.F. (1982) **Challenging the Men: The Social Biology of Female Sporting Achievement** Univ. of Queensland Press, St. Lucia, Qld.

Dyer, K.F. (1985) Making up the difference: some explanations for recent improvements in women's athletic performances **Search 16:**264-269.

Dyer, K.F. (1986) The trend of the male-female differential in various speed sports 1936-84 **Journal of Biosocial Science 18:**169-177.

Dyer, K.F. (1986) **Girls' Physical Education and Self-Esteem — A Review of Research, Resources and Strategies** Commonwealth Schools Commission.

Dyer, K.F. and Dwyer, T. (1984) **Running Out of Time: An Investigation of the History of Running Records** Univ of New South Wales Press, Kensington, NSW.

Egger, G. and Champion, N. (1986) **Fitness in Six Weeks** Allen and Unwin, Sydney.

Eichner, E. (1986). The anaemias of athletes **The Physician and Sportsmedicine 14(9):**122.

Elliott, B., Marsh T. and Overheu, P. (1984) The mechanics of the Lendl and conventional tennis forehands: a coach's perspective **Sports Coach 11:**4-9.

English, J. (Ed) (1977) **Sex Equality** Prentice Hall, Englewood Cliffs NJ.

Ey, W.M. (1982) The participation in school sport by girls and boys as it is influenced by the school environment. MA Thesis, Flinders University, SA.

Faulkner, J.A. (1968) New perspectives in training for maximum performance **Journal of the American Medical Association 205:**117-122.

Felshin, J. and Ogelsby, C. (1986) Transcending tradition: Females and males in open competition **Journal of Physical Education Recreation and Dance 57(3):**44-47.

Fitness Ontario (1981) **Low Active Adults: Who They Are, How to Reach Them** Fitness Ontario, Toronto, Canada.

Furlong, J.D.G. and Szreter, R. (1975) The trend of the performance differential between leading men and women athletes 1951-67 **The Statistician 24:**115-128.

Gillam, I. (1988) **The Science of Fitness for Squash** Video production, Phillip Institute of Technology.

Ginn, E. (1987) **Physiological Assessment of State-Level Hockey Players: A Report for the Queensland Women's Hockey Association** August.

Girls and Physical Activity Newsletter 9 issues 1985-88 including feature articles: March 1985, Action research programs; November 1985, Grouping participation in sport of ethnic children; March 1986, Equal opportunity in physical education and sport; June 1986, Sport in primary schools school organisation and structure; September 1986, Review of our experiences ACHPER Health and Fitnes Survey?; February 1987, What's in a name? or The names that people play; July 1987, Clothing — its influence on play, Girls and the outdoors; March 1988, Curriculum disabled girls program.

GPA Resource Kit (8 Units) Curriculum Development Unit 1988.

Gordon, S. and Smith, M.F.R.(1986) Perceived Determinants of Coaching Effectiveness in Gymnastics, Soccer, and Ice Hockey. Unpublished Report to Alberta Sport Council.

Gussow, J. and Contento, I. (1984). Nutrition education in a changing world **Wold Review of Nutrition and Dietetics 44(1)**.

Hahn, E. (1983) Tasks of welfare and guidance in the relationship between coach and female athlete. In **Report of the First IAAF Women's Athletics Congress**, Mainz.

Hall, M.A. and Richardson, D.A.(1982) **Fair Ball: Towards Sex Equality in Canadian Sports** Canadian Advisory Council on the Status of Women.

Hargreaves, J. (1983) Action reply — Looking at women and sport. In Holland, J. (ed) **Feminist Action 1** Battle Axe Books, London.

Hawkes, P. et al (1975) The state of play **Australian Journal of Health, Physical Education and Recreation** 678-16.

Hemery, D. (1986) **The Pursuit of Sporting Excellence** Willow Books, London.

Hill, A.V. (1925) The physiological basis of athletic records **The Lancet** 481-486.

Hughes, J.R. (1984) Psychological effects of habitual aerobic exercise: A critical review **Preventive Medicine 13:**66-78.

Inge, K. and Brukner, P. (1986) **Food for Sport** Heinemann, Australia.

Jaques, T.D. and Pavia G.R. (1976) **Sport in Australia** McGraw Hill, Sydney.

Jeannotat (1980) The emergence of women in sport **Olympic Review 151:**250-243.

King, H. (1979) The sexual politics of sport: An Australian perspective. In Cashman, R. and McKernan, M. (eds) **Sport in History** University of Queensland Press, St. Lucia.

Klafs, C. and Lyon, J. (1973) **The Female Athlete** C.V. Mosby.

Krise, R. and Squires, W. (1983) **History of Distance Running** Stephen Greene Press, Vermont.

Kudelka, S. (1986) Turning on the turned off girl in physical education. A CSC Project of National Significance. Education Department of Tasmania.

Kuscsik, N. (1978) History of women's participation in the Marathon. In **Annals of New York Academy of Science 301:**872.

Lames, M. and Letzelter, M. (1983) Present performance level, future development and prediction for the future in women's athletics. In **Women's Track and Field Athletics** IAAF/DLV, Darmstadt, FR Germany.

Lawrence, G. and Rowe, D. (1986) **Power Play. The Commercialisation of Australian Sport** Hale and Iremonger, Sydney.

Lee, C., and Owen, N. (1986) Uses of psychological theories in understanding the adoption and maintenance of exercising **Australian Journal of Medicine and Science in Sports 18(2):**22-25.

Lee, C., and Owen, N. (1985) Behaviourally-based principles as guidelines for health promotion **Community Health Studies 10:**131-138.

Lee, C., and Owen, N. (1984) Preventing dropout — a psychological viewpoint **Sports Coach 8(1):**20-23.

Lenskyj H. (1986) **Out of Bounds. Women, Sport and Sexuality** The Women's Press, Toronto.

Lloyd, B.B. (1966) The energetics of running: an analysis of world records **Advancement of Science 22**:515-525.

Lloyd, B.B. (1980) Athletic Achievement: Trends and Limits. Presidential address to the British Association, Salford.

Maccoby, N. and Alexander, J. (1980) Use of media in lifestyle programs. In P. Davidson and S. Davidson (eds) **Behavioural Medicine: Changing Health Lifestyles** Brunner/Mazel, New York.

MacIntosh, D. and King, A. (1976) The Role of Inter-School Sports Programs in Ontario Secondary Schools. Ministry of Education Ontario.

Miller-Lite Report on Women in Sports (1985, Dec.) New World Decisions Ltd., 120 Wood Avenue South, Iselin, New Jersey, 08830.

Mirror, Mirror . . . Educational Media: Adelaide College of TAFE (1987).

Mitchell, S. and Dyer, K.F. (1985) **Winning Women: Challenging the Norms in Australian Sport** Penguin, Ringwood, Victoria.

National Heart Foundation (1983) **Risk factor prevalence study No. 2.** NHF, Canberra.

Oglesby, C. (1978) **Women and Sport: From Myth to Reality** Lea and Febiger.

Olson, J.M. and Zanna, M.P. (1981) **Promoting Physical Activity: A Social Psychological Perspective** Ministry of Culture and Recreation, Ottawa, Canada.

Owen, N., Lee, C. and Sedgwick, A.W. (1987) Exercise maintenance: integrating self-management guidelines into community fitness programmes. **Australian Journal of Science and Medicine in Sports 19**:8-12.

Owen, N., and Dwyer, T. (in press) Approaches to promoting more widespread participation in physical activity **Community Health Studies.**

Owen, N., Lee, C. and Gilbert, A. (1987) **Getting Fit: A Do-it-yourself Guide to Aerobic Fitness** ACHPER, Adelaide.

Owen, N. and Lee, C. (1984) **Why People Do and Do Not Exercise** ACHPER, Adelaide.

Panagrazi, B., Chomokos, N. and Massoney, D. (1981) From theory to practice: a summary **Motor Development: Theory Into Practice Monograph 3** pp.65-71.

Pannick D. (1983) **Sex Discrimination in Sport** Equal Opportunities Commission, Manchester.

Perron, M.S. and Endres, J. (1985) Knowledge, attitudes, and dietary practices of female athletes **Journal of the American Dietetic Association 85(5)**:571.

Peters, M. (1974) **Mary P: An Autobiography** Stanley Paul, London.

Piscopo, J. and Baley, J.A. (1981) **Kinesiology — The Science of Movement** John Wiley and Sons, New York. p.152.

Poole, M.E. (1983) **Youth Expectations and Transitions** Routledge and Kegan Paul, Melbourne.

Powell, K.E., Thompson, P.D., Caspersen, K.J. and Kendrick, J.S. (1987) Physical activity and the incidence of coronary heart disease **Annual Review of Public Health 8**:253-288.

Rhodes, F. (1978) History of women's running. In **Complete Woman Runner** World Publications, Mountainview, California. p.241.

Richards, J.F. (1980) **The Sceptical Feminist** Routledge and Kegan Paul, London.

Ryder, H.W., Carr, H.J. and Herget, P. (1977) Future performance in footracing **Scientific American 212**:109-119.

Sands, R. and Ekberg, K. (1983) Little athletics **ACHPER National Journal 19**:22.

Smith, S. (1981) Talent identification and development. In V. Gambetta (ed) **Track Technique Annual '81** pp.41-45.

Steele, J. (1988) The effect of changes to passing height on the mechanics of landing in netball **Applied Sports Research Program Report** Australian Institute of Sport, ACT.

Stephens, T., Jacobs, D.R. and White, C.C. (1985) The descriptive epidemiology of leisure-time physical activity **Public Health Reports 100**:147-158.

Stoddart, B. (1980) **Saturday Afternoon Fever. Sport in the Australian Culture** Angus and Robertson, Sydney.

Summers A. (1975) **Damned Whores and God's Police** Penguin, Ringwood Vic.

Teraslinna, P., Partanen, T., Koskela, A. and Oja, P. (1969) Characteristics affecting willingness of executives to participate in an activity program aimed at coronary heart disease prevention **Journal of Sports Medicine and Physical Fitness 9**:224-229.

Thomas, G.S. (1979) Physical activity and health: Epidemiological and clinical evidence and policy implications **Preventive Medicine 8**:89-103.

Thompson, C.E. and Wankel, L.M. (1982) The effects of perceived activity choice upon frequency of exercise behaviour **Journal of Applied Social Psychology 10**:436-443.

Treutlein, G. (1983) Dependence and heteronomy in women's athletics. In **Women's Track and Field Athletics** IAAF/DLV, Darmstadt, FR Germany.

Ullyot, J. (1984) **The New Womens Running** Stephen Green Press, Vermont. p.97.

Van Swearingen, J. (1986) Iron deficiency in athletes: consequence or adaptation in strenuous activity **Journal of Orthopaedic and Sports Physical Therapy 7**:192-195.

Vines, G. (1988) Is sport good for children? **New Scientist 1622**:46-51.

Wells, C.L. (1985) **Women, Sport and Performance: A Physiological Perspective** Human Kinetics Publishers, Champagne, Ill.

Willis, P. (1982) Women in sport in ideology. In J. Hargreaves (ed) **Sport, Culture and Ideology** Routledge and Kegan Paul, London.

Wilmore, J.H. (1982) **Training for Sport and Activity. The Physiological Basis of the Conditioning Process. Second Edition** Allyn and Bacon Inc., Boston.

Winkler, R.C. (1986). Rights and duty: the need for a social model. In N.J. King and A.J. Remenyi (eds.) **Health Care: A Behavioural Approach** Grune and Stratton.

Wright, J. (1987) A Sporting Chance? Unpublished paper, Faculty of Education, University of Wollongong.